THE GUN IN POLITICS

THE GUN IN POLITICS

An Analysis of Irish Political Conflict, 1916-1986

J. BOWYER BELL

Routledge
Taylor & Francis Group

LONDON AND NEW YORK

First published 1987 by Transaction Publishers

Published 2017 by Routledge
2 Park Square, Milton Park, Abingdon, Oxon OX14 4RN
711 Third Avenue, New York, NY 10017, USA

Routledge is an imprint of the Taylor & Francis Group, an informa business

this book was written under the auspices of the Institue of War and Peace Studies, Columbia University.

Library of Congress Catalog Number: 86-30745

Library of Congress Cataloging-in-Publication Data

Bell, J. Bowyer, 1931-
    The gun in politics.

    Includes index.
    1. Ireland—Politics and government—20th century.
    2. Violence—Ireland—History—20th century.
    3. Firearms— Ireland—History—20th century.
    4. Terrorism— Ireland—History—20th century.
    5. Insurgency— Ireland—History—20th century.
    6. Northern Ireland—Politics and government—1969-   I. Title.

DA59.B428   1987   941.6082   86-30745

ISBN 13: 978-1-56000-566-7 (pbk)

For my Kerry wife Nora Browne,
who has made gentle the violent
Irish political seas.

Mo ghrá thú

Contents

Acknowledgments

The following publishers and journals are acknowledged for their permission to reprint the following previously published essays:

The Secret Army: The IRA 1916-1970, London: Blond, 1970, and New York: John Day, 1971 (variously republished most recently as *The Secret Army, the IRA 1916-1969,* Cambridge, Mass.: MIT Press, 1983, and Dublin: Academic Press, 1983

"American Writer in St. Mullins," in *The Nationalist and Leinster Times,* Centenary Issue, 1883-1983

"The Thompson Submachine Gun in Ireland, 1921," in *The Irish Sword* (Journal of the Military History Society of Ireland), vol. viii, no. 31 (Winter 1967)

"Proliferation: Sophisticated Weaponry and Revolutionary options— The Sub-State Perspective," in *Arms Control and Technological Innovation,* London: Croom Helm, 1977.

"Arms Transfers, Conflict and Violence at the Sub-State Level," in Uri Ra'anan, Robert L. Pffaltzgraff, Jr., and Geoffrey Kemp, eds., *Arms Transfers to the Third World,* copyright © 1979 by Westview Press, Boulder, Colorado

"Social Patterns and Lessons, The Irish Case," in *Civil War in the Twentieth Century,* Lexington: University of Kentucky Press, 1972

"Ireland and the Spanish Civil War, 1936-1939," in *Studia Hibernica,* Dublin, vol. ix (1969, annual)

"The Shadow of the Gunman," in *Sword of Light, The Irish American Review,* vol. 1, no. 1 (Spring 1974)

"The Escalation of Insurgency, The Experience of the Provisional I.R.A., 1969-1971," in *The Review of Politics,* vol. xxv, no. 3 (July 1973)

"Strategy, Tactics, and Terror: An Irish Perspective," in *International Terrorism, National, Regional and Global Perspectives,* New York: Praeger, 1976

"The Men with Guns, the Legitimacy of Violent Dissent," in *Legitimation of Regimes,* Beverly Hills: Sage, 1979

"The Irish Republican Army," in *Contemporary Terror, Studies in Sub-State Violence,* London: Macmillan, 1981

On Revolt: Strategies of National Liberation, Cambridge, Mass.: Harvard University Press, 1976

"Revolts Against the Crown: The British Response to Imperial Insurgency," in *Parameters* (Journal of the Army War College), vol. ix, no. 1 (1974)

A Time of Terror, How Democratic Societies Respond to Revolutionary Violence, New York: Basic Books, 1978

"The Gun in Europe," in *The New Republic,* vol. 173, no. 21 (November 22, 1975)

"Hostage Ireland," in *The New Republic,* vol. 174, no. 25 (June 19, 1976)

"Terrorism International Inc.: Academic Branch," in *Hibernia,* Dublin (September 7, 1978)

"Contemporary Irish Archival Resources," in *Administration* (Journal of the Institute of Public Administration of Ireland), vol. xviii, no. 2 (Summer 1970)

"The Chroniclers of Violence in Northern Ireland: The First Wave Interpreted," in *The Review of Politics,* vol. xxxiv, no. 2 (April 1972), and *Eire-Ireland,* vol. vii, no. 1 (Spring 1972)

"The Chroniclers of Violence in Northern Ireland Revisited: The Analysis of Tragedy," in *The Review of Politics,* vol. xxvi, no. 4 (October 1974)

"The Chroniclers of Violence in Northern Ireland: A Tragedy in Endless Acts," in *The Review of Politics,* vol. 38, no. 4 (October 1976)

"The Troubles as Trash, Shadows of the Irish Gunman on an American Curtain," in *Hibernia* (January 20, 1978)

"The Curragh: 1940-1945," in *Irish Times* (May 8, 1985)

Introduction: A Personal Memoir

This effort took considerably longer to reach print than anyone had anticipated. Originally it was simply the idea of republishing past work on Irish matters: a whip through past scripts, a bit of pasting, and a book thereafter. The rationale was and remained that much of my Irish work was often not really written for those concerned with Ireland but rather for those concerned with technology transfer or an appropriate democratic response to terrorism or the impact of civil war on society. Even those articles or chapters focusing particularly on Irish matters proved scattered, appearing in fugitive forums, usually far from the island. Using Ireland as example, of course, much had to be repeated for the innocent so that there was always considerable overlap—Easter rerun and the Provos rewrite. Still, it seemed possible that judicious scissoring and prompt publication would be possible. Like many Celtic matters, however, the project hung fire, and time drifted by—more to be written, more to be clipped, titles changed, conclusions postponed. The original Irish publisher, the elusive Seán Browne, withdrew from the scene into secrecy and rumor, carrying along various drafts and some enthusiasm. And so there were more delays, more editorial defections, more events, and more scripts.

Ultimately, heaped pages to hand, matters were pursued with the encouragement of various potential editors, not the least was Irving Louis Horowitz of Transaction. What has emerged is not only a collection of past work, as originally planned, but also, since clipping proved more complex, a mingled manuscript—some old, some new, much discarded, all edited, a medley rather than separate essays or a brand new book. The floor, despite the published length, is cluttered with cuttings and outs, repeats, but not articulate mistakes—faint predictions are included in the text, no error of judgment edited out, no flaw on the cutting room floor. And there are comments included, asides on the unfolding analysis, for the subjects would not stay within covers nor hew to predictable lines. There could thus be no coda, no neat end. And there are too few general conclusions, little wisdom to offer after a generation in and out of the island.

There are one or two small points. The present disturbances, now running deep into a second decade, I usually call the Ulster Troubles (the Northern Troubles would do as well) since there lies the core (the old

1

province: six counties and the border zone), even though the crisis is Irish and has lapped far shores: bombs in London, smuggling out of America, contacts in the Middle East, tours of Europe. An effort has been made to make the text uniform, despite the original style, and concise; therefore, bits and pieces have been edited out or a few words changed for reasons of style, but, overall, previously published material is as previously published. There is no point in trying to thank all those who have been kind over the years. Most of those who appear in these pages would rather have been skipped over if they played a role or more fulsomely praised if their works were mentioned. In twenty years a very long list of debts is accumulated and not a few admonitions; secret armies tend to prefer to remain in many matters secret. At the end, however, special thanks that are long overdue go to my Kerry wife—at last a valid Irish connection for an alien traveler— who has tolerated the IRA Army Council meeting in the kitchen, the police at the end of the lane, odd arrivals and strange gunmen for tea, and has provided a warm, Celtic, safe house for my ventures into violence. This book is for her—perhaps next time the gift will not come lumbered with Irish troubles but wrapped with a three-color ribbon of a more peaceful theme: fewer gunmen, however genial in person, more saints and scholars, however rare in real life, even in Kerry.

A Personal Perspective

My odyssey across the troubled waters, past and present, of Irish Republican politics began several years ago in Kilkenny. I drove over the River Barrow at Graiguenamanagh up the saddle of Coppanagh and down to Inistioge, the most attractive village in Leinster, to meet Paddy Murphy, then unknown to me, near the Spotted Dog. In the fullness of Celtic time and through various intermediaries, the Army Council of the IRA relayed to me in the regal Horse-Protestant atmosphere of the Russell Hotel on St. Stephen's Green their "utmost co-operation" in my projected history. Although this agreement was hardly binding on former volunteers and immediately assured that I would be regarded with deep suspicion is some quarters—in and out of the Republican Movement—nothing would have been possible without the tolerance and at times encouragement of the anonymous Army Council. As a result of the meeting in the Russell's upstairs lounge, I have spent more time on the IRA than a good many volunteers have spent in it.

—Foreword, *The Secret Army*

When I wrote those words nearly twenty years ago, I was nearly certain of at least one matter: that my course in Ireland had run. There might be further Celtic ventures but not for any analytical purpose. My interests were elsewhere. There was the NLF recently in power in Aden and mostly an unknown factor even to their late enemies the British. I wanted to see the old rebels like Grivas and Begin in what everyone assumed was comfortable if not rewarding retirement. There were, as well, rumors of new radicals in Italy and Germany. I assumed that someone else would take care of the history of the Algerians, and the Americans in Vietnam would undoubtedly carry academics and analyists in their baggage train while no one seemed to care about the South Sudan or Eritrea or Yemen. In any case there seemed ample, distant wars to measure against Irish revolutionaries. As for the IRA, the secret army might, as it so often had, re-emerge from penury and political ruminations at some future date; but in 1967 or 1968 the only movement visible in Ireland was the tide toward the use of civil disobedience and non-violent protest by some Nationalists. Ireland, once again, seemed to be in a time warp with the arrival of civil rights ten years late as a rallying cry for the angry and alienated. Well might Ireland soon supply those concerned with agitational politics a satisfactory case-study, but this was not really my concern at all. True, I strongly suspected that the only way to initiate a campaign of violence in the North was by recourse to the tactics of protest, an eventuality that did not seem to occur to the Irish practitioners. Imported fashions in protest hurriedly deployed to them seemed sufficient. They did not quite seem to realize that non-violence was often, usually, used as a means by the activists to ensure a violent reaction—only one side in the dialogue was non-violent. In any case an immediate role for the IRA, supposedly dedicated to physical force no matter the new political concerns of the leadership, seemed remote. Even secret armies seldom sit down in the face of provocation. Instead, for me, the secret army, the IRA, would be a model, an analytical base-line to carry on my revolutionary travels to real wars, old and new. And revolutionary Ireland with its long litany of rebellion, massacre, protest, and failure had been for this purpose a splendid foundation; and one that I had examined with great fascination, centuries of practice and retaining, all but a fly in amber, the same dedication to revolt made manifest in the IRA. Ireland, then, appeared an introduction, a gate, to a wider revolutionary world.

I had arrived in Ireland almost incidently to what was to become my major concern with contemporary revolution. In the course of writing on the sieges of modern cities, a most conventional work of military history, up one battlement, down the next, I had become interested in a relatively obscure Palestinian-Zionist group called the Irgun Zvai Leumi led by Menachen Begin. I felt with limited evidence that the Irgun had been far more pivotal in the establishment of Israel than the orthodox record suggested, a contention reinforced by work on a Middle Eastern book concerning conflict by various means but mostly military that emerged as *The Long War*. In the sixties anti-insurgency as both a military tactic and an academic subject had become trendy; the guerrilla, mostly rural since the urban variant was just emerging and the transnational terrorist far in the future, suddenly loomed large, certainly as a threat to Western, particularly American, interests—see Vietnam. The Irgun had certainly been urban guerrillas or terrorists, then an acceptable revolutionary name with a long Eastern European ancestry, and had even, largely, been successful. At least the British were no longer in Palestine and Begin was in the Knesset if not prime minister. I suspected that orthodox histories and governmental analyses were not going to be of much use in discovering how those rebels had worked. Yet, I did not want to live in Israel or learn Hebrew. Hence I was looking around for a more congenial revolutionary subject. A more attractive option seemed to be to spend several summer months in Ireland working on my siege book and checking up on the IRA, the longest-lived, unsuccessful revolutionary organization readily available and, probably, English-speaking. For some months through newspaper advertisements, estate agents, and correspondence we tracked down what seemed from thousands of miles a reasonable Irish headquarters. On the centenary of the Carlow *Nationalist* in 1983, I later wrote what we found other than the IRA's Republican Ireland.

Years and years ago, nearly twenty, my family—wife, daughter of eight, daughter of one—arrived for the summer in Rosemary Muldoon's house in St. Mullins, innocent not only of South Carlow but also of much of Ireland.

I was to finish in a pleasant place one book on violent matters and discover if there were something to be done on the IRA, then, to be mild, quiet quiescent but still more appealing than my other choice—Mr. Begin's Irgun Zvai Leumi.

And we had arrived in the last unspoiled village in Leinster at a special moment when little had changed in a generation.

The world began at Graignamanagh (fortunately for alien tongues reduced to Graig.) and ended at New Ross. Quite off the beaten track, no GB plates, even no Dublin plates, was our village: one pub, grocery store, telephone exchange, and community center.

There was a motte-and-baily, a mill, mill houses, a stump of a round tower, various ecclesiastical ruins and our Church of Ireland—everyone else's church was a mile away in Glynn next to the priest's house (or the reverse).

There was a village pump that people did not use and a sacred well that they did, and a green. Once a year in July was the Saint Moling's 'pattern' when the far flung returned. And that was it and more than enough to learn about.

Actually, Becky, eight, learned first and perhaps most because she could for the first time in her life run free—in New York City children do not run free unless heavily armed or beyond a parent's ken. Within miles everyone knew Becky even if Becky may not have known everyone.

Her knowledge increased on all sorts of matters—milk comes hot from a cow (heretofore always cold and in cartons) being the first revelation. Our knowledge came somewhat more haltingly for I was finishing up a book while we were settling down.

We went to church to see what it was like (a shrewd move since, of course, everyone went to church of some sort and thus the parish priest felt we were not a hopeless case and a hired girl was allowed down off the slopes of Mount Leinster to work for us). Morning prayer was an early shock for while the Prayer Book speaks of two or three gathering together I had always assumed this was theory, but at St. Mullins it proved practice—and it is difficult to pretend to sing when there are only four in the congregation.

Every other Sunday services were held at Borris House where many more gathered together—at the quite decent hour of half-twelve—but still not quite like our church in New York with more members than there were Protestants in all Carlow.

Of course, we were just as different although not quite so different as most rumours would have it. For early on after church in Borris, we stopped by to meet the O'Learys. Olivia, then much smaller and less famous (far from the RTE-*Irish Times*-BBC journalist.).

There was seldom a problem of driving on the wrong side of the road since most drove in the middle.

My wife managed to run more or less directly into a lamp standard, that I will admit was, probably is, planted in the middle of the New Ross road, while she peered out of the side window at a sign announcing BEWARE, DANGEROUS HOUSE, which did in truth loom directly overhead teetering on a cliff edge. After this I did all the driving on ventures to discover hidden ring forts and overlooked Norman castles.

And there were racing meets, with the horses running the wrong way round and leaping over fences, and hurling. I still favour the fortunes of Kilkenny but recall fondly the local parish teams making their way through the obstacles of a cow pasture in name of sport—and the mad scramble of doggie races (so many variants of doggies) and handball courts made out of medieval tomb stones and fishing about which I, then and now, know nothing.

On finishing typing at half five I would go down to the Barrow and "fish"—not to catch anything but because I like to cast—and half five is the best time to fish in America if a few hours too early in Ireland.

So like Becky I became known for miles for my ventures into the noonday sun (or drizzle) with worm on hook. I never caught anything actually but an eel.

In any case me catching anything was unnecessary since we discovered in Graig a gentleman who would take our salmon order to the nearest ounce and inch in the morning and deliver that afternoon.

The day I smashed in frustration the stove that nearly heated the hot water, I found a blacksmith beside the road whose workroom could have been painted by Goya—no tool fashioned after 1800—and learned he had made pikes for 1916.

Most romantic was the search for the IRA that culminated in a meeting in a pub with three proclaimed "Sinn Féiners" (who I later discovered made up the entire IRA population in three counties—the organisation being on hard times). There was even a suspicious detective to make the evening complete.

All this time later, one is a well-known "Sinn Féiner," one had a religious experience and takes no part in Republican politics, and one still farms the same farm—which is par for the course. With the IRA project on the horizon ("some American chap down in the country wants to write about us"), it was time to go home, summer holidays from the university being over—the summer in St. Mullins had been over since early June but that was another matter.

To a degree, however, St. Mullins had become an Irish home despite all the years to be spent in Dublin.

Two years after the St. Mullins summer, travelling toward Dublin on a Sunday, my wife wanted to stop mid-day to attend church at Borris House. No longer needing to keep up a local ecclesiastical front, I slipped off across the road to a pub. It was not your everyday, front-on-the-road pub but one that required an advance through a grocery, out a rear door straight through a hardware store, and a quick right to the place itself.

There were several customers strange to me and a novel barman. Curiosity seethed since the last stranger to find his way there probably was a refugee from '98. Cunning, subtle and quite polite questions drew forth that I was an American, even if I did not sound like an Irish-American (the only known variety) whose wife was at church across the road.

There was great relief. All nodded. The barman noted that, then, I must be the writer-fellow from St. Mullins. And not a bad reward for a summer on the Barrow, a name of my own and IRA fame, such as it would be, to come.

The St. Mullins site was an innocently astute move since, almost inevitably, for the visitor Ireland is a mix of Dublin and scenery. For me it was neither but rather people living in a lovely, if obscure, parish, more isolated in time and place than the actual mileage to the capital might indicate.

There might be fashionable priests on the television but not in the village. The new pump on the green, the retired bank director, and certainly visiting Americans were all regarded with some suspicion. I at least was a "writer" which explained a lot, excused a lot. Then, too, by attending the small Anglican church in the graveyard not far from Art, King of Leinster's tomb and the stump of a round tower whenever the rector could make his way up from Old Ross indicated that we were not quite heathens. So we were tolerated and I typed on until time came to do something about the IRA.

I drove up to Dublin and appeared before the catalogues in the National Library. There had been little enough on recent Irish matters in the American libraries that I had checked, but I assumed this was parochialism and priorities. On Kildare Street I discovered that Irish history apparently stopped in 1921. Some books ran a bit further and there were one or two minor ventures of a later date but not only was the IRA ignored but also everything else—history, politics, economics, sociology—was as well. Governments often have a fifty-year rule on releasing documents but apparently Ireland had an unwritten forty-year rule on discussing in print the history of the state. If I were going to find out anything, it appeared that I would have to talk to people; and I assumed, innocently, that St. Mullins would be as good a place to begin as any. There the general reaction to my questions was a faint uneasy, as if I sought news of a bad relation. There was, too, an aura of cunning conspiracy. No one might actually know anyone of the modern IRA but no one intended to admit as much. Most were truly ignorant of the Republicans except through rumor, exaggeration, and ballads. To be sure the IRA was rather thin on the ground at the time, certainly in South Carlow.

Eventually I managed to track down Paddy Murphy, south Kilkenny being somewhat more fertile Republican ground, and open a dialogue that was to continue with hundreds of people for endless years. It was not so much entry into a secret army as a secret world; for Irish Republicans seemed to have a different history, different priorities, and spoke a different language than the other Irish. Then, in the sixties, no one seemed especially interested in this world except, perhaps, the police. There, habit was probably the prime motive. Talking in the Inistioge pub with my first Republicans, Richard Behal from south Kilkenny and Al Ryan up from Waterford, I did not realize that I had cornered most of the actives—a fact that apparently was a matter of some interest to a detective at the other end of the bar. Although I almost never talked to anyone in a pub again, for analytical purpose that is, I was rarely out of sight of the police. Or so it seemed for, like my Republican friends, I soon became police-conscious, rather as Americans of note would be humiliated if their phone was the only one not tapped. Anyway, Paddy agreed to dispatch my request for a formal agreement by the IRA that I could do a history. Who knows what they thought in Dublin about a strange American down in the country who wanted to do a book. At least they were willing to listen. I fear that no one else, not even the police, had shown very much interest in IRA doings for some years; so I was rather a novelty.

The eventual meeting with a representative of the Dublin center took place at the Russell Hotel, a most unlikely venue but a quite splendid Irish institution with the best restaurant in the country (and like so many Dublin institutions it was to be destroyed, razed into a parking lot and then replaced by a ticky-tacky box). Later I found it an ideal place to meet people of interest to the Special Branch detectives since the clubby atmosphere in the tiny lounge was alien to law officers and the seating limited. Any of the paid watchers proved patently visible and most uneasy. In any case at the first meeting, I was delighted to discover that my contact, Tony Meade, who did not look like a gunman but an editor, which he was—of the *United Irishman,* thought the whole idea quite feasible. He had actually for some months before my St. Mullins advent been pushing the idea on Oliver Snoddy at the National Museum who had not bitten. And unknown to all Tim Pat Coogan of the *Irish Press,* who was about to come out with the first serious work on Ireland since the Rising—so entitled—had nearly decided that there was another book in the IRA. In my case the IRA Army Council felt that as an American with no Irish connection, and an Anglican to boot, I would be appropriately neutral—a blank slate. So all was agreed and Tony promised to dispatch a formal letter from headquarters agreeing to the project with which I had some small hope of interesting foundation support. In due time the letter turned up in St. Mullins and I was formally in the secret army business, observer status.

Back in New York I finished up my Arab-Israeli *Long War,* which was more than they ever managed, and read widely and, as it turned out, to absolutely no purpose, on guerrilla matters. As I was to discover, with rare exceptions the IRA had gone its own way whatever the foibles and fashions of the times or the theory and practice of revolution. Others read about the IRA while the IRA read not about others but Ireland. And for American foundations, ever inclined to pour money down last year's fashionable rat hole, Ireland was Yeats and Joyce and Guinness, not a fit subject for analysis. Worse, my subject appeared not only violence-prone (the term physical force charmed no one) but also illegal. Most of all for the smart foundation money Ireland and the IRA were irrelevant to the major contemporary revolutionary trends as read in Georgetown and Manhattan. No money. At Harvard Henry Kissinger and Tom Schelling were interested but I was not of Harvard. And the idea of appointing someone unknown who would appear in the Short Strand and Tralee but never in Cambridge seemed of limited merit. No money. So back we came on publisher's advances and odds and ends to be disgruntled that the rumor was soon about of vast American sums underwriting me and mine. They were the first of many rumors, all exchanged as gospel, over the years largely based on the mistaken assumption that someone in America cared enough to spend money on Ireland. Then—and largely now—no one of note in the United States, beyond the Irish diaspora, really cares much about contemporary Ireland and certainly not in the sixties about the apparently moribund IRA. Even at Harvard they seemed a bit vague whether the IRA was a movement or a marching society. Ireland was, as one of our American diplomats in the Park was to say later, small potatoes, a long way from vital American interests, a setting for literary historians and pub poets.

Certainly that first summer in the wilds of Kilkenny the movement had seemed moribund enough. Even the Irish seemed to know little unless they were involved. At the least the IRA needed a publicity agent or lots more people to paint "Up the IRA" on country walls. I had suggested to Tony that they do something spectacular like blowing up Nelson's pillar in Dublin so they could get on the front page of the *New York Times*. The Army Council was not interested in "stunts" but in serious matters like ground rents (whatever they were). My American friends were at least awed when they opened their *Times* the next April to find a grand photograph of the truncated pillar—an Easter Rising memorial. The IRA was not involved—and it took me ten years to find out those of "the splinter" along with their American financial backer who had been involved in that particular stunt. At least with that explosion on O'Connell Street there was an indication that there was some Republican movement if there could be active splinters—in revolutionary matters schism is often a sign of vitality. For my proposed history of the IRA, it was a comfort to know that the last chapter had not yet been finished since I was really concerned with future revolutions rather than a Irish revolution's past.

So in 1966 we settled into a mews in Ballsbridge on Pembroke Lane, Dublin 4. My oldest daughter, the Becky of St. Mullins, was dispatched to school in a tie and once there had to plunge into fifth-year Irish, eventually outdistancing a few colleagues before retiring from the field. The next two daughters (the oldest, Virginia, had taken her first step in St. Mullins the previous summer and the youngest, Elizabeth, began to speak in what might well have been Irish) filled up the house. I started off quite properly and academically reading newspapers in the National Library to put together some idea of the mysterious last forty years before tracking down the volunteers. It soon became clear that except for a sketchy outline the printed word was not going to be much help with Republicans. And among them there was no single valid source, no guardian of the corporate memory, no tribal historian. Each volunteer knew most of his own but many had spent time in prison and lost tract of the debates of the active. Even those figures who had been in the movement for a generation had often spent much of that time in isolation, in prison or detention, even in exile. Many, even at the center of the circle, had never exchanged stories or compared notes. By the time I began asking questions, no one could even make out a list of chiefs of staff after 1925. Except for a few with total recall, no one could easily remember the needed names from five or ten years before. Everyone—mostly—could remember their own story. So that is how I began, listening to stories that started at the beginning and came up to yesterday.

Many would talk with me in detail because the present IRA Army Council had so indicated. Others would not because the present IRA Army Council had so indicated. I soon discovered that for many the recent past was too painful for display, the splits and schisms still festering—and for most Republicans the recent past tended to run back to the year one. Many talked at length because they felt the project worthwhile. Some people gave me an inordinate amount of time while others I could track down for only an hour or two. A few simply refused to talk. David O'Connell, for example, however disastrous the previous campaign, believed that there remained a role for the IRA and did not want to become involved with a "history" that implied the movement was a relic. So he wrote a polite note. Others simply seemed to disappear into thin air. Mostly, however, people were willing to talk and their stories formed the core of what was to be the book—they were the major strand of my knowledge of the Republican movement. Another was my continued associations with active Republicans, endless tea seminars at the *United Irishman,* drinks at Hennessy's (a practice Cathal Goulding, then chief of staff, eventually discouraged since the pub was turning into a visible army seminar), and constant conversation throughout the country on political matters. I appeared at commemorations like Edentubber or Seán South's in Limerick and heard the Easter Sunday oration at Pomeroy in Tyrone, I went to cake-and-bake sales, to political rallies, orations and protest meetings. This was all research by osmosis as I slowly absorbed Republican reality. Academically it was really little different from field work by a social anthropologist investigating the mores of strange natives. Gradually my Republicans became less strange. Then the rest of the Irish, the normal neighbors in Dublin, the academics, the people up from the country, shopkeepers and Dáil members, St. Mullins friends and our church's congregation, became in turn strange. They all lived outside the secret world of the Republicans. Of course, so did the Republicans most of the time. Only the few at the center of the circle who were trying to hold the movement together in the sixties were as concerned daily about Republican matters. And a few Special Branch men aware that quiescence did not necessarily mean acquiescence.

Almost from my first unheralded appearance at various Sinn Fein seats of subversion, there had been official police notice. Historians tended to remain in libraries and anthropologists on Innismore and few Americans contacted Irish Republicans for academic purpose. Such notice, either in the pub in Inistioge or in the streets of Dublin, was hardly anticipated when I was absorbing the techniques of history in graduate school. The first time my car was followed home one night from Gardiner Place, I realized that I was going to make the evening for the Special Branch. Pembroke Lane, into which one tends to swerve suddenly, contained not just my mews but also further on down the headquarters of Mick Reardan's Irish Communist Party. Obviously a strange man in a strange car rushing straight from Gardiner Place where the Sinn Fein Ard Comhairle had met to Pembroke Lane was going to be a fascinating development. Sufficiently fascinating that someone was getting overtime at the end of my lane for a goodly while.

Even more exotic was a later trip north to Belfast with Tony Meade, Malachi McGurran and Tom Mitchell. Beyond the surface excitement that day was the beginning of the new Ulster Troubles. In view of the potential for distrubing celebrations of the Easter Rising of 1916—fifty years on—Northern Ireland Home Minister William Crag under the premise that the Republican Clubs were really just another name for Sinn Fein (which was true) and Sinn Fein was simply a form of the IRA (which was mostly true) and hence subversive (which was wishful thinking) had banned the organization. It was decided to hold a public Republican Club meeting with guests from concerned organizations as a protest—an act of non-violent disobedience in the name of civil rights. Tony and Tom Mitchell were to represent Dublin and Malachi was along for a ride home. He was let off in Lurgan and we went on into Belfast to the meeting off Divis Street—a rather cursory affair, nervous delegates, brief speeches, but the first real act of civil disobedience bringing together the tiny spectrum of radical Northern dissent that helped form the civil rights movement. As soon as we reached the street after the meeting, the RUC detectives descended and snatched up Tom Mitchell among others. Tony and I circled about in his all-too-visible white estate wagon and told Billy McMillan what was happening. Technically we seemed to be on the run. We drove out to Gerry Fitt, then the Republican-Labour Party member at Stormont, to see what might be done. There were a few telephone calls and no progress. Gerry played his campaign song. His friends to my delight seemed to feel I was some sort of imported Dublin gunman backing up Tony. Eventually we had a Chinese dinner of sorts with Kevin Agnew, picked up Malachi, and drove back over the border without incident, no longer on the run.

At Dundalk we stopped, as was Republican wont, at Mark's pub where flexible hours could be managed. One drink down and the door opened for Tom Mitchell and Paddy Kennedy. There had been no charges. The RUC had simply wanted to display a little force for Dublin's benefit and local appreciation. Tom had not been really questioned and not even searched. The later proved a boon. Just before we had crossed the border that morning, I had indicated that my research had revealed a universal truth that no one in the IRA carried "papers" except on the day they were arrested. So we stopped and checked the car for Republican "papers." No papers. Tom, however, had failed to clear out his pockets. Thus he had to sit in the Queen Street RUC barracks with the fatal "papers" contemplating more time in Crumlin Road prison—and after eight years of a previous sentence, the prospect was distressing. So he had arrived at Mark's in some shock. Ultimately, worse for the wear everyone reached Dublin. And since I was a disinterested historian it was possible for me a month later to interview Craig and other RUC officials in Belfast about the raid on the banned meeting. It was an incident that appeared to play a much lesser role in their life than in mine—after all *I* had been on the run for eighteen hours and they had merely been putting in a day's work. Ultimately, the incident could be seen to have played a much greater part in everyone's life as the small prologue to the long Troubles. And for the actors, Tony left the *United Irishman* to work in Tralee on the *Kerryman,* Malachi died much too young, Tom Mitchell left the movement and Billy McMillian was killed in a tit-for-tat Republican feud between the Provos and the Officials. William Craig is still an uncompromising Unionist politician while Paddy Kennedy became an uncompromising Republican one. And Kevin Agnew was always one. Most incredible of all Gerry Fitt of Republican-Labour is now Lord Fitt, a bitter opponent of Republicans, a man without a party but with a title. And there are bullet holes in the door of Mark's pub in Dundalk and bomb rubble in the Belfast streets near the meeting hall. None of us saw the sign, "Beware, Here-be-Dragons."

Actually I was less interested in the history of the IRA than its present state and future prospects as I had indicated at the beginning. History seemed a useful means to approach an Irish present. Hence Tony asked me to do an interim report on my impressions of the movement then attempting to ignore the division between the traditionalists who stressed physical force and past precedent and the futurists who were tempted by politics while the center of the circle attempted to stave off bankruptcy. In any case, while off on a trip to Egypt to see monuments and perhaps the NLF and FLOSY people from Aden, I produced a report—tombs and temples in the morning and the IRA in the heat of the afternoon. The end result was fifty pages that so delighted Tony he began to run off a set of copies each numbered. Others were not pleased to discover how much could be learned without asking questions. And Cathal Goulding having read my results confiscated all but a couple of the partly finished copies and kept my only draft of the entire report. It was the nicest compliment I had received since my arrival in Ireland. Subsequently, there was some concern since a substantial section of the sequestered reported indicated the ways in which a civil rights campaign could be manipulated into a physical force campaign. If the IRA rushed into the streets with ancient Thompson guns and homemade grenades, they would have been laughed off the streets. A sit-in would be a different matter. Actually when the civil rights campaign did begin, the IRA center was a swift convert, seeking not to manipulate marches and demonstrations into a low-intensity war but rather maintain the peace, join the protest. And their Republican rivals—the traditionalists—for some time had traditional doubts about any non-violent action, any politics, especially and particularly if the Dublin center was involved. No one had time for yesterday's sequestered report. In fact in my subsequent twenty years of discussions with all sorts and conditions of revolutionaries, gunmen, terrorists, militants, and activists, it has been my experience that no one pays much attention to suggestion, however well-meant or disinterested or even self-serving, from external sources. It is almost a universal that the *last* thing a rebel wants in advice. Most, like the Irish, welcome an interested ear, even more an interested, informed ear. And if the listener nods along, no matter how outrageous or improbable or even unpleasant the monologue, all will be well. That is, all will be well until the moment of publication, which usually can only engender disappointment that the listener misunderstood, misinterpreted, had been misled—had not, in fact, been converted to the revealed truth. It is so much safer to write about the dead or distant—little enough that Brian Boru or Lloyd George can do.

Actually the first two things I wrote on Ireland caused, for obvious reasons, no trouble at all. One was on Irish archival sources for contemporary history—there did not seem to be any—complete with questionnaire, a not very well received American academic innovation. It was interesting that in 1967 my first two prompt replies came from the, then, two most efficient institutions in Ireland: Guinness brewery and Seán Lemass. The other was an article on the purchase and introduction of the Thompson sub-machine gun into Ireland (used but once, legends and ballads apart, against the British) in 1921. And I put together bits for an article on Ireland and the Spanish Civil War—the first practice of neutrality by the government and more of the gun in politics by volunteers for both the Spanish Republicans and Nationalists. All of this rather conventional history was a sideline, the last academic residue of a proper career for henceforth I was seldom in a library and rarely far from a war. First, however, I had to get my secret army on paper in New York—finishing my final chapter just as the IRA and Ireland were beginning a new one in the North.

With trouble in the streets of Derry and Belfast, I was operating out of Harvard interviewing past rebels against the crown—Begin and Grivas, the Mau Mau and Nasser, the NLF and FLOSY—and contemporary practitioners from South Africa to Lebanon. There were the southern wars of the ANC and FRELIMO, ZANU, ZAPU, MPLA, UNITA, and insurrections in the marsh of the South Sudan and the uplands of Eritrea, the clashes in Yemen, the burgeoning Palestinian movement. There were new rebels in Italy and old guerrillas in Cyprus and Egypt and Israel. And Ireland seemed far away until civil protest began to be transformed into civil conflict. The Americans in general, having awarded white hats to the protesters and black to the police, became confused as matters drifted into chaos beyond comfortable generalizations. The Provos and the Officials were interviewed at length as were most everyone involved. Still there was no neat scorecard or grasp of the scope of the troubles. No one seemed to notice that part of the United Kingdom was be to be gripped by an open insurrection engendered by various Republican movements. Ireland might be news once again, but no observer seemed to know what to make of the island, the events, or future prospects. The journalists, no wiser, flocked in and out to the rhythm of the incidents. *Time* and *Newsweek, Stern* and *Espresso* came and left. French and Swedish television, BBC and NBC, came and filmed and left. And every European radical appeared to buzz about the honey of violence. And I, now at MIT, was about to depart for various wars in Arabia and the Horn of Africa, not yet news, not yet trendy, conflict as usual off the beaten path, when fate intervened in the form of a New York cocktail party.

There between drinks in the late autmn of 1971, I found those who wanted to film the new Troubles. I arrived in Dublin the week after Bloody Sunday with the ashes of the British Embassy still hot and the country seemingly in crisis. The reporters were back again in mass. All sorts of strange people had appeared, handimen of revolution, fashionable experts, the secret people often without secrets, rebels for any cause and surely agents for the threatened. All my old IRA friends had surfaced, the Stickies as the Official IRA still on Gardiner Place, and the others, the Provos, on Kevin Street. And Saor Eire gunmen, the mafia as Trotskyites. Some old Republicans were highly visible, public members and open spokesmen of various secret armies. Others had more discreet tasks. Instead of a dozen or so activists, the Specials now had to keep track of hundreds with more signing up daily. Kevin Street was jammed with journalists. Gardiner Place was jammed with journalists. Saor Eire did not seem to have an office. Times were a-changing. For most of the next six months, with a few weeks off now and again to attend to the wars in the Horn of Africa, I worked on the film with the Provos, attending bombings and snipings, training sessions and ambushes.

The result, alas, made neither fortune nor reputation largely because my colleagues' enthusiasm was far greater than their fiscal or marketing skills. Still, I could go back to the Red Sea trailing whiffs of cordite and an insight into the latest Irish misadventures. Over the next several years I managed to get in and out of Ireland to keep up on the Republican events. At times some of the involved showed up in New York, spreading the gospel or collecting funds or moving things from here to there. Finally while in Dublin at a Sinn Fein seminar, Richard Behal asked me some of the same questions I had asked him so long before in the pub in south Kilkenny. And so once again I brought *The Secret Army* up to date—rather like Grandson of Secret Army by then. Generally my Irish readers grumbled that it neither told them the inside story nor offered an analytical solution. They were probably right. First, the more I knew about the IRA the less, it seemed, I could write—that is if I ever wanted to learn any more. And second, in the words of my friend Professor Richard Rose, the problem in Northern Ireland is that there is no solution. Certainly I could offer none.

Beyond that plain tale of events that brought the secret army up to 1979, minus many of the goodies, there were also a great many pages, some different, in distant or obscure journals and other books concerning Irish matters used for other purpose. These with rare exceptions focused on special aspects of Irish matters, on sources and applications and particular incidents for more general purpose. Some were quite academic in title ("Technology Transfer and Non-State Actors") if not in content (the Provos' problem with the RPG-7 rocket launcher). At the same time during my revolutionary wanderings I regularly seemed to be involved in Irish matters. In Menachem Begin's Tel Aviv office I had to explain IRA intentions and in Rome the Provos' ideology and in Cyprus the impact of imposed partition on a small island. To academic audience concerned with the reality of revolutionary organizations or the legitimacy of rebels or the financing of subversion, I found Irish examples ready to hand. In fact in matters of political violence, one could pick and choose throughout hundreds of years of practice and theory—or focus solely on the most recent events.

Many of the articles, chapters, and reports were directed to an audience distant from Irish matters; others had limited circulation or none. Collectively they had something to say about one Ireland, the Ireland of the Troubles, and collectively something to say about a means to approach political violence—the wars and terrors of our time. Such a collection stitched together by my thread of concern with the gun in politics does not make a history nor the analysis of a single compelling proposition or even, perhaps, a coherent whole. It is rather a partial guidebook of my tour through twenty years of analysis of one long, blood red, skein of the rope of Irish history. One single strand. Picked clear of context, Irish violence, 1798, the Fenians, Whiteboys and murder from the ditch, Easter 1916, Invincibles, and the H-Block, may seem a coherent whole, much of the long story of the nation, a dominant strand. Political violence, Republican physical force, is actually but one and, not, always or often, a very important strand. There are other compelling traditions, many causes and factors, influence and practices, all swiftly neglected or relegated by the advocates of the gun in politics who would prefer not to reflect on the lineage of accommodation, the parliamentary tradition, the power of the monster meeting or the written word. What to do with the common people who cheered the royal visits, adored the quality, who stopped short of sedition, who loved Parnell and O'Connor, and voted for Redmond and presently would deny a united Ireland almost at any cost? Easier to ignore the Castle Catholic and Anglo-Irish. Easier still to ignore most history. And, of course, any cut of Irish history—and Ireland has increasingly been well served by historians too often read only by their own—reveals an enormously complex past, a meld of economics and demographics, social custom, external influences, categories of commitment, great patriot speechs and parish records, battle records and tax returns, a welter of events beyond heroes and martyrs and the comfortable litany of grievance and vengeance. Still Irish history is, if in part, a litany of grievance and vegeance, plague, famine, oppression, lost battles, flown earls, and institutionalized injustice. The gun, certainly, in this century had played all too prominent a part but, again, not to the exclusion of all else.

Mostly the Irish, like all others, have little time for politics beyond election day, parades, and the intrusion of the bureaucracy and less for the gun unless threatened in a most immediate way. Those who agitate for good causes or bad, organize and demonstrate, those who live by politics, forget how little others care in the press of real problems: a raise in pay, a marriage or a car accident, school leaving and a second mortgage. Those, too, who write of wars and rumors of wars, the rush to the barricades and great terror forget, especially, one suspects, in Irish matters, that mostly tomorrow is like yesterday, political slaughter is rare and erratic, screeching for attention even when irrelevant or marginal to the nation's course. Thus any approach to Ireland focused on the gun in politics, the recent Troubles, the immediate past as prologue to conflict is by necessity limited to exploring but one Ireland, one tradition, one strident, shrill instrument that moves events along.

These Irish events because they so often arrive packaged in English, nearly a mutual language for the various off-islanders, have a sense of undeserved familiarity. In political matters there are elections and blocs, parties with explicable traditions, judges with wigs for the English, campaigns involving kith and kin based on past favors for the Americans, and parliamentary practice hardly alien to the Commonwealth nations: and no strange Celtic tongue but in civil service examinations. Yet Irish politics like Irish-English is misleading. Real events, loyalties, trusts, and malice are quite often strange matters in familiar clothes. The simple language of governance curtains other often less comfortable matters, different nets and webs of power and influence, unarticulated values—and old myths made into new unavowed realities. A few months in a country parish, a few years in Dublin, a generation of concern will hardly be sufficient to trace the hidden paths of power or the convoluted basis of politics—but a beginning can be made. When the façade of charm, conventional habits, shared institutions and the lilt of phrase is recognized as only the first fence in a long hurdle toward the uncertain center of Irish society, then there are still other problems and still no solutions. In any case, once near the elusive center there is no great crowd beyond practitioners and strays. Most, certainly most of the Irish, have only intermittent time for politics, care little of the special ethnic hurdles, rarely are troubled by basics, historical practice, or hidden ikons.

This is everywhere valid. Politics tends to have a low priority with all but those involved unless violent change disrupts everyday life: money becomes worthless, foreign armies arrive by night, the meek are imprisoned or the devout punished. Power then has raw edges and ordinary people must live on the dangerous edge of events. Except briefly, episodically in the midst of the Tan War, in Ireland there has in this century been little violence: no great war, no invasion, famine, fiscal collapse, no plague or pogrom, no terror in the streets—until the Ulster Troubles. Even then the last twenty years have seen the chronic, daily anguish limited to a few fever sites sequestered by distance in the country and by poverty in the urban ghettos. Elsewhere in Ireland life moves apace. Occasional spectacular atrocity, patriotic sacrifice, or another distant death may mar tranquility; but novelty and sensation have been eroded by the long butcher's bill. So indignation is banked and anguish lost. In the North violence has been institutionalized and elsewhere largely ignored. Politics for most remains the erratic medley of voting and legislating, taxes, crime, entitlements; and power most readily seen in traffic regulation. Order is threatened by car thieves and random vandals, enhanced by royal visits or the All-Ireland final. Money is short and times hard, unemployment up and so politicians discredited; but revolution remains a school subject and a dream of Republicans not even a potential for hope or glory.

Ireland for most of the century has moved along, slightly out of phase with Europe, a bit behind in fashions, always on the narrow edge of penury even in times good for entrepreneurs with smart money. Largely the island has been tranquil with only the spectacular interruption between 1916 and 1922 that in contrast to the chaos on the continent was largely painless. The present Troubles, too, protracted, increasingly attenuated violence, limited in site and scope, seemingly tolerable without prospect of accommodation, have been reduced to murderous background music for real life except at the few nodes of conflict. Thus work focused on Irish violence, even and especially Irish Republican violence, will be blinkered, concerned with the few, the aberrant, the morbid.

Others, inside and out of Ireland, see an island in turmoil, a risen people, a nation on the march, a riotous present arising from an eight hundred year prologue. It is a special Republican vision. The people seldom mass in the streets except in the dreams of agitators. The masses seldom rise under rebel banners. Mostly now and in past centuries people stay home, tend their garden, wait out troubled times, live quiet lives in desperate times. The world of Irish patriots has crafted a rebel history, a glittering tapestry of legends and martyrs, villainous ebony and blood red threads, woven with dreams and dedication, that has little to do with the real world of milk prices, film queues, and leaving certificates. Still, there are those who go armed into the streets certain that such a world exists, that such a history is merely the plain, tale of events, that the present grievance and past dedication are not simply real but also a responsibility and validation. Everywhere, they see injustice and shame and so act in the name of a past that the disinterested find difficult to dissect and hard to weigh. Those disinterested observers, who doubt patriot history, even the most cautious of analysts, who come to pick at the threads of Irish reality, not one tapestry but many, not even one Ireland but many, must also accept that the politics of violence is not the same as Irish politics, that the spectacular and brutal are not dominant beyond the headlines.

Even more difficult than avoiding a special vision, no matter how carefully wrought, or an exaggeration of focus, no matter how prominent the turbulence, is the inevitable insidious appeal of the covert world of gunmen, the romance of cordite, the delicate taste, even second-hand, of the great game in narrow streets. For a historian all men are dead and the lure of power or easy money or state secrets unreal: the games dead kings play have no rewards for a contemporary observer but insight and understanding. For those concerned with real gunmen and tomorrow's massacre, secret armies may pay different and not so desirable rewards. It tends to take a very long time and regular prompting to eschew the attractions of that other hidden world, to find each time, the figure in the shadow, the man in the trenchcoat, the sniper in the ditch is simply the same lad down the lane sent to kill for the good or ill. The rattle of a Thompson gun may leave dreadful wounds; force-feeding is ritual strangulation; a target plays football at off-hours and prefers light ale. There is little romance in amputation, the impact of flying glass, the long years sealed in cold, dank, stone cells. The exhilaration of danger is brief, fleeting. The romance of the gunmen is best savored at a distance.

So over twenty years, then, in and out of Ireland, to and from various troubles, I have sought to remember the everyday Ireland eager for peace and quiet and a bit more than frugal comfort, and put aside the patriot's history written by the dedicated or exaggerated into a primary concern. Most of all, whether visibly or not, it is crucial to recall the costs of conflict, the maimed, the innocent ruined, the bright and brave humiliated, the roll of harm, yesterday's victims, to balance the lure of small wars in small countries. There is, of course, a special lure, for the young and bold an almost fatal lure, seeping from a secret army. Few volunteers in any crusade weigh the risks—and fewer still grow old in the service of those secret armies. Revolution is a young man's game directed by the very few serving life sentences, possessed by a vocation and denied alternatives. There, the center of that circle where a few covert, dedicated, often brutal and inept men move, has been the secret arena of my analytical interests. It is no more a romantic world than is the body crumpled in a country ditch wrapped in a black plastic bag waiting collection or the killer, now home, untouched by the operation, nearly as dead as victim, surely as much victim of the secret war. At times, just as the Belfast lanes or the hillsides of South Armagh seem a truly vast distance from the green at St. Mullins or Pembroke Lane, what I write about technology transfer or sociological leadership profiles, rebel legitimization or contemporary scholarly analysis seems divorced by time and distance and importance beyond reason from the secret world at the center of the circle, from that ambivalent dark arena at the heart of rebellion.

There is as well a risk at venturing into alien arenas that not only will the game appeal but so too the players' motives. Many scholars so venture under patent banners, *engagé*, their craft committed while others convert as the pages turn. In contemporary Irish matters there is a quite justifiable suspicion that most who express written concern are committed by heritage or class or wont. Many feel compelled within a preface to detail their religion, abhorence of violence, love of liberty before revealing the text, thus supposedly disinterested, a neutral gloss on contentious, killing matters. Others have no qualms, come from no neutral corner, flail about for any reader to note. A historian may write as if all players were dead but in Irish matters readers tend to breathe fire into a history all too living. No analyst, like a surgeon, comes sterile to the page nor can for long remain totally unmoved by recent, deadly events. No reasonable observer from afar can poke among the ruins of nearly a century of trouble, senseless murder, hypocrisy, denial and deceit, splendid dreams and repeated atrocity without some repulsion, some attraction beyond the weighing of evidence. The IRA vision continues to possess compelling allure despite everything, the lies, pretense and slaughter. And the IRA after a quarter century is not alien but people, friends, acquaintances, sources and an extended family, a Republican tribe and special band, not cut-out villains or ciphers, not criminal statistics or unpleasant headlines, blurred identikit pictures in a crumpled newspaper. And many I like not because or despite of their politics. And some I do not.

In the most ethereal terms, the Republican dream, based on the long ago fathers of the movement, seems, even to me, more valid than either most conventional visions for Ireland or all of the trendy revolutionary options proposed by Ireland's few dedicated radicals. The responsibility, assumed or inherited, to make that dream manifest is not mine. It is even easier to stand apart from real contemporary Irish political choices, parties based not on principle but grievance and choices of long dead men, movements and schism arising from imported fashions elsewhere discarded, loyalties to unpleasant tribes, jobbery. Even for the bold and dedicated—democratic, decent, and just—there are only crooked tools, warped institutions, and appalling problems not easily solved nor often even defined. It is often a wonder that so few opt for the gun and then, mostly, to use against outlanders instead of their own. Thus the Republican dream, Tone's Republic, still has a magnetism far beyond orthodox proposal for a new Ireland based on the present Jerry-built ruin of exploitation, greed, lost hopes and thwarted lives.

The deathless dream, the pure Republic conjured up on one summer Sunday afternoon each year before the grave of Tone by that secret army, does attract despite the betrayals, slaughtered innocents, and cant. Certainly it attracts more than the offers of the conventional, frugal comfort at best, a narrow vision of a new Ireland filled with old blunders. Certainly it is only a dream, but all too clearly worth the killing for the faithful, yet no more possible than reaching Oz by the Yellow Brick Road. Those who do, however, go down that road toward the Republic with its gutters awash with garbage, blood, and mire are, often, everyday people, some delightful, others not, but rarely mindless, psychopathic salesmen of violence. They go in a good cause which surely makes the necessary slaughter no less dreadful—more so, perhaps, because the luminous dream is just that, not a viable, potential political reality but a Celtic grail.

More than the Republican litany or the volunteers, the opposition is inclined to engender distaste from the balanced or the uncommitted. On the island and out of Britain these enemies of the Republicans have little appeal except to the threatened. Justifiably outraged at the pretensions of the Republicans, at the murder and arson, at extortion, armed robbery, maiming, and torture hastily clothed in piety and politics, the conventional have reacted as often as not by soiling themselves. Justice has been denied and seen to be denied, innocents punished, the guilty mistreated, suspects murdered, and the suspect harassed beyond measure. Seldom have democratic systems been revealed in less flattering a light than in the recent years of the troubles. Hence it is all too easy to be indignant at the outrages of the orthodox, more particularly at the hypocrisy that cloths institutionalized injustice. An alien eye tends to focus on the one lost sheep in the Irish flock—and on both sides of the border the responsible, the police, the army, the agents paid by the state, have strayed all too often. More was expected and so more the disappointment. The ensuing sympathy, however, does not need to accrue to the Republicans. They, individually appealing or no, in search of a truly fair Ireland of all the people or no, sinned against by the arrogant and dissembling or no, they have left a trail down the dirty brick road that few close witnesses would seek to excuse. So I have never been tempted, never been a volunteer *manqué* on the road to another's republic, nor especially fond of their avowed opponents.

In fact in Ireland, since I have not been a public advocate of Republican causes nor a secret supplier, there was and is a body of theoretically informed opinion convinced that there must, as is too often the case in such matters, be an ulterior motive. The most fashionable over the course of a generation has been that I represent CIA interests in Ireland. Where once British intelligence made the sun rise and the rain fall, now, the people at Langley in Virginia are responsible, opposing as well all good men and true who seek change, justice, revolution, the fine, fair things of political life. Alack, the CIA, even now cares almost nothing for Irish matters—the concern solely of our British cousins—beyond sending a man over to lunch with appropriate people every month or so. Ireland is just not very important not only at the CIA but also in Washington. If it were, the American imperialists would, the past being prologue, have long ago sent some conventional type to be attached to the Embassy at Ballsbridge and take notes from the *Irish Times*. So being an agent for no one I have the benefits neither of free lunches nor a stipend out of Ballsbridge, only the reputation among the trendy as the point of the capitalist lance. What is it, in any case, that the CIA would want to know about Republicans, after eight hundred years? The Republicans are no threat to the Great Satan or often even to their Dublin and London opponents. They are not even of great interest to the pragmatists along the Potomac; they are mere peripheral Celtic gunmen, the stuff of novels, easily parsed from public sources and borrowed analysis. So as I write not for Republican purpose so too is my interest my own, not that of those spiders at the center of the web at Langley—a web that often has as much reality as the Yellow Brick Road to Oz.

J. BOWYER BELL

PART I
The IRA Past as Prologue

I know no way of judging the future
but by the past.
—Patrick Henry, 1775

When all is said and done, I am concerned about Ireland because, through luck, I found a contemporary arena where some of the most unpleasant games of violent politics have been played out for years presenting examples and categories and cases all tightly focused in one small, usually pleasant, arena. In that arena much of the Irish audience has seldom paid attention to the game, and even that game for much of the time has been conventional, more accommodating than violent. Those who would use the gun in politics have appeared from time to time with mixed results—results almost always tilted and interpreted for special purpose. Those gunmen, now and then, have loomed large, romantic Ireland in a trenchcoat never quite dead and gone. They have thrown huge shadows on the contemporary canvas, but in reality have often played bit parts, and as players were not especially romantic in closeups, despite the Thompson gun and the ballads. Yet the Republicans, dedicated to physical force and the Republic, immersed in their history of martyrs and legends, crusaders often on real, not yellow brick, roads have played a significant role in contemporary Ireland. They have known, to their satisfaction, what is wrong with Ireland, what can be done about it, and, if successful, how to fashion the result. And hardly anyone else involved would be so bold.

Much more important, beyond the island, the long troubled history of the IRA, the entire spectrum of tactics and techniques, the various strategies of revolution, the flaws, the failures, the rare triumphs, the oversights and missed chances has done far more for observers than it has for the Irish. The Irish experience embodied troubled visions and dreams far from the Celtic killing ground. And, as the decades pass, the struggle for the Republic grows ever more protracted, the examples richer and more various. It is not the Irish alone who wait for the end-stage, the flickering out of the vital signs of

23

violence, an accommodation, a solution, an end, the gun gone, politics again solely getting and spending, keeping and dispersing, privilege and opposition. I once thought that by the end of the century, matters—if not settled—would be at least silent, the gun having been placed on the shelf. But Year 2000 is not that far away, and neither the Republic nor relief seems much closer than it was when first I came to St. Mullins.

St. Mullins was at a very special time, for events in Ireland had slowed down, and the village was closer to Victoria than "swinging London" or John F. Kennedy. Already the signs of change were about in Dublin with the construction of the glass-box, pagoda-topped headquarters of Labour on the Liffey—a new and irrelevant Liberty Hall; but for the time being the country rested. In popular theory this was as it should be, for Ireland was changeless, time moving through the Celtic mists, parochial, conservative, adamantine, unforgiving and unforgetting. Yet Ireland, the real historical Ireland, had long been the site of rapid and often horrendous change: in a century the language had been lost, much of the population dispersed, the rest largely incorporated into British ways and means, the economyy transformed and even the Roman Church shifting with the theological tides of the times. After 1922, however, there was a long pause partly from exhaustion, partly from penury; little was built, fewer fled, institutions decayed or ossified, jobs were scarce, money short, government distant and parish concerns major. After the first glass box appeared, change rushed into the island; the transformation in attitudes and habits was as great as the great waves of ticky-tack houses pulsing out of Dublin or the new dual-carriage ways and sprouting television antennas. Some things did not change, though, in St. Mullins or elsewhere: the Church remained, as did rural piety and public puritanism. And largely those of a more secular vocation within the Republican movement stayed the course, suspicious of novelty and sensation.

Even after the traumas of 1969-70, the core of the movement, the Provos, remained faithful to the old ways and ideals, isolated in time and place, rocks in a sea of troubles: South Armagh and the Sort Strand, the Ardoynne and the hills of Tyrone. That the Creggan and Andersonstown were new, state-built, planned, concessions to need, did not make the people new or their banners novel or their secret army different. The Fenians lived in Ulster just as the nineteenth century had lived in St. Mullins. And so my time in the country brought some indication of the nature of Irish time and the persistence of the past.

Perhaps, scanning the entire contemporary revolutionary spectrum, the

IRA's most curious aspect has been its persistence. There has been an ability to maintain the tradition, the grievances, solutions, and aspirations of previous generations largely in past form even at a cost in efficiency and appeal. Ireland may change, Europe may change. Revolution may change, demanding hi-tech skills and middle-class talents. The IRA has kept the faith at grave cost but with consistency. For it, history, the rendered past of its dreams, is a real, many splendored icon. For it, time runs at a different pace and its vision grows no less penetrating with age. Thus, in St. Mullins, in my unplanned, largely haphazard exposure to Ireland, I had been given a trip in time denied those who came later or even those whose native wit had been focused in a Dublin that swirled largely to London currents, a decade from fashion.

My concern with the present, the revolutions near and far of our own time, had special exposure to the Irish experience, to Fenian history that lived on, vital, respected, often effective, raw and dangerous. Thus each venture here into the recent Irish past is as much a journey into my evolutionary history with time twisted back and forth, the past often more real than present expectations. And for me insight into the real world of the present, the potentially troubled world of the immediate future, has often been founded on that past—and always so, as here, when Ireland is the subject.

1

Arms and the Volunteer

I'm off to join the IRA . . .
To the echo of the Thompson gun. . . .

There is never an easy beginning for a probe into history—no door labeled plainly "Once Upon a Time"—and no present has seemingly longer or more tangled roots than the Irish and particularly the Irish Republican Army. Everyone, even those most recently innocent, inevitably turns backward after a glance at the contentious present. The Irish past is not simply prologue but determinant; the future not simply held captive by the past but intricately to be shaped. History, like politics, is not an exact science; it exists as formed by man and is limited by the obdurate facts. An alien would see not clearer but differently, perhaps, noting the more visible as the more important Irish facts—the gradual removal of trees, the increase in Nordic blood-types, the use of sugar, the great trends of warming and cooling, the level of toxic pollutants, the increasing height of children, the disappearance of snakes, or the arrival of Asiatic microbes. The Republican would generally see special political events reflecting the centuries of clashing aspirations between Saxon and Celt, opponents who biologists or ethnologists would be hard put to define. The more orthodox, still seized on political matters, would see a long train of events, some certainly violent, that all but inevitably have led, through accommodation and confrontation, to the establishment in much of the island of an effective democratic state, monitor of free institutions, a frugal and pious people, guardians of the flame. This is not at all the way matters seem to those whose liberty, freedom, and civil rights seem at risk to those Fenian guardians of a hateful decadent Mediterranean culture made vicious and violent in recent years for Pope's purpose. Others dissect with very sharp instruments and great conviction the same past, finding class answers to political problems. There are as many Irish pasts as there are Irelands—North and South, Protestant and Catholic, rich and poor, old and new, rural and urban—and if not all, then too many seem to have a special past, special roots, plead special causes, explain, insist and predict, often in isolation but always with passionate conviction. Not only is there no consensus but also

27

present Irish straits have inclined advocates to move back into the past. Historians now harrow with bright new tools over peasant disorders, mercantile investment, patterns of local government, French intentions, the correspondence of the parish, the nature of rural agitators, city weavers, and Westminster votes. To explain a largely unpalatable present, to buttress programs of change, to shape the past for congenial contemproary advocacy, and often to simply discover the truth, a generation has been rewriting or at least reviewing the Irish past. There is now an Irish history for nearly every Irish cause. The IRA can offer reading lists and the Orangeman, the work of tractarians. Marxists, secure in spin-off British universities and Irish-Americans, out of the diaspora, have added studies of varying merit. The past is not so much prologue as battleground, where contending advocates struggle over scraps of legitimacy, fair precedents, old martyrs or the origins of historical forces apparent only to the saved. To the committed, now thick on the ground, history has become what it has always been for many: a means to fashion a proper past and assure the desired future. Confident of the proper tomorrow, many seek and find the inevitable yesterday.

In this strident battle of books, deployment of journals and volley of reviews, Ireland is generally well served. Much is awful, much contentious or contrived, much is passing matter, and some is exciting, revealing, skilled and novel. There is no consensus and no converting the convinced; but where once there was a void, a blank in bibliographies, a gap in library file cards, now the lists unravel across the floor, the shelves groan. If much remains to be done, much has begun. What is clear from afar is that the history of the Troubles is long and important. It is important for no other reason than that those involved and responsible believe it to be so. The crucial strand of the IRA stretches far into the past—another way of indicating that contrast to most of the world's revolutionary turbulence, the Irish experience is most protracted. All events, most especially revolutions, have deep roots but the Irish are particular, extending far into the past and greatly determining the direction of present growth. The very structure of the IRA can be traced without strain for over a century, and the dream is founded in the Enlightenment on even older Celtic relics. Within the Republican tradition, more particularly within the Irish tradition, can be found almost the entire spectrum of strategies and tactics of radical change—not just murder from a ditch and proponents of dynamite, but monster meetings, mass petitions, parliamentary disruptions, rural agitation, boycotts, diaspora politics and (as always) secret armies coupled with covert ambassadors and dedicated publicists. Centuries of practice and example lumber the present. France has had five Republics while the Army Council still seeks the same one. Britain has won and lost an empire and the Army Council still seeks to free the very first colony seized long before the crown at Westminster was imperial. Russia has had revolutionaries, revolution, and reaction, turned and turned again; and the Army Council has persisted. Once beyond the Pope, the descendents of Saxe-Colburg-Gotha, and a few persistent husks, the IRA has nearly as long a lineage as any in Europe.

By necessity history *must* matter. Certainly the IRA—Irish Republicans untouched by parliamentary power or present contentment—has fashioned its own history. Distant revolutionaries have sought to learn from the IRA experience what to avoid, what to employ and what is possible, probable and profitable. Some have been successful, even crediting Irish example. There may be too many examples for any one harried Army Council; too many options or alternatives; too much history to teach properly. In any case one should be wary of who would proffer the lessons of history. The IRA has often learned little; yet there is much to learn, even if it is not easy to apply. There is nothing more difficult than to watch present events fall into past patterns—not repeated, but surely reminiscent of past events. And, too often for efficiency, present purpose moves along, innocent of previous experience and potential; for so burdened with history, the IRA often does not have the time for reflection on contemporary application. The organization remains rather content with slogans and adages. For most, the history of grievance, the litany of martyrs and the convictions from past error—the big picture in shimmering colors—are sufficient.

Those within the movement who have advocated change, revision and novel direction, have explored the Irish past to seek not so much *truth,* as *validation* from the dead. They found Marxist ancestors in those of no property, or Celtic crusaders who sought out only British enemies. For many within the movement, such historical adventures led to communist contamination or conversion to parliamentary politics or alliances with monsters. Even the Provos' move to sit in parliamentary seats produced schism—one more Republican Sinn Féin opposed to violation of cherished principles. Thus the IRA history grows increasingly rigid; another orthodoxy that is not sufficiently pliable to include much from the past. Schism comes out of novel history, security from the comfortable. Even previous techniques and tactics, long neglected, are seldom unburied. Undisciplined shovels might dig up the unwanted. There seems to be too much history to absorb properly or to manipulate to novel advantage. The dangers of revisionist investigation have increasingly seemed too great. Tactics become principles that are considered morally just—history's gift, unquestioned by the wise. With patriot history—stark colors and past splendor, heroes and the perfidiously vile, a risen people, a nation on the march—there is no danger and some reward. Novel enthusiasm is saved for other struggles; distant, faint, and fashionable. The struggles of Palestinian Arabs or Latin American guerrillas teach only the same old Irish lessons. Irish historical ventures have for the movement seemingly required risks greater than the subsequent rewards.

This most traditional of revolutionary organizations has thus evolved only a rigid, conventional history—narrow, and parochial—which, if ideologically sound, is strategically barren. Others learn from Irish history because they need stand on the result, have no stake in a Celtic past and risk nothing poking into unsavory corners of the island boneyard. And so those involved in faint, distant, even fashionable struggles may come away from Ireland with applications—or so thought many past rebels who parsed the Irish scent. They learned what to do, what not to do, how to exploit their opponent, marshal their own, and most importantly, how to assure that victory changed more than the name plates on office doors and the crest on military stationery. They were intrigued not only with the techniques of murder from a ditch but also with the failure of the dream, left to the gunmen of the IRA, while the winners droned on in the Dáil contemplating hot dinners and share options. The IRA husbanded the dream, patriot history, the good old ways that were often neither old nor good, and let slip much of its strategic and tactical heritage. In hard times few read into the past beyond the simple annals of the martyrs. Involvement in past events, as the IRA was all too aware, did not necessarily reveal bright, blinking guide lights to future and immediate action. The time to conjure up the past was also sorely limited by the war, with a headquarters always on the edge of schism, a menu of pressing problems with no solutions, the demands of the insatiable and the dangers of an angry opponent. Yet this is always the case at the center of an active revolutionary circle, and some of those pressing problems with no apparent solutions had, from time to time in the past, found solutions.

To pursue, in whatever configuration, a strategy of physical force—insurrection, open rebellion, war-on-the-installment-plan—a necessary condition is acquisition of the material means, the tools. No revolutionary force ever feels that there are sufficient means at hand. The P.L.O. in Lebanon had more guns than the guerrillas, and caverns full of martial supplies, but they still wanted more. They had even managed to obtain tanks and heavy artillery, truly hostages to fate and clear evidence that to a secret army, acquisition often seems more productive than application. The IRA and their Fenian ancestors have always been deeply concerned with having the appropriate means to pursue a strategy of physical force and felt, justifiably, that Irish problems of supply were special. Certainly the arena of potential battle was an island tucked away lee of Britain, isolated without a local industry in a society that monitored weapons closely. On the other hand, the island had numerous isolated points of access, small harbors, empty beaches, port cities, and beyond Britain were the crown's enemies who were often willing suppliers to the restive. There were all sorts of strategic problems that would determine the nature of the supply problem: a French expeditionary force, a campaign of rural insurrection, bombs within Britain, or an attack on imperial Canada from America. Each presented differing technical problems. In the twentieth century, the IRB and then the IRA faced the problems of a general rising, fueled from abroad but aborted at an Easter insurrection in Dublin; an insurrection of a secret army throughout the island armed by various diaspora sources (The Tan War from 1918-1921); an internecine struggle by overt but irregular means (1922-1923); a holding operation with a steady erosion of spirit and resources (1924-1939); a bombing campaign in Britain (1939-1940); a guerrilla campaign in Ulster (1954-1962); and a few years of drift without visible assets.

In this century, the quartermaster of the IRA has often to seek abroad for the means to wage a campaign of physical force, and rarely has the result been sufficient for the avowed purpose or acquired with ease and regularity. The history of the IRA arms supply has been one of repeated failure, short falls, aborted transport, wasted funds and futile arrangements, brightened from time to time by a special success. Since there is no aspect of a secret army more secret than arms, except perhaps certain fiscal matters, the history of IRA arms procurement has hardly ever been plainly written. It is difficult enough to learn from written history—the agreed and accepted canons—but it is even more difficult to learn from hushed rumor, neglected court cases, colleagues' gossip, and newspaper reports of disaster. Thus it is hardly surprising that each new generation of Republicans has tended to approach the problem of supply with a halting grasp of the past as well as a few shared stories, a crumpled list of phone numbers abroad, a desperate need, and the odd idea. Britain's foes come and go. Once found everywhere, the enemies of the useful crown are now rare and obscure: Argentine officers, a scattering of Arabs, almost no noted government. Independent suppliers, congenial marketplaces, and agents of opportunity have a very short half life—yesterday's purveyor of grenades or time-fuses is today's long-term felon or retired resident of a Caribbean isle. What remains is the historical problem of fueling a revolution. Historical solutions tended to be just that—historical—screwed into past special circumstances of no use as guide, only goad. Yet within Republican history, there is a long, nearly invisible strand that might be label procurement, the province of the Quartermaster General on the headquarters staff. Most potential governmental suppliers are ignorant of Irish matters, insistent on plausible denial, doubtful of IRA capacity or the rewards from cooperation, and place such manuevers very low on their priority list. Most private suppliers are only looking for payment at more than the going rates, often to evade delivery, and at times, a secondary market in information sold to the British. Enthusiastic volunteers tend to be clumsy, too public, personally undisciplined, and more trouble than they would be worth if there were any alternative. Every revolutionary dreams of a risk-free supplier, capable of delivery, and possessed with a full and elegant array of the necessities. For the Irish, this mythical beast has yet to be found, leaving only a few rare, reluctant and uncertain governments acting haltingly at a low level, with no promises for the future; the odd revolutionary friend; or private dealers without scruples or ready addresses when matters go wrong. And then there are the faithful scattered through the diaspora; eager, often incompetent, they scramble for funds, learning procurement on the job, but find little but the police. So most often there are only the distant faithful, one step ahead of detectives with a life-time in the game and always one step from a coup. Together with the IRA, they must make do with retail purchases and dreams.

Sometimes even the blind hog finds an acorn. Sometimes the IRA puts together a splendid operation—elegant, effective, novel, sophisticated, and an intregal part of the greater strategy. This does not happen often, but then revolutionary triumph is generally rare. Sometimes even the halting, make-do collection of retail purchases shipped in erratic and irregular job lots, prove more effective than the hi-tech dreams of the headquarters staff. Sometimes matters do work out for the IRA but not often, not in this century, and never as a matter of course or even proper planning. When they do, the impact can be consequential, especially for the guardians of order suddenly outgunned or overawed by the scruffy gunmen in trench coats deploying much bigger guns.

The most elegant of all IRA ventures into armaments occurred in the glory days of the Tan War when, for the only time, nearly the entire spectrum of modern talents was available to the secret army: chemical engineers, import-export bankers, solicitors and journalists, foreign travelers, the wealthy and the skilled. A nation once again, it was an enormous and rich constituency for a rebel headquarters. In 1916 the rising had more poets than engineers or staff officers, but within two years there were all sorts of volunteers on the island and in the diaspora. The prospect of sending pistols by post or one rifle at a time held no charms for men with millions and vast entrepreneurial skills. What was needed was vision, gall, and competence applied to need. There was no better place to find all of this than in America, the great mill that ground huddled masses into consumers and richly rewarded producers—even the immigrant Gaels. So while pursuing simple matters of ambush and schism, I ran acrosss an old volunteer, Larry de Lacy, in Wexford who pointed out the origin of the

Irish affiliation with the Thompson gun. The IRA *Tommy gun* was not a concept out of pub history, a refined tale lifted from the patriots' book, or merely a source of ballads. I found that the IRA had not simply imported Thompson guns, the remnants of the Clan na Gael in the United States had also underwritten the weapon's development, made the first great purchase, arranged shipment, and oversaw subsequent supplies. Other revolutionaries are eager to acquire advanced weapons from conventional arsenals. The IRA had funded the research and development necessary for one of the world's great infantry weapons—the gun that became a myth and almost incidently an effective military tool for fifty years, and will almost surely still be in use on the periphery of great wars for decades to come. Of course, the myth was wrong, the ballads in error—the gun was barely used against the British and not often during the ensuing troubles; but the submachine gun did exist and its advent in Irish affairs was far more compelling than either ballad or myth.

> *I'm off to join the IRA*
> *And I'm off tomorrow morning*
> *And we're all off to Dublin*
>   *in the green, in the green,*
> *Where the helmets glisten in the sun*
> *Where the bayonets clash*
> *And the rifles crash*
> *To the echo of the Thompson gun.*
>   —The Merry Plowboy

Very few merry plowboys got to trade their picks and spades for Thompson guns, which was just as well for the British; but as example of what presently social scientists are prone to call non-state military technology transfer, few transactions could equal the early history of the weapon. And, true, few ballads have been written about technology transfer; but then it is all but possible to sing the history of the IRA, from the execution of Kevin Barry, who would not tell, past the hanging of the Boy from Tralee, Charlie Kerins, and Seán South of Garryowen, shot dead in Brookeborough under a northern sky, on down to the hunger strike death of Bobby Sands. So there is a song for the Tommy gun, excised by the editor of an article I eventually wrote off as unscholarly. But the IRA was a fit subject only for very contemporary scholars (and the few persistent police). And no one really foresaw that the IRA triumphs and subsequent tribulations with the Thompson gun were, as well as facets of modern history, living legend, patriot ballad, and prologue. The gun itself would appear after 1969; dug up, pulled down, brought back and used until, without nearly as much elegance or impact, the headquarters' staff found, in the Armalite, a replacement. In retrospect, the assets that previous GHQ had in the Tan Troubles could probably never be matched. Certainly the skills in America were impressive—no other revolutionary organization had ever been started with research and development instead of simple acquisition. Most certainly, as history or prologue, the Thompson gun's journey to Ireland was a fascinating adventure to trace.

2

The Thompson Submachine Gun in Ireland

The genesis of the Thompson submachine gun can be traced to the Spanish-American war of 1898. Lieutenant-Colonel Marcellus Taileferro Thompson accompanied General Shafter's expeditionary force against Santiago de Cuba. After a campaign of blunders, plagues, and victories, Thompson came away from Cuba convinced of the need to improve the fire-power of the average soldier. Thompson's various duties in the United States Ordnance Department limited his time for private research and development although expending his knowledge of military small-arms. After a conventional and successful career in the Ordnance Department, Colonel Thompson retired in 1914 to become Chief Engineer of the Remington Eddystone Plant. He began private research into the possibilities of an automatic rifle.[1]

In 1916 Thompson formed the Auto-Ordnance Corporation to exploit the potential of an automatic rifle. One of his partners was the former United States Naval Commander John Bell Bliss who held a vital patent on a physical principle of metal adhesion and repulsion which might make practical an automatic mechanism.[2] His other partner, a well known financier, was Thomas Fortune Ryan, who more vital for the future interests of Ireland was less widely known as an influential member of the Clan na Gael.[3] Whether Ryan in 1916 was motivated by the financial prospects of Auto-Ordnance or by the potential wedge into armament manufacture—or both—remains vague. In any case, Thompson's efforts to develop an automatic rifle had to be postponed when the United States entered World War I. Too valuable to remain in retirement, Thompson was brought back into the United States Army. In August 1918, he was promoted to Brigadier General; but with the end of the war in November, he again retired in the following month to devote full time to Auto-Ordnance.

By this time, Bliss in failing health had little part to play in the subsequent research and development. Experiments which had begun in Thompson's home in Pennsylvania were continued at facilities leased from Warner and Swazey Company in Cleveland. This company had developed some of the early testing devices for Thompson's autorifle which led inad-

35

vertently to an automatic submachine gun.[4] Thompson was soon applying for one patent after another, each representing significant modifications. Ultimately, Auto-Ordnance and Thompson would hold 285 patents relating to small arms manufacture. During 1919 the early prototype guns began to come out of the Warner and Swazey works in Cleveland. Designated Model-1919, these guns came out in three or four lots, each representing a modified version: for example, one could be fired only on full-automatic. The total number of Model-1919 guns probably came to no more than twenty-five or thirty, intended mainly as demonstration guns for potential customers.

By 1920 the question of ultimate sales became increasingly vital. Apparently, Thompson felt that the most practical use of his gun would be as a riot weapon in the hands of law enforcement agencies but he did not discount the military market. Model-1919 had already cost several hundred thousand dollars to develop and any responsible customer would be welcome. In 1920 the gun was test-fired by the New York City Police Department's Pistol Team at Camp Peekskill in New York. In August 1920, the Pistol Team demonstrated the gun publicly at the National Rifle Matches at Camp Perry in Ohio.[5] The gun aroused considerable interest. The United States Marine Corps began testing the gun at Quantico, Virginia. The New York police ordered ten guns, but an order of only ten guns from America's largest police force did not bode well for large sales to other law enforcement agencies. While many seemed interested in his gun, Thompson in 1920 was not finding customers capable of ordering a sufficient quantity of guns to recoup his massive investment in development.

By this time, of course, the interest of the leaders of Clan na Gael and various Irish representatives in military weapons of any sort had quickened considerably. At some stage, probably formally in December 1920, Thompson's partner Thomas Fortune Ryan put officials of Auto-Ordnance in touch with some prospective customers interested in placing substantial orders. Whatever Ryan's original intentions in joining Auto-Ordnance, he was quite capable of recognizing the potential value of the new gun for the IRA, then fighting a guerrilla war with a medley of mismatched and often obsolete weapons. In 1920 any military hardware was needed in Ireland. A brand new automatic weapon which could be acquired in considerable quantity was an incredible stroke of luck—or good planning. While the Auto-Ordnance officials were obviously very anxious for legitimate orders, any hint of extra-legal involvement would destroy the company and Thompson's hopes. Ryan and the Clan were confident that arrangements could be made for perfectly legal purchases by middle men which would leave Auto-Ordnance in the clear and the Clan in possession of the guns.[6]

On January 15, 1921, Frank Menkling, an official of the company and

Ryan's secretary, accepted an order for 100 of the newest model sub-machine gun from two dealers, George Gordon Rorke and Frank B. Ochsenreiter, in Washington, D.C. The gun ordered by the Washington dealers was designated Model-1921, using a box magazine of twenty .45 calibre cartridges or drum magazines of 50 or 100 rounds. The gun could fire either fully automatically or in single shots, semi-automatically; and although it had, technically, an extreme range of 600 yards, the gun was essentially a short range weapon with tremendous shock power from the heavy .45 calibre cartridges. In January, however, when the first order came in to Menkling, the gun existed only as a prototype. With the prospect of still more substantial orders not only from Ryan's friends but from both law enforcement agencies and military organizations, Auto-Ordnance's fortunes looked quite hopeful. Since the company did not have the facilities to mass produce guns, Thompson placed an order for 15,000 Model-1921 guns with the Colt's Patent Fire Arms Company of Hartford, Connecticut. Auto-Ordnance in New York would market the guns produced under Thompson's patents by Colt.

Behind the seemingly straightforward order by Rorke and Ochsenreiter lay the rapidly developing network of the Clan na Gael. The Irish intended to purchase 1,000 guns through intermediaries, stockpile them in New York, and at the first likely opportunity ship them illicitly to Ireland. Rorke and Ochsenreiter were disinterested agents of a mysterious Frank Williams, the man in charge of ordering and collecting the guns. Williams or Laurence Pierce was actually Laurence de Lacy of County Wexford, who had been operating previously in California as an Irish agent. Behind Lacy were other Irish agents confronted with the problem of financing the purchase of the guns.

Although various Irish organizations had been accumulating funds at a most impressive rate during the previous few years, the total needed for 1,000 guns at $225 apiece along with magazines and .45 calibre ammunition did not exist. Even with some juggling of various accounts, more money would have to be forthcoming. Harry Boland in New York took over the financial end of the problem and began quietly channelling Dáil Eireann funds into Lacy's hands. To a large extent the money problem presented no great difficulty. With Ryan on the inside and Lacy on the outside, even acquisition of the guns should cause no problems. The irregular nature of shipping arrangments also could be overcome in New York harbor, filled with nautical friends and allies. Barring the unforeseen, a major shipment of Thompson guns could be expected to arrive in Ireland in the summer of 1921.

In March the first seven Thompson guns came off the Colt line in Connecticut. The first two guns were immediately sold to a salesman in Chicago, a Mr. Wise.[7] The Clan had already arranged for two former United States Army officers, Major James J. Dineen and Captain Patrick Cronin, to travel to Ireland as instructors. Dineen acquired the two guns and Mr. Wise disappeared. At the same time two Irish agents met in New York to test the new acquisitions. Seán Nunan and Lacy took the chance to try out an early installment. The New York Clan made arrangements to use the local Sixty-ninth Regimental Armoury for a test firing. At the armoury, Lacy and Numan found the new Model-1921 fitted with a drum magazine. Nunan fired the first burst, Lacy the second, and then Nunan finished up the magazine. Lacy was impressed that the gun had no more kick than a Peter the Painter or parabellum. Neither had any doubts that the Clan's money was going to be well spent. Dineen and Cronin with the first two Thompsons in their luggage left for Ireland. The Clan returned to funnelling the money through their agents while Lacy collected and stored the guns as they arrived at the Auto-Ordnance offices in New York from the Colt plant in Hartford.

On April 5, Rorke and Ochsenreiter ordered 500 guns, 125 100-round drum magazines, 250 fifty-round drum magazines, and 1,000 twenty-round box magazines. Auto-Ordnance accepted the order. By this time the early production Thompson guns ordered in January began trickling into Lacy's hands. While a few guns might be sent over to Ireland when the opportunity presented itself, the safest course seemed to be to wait until a major shipment was possible. Not only would a single shipment reduce the chances of premature discovery but also once the gun was used in Ireland there were bound to be repercussions in New York. The United States Department of Justice would undoubtedly take a dim view of the Irish procurement and supply operations. Thus Lacy and his "brother" Fred Williams, actually Dan Fitzgerald of County Kerry, quietly continued their collections. Liam Peddler was responsible for transport and a man named Patrick Keegan from Enniscorthy, for the boats, when the time came for shipment.

Almost every gun off the Colt line went directly to Lacy, who picked them up from Auto-Ordnance and turned them over to John Culhane to cart out to his warehouse on La Fontain Avenue in the Bronx. There the Clan had a dump for all the odd armament being stored before shipment to Ireland.[8] According to the later records of the United States Justice Department, in April at least twenty-five guns found their way to the warehouse. By May, with Colt in full production the number, neatly stacked in their crates, began to climb. Thirty arrived on May 6, forty-five on May 11. Four lots totalling 240 arrived on May 18, 19, 20 and 21. By the end of the month Lacy had at least 400 guns in the Bronx warehouse.[9]

Simultaneously, arrangements for a shipment of at least 500 guns were nearing completion. The spring of 1921 was a perfect time for illicit shipping. A lengthy maritime strike had made it almost impossible for most ships in New York harbor to keep or acquire a crew. No owner or captain was going to be too concerned about the motives of men willing to sign on a struck ship. The Irish thus need not become involved with owners or captains or complicated paper work. All that was necessary would be to supply a crew for a vessel sailing for an appropriate port.

At Pier Two in Hoboken across the Hudson River the *East Side* had been hove to since April 13. Twice the captain had lost his full crew because of the strike. With the new Irish additions to the men he had already found, the captain planned to sail for Norfolk, Virginia, and then on to England with a load of coal. By sailing date, June 17, Keegan intended that he would also have an unconsigned cargo of Thompson guns carefully stored out of sight of the curious. The warehouse in the Bronx was cleared out. A steady stream of boxes, bags, and crates were brazenly carried onto the *East Side*, often during the day. No one paid any great attention. By June 16, the final total was thirteen bags, 289 crates and 175 small boxes all tucked away. This unconsigned lot contained 495 Thompson guns, spare parts and magazines, and a substantial amount of .45 calibre ammunition.[10]

On June 16, twelve hours before the *East Side* was to sail, a small army of customs men, Department of Justice agents, and local police descended on Pier Two. Although some uncertainty still remains as to exactly how the United States authorities learned of the shipment, the immediate explanation was that a curious non-Irish crewman stumbled against one of the bags and investigated. By the time the police and Federal agents arrived, the Chief Engineer and much of the crew had mysteriously disappeared but the Thompson guns remained. The American authorities began painstakingly trying to sort out the "Williams brothers," the incredulous Rorke and Ochsenreiter, who had sold the guns to "strangers," and the officials of Auto-Ordnance.

As soon as the news broke that the "Sinn Feiners" had lost 500 Thompson guns, several British newspapers immediately reported that Irish House in London claimed the raid as a coup for British intelligence. Journalists began speculating on the vague details of the British involvement. Apparently British agents had been circulating in the grey area of the international gun trade and ran into rumors of the Irish interest in Auto-Ordnance. The British government had immediately expressed an interest in the gun to Thompson's delight. In the ensuing negotiations someone had let slip the Irish connection. In point of fact, Thompson had approached the British as early as December 1920, as potential customers. The British had, indeed, expressed an interest. In April 1921, Thompson and his European sales manager, H. Morgen, conferred in London with British officials.[11] At one point, the gun was actually demonstrated in Dublin by the famous explorer, Mitchel Hedges, apparently in hopes of an order from the Royal Irish Constabulary.[12] Since considerable effort had been taken in the United States to see that the purchases were concealed by legal agents and since those few individuals in Auto-Ordnance who were aware of the guns ultimate destination were unlikely to discuss the "Sinn Fein" tie, much of the speculation of the prowess of the British secret service might have been no more than journalistic enthusiasm. More likely, although still unproven, was the story that the British had captured an IRA document written by Richard Mulcahy, referring to the purchase of submachine guns and the necessity for training camps. If this was the case, then the British interest in Thompson is understandable in terms of the Irish problem. The British government did, in fact, lose interest in the Thompson gun soon after June 1921; but, then, so had the United States Marines lost interest after considerable initial enthusiasm.

The blaze of publicity in the New York newspapers led directly to one of the strangest episodes of the entire affair, for British agents were not the only ones interested in Thompson's new gun. Some weeks after the seizure on the *East Side*, several small Oriental gentlemen approached "Frank Williams," who was still in New York. Most politely and firmly they requested that he accompany them. Rather mystified, Lacy allowed himself to be taken in tow. The strange Orientals took him along to a nearby restaurant where, amid vague mutterings and comings and goings, he was served an exotic dinner but given no reason for his polite "kidnapping." Eventually his hosts indicated that they were Japanese gentlemen and they were most anxious to acquire the blueprints of Thompson's new gun and could Mr. Williams help them. In California Lacy had had some contact with Japanese agents because of their mutual interest in assisting the Indian nationalist Gadhar Hindu party, but there had never been any previous contact in New York. Mr. Williams told the Japanese he would see what he could do. Neither Lacy nor Joe McGarrity, who had been brought in on the negotiations, could see any reason for not helping the Japanese. The Japanese were given a copy of the blueprint and soon thereafter word reached Lacy that his gift had been sent on by two different routes.[13] The Japanese promptly faded out of the picture and the Irish were left to pick up the pieces of the *East Side* disaster.[14]

While the Clan had put almost all of its guns in one basket, some Thompsons did filter into Ireland. In the middle of February 1921, a group of men with obviously Irish names, John J. Murphy, John O'Brien, and John Gallagher, ordered fifty guns. On May 25, these fifty guns were delivered to Murphy's agent, a P.J. Gentry. The guns, the Irishmen, and P.J. Gentry immediately disappeared. The United States Department of Justice never managed to trace either the men or the guns. It is highly probable that these guns arrived just before or soon after the truce in July 1921, too late to be used against the British.[15] Even before this there is evidence of another shipment arriving in Ireland. In Cork, Major Florence O'Donoghue, then Adjutant of Cork No. I Brigade, and his QMG, Joseph O'Connor, accepted a shipment of thirty guns sometime before April 26. The guns came carefully packed in several huge over-stuffed chairs and a sofa aboard a Moor McCormack ship. O'Donoghue kept twenty guns for Cork No. I and turned ten over to Joseph Vize to take back to Dublin. At approximately the same time an American, using the name Harty, contacted O'Connor about the guns, indicating that GHQ in Dublin knew of their arrival. There remains some doubt as to the specific date of this shipment, despite the independent recollection of O'Donoghue and O'Connor, because of the very limited number of guns available for shipment early in April 1921.[16] There is, however, no doubt that a trickle of guns was arriving in Ireland before the truce.

This trickle was not what GHQ in Dublin had anticipated. When Dineen and Cronin arrived in April, GHQ had foreseen a massive injection of a new armament by early summer. The two Americans were to be in charge of training a nucleus of Thompson gunners who in turn could instruct the IRA in the country when the major shipment arrived. In May, however, in Ireland few people outside the relevant departments of the Cabinet or GHQ knew of the gun. Thus, apart from Richard Mulcahy, Michael Collins, Seán Russell, Liam Mellows, whose title Director of Purchases should really have been Director of Foreign Purchases, and perhaps one or two others on the GHQ staff and Emmon de Valera and Cathal Brugha on the Cabinet, no one in Ireland had a hint of the guns' existence. When Dineen and Cronin arrived, a member of the GHQ staff, Seamus O'Donovan, Director of Chemicals, was asked to put up the Americans at his brother's flat at 2 Wilson Place. Dineen and Cronin remained with O'Donovan and his brother, "Charles Brown," on the top floor of Wilson Place for the next several months. Apparently both Dineen and Cronin had served with the United States Army on the Mexican border and had first hand experience with Pancho Villa's guerrillas. There was no doubt that Dineen, who had been a small arms instructor in the Chicago Police Department, was a first-rate marksman, capable of impressive accuracy after the time-honored American quick draw. Soon Dineen and Cronin began a series of lectures and firing demonstrations in the Pine Forest outside Dublin.[17]

One of the first formal demonstrations of the gun's capacities took place while Tom Barry, O.C. of Cork No. 3 Brigade, was in Dublin. On the evening of May 24, Barry was included in an inspection party of Collins, Mulcahy, Gearóid O'Sullivan, Adjutant General, and six men from the

Dublin Squad. They drove out to a house, sitting on its own grounds in the far suburbs, to see Dineen and Cronin perform. In an old basement the two instructors explained the gun, stripped it, reassembled it, and asked for volunteers to fire the first shot. Cronin asked Collins to have a go. Collins, reluctant to tackle the new gadget, replied "No bloody fear, Tom will do it." Barry, fearful of missing and letting down Cork No. 3, proved equally reluctant. Eventually badgered into volunteering, with the gun on semi-automatic Barry fired three times smashing, to his great relief, three bricks at the other end of the basement. Collins, Mulcahy, O'Sullivan and Barry drove back into Dublin, delighted with the gun. Barry particularly felt that the Thompson would be an ideal guerrilla weapon.[18] Flying Columns equipped with submachine guns would be a potent force. Ideal for short range work, the Thompson had the additional virtue for irregulars of being easy to disassemble—the stock could be removed almost instantly. A light, hard hitting automatic weapon, easy to carry and easy to conceal and soon to be available in quantity raised everyone's hopes.

Then the loss of the consignment on the *East Side* removed any chance of revolutionizing the armament of the IRA Flying Columns. After June 16, only a few guns coming in piecemeal could be anticipated and these would no longer come as a surprise to the British. Since a few guns were already in Dublin, GHQ decided to use them in an operation, an ambush of a train using the G.S.W.R. loopline in Drumcondra. Oscar Traynor, who would be C/O of the strike force, selected a site parallel to Whitworth Road which would give his men the cover of high concrete walls and heavy wooden palings skirting the railway line.

On the morning of June 16, 1921, 300 men of the West Kent Regiment, who had come direct to Ireland fom Silesia, were aboard a troop train moving from Amiens Street to Kingsbridge. At eactly 8:30 the train moved into Traynor's ambush. What seemed like heavy revolver fire opened from St. Brigid's Road on one side and St. Clement's Road on the other. Bombs began bursting, one directly under a carriage. The West Kents could do nothing. They could see no one. For 150 yards the train rolled on, racked by heavy fire. Men on Claude Bridge fired down through the roof of the train. When the train arrived at Kingsbridge minutes later, the coaches were wrecked, woodwork splintered and torn, windows smashed, bullet holes everywhere. The carriage next to the engine suffered particularly, being practically riddled with bullets. Inside there was a pool of blood, but the British admitted only three men wounded, one seriously. While the wounded were being removed, the West Kents were met by a detachment of other troops and played to the Park. One anonymous West Kent was more impressed with the IRA's reception, "We were not a half-an-hour in the

country before we ran up against the 'Sinners'." That evening, more lac-
onically, British GHQ issued a communique concerning the ambush.

> About 8:30 A.M. today bombs were thrown and revolver shots were fired at a
> troop train as it was in the vicinity of Old Drumcondra Station, Dublin.
> Three soldiers were wounded, one seriously.[19]

A more detailed description of the ambush was contained in the IRA
report captured, and later released, by the British:[20]

> To the President.
> From M/D (Minister of Defence).
> In accordance with orders received the troop train was attacked this morning
> at 8:30 A.M. at a point halfway between Drumcondra Road and Botanic
> Road. The Ambushing Party consisted of the O/C and eleven men, two
> Thompson Gunners, eight bombers, one motor car driver.
>
> The bombers were extended from 150 yards on the north side of the railway;
> from St. Joseph's Avenue to Upper St. Columba's Road. The attack was
> opened by bombers, two of them put two large grenades into two separate
> carriages. I cannot say how successful the remainder of the bombers were as I
> could not see them all from my position. The bombers had a very good
> position and should have done good work as the train was moving at a slow
> rate, approx. twelve miles an hour, and they bombed at fifteen yards' range.
>
> Of the two machine guns that we engaged, one failed to come into action.
> The reason being that the original gunner turned up late, and the substitute
> man never handled a gun before and he perhaps made some mistake. The
> second Thompson gun checked when four bursts had been fired. The fifty or
> sixty rounds that were fired appeared to take good effect. I know for a fact that
> the enemy had casualties in four carriages. We suffered no casualties and all
> our men and guns returned safely.
>
> (signed) O/C Guard.
>
> NOTE:—I went to Kingsbridge after the attack, three ambulances arrived after
> 9 A.M. There was a lot of enemy activity so I retired.
>
> (signed) O/C Guard.
>
> 12:30 (mid-day).
> 16th June, 1921.

Thus at Drumcondra in Dublin on June 16, 1921, the Thompson gun
was fired for the first time in military action. The legendary career of the
Tommy gun had begun in earnest with fifty rounds from the drum of a
1921-Model. In the fullness of time the gun would be identified with Al
Capone and his Chicago gangsters, adopted by a score of countries, modified to use rifle cartridges or to take a bayonet, and fired at or by almost all
of the world's armies. Yet, even now nearly fifty years after the first hand-

made Thompson was fired, it seems unlikely that any of the legends surrounding the Tommy gun can match the reality of the IRA's connection,
involving Irish agents, British spies, inscrutable Japanese, aborted smuggling and, finally, that first Irish echo in Dublin.

When the troubles began anew in August, 1969, and the Nationalist
population in the North came under threat, the IRA was more myth than
reality; the few scattered guns, often rusty and without proper ammunition. The Thompson gun actually returned briefly in Belfast streets as a
retired volunteer opened his private dump as a result of the emergency. The
Northerners, who became the first core of the Provisional IRA, had pursued the arms problem before August; after that the dominant task was the
search was for guns—contacts were made with individuals and groups in
the South, with the Fianna Fail government, with agents in Europe, and
most of all with old friends in the United States. For a generation, the
search for arms would continue with spectacular failures and muted successes, with nothing to equal the Thompson gun. But it was not for lack of
trying—rather from paucity of appropriate skills: the Provisional IRA's
catchment area of talent was small.

These IRA efforts, however, attracted enormous attention; for arms shipments were romantic, at least in the opinion of the media, and dangerous,
surely in the opinion of law enforcement officers. There were regular ex-
posés, investigations, and revelations that, except for the open record of
court cases, revealed little, exposed less, trampled old ground. The problem
for any analyst seriously, if academically, concerned with such matters is
that there is no advantage to a secret army in revealing sources, describing
acquisition methods, detailing successes and particularly failures. So the
IRA sees no benefit in publicity, nor do the police, custom officials, agents,
detectives, and intelligence officials. It took more than fifty years for the
Thompson gun's arrival in Ireland to be a historical matter; and not until
1972 was the weapon in use, and then only in training sessions. It may take
another fifty years before some of the details of procurement and technology transfer in these Troubles to become public. Presently, arms, as is
almost always the case with covert revolutionary organizations, are a killing matter. And, too, the authorities take extraordinary pains to limit
shipment, apprehend the suspect, sit on the suspicious, watch for a year a
single impounded refrigerator with dubious provenance just in case someone comes to collect. In sum, the more one knows the less that can be
written, if more is to be known. And even on publication, there are bounds
and reticence.

In 1969 the word *terrorist* did not appear in the *New York Times Index.*
Then terrorists were a certain variant of middle-European revolutionary
following specific tactics; their descendents could be found in the late Irgun

Zvai Leumi in Palestine. After the Irgun came guerrillas, freedom fighters, and national liberators. Finally, the outraged and the threatened classified all rebels, particularly those who targeted the ordinarily innocent, as *terrorists*. The new threat, largely to the West, became a major concern to many Western governments administered by bureaucrats largely ahistorical and conventional. Into the great alphabet soup of violence— PLO, FRELIMO, ERP, ETA, MPLA and on and on—the British dumped the IRA—Provos, Stickies, Saor Eire, INLA, whatever. Hence even those not threatened, especially by the IRA, like the United States government, wanted to know more about the organization, especially those matterss of particular concern to American interest, small for Ireland despite the exaggerations of those on the island who saw NATO plots and ambitions everywhere. The resulting conferences, seminars, papers, reports, meetings, conclaves, and mounds of unread terror summaries, mostly produced by Americans, accumulated under the glazed eyes of the responsible.

One of the few American concerns with IRA matters was the question of arms shipments, not simply those from the United States but as an insight into the problem of covert acquisition of hi-tech weapons—the most awesome being a nuclear device, nearly everyone's great concern. At one point, the U.S. State Department held a conference of various specialists, real and proclaimed, and interested parties, eager and bored, concerning the problems and prospects of terrorism. Focusing on the matter of sophisticated arms and conventional revolutionary organizations, the burden on my comment was not to worry unduly. What appeared probable and drear to the ivory tower looked rather different walking down the Falls Road:

> I thought it might be wise to focus on one specific area in some detail: the problems and prospects involved in weapons technology transfer for the revolutionary-terrorist. The major burden of this comment is that such transfers are not simply the acquisition of a piece of hardware and consequent increase in revolutionary capacity but rather a more complex process. In point of fact, the procurement of a novel and a more complicated weapon may cause more problems for the revolutionary than it solves. Leaving aside the aspirations of those waging limited wars or rural guerrilla campaigns, I will examine one particular organization: the Belfast Brigade of the Provisional IRA, an organization that would not welcome being discussed in a conference on terrorism. Still, the Provos in Belfast face weapons procurement policies not unlike those of many revolutionary groups operating without liberated zones or sanctuary. . . . In early days weapons came into Ireland in golf bags and coffins, were shipped to England and back to Ireland, arrived in crates and disappeared from the docks, slipped by customs at Shannon airport or transfered to fishing boats. The most effective new weapons to arrive in Belfast were the Colt-AR-15 and the AR-180 Armalite, semi-automatic civilians' versions of military weapons. These rifles, however, do not really give the IRA a greater capacity than would an M-1 or even the old Lee-

Enfield. Their virtue is that they are easy to use. It must be remembered that most urban guerrillas learn on the job. Very few have fired a shot except in anger. Very few have had any formal military training—and that in the British army. Very few handle weapons with special competence. And the Armalite compensates for incompetence. . . . The use of the Russian-made RPG-7 rocket launchers intrigued the press but the entire exercise proved futile for the IRA; some of the weapons were lost, others went into dumps, and the volunteers went back to rifles and infernal devices. . . . The IRA difficulty in absorbing new weaponry is hardly unique. And it is not only hardware that complicates revolutionary life but new tactics and new ideas. . . . Mostly, however, the revolutionary who is going to operate on the transnational stage or in major cities can make do quite well with the present generation of weapons. It is easier to destroy an airliner with a conventional altitude bomb in the luggage compartment than to sneak about the airfield with a rocket launcher. It is easier to make your own bombs as do the IRA—although somewhat more dangerous—out of fertilizer and stolen gelatinite than set up a chemical factory. . . . And revolutionaries, like most, prefer the easy life, opt for the conventional response, and regard innovation, especially if it requires a training course, with suspicion. Anyway, as a former IRA Chief of Staff remarked, a match can be a guerrilla's most potent weapon.

The idea that weapons transfer, especially and particularly sophisticated weapons, to revolutionaries should be given a minor place in the terrorist menu of threats, was not especially popular. It was not only against analytical fashion, but also raised suspicions among the orthodox who assume that their opponents possess their own attitudes, skills, options, and priorities. If we scientists could make a diabolical hi-tech device, why shouldn't *they* do so? In theory, of course, the IRA wants not only more but also better, more awesome weapons, state-of-the-art explosives; but in practice such acquisition is at the edge of GHQ capacity and deployment more complex than weapons specialists assume. The IRA volunteer is not even a mirror image of a commando, much less an American weapons designer, and his Belfast is quite different from that seen by a British officer.

All this is difficult to explain in Washington—as, I would imagine, it would be in a discusssion at IRA GHQ. It is always difficult to explain reality to a realist familiar only with his own. It is equally difficult to persuade academic analysts concerned with theories and models often far divorced from the reality of the streets of Belfast. Still, an academic conference, like the one held by the Fletcher School of Law and Diplomacy on Arms Transfers to the Third World, allows a more extended argument and assures a mix of academics and practitioners in the audience. More to the point, the end result—an article—reveals how recent Irish history is molded to other use rather irrelevant to the concerns of the IRA quartermaster or even Irish history. The script given at the Fletcher School and later published and edited for present purpose follows as chapter 3.

Notes

1. The information concerning Thompson's career is derived from his own Vital Statistics Questionnaire at the United States Military Academy and various clippings supplied by Joseph M. O'Donnell, United States Military Academy Library, West Point, New York.

2. Commander Bliss' patented principle concerns metalic adhesion in which certain metals set at certain angles by themselves without aid alternately become adhesive and repellant under high and low pressure. Thompson saw the possibilities of applying Bliss' idea to the mechanism of an automatic rifle and devised a self-operating and self-oiling breech closure. Apparently beyond the patent Bliss' contribution to the ultimate submachine gun was minimal.

3. Although in 1920 and 1921, the old monolithic Clan no loner existed, having become prey to clashing personalities and policies and weakened by the creation of new organizations, the harsh in-fighting of Irish-American politics does not seem to have disrupted the Auto-Ordnance negotiations. Thus Ryan and several of the individuals concerned were in the Clan na Gael in 1916 and I continue to refer to "the Clan" when often Irish agents in America would be as appropriate. Laurence de Lacy (Country Wexford) recalls that in 1920 Ryan was one of a group of several important Clan businessmen but the passing of the years and the secrecy of the negotiations has clouded Ryan's contribution.

4. One of the earliest guns was a handmade prototype which could be magazine-fed or operated by a belt. The gun is at present in the United States Military Academy Museum catalogued as Model-1918 (?), Gerald C. Stowe, U.S.M.A. Museum, West Point, New York, "Letter", July 12, 1967.

5. Lieutenant Joseph A. Nardoza, New York City Police Department, "Letter", May 18, 1967.

6. The information concerning the acquisition and shipping of the guns was largely supplied by Laurence de Lacy during the course of two interviews and supplemented by correspondence.

7. William J. Helmer has been particularly helpful in checking the early records of Auto-Ordnance Corporation (his own work on the Thomspon gun was then in progress).

8. Some of the arms were very old, indeed. Among a considerable array of mismatched rifles, obsolete pistols, surplus ammunition and tag ends of equipment was a weirdly diabolical device: a metal container in the shape of a large football with holes on the outside and a central chamber. When exploded the "bomb" was supposed to scatter forty or fifty bullets in all directions. No evidence has been forthcoming on the origin of the device or its ultimate fate.

9. Details are from the Federal Grand Jury indictment brought against Laurence de Lacy, his "brother", Rorke, Merkling, Ochsenreiter, Culhane, Brophy and Marcellus H. Thompson, son of General Thompson, of April 1922. The copy was supplied by Laurence de Lacy.

10. *New York Herald,* June 17, 18, and 19, 1921.

11. A full account of the British coup is given in *The Gaelic American,* June 25, 1921. *v. The New York Times,* June 18, 1921; *The Daily Sketch,* June 17, 1921; *The Pall Mall Gazette,* June 17, 1921. The London *Express* published a marginal note—in an IRA leader's handwriting—referring to the guns: "A preliminary class could be held in the Dublin area, where numerous suitable targets are to be found at all times."

12. Strangely enough, one of these early Thompsons given to the British government in hopes of subsequent sales may be the gun depicted on the photo-cover a Penguin edition of Hemingway's *To Have and to Have Not.* The gun on the cover has Serial Number No. 66, which suggests an April manufacture date. Thus it would have been a likely candidate for Thompson to have brought to London in 1921. The gun is now in the possession of Bapty's & Co., London, but had no history before 1940 when it was acquired by Bapty's in an odd lot of weapons returned to replace items sequestered in 1939. Mark Dineley, Bapty & Co. Ltd., London, "Letters", June 21 and June 27, and interview, July 31, 1967.

13. In a request for more detailed information, Susumu Nishrura, Chief, War History Office, Defence Agency, Japan ("Lettter", April 28, 1967) could supply no additional information: "I regret to say that we have not any document pertaining to the smuggling trouble of Thompson gun . . . " As a matter of curiosity, one of the most perfect examples of foreign manufacture was an excellent Chinese version of the 1921-Model.

14. In April 1922, a Federal Grand Jury at Trenton returned an indictment against most of the individuals involved in the *East Side* affair. The United States Department of Justice subsequently decided that in view of previous interpretations of the American neutrality statutes that no case existed and filed a motion to *nolle prosequi* the case against all the defendants. Thus no one ever came to trial. On June 21, 1922, a warrant was issued for the seizure of the 495 Thompson guns. In turn the guns were claimed by "Frank Williams" on August 18, 1921. Libel proceedings against Williams were dismissed upon motion of the government previous to trial; but the guns remained in the custody of the Collector of Customs until on September 14, 1925, an Order of Discontinuance was entered by United States District Judge William Clark. The order directed the Collector of the Customs at New York City to deliver the guns to "Frank Williams, claimant and owner, or Joseph McGarrity, his duly authorized agent and attorney-in-fact". Fred M. Vinson, Jr., Assistant Attorney General, United States Department of Justice, "Letter", May 17, 1967, and enclosure, a copy of a letter of April 22, 1964 from J. Walter Yeagley, Assistant Attorney General, Internal Security Division, to William J. Helmer, Austin, Texas.

15. Piaras Beaslai, *Michael Collins and the Making of a New Ireland,* Dublin, 1926, vol. I, pp. 45, 62; vol. II, p. 215, mentions a small shipment of fifty Thompsons coming into Ireland around the July 9, 1921 truce. T.P. O'Neill found references that from July 11 to December 17, 1921, fifty-one machine-guns were imported and distributed; that there were forty-nine Thompson guns in Ireland with seven Lewis and five Hotchkiss on October 31, 1921, and that between August 6, 1920 and July 11, 1921 six machineguns (make not specified) were imported. While it is impossible to tell which guns came into the country at that time, it is possible that Murphy got his fifty into Ireland around July 9. In the Enniscorthy Museum there is a Thompson, known to be in Ireland in 1922, with the serial number 1080. Since two of the serial numbers of the guns seized on the *East Side* were 701 and 901, number 1080 was produced at approximately the right time for it to have been included in Murphy's lot. Simply checking all available serial numbers of Irish 1921-Models to discover which guns were, in fact, in Ireland before July 1921 is of limited value in that there is no way to tell from how many the serial numbers were actually removed. The R.U.C. picked up several with numbers between 700 and 800 (Interview: Inspector-General Albert H. Kennedy and County Inspector W. Meharg, July 21,

1967). The Irish Army has only one with the number removed ("Letter", August 4, 1967, Rúnaí Aire, Oifig an Aire Cosanta). Unfortunately, access has been refused to the Model-1921 Thompsons still held by the Garda Síochána, most of which have no numbers in any case, thus making further cross-checking in Ireland impossible. The largest remaining file of Irish 1921-Models is held by the Virginia, United States of America, branch of Interarmco (Monte Carlo, Monaco). Interarmco purchased a considerable lot of obsolete Irish Army weapons in 1957 and fortunately kept a file of the serial numbers ("Letter", August 11, 1967, Samuel Cummings, president, Interarmco).

16. The independent recollection of O'Donoghue and O'Connor, carefully verified by specific dates, concerning guns arriving in Cork (Interview: Major Florence O'Donoghue, May 6, 1967, and subseqent correspondence) in the light of the very limited Colt production up to that time is something of a mystery. Most of the production of Auto-Ordnance, with the exception of Murphy's fifty guns, was traced by the Department of Justice. Neither Federal agents nor, certainly, the books of Auto-Ordnance can be considered infallible but to get twenty or thirty largely undiscovered and undocumented Thompsons to Cork by April 26 would have been very difficult. If Murphy did get his fifty guns into Ireland the total number of around fifty guns given by various sources should have been greater—unless Dublin G.H.Q. never learned of Cork's guns. All the problems of serial numbers apply to the Cork guns as well, although a few Irish numbers below 300 would at least buttress personal recollections. Nevertheless, a Cork shipment cannot be discounted, even without collaborating evidence in either the United States or Ireland, mainly because of the substantial independent evidence supplied by O'Donoghue and O'Connor.

17. Seamus O'Donovan (Interview: May 21, 1967) distinctly recalls that Dineen and Cronin trained the Engineers, 5th Battalion, Dublin Brigade; but Liam Archer ("Letter", July 3, 1967), formerly O/C 5th Battalion and Deputy Director of Engineering in June 1921 has no knowledge of the 5th Battalion having been trained on Thompsons, nor does Liam O'Doherty, another O/C, 5th Battalion.

18. Interviews with Tom Barry, March 10 and May 6, 1967. Cf. Tom Barry, *Guerrilla Days in Ireland,* Cork, 1955, pp. 189-190.

19. *Irish Independent,* June 17, 1921.

20. C.J. Street ("I.O."), *Ireland in 1921,* London, 1922, p. 87. (O/C Guard should be read as O/C squad).

3

Proliferation: Sophisticated Weapons and Revolutionary Options

In an uncertain world, one of the presently agreed verities is that revolutionary violence, terrorism and irregular war are growth areas. Efficient democratic states that can accommodate rational dissent and effective totalitarian regimes that can crush any open dissent may for the moment be immune to indigenous revolutionary violence, but vast areas—including several post-industrial states—may not be so fortunate. And any state, including and perhaps especially democratic ones, with an unresolved nationality problem cannot rest easy.

The most important factor, perhaps, is not the strategy and tactics of the various revolutionaries, whether they seek power or only an audience to their despair, but rather the arrival of a patron and with a patron a new and deadly weapon. If a revolutionary can make an appropriate connection in Havana or Washington, with the Russians or the Libyans, his capacities are greatly increased, his prospects enhanced, and his challenge to order heightened. If the new patronage sparks a zealous response, what had been a small, tolerable armed struggle, waged in isolation, may become an area for the clash of major power ambitions quite removed from the parochial issues. Consequently, the aspirations, intentions and capacities of revolutionary organizations may suddenly matter a great deal. And one means to make them matter to advantage is to inject more and better weapons into the armed struggle.

Weapons procurement procedures for revolutionary organizations must take into account certain factors rarely of concern to conventional governments. Essentially the revolutionary spectrum of acquisition runs from scavenging, theft and construction on a local level to illicit shipments by agents, by friends or by patrons. Some groups begin with almost nothing. The paucity of weapons was such that each was cherished, never discarded even at the risk to the bearer. When the Stern Group assassinated Lord Moyne in Cairo in November 1944, the British authorities discovered that the Nagant revolver used had been also used to kill a policeman in

Jerusalem six weeks before, a police inspector and constable in Feburary 1944, a police constable in March 1943, another constable in May 1944, an Arab in Jerusalem as far back as November 1937, along with still another murder of an unknown date. "You don't think we would be so silly as to throw it away when it still worked?" Other revolutionary groups have had the immediate support of a patron eager to achieve influence or position by stocking the revolutionary arsenal—in fact in some cases the revolutionary organization is little more than an agency of the patron.

In any case most revolutionaries would like more, even if the new weapons may create problems. The necessary skills may not be available and technicians may thus have to be imported; the new weapons may determine inappropriate tactics; and the ease of acquisition may not inculcate effective revolutionary habits of mind.

The acquisition of weapons by revolutionaries is a form of technology transfer—proliferation to the fearful—that almost inevitably presents the same difficulties as the conventional movement of technology from the skilled to the unskilled. A weapon is not simply a piece of hardware to be acquired and immediately used to effect—a hat that fits any head. For revolutionaries are self-elected and self-taught. The new revolutionary variant in democratic or Western societies reflects a combination of intellectuals and men of no property—few with real military experience. Most revolutionaries learn their business on the job; the incompetent guerrillas or bomb-makers have a high attrition rate. In the campaign in Ulster nearly as many IRA volunteers have been killed by their own bombs as by British security forces. Other than carelessness that comes from familiarity and limited original training, the necessity for speed and the quality of the materials are the major reasons for premature explosions.

Many members of the Provisional IRA have never fired a shot except in anger. In any conventional military terms they are badly trained—which is one of the reasons that revolutionaries prefer to rely on unconventional tactics. This level of competence severely limits what sort of weapon can be absorbed effectively. Terrain is also a limiting factor—an urban guerrilla cannot make use of a tank, or even a 30-calibre, air-cooled machine gun. Even in a rural guerrilla campaign with secure bases, the introduction of even relatively simple new weapons can cause difficulties. The Viet Cong rocket attacks on Saigon were effective simply because no one knew where they would land, least of all the Viet Cong; thus military targets were regularly missed and the entire civilian population intimidated.

Despite any difficulties in acquiring and effectively absorbing more sophisticated weapons, every revolutionary movement, almost without exception, avidly wants new, elegant weapons. And just as weapons systems have grown larger and more complex and more expensive so have systems grown smaller, but no cheaper. Each new generation of precision-guided missiles includes still one more set, more accurate, easier to carry and more flexible than the last. One or two men with a slim metal tube and a bit of courage can destroy at distance an immeasurably more expensive and complex bit of equipment. There are tiny grenades no larger than a 35mm. film capsule, a submachine gun that is totally silent and fires 3-shot bursts, hand-held flame throwers, gas guns, cunningly miniaturized bombs to pop in the mail, even tactical nuclear weapons in a suitcase. And doubtless the ingenuity of those involved in weapons technology will contrive even more elegant devices. Not unreasonably a great many of the concerned have become alarmed that these new, deadly and sophisticated weapons will, sooner or later, appear in the hands of the unauthorized. Somehow for many the idea of such weapons in the hands of those not legally authorized to kill by recognized governments strikes terror. And it is abundantly clear that in the immediate future the world will be filled with those engaged in armed struggles under an unrecognized flag for an alien cause. It seems equally clear that each new generation of light weapons will almost surely find its way into such hands. Certainly there is no doubt that frantic men will seek any and every means to advance their cause. If they cannot find patrons to donate the new weapons, they can depend on theft, extortion, the spin-off residue of bigger wars. Proliferation of the new light weapons is—seemingly—assured. Yet such arms procurement is not a simple conduit from patron to recipient. If a new weapon becomes available, there are three options: the device can be ignored or misused, volunteers can be dispatched outside the area to acquire the needed skills, or instructors can be imported. In the first case the level of violence remains the same. In the second, the returning members may introduce a variety of personal, political and ideological problems. And in the last case alien instructors guarantee less freedom of action, a greater dependency on the distant patron. Moreover, the new instructors almost always also guarantee an escalation in the conflict. They provide a more significant international component, as the patron becomes more visible, and perhaps inspire intervention by the friends of the threatened.

As an example of the difficulties and dangers for revolutionaries, the trials and tribulations of the Provisional IRA in Northern Ireland specifically reveal certain trends. The Provisionals, fluctuating in size from several hundred to several thousand volunteers, were armed largely by scavenging in Ireland and Europe, from the United States, and later with the help of the Libyan government—although the latter source was more visible than viable.

There has been in recent years a sporadic trickle into Ireland from these sources, but never a flood. Even though the IRA has come into flush times with over a million dollars funneled in from America alone to the financial officers of the GHQ, the funds have not assured a constant source of weapon supply. The most notorious single attempt, however, cost the IRA little or nothing. Colonel Muammar Qaddafi of Libya, seeing the Provisionals as an antiimperialist force, arranged for both arms and money to be handed over to appropriate representatives. Joe Cahill, the IRA Quartermaster, leased a vessel, the *Claudia,* picked up the arms and, carefully followed by the British, sailed off to be met in Irish waters by the Irish Navy. Consequently, the Provisional IRA has had to depend largely on the American connection to supply weapons as well as money.

The most effective weapons to arrive in Northern Ireland have been the civilian version of the M-16, the Colt AR-15, and the AR-180 Armalite, first manufactured in Japan for an American company, Armalite Corporation of Costa Mesa, California. (When the Japanese run was shut down, Armalite subcontracted another run of fifty thousand to Sterling—a British arms manufacturer, which must prove something about the British need for foreign exchange, since it is now well known where many Armalites end up.) Both the Colt AR-15 and the AR-180 Armalite may be purchased legally and openly in the United States. For IRA purposes the weapons are ideal. Neither is automatic, which is a virtue in untrained hands, and again in any conventional sense the IRA volunteer is badly trained. They are light. The AR-180 Armalite with a folding stock can be reduced to a two-foot length ("Fits inside a cornflake box, it does") and the high muzzle velocity (3,250 feet per second) permits the .223 bullets to penetrate standard issue British body armor and the armor of British personnel carriers. It has a very flat trajectory, and the rate of fire gives the inexpert marksman a chance of hitting the target. The two are in fact perfect urban guerrilla weapons. An Armalite, however, does not really give the IRA a greater capacity than would an M-1 rifle or even the old Lee-Enfield. The virtue is that it is easy to use. It must be stressed again that most urban guerrillas learn on the job. Very few have fired many shots in practice. Very few have had any formal military training. Very few handle weapons with special skill. The Armalite, in particular, does not need very special skills.

Once the level of weapon sophistication is increased this problem of competence becomes more serious. In the autumn of 1972, the IRA managed to get a shipment of arms into Ireland that included Soviet-made RPG-7 rocket-launchers. To anyone with an exposure to the military, a bazooka or a PIAT is quite a simple weapon used for obvious purposes. The IRA had never been trained to use a launcher. The GHQ was not about to practice with the few rockets available. Instead the RPG-7 was used for IRA purposes rather than in the way the maker had intended.

Fired into military and police posts the armor-piercing rocket zapped in one side and out the other. The entire exercise proved futile for the IRA. Some of the weapons were lost, others went into dumps, and the volunteers went back to rifles and infernal devices. Assuming that the IRA had persisted, the solution would have been to import skilled instructors—the obvious candidates being Irish-American veterans of Vietnam. This has almost always been the only option open to revolutionaries unless the opportunity occurs to send volunteers abroad for short courses. And such "graduates" introduce problems along with the skills. There is, however, the possibility in certain areas of learning on the job.

The IRA explosive devices at first were often crude, two decades behind the time, and a danger to transporter and detonator. As the supply of commerical explosives dried up, the IRA engineering officers had to become more ingenious—and the libraries supplied the first step. Although competence has improved, the mixtures of diesel oil, nitrobenzene, sodium chlorate, water, oil, calcium carbonate and ammonium nitrate often leave something to be desired. But, again, they generally work well enough.

For most urban guerrilla operations sophisticated weapons are not of any great help. A Browning 30-calibre machine gun may cause more problems than solutions. Once fighting has gone beyond incidents and operations to an irregular war, then heavier weapons—mortars, heavy machine guns, bazookas—are highly desirable. At that stage, however, the whole problem of revolutionary strategy has been transformed. Many revolutionary organizations, like the IRA, cannot aspire to fighting an irregular war. Most revolutionary organizations in advanced countries like the IRA can manage quite well with conventional infantry weapons, stolen, scrounged, even in some cases turned on lathes, coupled with home-made bombs and great ingenuity. Less is often more.

It appears that in the immediate future there will continue to be urban guerrilla conflict. For the urban guerrilla, the terrorist, the assassin, while not adverse to trading up, all the new, elegant sophisticated weapons will not especially add to his capacity. It is easier to put an atmospheric pressure bomb on a jet airliner than go to the trouble of acquiring and using a missile launcher. Certainly the new weapons will dribble into the arsenals, even the IRA, but such groups are seeking a victory over the will at the center rather than in the field. This they can achieve with matches and knives if they can just persist until the shifting tides of history favor the cause, or the masses mobilize, or the tyrant flees.

The key moment in illicit and covert weapons acquisition comes when the struggle in the ghetto or the bush makes a leap in capacity so that more elegant and lethal weapons can be deployed to effect. Then, as the guerrilla evolves into a soldier and the irregular war becomes more regular, the new skills can most swiftly, if speed is to be a factor, be supplied by a patron for a patron's purpose.

In this pattern of escalation and proliferation there has been increasing concern about the most elegant of all weapons—a nuclear device. Certainly for many academics the prospect is a real one. In point of fact, few presently active revolutionary groups have the time, capacity or interest in "going nuclear." Fashioning bombs in an MIT laboratory is quite different from building them in Belfast or Beirut. Even the new breed of transnational terrorist is not really interested in killing people, especially large numbers of people, but rather attracting attention to a troubled cause. The nuclear option has long been that of the centers of imperialism. Ideologically, the prospect is not attractive. Strategically, it would absorb too many resources, warp existing strategy, alienate potential support. It appears an unattractive option. Conventional means will do as well, perhaps better. There is and will be serious, perhaps excessive, concern about this particular revolutionary "option" on the part of those with trained minds but little understanding of the nature of revolutionary options, revolutionary talents or even of the real world beyond the seminars and laboratories.

Over the next decade there seems every likelihood that there will be literally hundreds of revolutionary oranizations—non-state actors—seeking the means to lever themselves into power. If the scope of inquiry were limited, for example, simply to Western European democratic countries, the number of active or recently active indigenous groups almost boggles the imagination. Certain of these groups face obstacles so severe that the major impetus of their revolutionary strategy will be to seek prominence rather than power. As noted, these groups may opt for spectacular transnational terrorism and might, therefore, like spectacular weapons. Yet much of the violence will be on a lower level. The new weapons for a time will not be a serious component. The real danger for those in favor of an easy life will come when revolutionaries need steps beyond revolutionary capacity. Then an eye must be kept on new characters in the revolutionary drama— as small as the IRA arms ship *Claudia*. Arms may not make the man or the soldier, but at that stage they are the foundation for escalation.

And, basically, it is escalation, not proliferation, that will threaten stability. Life may be made simpler for the assassin or the guerrilla with the injection of a new weapon, but order will not be unduly threatened. The danger or—more threatening—the opportunity comes not with the weapon but with revolutionary incapacity. Perhaps military technology will sooner or later devise still another generation of dreadful and elegant weapons especially for the untrained and incompetent, but until then the concern of academics and analysts may be excessive. In this one small area proliferation may not be a danger and in fact too elegant weapons in the hands of the untrained may be a blessing for those dedicated to peace and quiet. In the real world, not in the lecture hall, a revolutionary with an elderly pistol may be a greater danger than several men staggering under a portable precision-guided missile—cold comfort in a threatening world but some comfort nevertheless.

The IRA is naturally not comforted with make-do weapons and failed shipments and as in most matters has persisted in seeking more and better. The problem is that the Provos have become the dream of most radical Western intellectuals—a working-class movement tolerated but not abetted by the middle class Nationalist of the North for various reasons. As a working-class movement the necessary skills to find, acquire, ship, maintain, and deploy advanced weapons—or any weapons—are largely lacking. Everything else is in place: dedication, determination, persistence, money, need, commitment—even a useful image. Consider "IRA" as a logo to be imprinted on television scripts, novel plots, scare headlines, rumors of wars and conspiracies, or aspects of private enterprise (John De Lorean claimed among other improbables a Provo connection in Belfast). What remains elusive is a pool of import-export volunteers, those skilled in covert transactions, secret purchase, bills of lading, front institutions, and customs law. Neither extortion nor intimidation can move shipments through legal barriers for long in the face of determined governmental opposition. Neither persistence nor dedication can compensate for a nearly complete failure to understand the nature of the game. In America at least, some of the more avid advocates of the Provo cause are a few with middle-class occupations. Few, however, seem willing to risk more than contributions and few Chicago dentists or small town attorneys or accountants living in Queens possess the skills needed, much less the commitment. Second, money laboriously acquired from Derry dues or armed robberies at great risk to volunteers and reputation, from fundraisers in Detroit and Chicago, from all sorts of places has been zealously restricted to payment for things, guns. And in the real world of effective supply, a considerable portion of the money should have been spent not on things but paper; for paper can turn illicit weapons into legitimate farm machinery, move lethal items with dispatch, with special handling, along express routes, through customs, out of the dockyard—mostly legally. Those who work for their pennies do not, however, like to waste money in what to the innocent appears to be gift wrapping but to the knowledgeable is simply postage guaranteeing delivery not to the dead letter office but ultimately to the IRA. So, mostly, IRA shipments have not been delivered: those sent to find the weapons are innocent, loud, and clumsy, those who pay are obvious, those who transport think of romantic drops or cunning packaging, never documentation, and those who would collect them in Ireland find nothing to pick up and are often picked up instead.

During the entire span of the present troubles, the IRA GHQ has never come close to solving the procurement problem. The same limitations apply, the same mistakes made, the same penny-wise problem exists and nearly the only novelty is the names of those volunteers and agents sentenced for violation of arms laws. The very few foreign friends, once enthusiastic concerning Provo prospects, who had the capacity to aid, have lost interest when their involvement became public, their volunteers put at risk, their weapons confiscated. In point of fact, much of the IRA's armament in the 1970s arrived through a small, private group of Republicans who largely isolated themselves from GHQ in Ireland and the visible Americans. They spent on paper. They could legitimately move their crates quietly off the Dublin docks. They managed "legitimate" shipments moved to safe dumps—then notified GHQ. One natural death and the flow sputtered to a stop—proper paper was lacking. And one decade was long enough for the nerves of the concerned.

Mostly, however, the GHQ efforts floundered—money was lost on the continent, the Palestinians were often outraged, the Libyans furious, and the agents with Bulgarian submachine guns or access to Skoda were untrustworthy. Some arrangements did, of course, go through. Weapons came in from time to time: the famous RPG-7 rocket-launchers spectacularly, a few Berretta submachine guns less so, and always the sputtering flow from friends in America, whose shipments often did not reach their destination. Thus the GHQ Quartermaster could never track down ground-to-air missiles but did manage to get a few M-47 machine guns from America; found even cordite difficult and more sophisticated explosives impossible; and often made do with increasingly sophisticated home-made fuses and the American connection, no matter how small the results.

The Thompson gun past has not been prologue for the Provos because there is no American remotely like Thomas Fortune Ryan or a staff like that of Michael Collins. Even reading of the procurement procedures of the Tan War would do the QMG little good—the glory days are over. Thus book-history is neither prologue to present policy, foundation for future action, nor even a comfort in troubled times. It is irrelevant, a matter of books. More to the point, the immediate history of the IRA—a complete adult lifetime for the present leadership—seems to have taught none of the fabled "lessons" available to the discriminating. Procurement policies have changed little since a few verterans made contacts in the United States in the late 1960s and a bit later others without introduction met kindred spirits in the Middle East. Attempts to adopt conventional subversive means to handle covert shipments have not worked when repeated. The British have too many friends, too much experience. Most large IRA shipments have been carefully monitored, especially when the final stage of a drop is reached. While the poorest fencer in the land may frighten the orthodox champion, arms shipments are, as the GHQ can attest, nearly impossible without some grasp of the basic principles, some skills, some agents beyond those readily found at the end of the bar or working for Con Edison as a lineman in the Bronx.

Thus the GHQ may recognize the problems, but parsing the immediate past has as yet found no solutions. Even then, even if the long-sought missiles were to arrive, deployment is no sure thing, as the RPG-7 experience would indicate. And such weapons have to be maintained properly and resupplied, not to mention deployed to tactical purpose. As it is with home-tooled mortars, a police station can be devasted, with home-fashioned timers and radio-activated fuses, the British prime minister can escape death largely because of the luck of the room reservation. This for GHQ is, of course, insufficient: what is wanted are more and more elegant weapons, the clarion cry of even overt armies. And what, after fifteen years, has not been learned is that existing procurement is futile.

Once again in very crucial matters the IRA has been content with the patriot past, the old ways in new circumstances. The returns in comfort and control have not paid dividends in weapons or scope for destruction. The immediate past, yesterday, the last decade, are not grasped as prologue, an arena for instruction; so faulty procedures have become policy. There has been no echo of the Thompson gun, no Ryan to oversee procurement of advanced weapons shipped through loopholes in American law. There has not even been a proper reaction to past failure, to their own history. Persistence, dedication, sacrifice, and determination may be vices, inappropriate virtues, if the guide is following the yellow brick road rather than the twisting lane to effective procurement—a toll-road, with entry limited to those with proper papers, special skills, and necessary accounting practices. The Merry Plowboy may prove a good soldier, a dedicated volunteer, even a hero and a martyr, who in time can fire his Thompson gun to effect; but recent IRA history indicates to the distant if not to the involved that insurrections are no longer won with plowmen's skills: maintained, yes; won, no.

PART II
The Irish Past as Prologue:
Patterns, Probes, Wars, and Warriors

> *Politics is not an exact science.*
> —Otto von Bismarck

For political analysts probing the past for present academic purpose, history is often, quite mistakenly, assumed to be real, a plain tale of events to be read by all, a case study writ in simple black and white. It is, perhaps, the kindest compliment that the social scientist can pay to history's muse that such narrating is accurate, the base for theory, the stuff of paradigms. Historians are by training and nature suspicious of patterns, ever ready with exceptions and peculiarities, all too familiar with the singularity of their specialty. Still, if there were no patterns in reality, no general rules across time and distance, all would be reduced to motes and musing. So even historians are capable of generalization, certain, of course, to outrage each particularist. At the top with the great models are the philosophers of history who note the ceaseless play of God's will or the constant movement arising from challenge and response, those of the dialectic or advocates of the power of great men to adjust events. At the bottom are those who find it extraordinarily difficult to make simple statements about the priorities of the peasants in France in 1789—much less those of all peasants on the eve of social revolutions.

In the Irish case, in recent years especially, probes into the past have been founded on very real present predilections so that the contemporary tools of history, sociology, or political science are put to use to prove as well as to probe. In Ireland, more than most arenas, this to some degree has always been the case. It is certainly true that those who use a gun for political ends, whether sanctioned by the state or not, especially not, seek justification in history's example. More to an analytical point, those further afield have found both Irish reality, however disinterned, and Irish historiography, however elegant, useful. That there is no consensus on the plain tale of events, much less the direction of Irish historical tides, has seemingly ham-

59

*pered no one. After all, Ireland has been well served by historians, much is
already known—and every year more—and an enormous amount of data
must be accepted as real, not postulated. If so inclined, and many have
been, Irish history as presently written is a rich lode for model builders.*

*For political historians, contemporary Irish experience—this century's
plain tales—need not be particularly singular or uniquely Celtic, but should
fit far broader patterns. A nation partitioned by class, religion, and ethnic
roots seeking freedom in a century of postimperial nation building is hardly
novel. The problems of economic development, social change in a postindustrial Europe, secularization in a devout country, democratic stability in
troubled times, nonalignment in a committed world are hardly special problems. Even the use of the gun in politics has been in almost all nations a
factor, even if at times less than compelling. Even those few resolute and
successful neutrals have to have military policies and occasionally suffer the
shoot-outs of alien gunmen attracted to their quiet streets. Ireland as a case
study has managed, in fact, to combine neutrality with commitment, the
gun with democracy and civil liberties, free elections with internment, and
international concern with isolation. There is in recent Irish history something for everyone: innumerable elections, enormous social and economic
shifts, confrontation and accommodation, social conservatism and radical
change, and a highly visible thread of violence through the social fabric.
What is interesting at the beginning is that amid all the turmoil of this
century, the level of violence on a small island, so bitterly divided and seized
repeatedly on deadly quarrels has been, despite provocation and opportunity, very low and the casulaties relatively small if not inconsequential.
The analyst, however, is far more concerned with the event, the deed, the
incident of protest or war or symbolic alienation rather than a butcher's bill.
So, because Irish politics has been so various, so bitterly fought, so broad of
spectrum, the island experience is enormously useful even when, as was
almost always the case, the level of violence was low. In Ireland each death
somehow becomes magnified; martyrs and patriots have names; each ambush or assassination, every hunger strike, most boycotts or pogroms, every
small war is exaggerated, echoing through the island and out on the world
stage, filmed, transmuted into poems and plays, added to scholarly
agenda—a special case for use by all.*

*In this century the events after the negotiation of the Anglo-Irish Treaty that
ended the Tan War and ultimately culminated in the end of irregular armed
opposition and the triumph of the new Free State government in Dublin
have engendered generations of bitterness that will still poison Irish politics
into the next century. To the external eye, unconcerned with the analysis of*

the participants, such a conflict was not special; many revolutions, especially great ones, have seen the purists purged after victory. There is often a lurch toward conserving instead of transforming and often a civil war of sorts with revolutionary élan tamed by convention, a reaction led by those who would exploit rather than expand the dream. Such civil conflicts tend to be most divisive, and the winners seldom magnanimous. In Ireland even today, the heirs of the defeated deny even a civil war, only a losing phase of the struggle against British imperialism when co-opted Irishmen destroyed the dream, drew a line to the march of a nation for limited power and narrow rewards. For the pure Republicans there was no civil war, only betrayal. For others less commited there was simply a conventional civil war after a period of revolutionary turmoil. The more conservative, the winners, could see only criminal violence by a minority of the romantic and irresponsible who would have lost all gains to strive for the impossible. For them the irregular opponents were old friends gone wrong or misled, brigands and fanatics, not the other side of the Irish coin.

Surely, except for present ideologues, there was a civil war, not unique, that might offer certain societal patterns and lessons when other such conflicts are contemplated. In the Irish case the war, however bitter, was not a slaughter—in fact the number of Irishmen killed in a few days at the Somme totals more than all the political deaths on the island this century. And despite a real residue of bitterness, the societal accommodation in the decade following the "Troubles" was swift, effective, and largely conscious. Ireland did not sleepwalk into conciliation; the process was contrived and pursued by all the involved except the unrepentant Republicans. The result was that by the late 1930s, twenty-six counties of Ireland became a nation once again: hardly the dream of Easter 1916 made real and certainly not the Republic, but adequate for the time being. And the confrontation, conflict, and accommodation were played out almost solely in one Ireland; the Unionists were ignored except as a potential target for tactical purpose. Those nationalists trapped in the isolated zone of the six-county province of Northern Ireland were largely ignored. The Unionists hurried to institutionalize their potential domination, and the Nationalists waited on the results in the South—in vain. The civil war was between those of one Ireland, and that was what the Free Staters gained, the opportunity to manage one Ireland. In this, as well as in the low violence level, Ireland was special, but in other ways the 1922–1923 war could be moved about a pattern and used to proffer lessons about such conflict in general.

4

Societal Patterns and Lessons

A prolonged civil war is the most overt indication of an attenuated societal schism. In the preliminary civil discord—no matter how divisive and mutually contradictory are the elements involved, no matter how long-standing the opposing values or how deep-seated the distrust—a society, however strained or artificial, continues to exist. Once civil strife has passed the point of no return into civil war, however, the prewar society has, for better or worse, committed suicide. There can be no restoration of the uncomfortable but familiar past, for civil war can lead only to the ultimate triumph and imposition of a new society, cherished by the victors, inconceivable to the vanquished. Thus, every civil war ends with the effect of a revolution: the construction of a society with institutions and values that create an intolerable life for a substantial portion of the defeated, whose very identities had been first transformed by the polarization and then shattered. The vicious, almost permanent psychic wounds of civil war are less a result of the cruelty of the contest, the extensive violence, battles of vengeance, judicial murder, and wanton destruction, than of the "intolerable" terms of defeat, which must be "tolerated" by one side and imposed, year after year, by the other. There remain two societies: one hopelessly excluded from the reality of the old dreams and full participation in a new and abhorrent world; the other, arrogant in triumph, secretly insecure, twisted by constant coercion, grasping for the future. To sew up the raveled ends of these two societies into a single, even if patched, garment requires decades, often generations.

Most advanced societies, organized politically into nation-states, have serious or at least recognizable differences. Many new nations, particularly in the Third World, can scarcely be considered societies organized as states at all, but rather highly artificial umbrella structures tying together a clump of divergent societies with fragile and alien institutions. While the tensions of diversity may give an advanced, pluralistic society flexibility or creativity or stimulating variety, they may also impose strains so severe that two societies emerge. Thus, there were two Englands in the nineteenth century, the rich and the poor; two Americas, the North and the South; two Frances, the Monarchist and the Republican. Around some nodal point of difference, such as Catholicism or poverty, a variety of values, customs, habits, and attitudes may accumulate, engendering a subsociety still not politically visible but having less and less in common with the rest of the country. Such a society under special circumstances may either seek to impose its particular values or secede. Either undertaking polarizes the previously "united" society; if either pole has or develops the military capacity to oppose and thus to postpone an ultimate decision, then civil war becomes likely.

Many deeply divided societies are commonly wracked with violence or near-violence; some nations have endemic fighting or habitual coups or massive disorders but lack the combined polarization of society and reciprocal military capacity to prevent integration. The capacity of both societies to wage war, but without the power to secure swift victory, means a struggle within the old society's husk for the future. The civil war that ensues will be a violent military struggle between two societies so committed that victory for one means extinction for the other. Thus, a society organized as either envisions would be incompatible with the continued existence of the other: the alternative becomes Victory or Death, God or the Devil, Freedom or Slavery. Once the battle has been joined, the war is total and the outcome is seen only as total victory or total defeat. Neither side at any stage can seriously contemplate any alternative to victory except death—if not of the body then of the soul.

One of the most bitter and complicated of these civil wars took place in Ireland between 1916 and 1923, encompassing coups and pogroms, a war of national liberation, terror, communal violence, and ultimately a variety of imposed and contrived solutions that still haunt the island. On Easter Monday, April 24, 1916, a small band of Irish conspirators attempted a rising against the British, then otherwise occupied in France. Planned as a national insurrection, a variety of ill-favored accidents largely limited action to Dublin, where a few hundred men siezed and held the city for a week. In Irish terms these men were nationalists, intent on establishing the Irish Republic and defending their country by force of arms. For them, Ireland, though organized openly as a republic, had long existed as a submerged and occupied nation. The long procession of previous risings, nearly one a generation, was an outward sign of the peculiar integrity of an Ireland held in alien domination. Knowing that the Dublin rising would be crushed, they hoped that their blood sacrifice would awaken another generation, would water the roots of the "real" Ireland, would strip away the shell of assimilation, would in fact inspire a more successful war of national liberation. The British in turn were appalled at the senselessness of the rising, the pointless destruction of Dublin, the lost lives, the cost of fanaticism inflicted on Britain at a crucial moment by a tiny, unrepresentative band of rebels. For the British, the men of the Easter Rising *were* rebels. Britain had century after century absorbed diverse races into a single body politic and largely a single society. Ireland was an integral part of the United Kingdom, not a potential and distant dominion, like Canada or Australia. The Scots could be Scots, the Welsh, Welsh, but all were British, all were citizens of the United Kingdom. The king, the parliament, the army, and all enlighteded opinion accepted the indivisibility of British society. The Easter Rising was rebellion; the rebels had sought to instigate a fratricidal civil war.

Momentarily it seemed that all decent people, the Irish included, would agree. Ireland had been promised home rule. There had been no violence for a generation and in the spring of 1916 no indication of sudden mass support for further "rebel" adventures. Vast numbers of Irishmen were fighting in France alongside the Welsh and the Scots and the English—no greater proof was needed of the loyalty and unity of Britain. The leaders of the Easter Rising were executed as traitors and the rebels interned. As usual, the British had misjudged the Irish—in fact the Irish had misjudged themselves. Under the superficial accommodation with Britain, behind the seemingly irreversible assimilation into Britain, the Irish found all their old values, their ancestorial aspirations. Within a year, Irish society changed utterly, transformed allegiances, and opened the door to civil war. The irresponsible rebels became martyred patriots, the released internees heroes. After the December 1918 elections for the Westminister Parliament, 73 of the 105 Irish winners agreed to form their own Irish Parliament, the Dáil, which met on January 21, 1919, with by then 36 members in British jails. The threads of conspiracy and resistance had been gathered by the survivors, joined by eager new recruits to the cause of the Irish Republic. The "Troubles" came to Ireland, years of bitter irregular war, assassination, and violent repression, guerrillas in the hills, shadow governments, religious pogroms, executions, and arson. The British were determined to restore order, maintain the authority of the crown, protect the security of the realm, and defend the loyal Irish unionists, largely Protestants. Either there was a united kingdom or there was not—and the Irish Republicans with their recourse to arms insisted there was not.

The seemingly insurmountable obstacle facing the Irish Republicans was the overwhelming military superiority of the newly victorious British Empire. The means available to the Irish Republican Army to wage open war were limited indeed. The futility of seizing and holding part of the island had been underscored by the failure of the Easter Rising and a long series of earlier, abortive risings. Simple terror, bombs in the night, and murder from the ditch seemed unlikely means to coerce the British Empire. If the

Irish Republic was to become a reality, the IRA had to discover an effective means of waging a war.

Pragmatically, with little recourse to theory, the Irish evolved a form of internal war that in time would be the archetype for national liberation movements. First, the structure of British control and intelligence was hit repeatedly: the Royal Irish Constabulary, the paramilitary police, became prime targets, as did British secret service agents. As British knowledge of the countryside declined, it became increasingly easier to maintain small guerrilla columns in the hills, men who struck at barracks and transport and disappeared when pursued. The more British troops moved into the island, the more the targets available for ambush. Within the cities, terrorist operations were carried out with sufficient frequency to force the British into increasingly repressive measures. The more stringent British regulations became, the more brutal the searches and seizures, the more harsh the restrictions, the more "immoral" the British presence became, first to the Irish and gradually to international opinion. And while the IRA sought to accelerate the "military" campaign, an effort was made to create parallel governmental structures—Irish courts instead of British, Irish tax collectors, Irish diplomats. Abroad, Irish representatives poured out their story and churned out endless papers, pamphlets, and manifestos. Despite their ingenuity, however, and despite the British inability to restore order, after nearly three years the Irish were still no closer to expelling the British by force of arms. The Irish had discovered only how to evade defeat, not how to impose victory.

Increasingly the British public appeared to have doubts about the repressive policies of the government, particularly since they had so far been ineffective. Cork city had been burned and young Irish lads hanged, while the struggle between Irish Catholic "rebels" and Irish Protestant "loyalists" in Northern Ireland resembled medieval religious massacres. Most of all, the "moral" right of Britain to impose order through brutality began to be questioned. The difficulty for the British government remained not so much the distaste of yielding to rebel violence and opening negotiations, as belief in the indivisibility of the United Kingdom. There seemed no common ground between an Irish Republic and a British crown: local autonomy, home rule, even federalism might yield a formula but either there was an Irish Republic or there was not. Still, the British cabinet decided to explore the prospects of diplomacy, hopeful that some of the more responsible rebels would accept less than a whole loaf. In Ireland, some of the leaders of the IRA and the shadow government increasingly felt that with victory as illusive as ever, a British initiative for a compromise solution would not be unwelcome. Beginning in October 1920, even while the war continued, negotiations were opened by a variety of agents and agencies.

These eventually led first to a truce, July 11, 1921, and then to the arrival in October of an Irish delegation in London.

Under the shrewd and cunning leadership of Prime Minister David Lloyd George, the experienced and talented British delegation, which included among others Winston Churchill, managed to produce a solution that not only satisfied London's minimal demands, now far, far less than they had been a few years before, but also might not necessarily deny the basic Irish aspirations. A complicated, hybrid institution named the Irish Free State was proposed, which would be outside the United Kingdom but inside the British Empire. The government in Dublin would have to take an oath of allegiance to the crown but would have almost all the other attributes of an independent nation, as much as, if not more than, other British dominions. For some of the Irish delegation, the Free State seemed not to be the Republic or Freedom but a necessary means to achieve both in time. The responsibility for the loyal unionists, adamant to the point of rebellion in their refusal to accept absorption into a Catholic Irish Ireland, was accepted by London with the creation in six Ulster provinces of Northern Ireland—home rule within the United Kingdom for a majority of the unionists. Finally, the acquisition of military bases in the Free State satisfied British security requirements. Essentially the British had recognized the existence of an Irish society, organized as the Irish Free State in twenty-six of the thirty-two counties, but by a variety of legal and strategic ties retained that "society" within the British Empire if not the United Kingdom.

For a great many men who had spent years living on their nerves, seen their friends executed, and fought a long and bitter war, the legal ties that satisfied the British and some of their colleagues were chains. For them the sacrifices had been for recognition of the Republic, proclaimed Easter Monday, 1916, not a slick British formula called the Free State, which was not free as long as an oath to an alien crown was included and not a state as long as six counties were annexed and foreign bases imposed. During the bitter debates on the treaty, tensions grew within Irish society and the IRA. On January 7, 1922, when the treaty scraped through the new Dáil, sixty-four votes to fifty-seven, the Republican purists felt betrayed. Although they refused to recognize the existence of the "Treaty State," the advocates of compromise went right ahead organizing the new Free State. The British army evacuated the south, and a Northern Ireland government was set up in the north. The Troubles, however, were not at an end.

The Republicans, not unexpectedly, could not give up the Republic so easily. The IRA remained in existence. The old Republican government refused to fade away. Reluctantly, despairingly, two Irelands began to emerge. Through months of failed compromises, plots, meetings, and endless informal discussions, a middle way could not be found. Once more it proved a case of either/or: a Republic or the Free state, an oath or not. The breaking point came largely because the new government in Dublin could no longer tolerate the independent, potentially rebellious IRA. Either the Free State government was master of Ireland, at least of twenty-six counties thereof, or it was not.

The Free State army, with artillery borrowed from the British, opened fire on the IRA headquarters at Four Courts in Dublin on June 28, 1922, and the last act of the Troubles began. While many of the most brilliant guerrilla leaders and articulate spokesmen had remained loyal to the Easter Republic, the Free State—recognized as the legal government, possessed of the assets of the state, and directed by solid, efficient men—proved the stronger. Aided by a series of IRA strategic blunders, the Free State army first broke the IRA's thin, linear defenses and then forced the Republicans into guerrilla warfare. Whatever their sympathies, most of the Irish people were exhausted, felt they had sacrificed sufficiently, and were unwilling or unable to support the IRA's desperate struggle. By use of judicial executions and massive detentions, the IRA was intimidated, reduced to arson and ambush. Free State repression became sufficiently efficient that the IRA became little bands of armed men on the run. Finally the Republicans were forced on May 24, 1923, to issue an order not to surrender but to dump arms and disband. The shattered remains of the IRA were hunted down by the Free Staters. The jails were filled with internees, the emigrant ships with a new generation of exiles. The practical men of the Free State had crushed the pure of heart. There was to be no republic.

On the morning after final victory, the triumphant are faced with the task of securing that victory. Since few defeated societies have been totally annihilated on the field of battle, victors have to face the problem of assimilating or eliminating the remnants. The Irish situation was particularly complicated because of the variety of victories and defeats. First, when a war of national liberation is successful, then it is clear to the victors that no civil war took place. If Ireland had been intimidated by the British army, resistance ended, and order restored, then the civil war would have been won and the national liberation struggle denied. Normally, even logically, these alternatives are mutually exclusive—except in Ireland. In twenty-six counties the Irish forced a solution that largely recognized the independent existence of Ireland, that is, that the war had not been a civil war and that neither the new government in Dublin nor the old in London had to assimilate a defeated society. In Ulster, however, the loyalists emerged triumphantly dominating the new Northern Ireland government with their two-to-one majority, discriminating against their potentially disloyal Irish-Catholic neighbors, imposing, as one indiscreet spokesman noted, a Protestant parliament on a Protestant people. In the North the civil war had been won in the name of unity with Britain, and so the "rebels," doubly dangerous, for they could look south for aid and comfort, had to be closely controlled. Since assimilation was impossible without wholesale conversion to Protestantism, rather unlikely, the Northern Ireland government and the loyalist society by a tangle of legal and extralegal restrictions and practices set up a machine of domination, determined that their society would be safe by isolating and restricting the "other" minority society. With no other choice, the Catholics of Northern Ireland were forced to endure sullenly, too weak to rebel and too devout to convert.

In the Irish Free State, the victorious government after the real but brief civil war felt far less threatened than its Northern counterpart. The war had been vicious but not exceedingly bloody, with less than 700 killed. The irreconcilables of the IRA could in time be absorbed, once they recognized the futility of continued armed resistance. The hatred was deep and likely to be long lasting, but it was Irish hatred between Irishmen. The detention camps remained but for a year. The Republicans were permitted back into political competition. After various evasions and rationalizations the more practical Republican wing under Eamon DeValera entered the Dáil and after their party's 1931 election victory formed the new government.

The die-hard Republicans, however, refused to recognize the Free State or to participate in parliamentary politics. The IRA remained in existence as a secret army but not only declined as a threat to the security of the state but also showed very considerable reluctance to reintroduce the gun into Irish politics. Thus, despite the old and very real grievances, the Republicans were largely absorbed into the new Free State, and so successfully that in less than a decade they had taken over the government. The hardcore Republicans, who remained outside the governmental system, did not become a dissident society, but only a dissenting current within Irish society. The unreconstructed IRA did carry out a bombing campaign in England in 1939 and 1940, forcing not only the British and Northern Ireland governments to institute harsh repressive measures but also the government of De Valera in Dublin, fearful of the IRA's jeopardizing Irish neutrality. In 1956, after a series of spectacular arms raids, the IRA opened a six-year guerrilla campaign in Northern Ireland, again resulting in repressive measures north and south of the border, but again failing seriously to disrupt society. The hard core did and does exist, but without sufficient support to impose its solution on Britain or polarize Irish society.

Not all victors in civil wars select toleration as a method to secure a stable society; in fact, very, very few do, although a system foreseeing permanent repression is not necessarily a favored option. In fact, the most efficacious solution to disposing of a subsociety is genocide. At one level of efficiency or another, this has not always been discarded: Cromwell almost "solved" the Irish problem once before, and in more recent times the Soviet regime eliminated two classes, the nobles and the bourgeoisie, who were without function or place in their new society, relegating them to the garbage heap of history. A somewhat less severe policy is the transfer of the potentially dissident population, as occurred between Turkey and Greece after World War I, or their expulsion, such as that of the Germans in East Prussia. A discreet balance between terror and expulsions may either completely eliminate the undesirable society or so bleed off the bold and daring as to emasculate the remainder. In both cases, however, moral considerations aside, the victors may not wish to eliminate the defeated society entirely, thereby also eliminating the possibility of exploiting the losers. After the long, bitter Spanish Civil War of 1936-39, Franco and the Nationalists could hardly eliminate or expel well over half the Spanish population. They could and did follow a policy of harsh repression, but the suspect classes and sections within Spain, if not reconciled to the victorious society, at least became resigned to the futility of opposition.

In some cases, once purged of active dissidence, the old society is simply ignored, feeble, and frustrated, while the new society is created around them or, as the case may be, on top of them. Thus, in America the "rebels" were largely ignored and excluded during the post-Civil War reconstruction period. When the reconstructed society proved too feeble and too expensive for the victors, increasingly involved in the expansion of the new postwar industrial society of the North and West, the former rebels were allowed limited control over the devastated South. In the fullness of time, the Southern "society" evolved into Southern sectionalism and was gradually absorbed into the mainstream of America. No matter whether the relatively magnanimous policies of the Irish Free State or the United States or the harsh repression of Spain or Northern Ireland are followed, the residue of a defeated society remains well into the following generations.

Although recourse to rebellion no longer holds any lures for most of the defeated (civil war inoculates a nation against a second attack), a not-always-conscious attempt is made to discover alternatives to defeat. In America, with the Confederacy crushed and the South devastated, General Robert E. Lee could only offer acceptance. The South had fought the good fight and far longer than reasonable because there seemed no alternative. Said he: "We have fought this fight as long as, and as well as we know how. We have been defeated. For us, as a Christian people, there is now but one course to pursue. We must accept this situation." Understandably, to most shattered societies without hope in the future, simple acceptance proves scant comfort. The Lost Cause is enshrined in myths, becomes pure, a bold act of the spirit smashed by overwhelming, materialistic force. These legends of the past—dashing cavaliers, brave grand dukes, kings across the waters, workers on the Madrid barricades—often provide fertile ground for subsequent generations' creativity, producing a rich artistic lode, rather the case of the sand transformed into the pearl. Even a "mild" civil war with relatively rapid reintegration will produce a society wedded to the issues of the past long after there is any viability in the old arguments. Men not yet born at the crucial moment of battle will in Ireland or Alabama vote basically for vengeance, rallying behind political symbols irrelevant to the issues of the day.

In summary, then, in social terms civil war is a struggle between two societies incapable of coexisting in the husk of previously unified institutions. Essentially the struggle is over either the purity or the unity of society, a battle for a Communist Russia or a free Ireland. With neither side militarily capable of enforcing a swift decision, the confrontation between totally contradictory aspirations must be fought to the bitter end. Such a war inevitably means total denial for the most cherished goals of one side. The process of accommodation for the defeated under even favorable circumstances almost always requires sufficient time for a generation no longer committed to the past to mature. In some cases, because of the adamancy of the differences, accommodation is not really possible, and the unreconstructed rebels are relegated to an almost permanent subcaste. New options or the decline of former advocacies may in the fullness of time mute the old bitterness, and exhaustion or sudden wealth or an external threat may bring toleration and then integration.

In Ireland, after 1923, the complication was that both sides in the conflict proclaimed their devotion to the same ideals; achievement was the matter of contention. Those, especially among the victors, who thought the 1916 dream either unwise or unlikely tended to mute their advocacy. As a result Ireland as a Commonwealth country was really a nonstarter, despite some support and considerable toleration for the concept, for the appeal of the Republic was enormous. Those who could not or would not be satisfied with the interim comfort of the Dublin institutions were as isolated as the Commonwealth core; they, however, claimed to embody the pure dream, the absolute Republic. This meant that the great middle ground of Irish politics that incorporated much of the Nationalist North had the same ideals but differed on means. No matter what means were selected by Dublin, it became increasingly obvious in private, if not on the platform or in the parliament, that the state did not and would not possess compelling force to impose a united Ireland and that the people seemed unwilling in any case to make the necessary sacrifice. In the meantime they could transform the existing limited possibilities into real steps toward independence—break the connection between Dublin and London at least—transform what could be reached and use the freedom to be free to liberate one Ireland if not all Ireland.

While this process, coupled with efforts to develop the economy and improve social conditions with most limited assets, absorbed Irish energy, events elsewhere beyond Britain often seemed very far away. The fact that bank failures in Vienna or New York had an effect on milk prices was often difficult to grasp in Mayo or Leitrim, even as the extra sons continually immigrated to distant unemployment lines. And the fact that political ideas of the corporate state or racial purity would affect Irish politics focused on the Crown's prerogatives seemed unlikely. There were, however, always some in Ireland deeply concerned about foreign events. The radicals worried about the rising tide of world fascism and the meaning of events in the Soviet Union. The reactionaries were concerned about the threat of secular communism and the future of the Church. Many were disturbed by the nature of the international depression and nearly all by the quarrel with Britain. Mostly, as always, parochial matters loomed large and time moved slowly, bleak and grey for the isolated without prospects, comfortable in the allotted seasons for the conservative.

All of this hardly changed during a few weeks in 1936 when Spain collapsed into war and chaos. For most in Ireland, Spain was a distant country with shreds and tatters of Irish links but no pressing image of importance. As isolated behind the Pyrenees as Ireland was by the sea, Spain had seldom of late played any great role in Europe and almost none in Irish eyes—a poor Catholic country prone to local violence with a glittering history but few prospects. Spanish events, however, would in Ireland as much of Europe awake those spread out along the entire spectrum of ideological commitment: radicals of all flavors, reactionaries, the devout and dedicated, the romantic, and even the orthodox. In Spain the future to many seemed at stake, and Ireland, however provincial and parochial, involved in a potato war and a language revival, was not immune. Thus, at a period when the gun had been largely removed from Irish politics (a period of ideological exhaustion and strategic frustration) a new violent arena opened unexpectedly. The variegated Irish response would give some indication of the island's values, aspirations, and prospects. There were many roles and many Irish actors eager for a part—at least until a place for the gun could be found locally. So, barely over an Irish civil war, the country became, like much of Europe, involved in a Spanish civil conflict little understood but much exploited.

5

Ireland and the Spanish Civil War, 1936-39

On 20 July 1936, Irish newspapers began publishing reports of some sort of serious disturbance in Spain. This was hardly novel since for over a century the politics of Spain had been little more than a catalogue of failed governments, aborted coups, and institutionalized instability. The new Spanish Republic, established in 1931, had been no exception and by the summer of 1936 had already survived two unsuccessful risings, one by part of the army and one by the Asturian miners. Spain's internal difficulties, however, had long been of concern only to the Spanish; for the major clashes of international rivalry had taken place elsewhere, leaving Spain isolated in chronic chaos. At the first reports of trouble, there was in Ireland as elsewhere in Europe sympathy for the tribulations of the Spanish people but no immediate recognition that Europe stood on the eve of a major crisis. Although Ireland had long and often intimate historical ties with the Spanish people, the Irish Free State had few political interests in Spain despite the presence in Madrid of one of the few Irish Free State diplomats. Sentiment and tradition were the prevailing factors in Irish-Spanish relations. Until July 1936 European-Spanish relations were largely based on the same considerations, for if Africa did not actually begin at the Pyrenees, at least European interest ended there.

In the summer of 1936 Spanish politics suddenly engendered far wider concern than anyone could have anticipated because of the sudden and belated realization of the nature of the various Spanish factions. With the rise of militant ideologies after World War I, there had developed an intense international partisanship in the outlook of certain parties within most European countries, so that they often found themselves in close accord with the aspirations of their foreign counterparts. In the case of Germany, Italy, and particularly the Soviet Union, the ideological identification was often paramount in determining foreign policy. As the open clash of ideologies in Spain had become more apparent during 1936, there was an increasing tendency toward partisanship in regard to Spanish affairs. Perhaps no country in Europe had as broad a representation of the political spectrum as did Spain during the days of the Republic. There were not only the usual collection of moderate parties of all shades and persuasions, but an embryonic Fascist party, two rival Monarchist groups, several varieties of Marxist parties besides the orthodox Communist, and the largest Anarchist party in the world. Hardly a European faction or creed was without Spanish representation, so that when the rebellion began in July, much of Europe was almost at once emotionally involved, backing vicariously, at first at least, their own particular horse.

Ireland was no exception, although being insular and isolated, the major continental ideologies had largely fallen on barren soil. For over a decade the political divisions in both the Irish Free State and Northern Ireland had been almost totally determined by the implications of the Anglo-Irish Treaty of 1921. There had been and still were in 1936 representatives of both the far Left and far Right in Ireland who saw Spain through their own peculiarly tinted spectacles.

In the North there was a scattering of Communists and Socialists in Belfast but what few radicals there were could be found in the Northern Ireland Labour party. The Protestant Unionists and Catholic Nationalists continued to devote their total energies to the issues of 1921. Essentially both parties were deeply conservative, little interested in broad economic and social issues but only in the all-abiding constitutional question—the ultimate status of the six counties. Both were embedded in the past, neither concerned with the radical ideologies of continental Europe nor the world outside Ulster. Their vision was largely limited to sectarian Irish affairs and their response to Spanish events fell into the same pattern.

In the Irish Free State the Left was tiny but articulate and the Right hazy and disorganized. Orthodox Marxists were rare indeed, the trade unions largely conservative, and the Labour party almost reactionary. Despite the opposition of the Church, the suspicion of the traditional parties, and the apathy of the masses, a Republican Congress incorporating the Left of the Irish Republican Army and a scattering of radicals had been formed in 1934. This uncertain umbrella of the Left had been split almost at once on ideological issues that seemed sterile to most of the Irishmen who cared to follow the arguments. Thus, by July 1936 much of the agitation and activity of the divided Left seemed to be tapering off in the face of growing support for Fianna Fáil's moderate but visible reforms.[1] The Left still remained, however, aggressive, determined, and perpetually hopeful and with a new cause in Spain, where the forces of democracy clashed with fascism. The Irish "Fascists" had all but faded from the scene by 1936. The Blue Shirts movement under General Eoin O'Duffy had mushroomed briefly, creating what some saw as a real threat to Irish democracy, only to collapse in the face of internal schisms and administrative incapacities. By July 1936 the movement was dead if not buried, either absorbed in the new

Fine Gael party or clumped nostalgically around O'Duffy, a proven political failure. Many former Blue Shirts, however, saw in Spain an issue to revive the movement, a cause to reactivate a crusade, a rallying cry for the Right.

While the spectrum of Irish politics was wide enough to include both Communists and Fascists—of a sort—the mass remained huddled in a narrow band near right-center. Tory paternalism based on sectarian considerations in the North and a Fianna Fáil government dedicated to achieving the national aims of 1916 by parliamentary means left little room for new ideas. Irish politics were directed solely to maintaining or to undoing the past. On these questions, events in Spain could play little part. Yet there was something for everyone in Spain. If the theories of the Spanish Left or the Right found few partisans, the fate of the Spanish Church concerned all. As so often in the past, religion not politics would largely determine the Irish response.

The immediate Irish reaction to the Spanish crisis was vague.[2] The newspapers were cautious since the editors had little idea of exactly what was going on in Spain. If there was a general immediate reaction, it was that events boded ill for the Spanish caught between unpalatable alternatives.

> It is of no great importance to us in Ireland whether Spain decided to throw in her lot with Communism or with Fascism: for either alternative is equally destestable to people of a liberal tradition.[3]

Within two days, on July 22, the *Irish Independent* made it clear that the fate of Spain was of great importance to Ireland. Spain was not the battleground of alien ideologies.

> All who stand for the ancient faith and the traditions of Spain are behind the present revolt against the Marxist regime in Madrid.

The editor of the *Independent*, reacting to the persecution of the Spanish Church, saw in Spain a desperate clash between the atheistic Reds and the Church. In time many others would agree, but for a while uncertainty remained.[4] On the next day the *Irish Press*, an unswerving advocate of Fianna Fáil government, noted that "no really authentic information as to what is taking place" existed as yet, although with the Madrid government's "connivance, if not under its aegis, churches have been burned, schools secularised, communist schemes carried out."

Other Irish newspapers did not necessarily see the religious question as the major factor. *The Irish Times*, supposedly the organ of the Protestant ascendancy, began to publish some of the most factual, balanced editorial analyses to be found in Europe, but there was no emotional commitment, none of the *Independent*'s dedication to the patriot's Christian crusade or the *Press*'s concern with the fate of the Spanish Church. For the *Times*, Spain was an international political issue, endangering the European peace but not the Irish conscience. The *Cork Examiner,* more royal than the king, viewed the war as an event disruptive of the policy being followed by the British government, taking little note of the impact on either Irish policy or Irish Catholicism. The *Belfast Telegraph* reacted as would any provincial British paper loyal to the government in Westminister with editorial support for the official policy of neutrality: "On the whole it would not be right for any Power to take sides openly with either of the combatants."[5] Thus, the Irish Protestant press saw no religious issue in Spain, only a political problem.

The problem was, of course, to avoid a general European conflict over Spanish issues, which was far more important than the sectarian excesses of the Madrid government. This stance was a reflection of the attitude of the Conservative government fearful that foreign intervention in Spain would lead to chaos and war. On July 30 three Italian army planes were forced to land in French Morocco on their way to General Francisco Franco, the insurgent commander in Spanish Morocco.[6] This confirmed the suspicions of many that Mussolini and probably Hitler had come to the aid of the insurgents.[7] In Moscow the Soviet Union was showing increasingly vocal support for the Spanish Republic, a support many felt would evolve into specific intervention of offset Italian-German aid.[8] In France the *Front Populaire* government of Leon Blum seemed to waver between aiding the Spanish Republic and remaining neutral to maintain Franco's special relationship with the Conservative government in London. All Europe seemed to be taking sides over Spain where fascism fought democracy or God met the anti-Christ or tradition wrestled with revolution. British hopes for disinterested neutrality seemed to evaporate in a wave of bitter political partisanship and ideological self-interest.

In Paris, with his nation torn by dissention, Blum feared that French support of the Spanish Republic might lead to civil war and surely to the collapse of the British alliance. Yet, if he failed to aid his collegues of the Spanish *Front Populaire*, as he legally could and morally should, he might well be discarded by his own party. If Italy and Germany supported the insurgents, he would be driven into the arms of the Spanish Republic. Desperately he devised a formula for European nonintervention that would solve his domestic difficulties, reassure the British government, and isolate Spain from the rip tides of European competition. If all the European nations agreed not to intervene in Spain, no one could fault France's contribution to European stability except the Spanish Republicans who could be uneasily ignored. On July 30 Blum presented a nonintervention declaration to the Foreign Affairs Committee of the Senate. The declaration was contingent upon the attitudes with other European powers. The British government, delighted with Blum's initiative, suggested including other powers. On August 1 the French government issued an appeal of the interested powers for the rapid and rigorous fulfilment of rules of nonintervention. In close co-operation with the British, the French diplomats began an intensive campaign to secure acceptance of nonintervention as a European policy.[9]

In Ireland as in Europe, neutrality seemed to have evaporated as the reports from Spain became more specific. Among most Catholics the overriding consideration was the plight of the Spanish Church. Even those who did not see the war in religious terms were forced to comment on the persecution of the Spanish Church.[10] In the Free State many insisted that in some way Catholic Ireland must lend its moral support to Catholic Spain. Others, while sympathetic to the plight of the Spanish Church, felt any such gesture would do little to help the Anglo-French efforts to secure a European nonintervention policy. While in the North the Unionists held strictly to a policy of nonintervention, the Nationalists identified themselves with the persecuted Spanish Church. As might be expected among the more intolerant believers, events in Spain were fuel to add to old fires. In Belfast, Rev. Lawrence Elder informed the parishioners of Clifton Street Presbyterian Church that the Vatican was in a large degree responsible for the appalling state of Spain.[11] In Kerry, Father Garrahan, s.j., at a lecture insisted that the desperate upheaval was a result of the Reformation.[12]

On August 11 the *Irish Independent* demanded to know why the Free State government continued to maintain diplomatic relations with the Red government of Madrid. Fine Gael supported this stand as did a variety of conservative politicans and vocal priests. DeValera's government, supported by the editorials of the *Irish Press,* contended that this would violate normal diplomatic procedure, hinder efforts to secure nonintervention, and even go further than had the Vatican. While there was within the ranks of Fianna Fáil sympathy for the Spanish Republic and a considerable distaste for the reactionary insurgents, everyone supported a policy of proper neutrality.[13] To the cynical the insistence of the *Independent*, apparently with the support of Fine Gael, on an Irish commitment to the insurgents seemed more like politics than principle, an effort to take partisan advantage of religious feeling. Even the generous could see no advantage to Europe, to Ireland, or even perhaps to Franco, in such a unilateral gesture. Blum's nonintervention policy thus fitted neatly with Fianna Fáil's inclinations, adding international authority to the government's policy. On both the Left and Right of the two major parties, there were those who felt that

disinterested neutrality or newspaper debate on formal diplomatic relations held no charm. These Irishmen believed that intervention in Spain
was a duty, that no one could stand aside when the forces of good and evil,
however defined, clashed in open battle. For the time being, however, the
activists worked in silence while public debate centered on the proposals of
the *Independent.*

In all parts of Ireland, honest men saw Christianity threatened by communism in Spain. E.T. Keane, editor of the *Kilkenny People*, saw the war as
a struggle "between the forces of Christ and the forces of anti-Christ."[14]
Many agreed. The *Derry Journal*, a Nationalist paper sympathetic to De
Valera and Fianna Fáil, urged on August 5 that the Irish Free State should
recognize the insurgents.[15] Throughout Northern Ireland the Nationalists
were embittered by the apparent lack of Protestant concern for the fate of
Spanish Christianity. Instead of sympathy, the Unionists offered nasty little
lectures. On August 31, the *Belfast Telegraph* editoralized that "Most people will agree there is little real religion on either side, and it is a sad
reflection on the influence of the Church . . . that so many of its members
or nominal members should descend to deeds that are usually associated
with the Middle Ages." The theme repeated from pulpits and in the more
biting weekly papers that the Spanish Church was to blame for its own
plight violently antagonized Northern Catholics. For them there was no
neutrality in the face of a persecution with which they were all too familiar.
For them the editorials of the *Irish Independent* made sound sense.

The first practical step to implement the breaking of relations with
Madrid was a movement to secure resolutions from various local government bodies. What became known as the Clonmel Resolution was introduced, usually by Fine Gael members, urging the Fianna Fáil government
to cut the diplomatic tie with the Red Government. Avidly supporting this
maneuver was the new Irish Christian Front, whose director, Patrick
Belton, an independent member of the Dáil from Dublin, led a nonparty
movement to turn back the threat of international communism.[16] In Spain
Belton found an ideal target for the Christian Front's activities, in the
Clonmel Resolution an ideal first step in rededicating Ireland to Catholic
principles. During August an impressive number of councils passed some
form of the Clonmel Resolution. Opposition, facing the choice between
communism and Christianity, was sketchy but present. In the highly
charged atmosphere of excessive piety, the risks of standing against the
resolution were considerable.

> Mr. W. MaHon (Chairman of the Athy Urban District Council): We will take
> this resolution as adopted unanimously.
> Mr. T. Carbery: I am dissenting.
> Mrs. S. Doyle: Are you a communist?[17]

In the midst of this seemingly spontaneous upsurge wrapped in impregnable devotion, the Fianna Fáil government remained unmoved. Belton's new Irish Christian Front looked to some like the old Blue Shirts clad in tweed. The resolutions often seemed to derive their support from solid Fine Gael men with an eye on the Dáil. Then, too, the leadership had more than once experienced the slings and arrows of previous anti-Communist campaigns to flinch when the "Red Menace" was rediscovered. There was no doubt that the Church was deeply disturbed by events in Spain and by the supposedly fatal attraction of Communist ideology and that many conservative Irishmen, in and out of Fine Gael, sincerely believed Ireland faced a Communist threat of some sort. Mexico yesterday, Spain today, and Ireland tomorrow.[18] As P.J. Curran said at an Irish Christian Front rally at Balbriggan, "Communism has approached very close to Balbriggan."[19] While the Right in general desperately feared the Reds, the major problem was to find them in Ireland.[20] Other than a few self-proclaimed Communists, Ireland has remained hostile to the wiles of Marx. No one in his right mind could accuse the Irish Labour Party of extremism nor were the small covey of Left sects a clear and present danger. A call for action based on Catholicism, which all professed, and against communism, which few could define or even find, appeared either emotionalism without content or, worse, an attempt to secure partisan advantage by sectarian means. Thus, the Fianna Fáil government ignored the furore.

On August 26 the Government Informaion Bureau announced that on the previous day the government had informed the French Minister in Dublin that the Free State accepted the principle of nonintervention in the affairs of Spain.

> They have informed the French Government that they propose accordingly to take the necessary steps to prohibit the exportation of arms and ammunition to Spain and Spanish possessions.
>
> The majority of the governments of Europe have notified the French government in the same sense. The policy of nonintervention had been adopted in the conviction that it is in the interests of Spain itself, and that it is in the present circumstances the policy which will best serve the cause of European peace.
>
> The government of the Saorstát Éireann, in common with the Irish people and the Christian world, are profoundly shocked by the tragic events that have been taking place in Spain and by the excesses by which these events are reported to be accompanied.
>
> Their sympathy goes out to the great Spanish people in their terrible suffering. They earnestly hope that peace may soon be restored, and they would gladly participate in any practical effort directed toward that end.
>
> To those public bodies, however, and to others who have requested the gov-

ernment to sever diplomatic relations with the Spanish government the government of the Saorstát Éireann would point out that diplomatic relations are primarily between States rather than Governments, and that the severance of diplomatic relations between two countries would serve no useful purpose at the present time.[21]

While a policy of nonintervention attracted considerable spport, including that of Fine Gael if not the *Irish Independent*,[22] efforts to persuade the government to break relations with the Spanish Republic continued. Basically Fine Gael wanted nonintervention without ties to Madrid. Fianna Fáil spokesmen and the *Irish Press* continued to point out that this would break diplomatic precedent, fail to aid the cause of peace, and be at odds with the policy of the Vatican, which still maintained ties with the Spanish Republic. The relevance of the dispute began to fade as the public realized that other Irishmen intended to intervene in Spain regardless of the supposed enthusiasm for neutrality.

Peadar O'Donnell, one of the founders of both Saor Éire and the Republican Congress, had been in Spain on the outbreak of the revolt and had returned to Ireland eager to aid the Madrid government in its struggle against fascism.[23] In Dublin he found that considerable support for the Spanish Republic already existed. This was generally the case throughout Europe where no sinister prompting was necessary for the Left to identify with the Spanish republic. One Irishman, Bill Scott, a member of the Irish Communist Party, had not waited for formal intervention but had gone directly to Spain to volunteer his services. The leaders of the Left in Ireland decided to send George Gilmore to Spain to find out what could be done; however, Gilmore was accidentally injured in the Basque country and later interned before achieving any positive result. The most obvious candidate remaining was Frank Ryan, former editor of the Irish Republican Army newspaper *An Phoblacht* and an effective and dedicated agitator for the Left. Ryan, immensely popular in Dublin even with his political opponents, set to work to organize an Irish volunteer movement. With men like Ryan, O'Donnell, perhaps contemporary Ireland's most gifted agitator, Frank Edwards, Kit Conway, and others, the cause of the Spanish Republic was well served. Offers from all over Ireland to volunteer for Spain began to come into Dublin. During the autumn volunteers were processed and quickly sent on their way to Spain to join the newly formed International Brigades. Few of these Irishmen could be called orthodox Communists, but all saw Spain as a battleground between democracy and fascism and felt that they must participate.[24]

Others in Ireland, often equally dedicated, saw Spain as a battleground between Christianity and communism, and they, too, felt they must participate. Early in August Count de Ramirez de Arellano, an avid Carlist monarchist, wrote to Cardinal MacRory, Primate of Ireland, concerning his hope that Ireland must play a more direct part in the Spanish struggle against communism. On August 6 Cardinal MacRory replied and suggested that for practical action the man to contact would be General O'Duffy, then in partial political retirement after the decline of the Blue Shirts and his split with Fine Gael. On August 12 the Count wrote to O'Duffy:

> You will be pleased to know that your splendid Cardinal Primate has written me a glorious letter, wholeheartedly and enthusiastically agreeing with my views and intentions. Oh, please God, that we may be able to do something. What a glorious example Ireland would be giving the whole of Christendom.[25]

The idea attracted O'Duffy. The romance of the historic ties with Spain, the atrocities of Spanish communism, the need of the Spanish Church and the blessing of the Irish Cardinal Primate added to his own isolation, made the idea of an Irish Brigade appealing.[26] O'Duffy conferred with those sympathetic Irishmen and flew to Europe to see what the prospects were going to be. By mid-August branches of O'Duffy's National Corporate Party were calling for volunteers and soon reporting an overwhelming response. Not only O'Duffy's old Blue Shirts were volunteering but also a wide variety of Irishmen attracted by the idea of a modern crusade.[27] O'Duffy flew to Spain to contact the insurgents and complete the formal procedures for the intervention of an Irish Brigade. O'Duffy's major reservation was that the Irish Brigade should not fight on the Basque front in view of the fact that the Basque Catholics had remained loyal to the Spanish Republic. The Spanish insurgents, apparently with some doubts about the wisdom of O'Duffy's project, agreed to a volunteer Irish Brigade. During the early autumn recruiting continued amid a blaze of publicity, not always favorable even by the insurgent's Irish advocates who found no romance in the legend of the wild geese dying in exile for alien causes.

To prevent just the sort of intervention being organized in Ireland, the British and French felt something more effective than unilateral declarations of nonintervention was necessary. To oversee European nonintervention a formal committee was organized. On Wednesday morning, 9 September 1936, the newly formed Non-Intervention Committee met for the first time in the Locarno room of the British Foreign Ministry. Twenty-five delegates were present including the Irish High Commissioner in London, John Whelan Dulanty. As with most of the small powers of Europe, the Irish Free State had been more than willing to cooperate in any new concert of Europe to lessen the abrassive tensions arising from the

Spanish war. Dublin, too, was pleased to have Ireland present in an international forum, particularly a forum dedicated to peaceful negotiation. Actually the Irish contribution to the intricate and often vitriolic committee negotiations proved to be negligible, but through no fault of the Irish government. The meetings of the full committee of twenty-six nations soon proved unwieldy. A smaller chairman's subcommittee was created on September 14, seating the five major powers along with Belgium, Czechoslovakia, Sweden, and later Portugal. The full committee was relegated to little more than the role of a ratifying assembly, always voting favorably on the recommendations proposed by the subcommittee, which in turn were dictated by the major powers' decisions. Ireland was, nevertheless, participating in the European effort to cordon off the Spanish crisis.[28]

While Irish adherence to policy on nonintervention was accepted as desirable by both Fine Gael and the Labour Party, the question of relations with Madrid had for many not been settled. The Clonmel resolution in some variety continued to appear before local bodies. Many local newspapers followed the lead of the *Irish Independent*. In other areas priests and politicians spoke on the dangers of communism and Ireland's spiritual unity with those defending the Spanish Church. Several trade union branches passed resolutions condemning their leadership's support of the Spanish Republic. Irishmen were not, as yet, intervening in Spain; but few were neutral. The most ambitious programs were undertaken by the Irish Christian Front, determined to secure mass support for the cause of the Spanish insurgents, and the hierarchy of the Irish Church, eager to combat communism in general and defend the embattled Spanish Church in particular. Both, however, were more concerned with rallying Irishmen to a new militant Christianity than in following O'Duffy's trail of direct intervention in Spanish affairs.

The Irish Church had almost from the first reports of the atrocities against the Spanish Catholics shown intense concern but also intense partisanship. While the leaders of the Church of Ireland were prone to take a balanced view, pointing out the excesses of both sides and the unsavory political philosophy of the insurgents, the Catholic bishops embraced the insurgents. Some felt that Protestant neutrality was directly related to the limited number of Protestants available in Spain for persecution. On August 18 Dr. Fogarty, bishop of Killaloe, praised the editorial position of the *Irish Independent* on Spanish affairs. On August 30 Dr. Mageean, bishop of Down and Connor, in a letter to his diocese called for a crusade of prayer in aid of the Spanish Catholics. From the pulpit, in the letter columns of the newspapers, on the platforms of mass meetings, the spokesmen of the Church increasingly identified the Irish Church with the cause of the Spanish insurgents. Provoked by the massive interference of the Church in what they considered a political issue, the leaders of the Republican Congress defined the war in terms the Irish hierarchy would not accept and sent a telegram of support to a "Red" government that the Church anathematized.[29] At Drogheda on Sunday, September 20, Cardinal MacRory said that "it is a scandal and an outrage that an Irish Catholic body should be guilty of pledging support to such a campaign." The Cardinal felt that prayer was the only hope for the misguided souls of such Irishmen.[30]

The hierarchy insisted that it was "a question of whether Spain will remain, as it has been so long, a Christian land or a Bolshevist and anti-God one."[31] On October 13 the hierarchy issued a statement calling for a collection on October 25, Feast of Christ the King, "to make atonement for the sacrilegious outrages committed against Christ and in supplication for the victory of Christianity over Anarchy and Communism."[32] On October 19 Cardinal MacRory suggested the secondary schools give instructions to offset the teachings of communism. On October 25 the Cardinal's fund collected over £40,000.[33] To the militant Left this appeared a forced levy to support the political views of the hierarchy. To many British and Irish Protestant clergy the Irish Church's commitment to the insurgents seemed unwise.

In this atmosphere of militant ecclesiastical conviction, the Irish Christian Front found a fertile field for its efforts. A manifesto was issued at the end of August incorporating most of the positions taken by the advocate of the insurgents. Under Belton's direction and with the cooperation of local sympathizers and a variety of priests and bishops, the size and influence of the Christian Front mushroomed. The Front organized a series of monster rallies in support of the Spanish Church and in opposition to the Red Menace. These meetings were intended not only to raise money for the relief of Spanish Catholics but also to rededicate the Irish people to the militant Catholicism necessary to turn back communism. On August 31 a large emotional rally was held at College Green in Dublin revealing the attraction of the new movement. During September new branches were announced regularly.[34] Huge throngs were reported at the Cork meeting. On October 26 another great anti-Communist rally was again held in Dublin complete with processions and mass responses. By November the Irish Christian Front had collected over £30,000 and a host of new members. Belton left for Spain to arrange for the shipment of medical supplies to be purchased with the money. While the monster meetings tapered off, another great rally was held in Galway on November 22. The typical resolutions passed by acclamation: militant anticommunism, sympathy for the Cardinal Primate of Spain, and congratulations to General Franco, the new head of the Nationalist junta; however, at Galway a resolution pledged the Irish Christian Front to bring about an economic system based on the

Papal Encyclicals. To some, particularly in Fianna Fáil, there was some indication now that Belton and the leaders of the Christian Front had wider and more political ambitions than their apolitical claims.

Neither the emotionalism of the Christian Front nor the position of the hierarchy produced a reappraisal within De Valera's government. Nonintervention remained a satisfactory as well as proper policy. Diplomatic ties could not be discarded as a gesture. What was concerning men both within and without the government was the rapidly maturing plans for an exodus of Irishmen, volunteering to fight on one side or the other. During the autumn, grave doubts were made public even among those deeply committed. Belton suggested that advocates of intervention "should think before urging more wild geese." On November 31, back from Spain, he announced that "I did not agree with the wisdom of Irishmen going out to Spain,[35] but the Christian Front would guarantee medical supplies to O'Duffy's Irish Brigade. The illegal Irish Republican Army, too, felt that the place of Irishmen was Ireland and prohibited its members from volunteering for Spain.[36] For the moment De Valera's government could do nothing about the volunteers, still a trickle in November, but in the Dáil turned back a demand to sever relations with the Spanish Republic.

Essentially the Dáil debates on the Spanish question revealed nothing that had not already found a place in the various newspapers' editorials. Many could sympathize with Cosgrave's reasoning, but Fianna Fáil spokesmen insisted that the Irish Free State must follow traditional diplomatic norms. Although Germany and Italy had recognized Franco's government,[37] this should not determine Irish policy. Again the continuing ties of the Vatican State with the Spanish Republic were noted and immediately picked up by the Protestant press of Northern Ireland as ample evidence of Catholic power over the Irish Free State.[38] There was, of course, never any doubt about the government's majority. The Irish Labour Party, unlike its counterparts in Great Britain and Northern Ireland, favored nonintervention and voted with Fianna Fáil. The result was that Cosgrave's amendment failed sixty-five to forty-four on November 27.

By December the main impact of the Spanish war had shifted to the question of the Irish volunteers. In London on December 9, the nonintervention committee discussed the question of volunteers, but as usual without any immediate results. From all over Europe volunteers had been arriving in the Spanish Republic with the enthusiastic support of the liberal and labor press of Europe. General Franco's Nationalists did not attract the same individual enthusiasm but were more than compensated by a growing stream of Italian and German equipment and "volunteers." By the time of the crucial battles around Madrid in November and December, none but the willfully or diplomatically blind could ignore Russian advisers, German aircraft, the polyglot International Brigades, and Italian artillery.

The Irishmen organized by Ryan drifted into Spain and eventually arrived at the camps outside Albacete where the International Brigades were trained. These Brigades were filled with idealists, intellectuals, and exiles holding a variety of beliefs and coming from scores of countries. All were united in their dedication to the cause of the Spanish Republic. They were convinced that the future of man would be decided in a Spanish Armageddon between the forces of democracy and fascism. With few exceptions the leaders of the Brigades had long careers of revolutionary agitation in the violent jungles of Communist politics. They had already survived much, and those who survived the Spanish war would often go on to dominate the Communist world of the future.[39] Led by the determined, already tempered in violence, the volunteers had their own courage and their own convictions if little formal military training. Yet the virtue of faith produced shock troops, unshakeable in morale, able to accept enormous casualties without crumbling. On December 11 a large levy of eighty men left for Spain under Frank Ryan bringing the total number of volunteers to about two hundred. The Irishmen formed the James Connolly Battalion and were attached to the English-speaking Abraham Lincoln Brigade.[40] On December 22 the first casualty reports came into Dublin. The brutal attrition of the Spanish war on the International Brigades had begun for the Irish as well. It was the reports of these heavy casualties seeping back to Ireland that focused attention on a not particularly welcome Irish involvement in Spain. No one could ignore Spain when hardly a week passed without one or more reports of Irishmen killed or wounded.

Those Irishmen who volunteered instead for O'Duffy's Irish Brigade embarked on a far different expedition into Spain. The first effort to transport his volunteers in October failed, and O'Duffy was forced to go to Spain to rearrange shipping preparations. Although a few members of the Irish Brigade arrived in Spain during November the major body of 700 left from Galway in mid-October. Some indication of the tribulations in store for O'Duffy occurred at Galway when some fifty men opted out even before the ship sailed. Once in Spain, many of O'Duffy crusaders found fault with their rations, with their officers, with their quarters. Finally, on 16 February 1937, the Brigade was ordered into action on a quiet sector of the front. After twenty-six hours on the train and a long march, the Brigade on February 19 had its first taste of action, a brief, confused fire fight with a Nationalist unit from the Canary Islands. Two Irishmen were killed. Things got no better. There was one disorganized, aborted attack under Republican artillery fire, which O'Duffy refused to repeat despite a direct order. Withdrawn from the line, refitted, and returned again to a quiet sector, the Brigade rapidly lost any residue of enthusiasm for the Nationalist cause. Cliques formed, mutiny was muttered,[41] and O'Duffy attacked for his proven incapacities. The men were sick, tired, homesick, and disgruntled. Their withdrawal was only a matter of time.

The whole question of volunteers had become a major threat to the existence of the nonintervention committee. Everyone recognized that official and unofficial volunteers had arrived in Spain despite all the denials. The committee had become little more than a facade held together by British determination and a general reluctance by the intervening powers to admit publicly their hypocrisy. From December until February the committee was seized on the problem of volunteers, but after seemingly endless negotiations a formula was produced. On February 16 the committee agreed to extend the nonintervention agreement to cover volunteers leaving each country. The Irish government welcomed the step, and on February 17 De Valera introduced a nonintervention bill into the Dáil. Once again, as in November, the Dáil became the scene of a lengthy debate on the proper procedure for Ireland to follow in Spain. This time the debate was more slashing, with a growing feeling among some Fianna Fáil members that Fine Gael was following sinister tactics in all but calling the government Communist for not accepting the Fine Gael and Belton position. On February 24 the accusation that some were using religion for party advantage was heard. The bitterness of the debate had no effect on the outcome.[42] The Spanish Non-Intervention Bill passed seventy-seven to fifty with Labour again voting with the government. Belton's various parliamentary maneuvers had led to nothing but the anticipated publicity for his distaste for the government's strict neutrality.

A further effort to ensure a strict European neutrality was accepted by the nonintervention committee on 8 March 1937. A control scheme to be administered by a nonintervention board hopefully would cut off intervention in Spain by increasing the risk of discovery. Administered by Dutch Vice-Admiral Van Dulm the plan provided for observers on all ships sailing to Spain as well as observers along the French-Spanish border. The Portuguese-Spainish border was to be controlled by a separate Anglo-Portuguese Agreement. The Irish Free State again welcomed the committee's initiative and enacted The Merchant Shipping (Spanish Civil War) Bill 1937 embodying the control scheme into Irish law. For the first time, however, the Irish had a responsible part to play in the activities of the nonintervention committee.

On March 8 the *Irish Press* reported that the Free State would be asked to send some observers to participate in the control scheme. Francis Hemming, secretary of the nonintervention committee, intended to rely on British observers, whose judgment and neutrality he could trust, but wanted a scattering of small power representatives as well. The Free State was one of Hemming's more obvious choices along with men from eight other small nations.[43] On March 25 it was announced that the Irish would supply eleven sea and six land observation officers. The first appointee was Captain Michael Doyle, selected as Administrator at Marseilles. The control scheme, as might have been expected of any nonintervention committee project, took longer to put in action than had been anticipated, but by April 14 most of the Irish observers had been selected by the Minister for External Affairs. The observers in time took up their positions and served during the remainder of the crisis or at least at those times when the ill-fated control scheme functioned. Such duty was not simply a safe sinecure for the retired or the faithful since Franco's air force developed a habit of bombing merchant shipping in or near the ports of Republican Spain. On May 25 the British steamer *Thoroehall* with J.M. McDermott of Dublin on board as obsever was bombed. McDermott was unhurt, and no Irish observer came to grief, but the next month on June 11 a Belfast ship was sunk off Spain and the British observer John Edwards later died of wounds. While the control scheme, for which the British had such high hopes, never really worked, once again Ireland had made a contribution to international harmony by providing volunteers for an emergency peace-keeping force.

In Dublin keeping the peace was the last item on the agenda of the supporters of the Spanish Republic who had not given up hope of converting Irishmen to the Spanish Republic's cause. The usual number of committees, fronts, and organizations were spawned, usually with interrelated memberships. Existing groups, from the Republican Congress to the Northern Ireland Socialist Party, dedicated most of their energies to Spain. Money was raised by groups like the Spanish Republic Women's Aid committee, whose chairman was Mrs. H. Sheehy-Skeffington. With only the small weekly *The Worker* available, the letters to the editor began to flow, engendering if not conversions at least controversy. One of the great handicaps was the public position of the hierarchy. Neither Ryan's newspaper correspondence with Cardinal MacRory nor the intervention of the militant Republican Father Michael O'Flanagan had much effect in the face of hundreds of parish priests. In January 1937 the Republican Congress arranged for Father Ramon Lamborda, a Basque priest, to come to Ireland as a living example that God was not entirely on the side of Franco. Father Lamborda, who spoke little English, appeared at a variety of meetings without apparently converting the hierarchy. In the North the Irish Labour Party organized various funds and meetings supporting the Spanish Republic, to the irritation of the Unionists supporting nonintervention and the horror of the Nationalists supporting Franco's Christian crusade. In March 1937, Peadar O'Donnell began editing the *Irish Democrat*,[44] a weekly espousing the policies of the Irish Left, but by then it had become apparent that no great mass-backing for intervention in Spain was going to appear. There was a vague sympathy for the Irish volunteers fighting and dying for the Spanish Republic, but the majority of Irishmen seemed to favor neutrality despite the highly articulate efforts of the Left.

The Right did no better. All the sound and fury of the Irish Christian Front had not produced the militant mass movement Belton had envisioned. No one seemed to know where to go after the monster meetings. Belton was too poor a speaker to vitalize crowds endlessly, particularly wthout a new script. The masses were bored and the middle class embarrassed. With the decline in the fortunes of the Christian Front and the continual failure of the Left to gain any ground, the urgency of the Spanish crisis receded. Spain had never became a central issue in Irish affairs and other crises, other news, other disasters, attracted the attention of the press and people as well as the politicians and priests. Spain by no means disappeared from public consciousness, the new battles in Spain and the ensuing casualty list of Irish volunteers alone would have prevented that. Then, too, that somehow Spain could still spark a general European conflagration that would involve Ireland could not be discounted by either private citizens or the government. None of the major powers seemed interested in any new initiative so the Spanish war dragged on bleeding the country white, while ever so slowly Franco nibbled away at the Republic. Ireland could do no more than had been done. De Valera was dedicated to nonintervention and unlikely to reverse himself. Ireland watched in compassion or fascination or frustration as the war dragged on indecisively.

Spanish events continued to interest many, some vitally, and whatever the lack of movement in the center of Irish politics, the dedicated fringes remained active. On March 8 O'Donnell and Father Lamborda were banned at Queen's University in Belfast. On March 9 the Longford County Council debated whether a resolution of sympathy to the two members of the Irish Brigade killed in Spain should be extended to include all Irishmen who died in Spain. On March 14 the Free State Minister to Spain, Leopold H. Kerney, took the rather unusual step of visiting Franco's headquarters at Salamanca. On March 15 the last installment of Irish Christian Front medical supplies left for Spain from Dublin. On March 20 headlines reported two more Irish casualties in the International Brigade. Nothing essential, however, changed in the Irish scene.

At the end of April reports began to circulate that the Irish Brigade was to return. In time the rumor was confirmed. O'Duffy contended that his agreement with Franco was to serve for a maximum of six months and because of the ban on volunteers renewal was impossible. The Brigade had been decimated by a variety of Spanish ailments, weakened by long months in the front line, and in any case fulfilled its commitment. While all this was true, there is little doubt that the Brigade was fed up with the Spanish adventure, teetering on the edge of mutiny. The great crusade had turned into miserable months of little purpose and great muddle. The Brigade voted practically without dissent to withdraw and by the middle of June was on the way back. By then reports of the Brigade's problems had appeared in the press. O'Duffy and Belton soon engaged in a long public debate over allocation of Irish Christian Front Supplies and as soon as the Brigade arrived in Ireland further divisions were revealed. Neither the praise of cardinals nor the editorials in the *Independent* nor the reception at Kilkenny could cover up the transformation of the great crusade, started with such high hopes and pious idealism, into a futile and chaotic disaster.

Nothing revealed the lack of political capital to be mined in Spain more than the results of the July 1937 elections for the Dáil. Instead of Belton moving on to a higher plane from his Irish Christian Front base, he lost his seat to G.L. McGowan of the Labour Party. Frank Ryan, running for Dublin City South as the candidate of a United Front against Fascism, campaigned vigorously. He polled only 875 votes. The Irish simply refused to become involved in crusades to save either Christianity or democracy.

The depth of De Valera's commitment to neutrality was revealed at the meeting of the League of Nations at the end of September. By 1937 the League was in an advanced state of decay and, as a source of friction rather than conciliation, had been by-passed by the nonintervention committee. Mainly as a result of British and French pressure, the League Political Committee considered a resolution that, subject to certain conditions, provided that "the members of the League will consider ending the policy of nonintervention."[45] In actuality the resolution was intended to placate the Russians and Spanish so they would not condemn the Germans and Italians as aggressors, thereby complicating Anglo-French negotiations with Italy. De Valera insisted that this section must be removed since the Irish Free State had no intention of even considering the end of nonintervention. Actually, neither did Britain nor France, but some gesture was necessary to allow time to further the appeasement of Mussolini. In any case, although others protested as well, the resolution passed. The Irish Free State and five other small states for various reasons abstained. For the Irish government nonintervention was a positive policy not to be discarded even if its founders and major proponents had second thoughts.

Whatever happened in Geneva or in Spain, Irish interest had been largely confined as previously to Irish affairs. First had come the removal of the British crown from the Irish constitution in December 1936, followed by the new De Valera Constitution, accepted in a plebiscite at the time of the July 1937 Dáil elections. By December 1937 the Irish Free State had disappeared and there were indications that De Valera was seeking to persuade the British to withdraw from their Irish military bases. Anglo-Irish negotiation led to an agreement on 22 April 1938, which was formally signed three days later. Not only was the long drain of the "economic war" ended but most important the British did in fact agree to evacuate the Treaty ports. Ireland could, perhaps, remain neutral in a Europe apparently determined in war. On 12 March 1938, German troops had occupied Vienna. Hitler made no secret of his designs on Czechoslovakia. Franco's airplanes bombed British shipping off Spain. Mussolini appeared unappeasable despite Prime Minister Chamberlain's best efforts. Spain had become only one facet of the rapidly whirling European kaleidoscope.

There was always Spanish news. On 4 April 1938, Frank Ryan was reported captured in the Aragon front; confirmation came from the Republican Congress one-issue paper *Easter Week* on April 18. The nonintervention committee's efforts to get the volunteers out of Spain had dragged on with little real results. The International Brigades continued to act as Republican shock troops and the casualty figures still arrived in Dublin. By the summer of 1938, however, most of the reports concerned prisoners, for the heavy fighting had greatly depleted the ranks of the Irish volunteers. Eventually, at the September meeting of the League of Nations,[46] Premier Juan Negrin announced that the International Brigades would be disbanded. The Brigades had been badly battered and such a step might lead to the withdrawal of the Italian and German troops. By the fall of 1938, some dramatic reversal in the fortunes of the Spanish Republic was obviously Negrin's last real hope. None came. Franco and his allies saw no reason to quit while they were ahead. The International Brigades were dissolved on September 23 and 24, and the remaining Irishmen started home. On November 11 over two hundred people welcomed home forty-four members of the International Brigade at Molesworth Hall.

Despite the declining military fortunes of the Spanish Republic, the Irish Republicans continued their activities. Negotiations were undertaken to secure Ryan's release. Rumor had it that he had been sentenced to death but that this had been commuted to a thirty-year sentence. Very little firm information could be discovered despite a variety of intermediaries and disinterested appeals to the Franco government. Franco, hardly magnanimous in victory, showed no inclination to pardon so dangerous an opponent. Ryan remained in jail until much later, when the Germans, for their own purposes, pried him loose.[47] Other than the Free Ryan Campaign, all that could be done was to ship food to Spain and hope for a miracle.

No miracle occurred. With the collapse of resistance on the Barcelona front in January 1939, the end of the war was at last in sight. No one but the very faithful felt there was any chance of victory or even of a stalemate. On

Saturday, 11 February 1939, Ireland formally recognized General Franco's government. De Valera explained that the conditions now existed for normal diplomatic relations with Franco:

> After recent events in Spain it became apparent that the establishment of General Franco's authority over the whole of Spain was but a matter of time.[48]

Fine Gael expressed satisfaction that at last the government had done the proper thing although the bishop of Killaloe felt that Fianna Fáil had "kept bad company during the crisis."[49] The Republican Congress, as was to be expected, was horrified and cabled the Spanish Foreign Minister Alvarez del Vayo their continued support:

> Irish Republicans repudiate Franco recognition by De Valera Government. Your decision to fight on inspires all subject nations and must rouse all free democracies to break through hurriedly to your aid. *Salud.*[50]

No one did come to the Spanish Republic's aid. The troops in Madrid mutinied. The government was forced to flee from the temporary capital at Valencia. Franco moved into an undefended Madrid at the end of March. On April 1 Franco issued a communiqué from Burgos announcing the end of the war.

The last frazzled ends of the crisis were tidied up. On March 23 the nonintervention board was closed down. Although many of the members had already withdrawn from the nonintervention committee, since as the Russians had pointed out it "long ago ceased functioning," one last meeting was held in April at which the committee dissolved itself. On April 10 the Irish Minister Kerney was received by Franco, who announced that he was appointing the Spanish Consul-General in Hamburg, Senor Ontiveros, as Spanish Minister to Ireland. For the first time in three years, Spain ceased to trouble Irish life.

In retrospect the Spanish war had acted as a scalpel laying bare the Irish body politic. The relative strength, potential, and efficiency of all Irish parties were exposed by the Spanish problem. The Right was revealed as a group of limited if devout men incapable of transforming their hazy world view into practical action. The Irish Christian Front collapsed from a lack of ideas.[51] O'Duffy's Irish Brigade disintegrated in the wake of administrative chaos and the rank and file realization that a crusade, however just, requires more than piety to succeed.[52] From the Right came no great regeneration, no new party of principle, nothing at the end but the quarrels of the disappointed and discredited. On the Left the militant Irish Republicans had proven dedicated in their support of the Spanish Republic but no more successful than the Right in disturbing the equilibrium of Irish politics. Spain had claimed some of the most talented and most determined, but those in Ireland increasingly found themselves isolated on the fringe of power. In the North nothing could distract for long the forces of the old order. By 1939 it was clear that despite the sound and fury of the men involved in the Spanish crisis, Irish politics would continue as before.

A potentially significant factor for the future had been the refusal of the Fianna Fáil government to panic in the face of the Irish Church's espousal of Franco. The government had chosen to ignore what appeared a spurious issue and continued to maintain ties with the Spanish Republic despite the emotionalism of the moment. While there was never an open confrontation, there was ample evidence that the Church had little liking for De Valera's position. Fianna Fáil comfortably weathered the storm largely by ignoring the issue, thereby demonstrating that the party could distinguish clearly between what should be rendered to the Church and what should not.

Ireland's adamant neutrality foreshadowed neutrality under far more trying circumstances. Although within Fianna Fáil there were many who favored the Spanish Republic for political reasons and others who did not for religious reasons, all soon accepted the need for neutrality. Over the three years of the Spanish crisis, the government had ample opportunity for exposure to the pressures against neutrality when it conflicted with the interests and ambitions of the great powers. At the League meeting in October 1937, the Irish had to oppose the very nations that had urged a policy of nonintervention on Dublin in the first place. The ties of faith, the tug of tradition, the heritage of past favors and feuds, the rewards and penalties of the present, all had to be ignored. A policy of neutrality in a world moving toward violence was no tranquil negative act but a constant twisting and turning to evade commitment. When De Valera came home with the Anglo-Irish Agreement of 1938, the major obstacle to Irish neutrality had been removed—Ireland could not be a British base in a general war. The lessons of Spain could be applied on a far greater scale to a far more dangerous situation. In the Spanish crisis Ireland had little to lose, but in a general war Ireland could lose everything.

Thus, in many ways the Spanish war had been a harbinger of Irish foreign policy for the future: disinterested neutrality, a distaste for the ideological extremists and their entanglements, sympathy for the democracies but no binding commitments. Even the Irish contribution of observers to the control scheme foreshadowed a later contribution to the peace-keeping activities of the United Nations, which would prove that responsible neutrality could include a positive contribution to international conciliation. Simply because Ireland was small, insular, and often parochial, her contribution at moments of crisis might be more significant than her rank in the world's power structure might normally warrant.

From 1936 to 1939 Ireland found that her political system was more secure than some detractors had assumed, that her government need not be on call to the Church, and that there was an honorable place in the jungle of world politics for a small nation. None of this was brand new, but the Spanish experience did reinforce the faith and convictions of many in a fair future for Ireland. In 1939 few nations had learned as much from Spain at so little cost as had Ireland.

In a real sense the Irish response to the Spanish Civil War institutionalized a national attitude toward external conflict that was not immediately apparent when first approaching the 1930s. Essentially, Ireland was on its way to becoming not just a nonaligned nation, a neutral in a contentious world, but also a pacifist state. In the particular, Irish neutrality in Spain and subsequently during the Second World War had very little to do with war and peace and international issues and a great deal to do with the government's effort to assert national sovereignty in full public view. In Spain Ireland could play an honorable part in a European congress—albeit one structured on the duplicity and self-interest of the great powers—despite the involvement within the war of Irish militants. As a neutral, Ireland could be independent, pursuing a policy that merely happened to parallel British interests. It was practice for the far more difficult assertion of independence that neutrality in World War II required, since such a policy was very much opposed to British interests. Irish neutrality, then, was not a cunning manuever within a troubled global complex, not a high moral stand, not involved with war and peace or internal law except in passing; the stand was an outward and visible sign of Irish unfettered nationalism, much of the island a nation once again. The neutrality practiced in the Spanish war and perfected after 1939 under most trying circumstances evolved as a proper, Christian, Celtic posture for a small nation in a troubled world. Ireland stood back from wars, crusades, and strife as a moral choice of options. Neutrality as an assertion of nationality slipped away as the years passed and instead became an unstated sign of Irish purity in a mean world. In time, as the decades passed and Ireland remained nonaligned but deeply involved in various international organizations dedicated to peace and development, "neutrality" somehow became a grand Irish tradition stretching deep into the past. Thus, the Irish army became a mean sinecure for garrison soldiers without mission until United Nations peace-keeping opened up some mild directions. The Irish establishment was appalled at the very idea that Ireland might become involved in alignments or alliances, might tolerate, much less sponsor, any military production. Ireland did not need Switzerland's huge militia system with its intricate defenses, elegant weapons, and war industries to maintain neutrality. Ireland did not need to manufacture advanced weapons like Sweden or even small arms like Finland to maintain neutrality. All that needed to be done was to proclaim the policy and watch the moral interest accumulate componded without risk.

The greatest risk to Irish neutrality from the first was to be found in those who, as their various ideological ancestors had done, would entangle their parochial dreams within alien interests. Mostly those fascinated with the corporate state or Soviet prospects could be monitored and ignored. They dealt in ideas and fancies, not power. The only real problem was that orthodox, militant Irish Republicans, who had largely ignored Spanish sirens, would find foreign friends eager to play in Celtic pastures. This did, indeed, occur in 1939–40 when the IRA GHQ had contacts with the Germans that, due to mutual incompetence, led to little but acute anxiety in Dublin.

NOTES

1. The stability of the Fianna Fáil government had increased remarkably with the decline of the Republican Congress and the Irish Republican Army, which had been banned and its Chief of Staff Maurice Twomey imprisoned. During the summer of 1936, the Fianna Fáil candidates in two by-elections won substantially and the militant Republicans (Hayes in Wexford and Plunkett in Galway) fared very poorly indeed. Thus, the threat of the Republicans and the extreme Left faded, as had the danger of the Blue Shirts, consolidating Fianna Fáil's position.
2. The difficulty of discovering Irish opinion on any subject is considerable. The techniques of polling were not applied to Irish politics in the 1930s leaving the investigator dependent on retrospective opinions, newspaper editorials, and various hints and guesses. Newspaper editorials are a crude indication of party position and personal prejudice but hardly a refined tool. In any case, use has been made of the following newspapers: *Irish Times, Irish Press, Irish Independent, Cork Examiner, Belfast Telegraph, Irish News* (Belfast), *Derry Journal, The Northern Herald* (Co. Down), *Fermanagh Times, Kerryman* (Tralee), *Kilkenny People, Worker* (Dublin), *Irish Democrat* (Dublin), *Easter Week* (Dublin).
3. *Irish Times*, 20 July 1936.
4. Essentially the points at dispute, which have been hidden by a fog of controversy for a generation, were the nature of the coup, the composition of the Madrid government, and the extent of foreign intervention. Despite the fine studies by David C. Cattell (*Communism and the Spanish Civil War* and *Soviet Diplomacy and the Spanish Civil War*) a mass of myths concerning Communist plots and programs remains undemolished (cf. Burnett Bolloten, *The Grand Camouflage, The Communist Conspiracy in the Spanich Civil War* (London, 1961). Contemporary advocates of the Spanish Republic have proven no more disinterested in much of their work—this is particularly true of those who fought for the Republic, most of whom seem to have written on Spain. In

Ireland between 1936 and 1939, few seemed interested in more than buttressing their prejudices. The *Irish Times* received small thanks for its excellent, balanced analysis of the Spanish war.

5. *Belfast Telegraph*, 31 July 1936.
6. Almost alone Italy had been involved in recent Spanish politics (v. W.C. Ashlew, "Italian intervention in Spain: The Agreements of March 31, 1934 with the Spanish Monarchist Parties," *Journal of Modern History*, vol. xxiv, no. 2, [June 1953] and Mussolini was more than willing to fish in the troubled Spanish waters again. Essentially he wanted the prestige of victory and eventually his "volunteers" would total 60,000 troops on the mainland and an additional 10,000 on Majorca.
7. Hitler had, in fact, agreed to lend Franco planes to fly his troops from Morocco to Spain on July 22. The decision was taken between acts of the Wagner festival at Bayreuth (*Documents on German Foreign Policy (1918-1945)*, Series D, iii, "Germany and the Spanish Civil War, 1936-1939" (Washington, D.C., 1950, pp. 1-2, footnote) and led to an eventual German commitment of 14,000 men, The Condor Legion.
8. Soviet intervention came later than Italo-German and although significant never redressed the balance. v. Cattell's books and D.C. Watt, "Soviet Military Aid to the Spanish Republic in the Civil War, 1936-1939," *The Slavic and East European Review*, vol. xxxviii, no. 91, pp. 536-38.
9. v. J. Bowyer Bell, "French Reaction to the Spanish Civil War, July-September 1936" in *Power, Opinion, and Diplomacy* (Durham, 1958).
10. Although violent atacks on the Spanish Church are a rather long-standing if appalling tradition, the year 1936 marked a high point in terror. Despite considerable efforts by the Franco government to detail the Red terror, no final estimate for formal and informal executions has been made. Hugh Thomas (*The Spanish Civil War* [New York, 1961] pp. 169, 173) estimates 75,000 Spaniards of all varieties were executed by the Republic. For their part Thomas credits the Nationalists with 40,000 executions and they added more to the total after the war. There is no point in matching one brutality against another, but there is no doubt that the sorry tale of murder, rape, and arson inflicted on the Spanish Church gave all Irishmen cause for concern.
11. *Belfast Telegraph* 14 December 1936.
12. *Kerryman*, 17 October 1936.
13. Seán Lemass (Interview) recalls that there was far more sympathy for the Spanish Republic both within and without of Fianna Fáil than might be apparent from the newspapers. There was no doubt, however, that nearly everyone in Fianna Fáil felt that De Valera's nonintervention policy best suited Irish needs.
14. *Kilkenny People*, 15 August 1936.
15. Although the *Derry Journal* continued to support De Valea in general, on the issues of Spain the editorials were pro-Cosgrave and on 30 November 1936 an editorial noted that "the analogy with the Vatican leaves us cold."
16. Belton had fought during Easter Week 1916, joined De Valera's Fianna Fáil but left it to go into the Dáil and sit as an Independent. Briefly connected with the National Centre Party and Fine Gael, he had sided with O'Duffy in 1934 when the ill-matched party of Cosgrave-MacDermot-Cronin-O'Duffy splintered.
17. *Irish Independent*, 11 September 1936.
18. The lack of a strong secular Socialist party or a general strain of anticlericalism has long been explained by recourse to an interpretation of "Irish" character

and "Irish" history based as much on sentiment as on fact. The Church as the last resort of patriots is not solely an Irish phenomenon. Perhaps a sociological comparison with the relation between nationalism and religion in Wales and Scotland might be more productive than analogies farther afield in Italy or Poland.

19. *Irish Times*, 12 September 1936.
20. No one doubted that there *were* Communists, but the exact number varied somewhat in different reports. J.H. Morgan addressing a meeting of the Irish Loyalist Imperial Federation in London estimated "that there are 40,000 Communists in the Free State. The Communist Party is large and growing" (*Belfast Telegraph*, 27 November 1936). On the other hand Kirwin in *G.K.'s Weekly* could find only 53 native Communists and these were working to control the Orange Lodges.
21. *Irish Press*, 26 August 1936.
22. The Irish acceptance of the Non-Intervention Committee is "contrary as we believe, to the wishes of the Irish people, falling in line with Socialist France and Soviet Russia." *Irish Independent*, 8 September 1936.
23. *v.* Peadar O'Donnell, *Salud, An Irishman in Spain* (London, 1937).
24. Interviews Peadar O'Donnell, George Gilmore.
25. Captain Liam Walsh, "General Eoin O'Duffy, His Life and Battles (typed manuscript, 1946?) p. 205.
26. O'Duffy almost immediately wrote his own history of the Irish Brigade (*Crusade in Spain* [Dublin, 1937]), which bears only marginal relation to the actual events in Spain. Even the pro-Franco reporter Francis McCullagh in his article (*v. New York Times,* 6 May 1937) and his subsequent book, *In Franco's Spain* (London, 1937) indicated that all was not well with the Brigade. A series of articles by T.P. Kilfeather in the *Sunday Independent* (May 15, 22, 29, June 5, 12, 119, 26, July 3, 1960) are in the O'Duffy tradition.
27. As an example of the universal attraction of the Irish Brigade, Brendan Kielty of Belfast, a long time member of the militant Republican movement and an IRA man, joined O'Duffy, went to Spain, and returned to Ireland to rejoin the IRA (Interview Charles McGlade).
28. J. Bowyer Bell, "The Non-Intervention Committee and the Spanish Civil War, 1936-1939" (Ph.D. dissertation, Duke University, 1958); Cf., for more partisan accounts, Ivan Maisky, *Spanish Notebooks* (London, 1966), or Count Dino Grandi, *La guerra di Spagna nel Comitato di Londra, Luglio 1936-Aprile 1939* (Milan, 1943, proof-copy only).
29. *Irish Press,* 16 September 1936.
30. *Belfast Telegraph*, 21 September 1936.
31. *Irish Press,* 21 September 1936.
32. *Irish Press,* 14 October 1936.
33. The eventual total in the Cardinal's Fund was £43,331. *Irish Independent,* 5 December 1936.
34. Just how monster the meetings actually were depends on the source since the *Irish Times* could only count 40,000 heads in a crowd the *Irish Independent* insisted contained 120,000 Irishmen.
35. *Irish Press,* November 26, December 1, 1936, cf. *Irish News,* 30 September 1936: "To-day Irishmen can gain for their own country a high reputation if they concentrate on their own and their country's needs and leave cloak-and-sword romance to the novelists."

36. Many members of the IRA were sympathetic to the cause of the Spanish Republic and several members of the Dublin Brigade as well as others elsewhere in the country resigned to join Ryan in Spain while they had not resigned in 1934 to join him in the Republican Congress (Interviews Michael Fitzpatrick, Myles Heffernan). One of the few pro-Franco Republicans was Sceilig (J.J. O'Kelly), a long-time Sinn Féin leader.

37. Italo-German recognition had been based on the assumption that Franco had already captured Madrid, a common illusion in early November 1936.

38. The *Fermanagh Times*, December 3, pointed out the hopelessness of a united secular Ireland while in Dublin Irishmen were "accepting the final arbitrament of the Pope in home and international affairs—as the Dáil is doing for instance, in regard to its attitude towards Spain."

39. From Italy along, for example, came Palmiro Togliatti, future head of the Italian Communist Party, his successor Luigi Longo, Giuseppe de Vittorio, future Secretary-General of the General Confederation of Italian Labour, Pietro Nenni, future leader of the Italian Socialist Party, and scores of lesser figures. In Yugoslavia in 1960, twenty-four generals had fought in Spain and similar figures could be produced throughout Eastern Europe.

40. The organizational structure of the International Brigades constantly shifted under the impact of heavy losses so that the common usage of "battalion" and "brigade" is no indication of strength.

41. Before the Irish Brigade departed, Peadar O'Donnell had organized a small cadre of Irish Republicans to accompany O'Duffy seemingly as dedicated volunteers but actually for the purpose of formenting mutiny. According to O'Donnell and George Gilmore (Interviews), O'Duffy's men needed no prompting and proceeded to mutinous plans before the Republican "volunteers" could act.

42. *Dáil Debates*, lxiv, 1197, lxv, 597-1024.

43. Interview with Francis Hemming, secretary for the Non-Intervention Committee.

44. The *Irish Democrat* was a shoestring venture backed by much of the Irish Left (Sam Haslett, chairman of the Socialist Party of Northern Ireland, Seán Murray, Communist Party of Ireland, P. Byrne, joint-secretary of the Republican Congress *et al.*) and collapsed in December 1937 from lack of funds.

45. *Survey of International Affairs* 1937, vol. ii (Oxford, 1939) p. 360.

46. During this meeting of the League, the Irish delegation continued to urge a policy of nonintervention, but as always decisions concerning Spain were being made elsewhere.

47. An account of Ryan's subsequent career can be found in Enno Stephan's *Spies in Ireland* (London, 1965) pp. 141-52, 203-5, 216-27, 261-64 v. Francis Stuart, "Frank Ryan in Germany," *The Bell*, November and December 1950. Cf., Seán Cronin's *Frank Ryan* (Dublin, 1980). The efforts to free Ryan included a telegram by De Valera and an official Irish effort after the end of the war in March 1939. Many of Ryan's colleagues, scattered to the winds in 1938, assumed with ample evidence that Ryan had been shot out of hand.

48. *Irish Press*, 16 February 1939.

49. Ibid., 20 February 1939.

50. *Irish Press*, 14 February 1939.

51. Donal O'Sullivan, *The Irish Free State and Its Senate* (London, 1940) p. 475, suggested that it is fortunate that the Irish Christian Front did not evolve into a

clerical party that would have "as its inevitable concomitant an anticlerical party." It is curious that a Christian Democratic party of some sort was never a factor in politics as has proved to be the case in most democratic Catholic states in Europe. On the continent, of course, anticlericalism needed no new challenge from a clerical party; and in Ireland it is highly speculative if an "anticlerical" party would have responded to the creation of a Christian Democratic party. In any case, it is clear that there has been too little quantitative analysis of the Irish political process and too ready an acceptance of generalizations, perhaps accurate but as yet unsupported by adequate documentation.

52. Some indication of O'Duffy's limitation can be found in his instance that his lads could not march to Spanish music. At considerable expense the St Mary's Anti-Communist Pipe Band was imported so that the Irish Brigade could march to and from the front lines to authentic Celtic airs. What the Spanish Nationalists thought of all this boggles the imagination.

6

The Curragh: 1940-45

After the flutter and failure of the British bombing campaign of 1939-40, most of the IRA would sit out the war isolated in detention camps or prisons—none more bleak than the Curragh in County Kildare. One of the recurring artifacts of the twentieth century has been the internment camp, a holding pen for the unwanted or dangerous or guilty. Devised, if there is a special beginning, by the British to remove the civilian Boers from any role in the South African war and repeatedly recreated to fill the perceived needs of uneasy states, such camps are everywhere to be found.

In Russia they have been institutionalized in the Gulag archipelago. In Spain the victorious Franco put Spanish Republicans in camps for years— and those who escaped across the border were put into camps by the French. The Americans put the Japanese, citizens or no, in camps in World War II and the British the Germans, refugees from Hitler or no. And the Germans devised death camps for the millions, mostly Jews, but also gypsies and homosexuals and political deviates and dissenters. And in the century of camps, Ireland, North and South, has had ample experience, from the instigators of the "mad folly" of 1916 interned as failed and future rebels at Frongoch in Wales, to those moved into Long Kesh in the present Troubles.

People like pieces are swept off the board, no longer players but perceived as dangerous or wicked or beyond immediate redemption, pushed aside, boxed away for the uncertain duration or marked for future slaughter. And in Ireland, where for most the green and pleasant fields of Kildare evoke the horses or, for the more perceptive, the playing ground of the Irish army, for some the very word, the Curragh, has become not only a corrosive memory of internment but also a descent into futility for years of internment.

The classical years of Curragh internment, the endless months and finally years of irrelevance, were those during the Emergency, elsewhere World War II, when Dublin and De Valera had to protect the novelty of neutrality from any real and some imagined threats. Later there would be other Curragh years. In 1940 the threat of subversion was generally viewed as crucial and the internees a clear and present danger to Irish independence.

And for De Valera and a great many others, Irish independence, an inward grace, could be made visibly manifest by the outward sign of neutrality—a free Ireland no matter what the practical pressures would not be swept into the Empire's train. Obviously, for De Valera on political matters was a most practical man, there had to be a balance between being proper toward the Axis, in practice the distant but awesome Germans, and within limits accommodating to the British. And most of all giving no one German, British, and later American, an excuse to intervene.

Neutrality was not a moral stance nor a political program nor even a strategic response to reality but rather a symbolic stele over a resurgent Irish nation. And yet neutrality had to be defended on Irish ground with very considerable political cunning, restraint mixed with ruthlessness, with tact, with diplomacy, with special formulae and particular exceptions, with notes and conferences and with the removal from the Irish board those whose ideals might endanger the policies of the State.

The obvious candidates for incarceration were the activists of the IRA who had declared war on the United Kingdom on 12 January 1939 and then undertaken a largely ineffective bombing campaign in England. In Ireland the result was intense police activity, searches, and arrests. On August 22nd, parts of the Offences Against the State Act came into effect. As the English campaign wound on, the Irish police swept up active volunteers and most of the IRA leadership. There were, however, two setbacks. Seán MacBride, a former IRA Chief of Staff, instituted *habeas corpus* proceedings that led on December 1st to the release of fifty-three men. More ominous, on December 23rd the IRA raided the Magazine Fort on Islandbridge and got away with thirteen lorries of ammunition—over a million rounds.

In the first case the Minister for Justice Gerald Boland pushed the Emergency Powers Act through the Dáil and, so empowered, directed an intensive IRA hunt—a hunt that among other things produced more bullets than had been stolen from the Magazine Fort. Although convicted members of the IRA went into prison, especially Arbour Hill, the internees were placed in a ramshackled army camp in Curragh—Tintown—or as punishment in an even more unsavory Glasshouse.

While outside the searches and sweeps continued, the center of the IRA circle organized and reorganized under pressure, the English campaign faded away, and the hints and guesses of an IRA-German connection became more than rumor but a constant concern of the Dublin government, nothing of consequence seemed to happen in the Curragh. The internees became irrelevant.

Of course the internees did not feel irrelevant. They had their own problems and priorities—and as always with Republican prisoners, causing trouble was often one of the latter. Although Billy Mulligan was the first C/O of prisoners, when Larry Grogan and Peadar O'Flaherty, recent members of the IRA Army Council, arrived in camp after finishing sentences at Arbour Hill, they announced that as members of the Irish government, courtesy of the scant remains of the Republican Second Dáil, they were taking over command of the camp.

The Curragh "Camp" was merely a cordoned-off section of low, dreary wooden huts, badly heated, furnished only with beds, dreary as the surrounding mud field and barbed wire. There had been little to do but wait and quarrel and eat the equally dreary food—rations for Free State Army privates. Grogan decided on pressure. On 14 December 1940, fires were set in selected buildings; however, the wind carried the flames and more of the camp burnt than had been intended. Any defiance was too much as far as the authorities were concerned.

The suspected leaders were run through a gauntlet of soldiers to arrive at the Glasshouse beaten and bruised. The rest of the internees were locked in the remaining huts from Saturday evening until Monday morning. They stumbled out, then, and began to line up for breakfast.

Apparently the soldiers had been told there would be no line up but, whatever the reason, they fired into the crowd of internees. Barney Casey was shot in the back. A bullet grazed Martin Staunton's face and another struck Walter Mitchell's shoe, bruising his heel. Bob Flanagan and Art Moynihan were hit. The firing stopped.

The prisoners stood stunned. Billy Mulligan walked directly to the gate and demanded a stretcher for Casey who was lying crumpled on the ground, his face and chest covered with bloody froth. He died two hours later. The Republicans were always to claim he was the victim of an unprovoked and inexcusable attack.

At the subsequent inquest Seán McBride was permitted to ask only one question, "Why was Barney Casey shot in the back?" The inquest was adjourned at once. The government wanted no scandal, no incidents out on the Curragh from those pieces removed from the board. And there was no "scandal," then or later. Tintown and the Glasshouse could have been in another country for all the Irish public knew or cared as the nation moved into the second year of the Emergency.

In the camp, Liam Leddy of Cork became C/O of prisoners, an increasingly thankless job. From the outside there was no good news, only rumors of arrests, North and South. The internees were no longer waiting out a "campaign"—the English bombs no longer detonated—or serving as silenced witnesses for a just cause. They were in the main simply waiting. And among them were a few who were not even Republican volunteers.

During the sweeps, a few of the militant Left had been lifted—symbolic of Marxist-Leninist subversion and suspect to police and politicians who despite all the evidence believed in a "Red Menace" to Catholic Ireland. The level of that menace might be judged by the vote in dissolving the only Free State branch of the Irish Communist Party in 1941—reputedly eleven to nine and not all of those Irish. No matter, the police had interned a chosen few Marxists into the Curragh: Michael O'Riordan, Johnny Power, and Dermot Walshe, who had fought in the Spanish Civil War, and Neil Gould Verschoyle, a dedicated if independent communist who had studied in Moscow and married a Russian woman.

Police attempts to go further in nibbling at the "Left" in the name of security were not as successful when something other than symbols were to be interned. In April 1940, Tom Dunne and Steve Daly, leaders of the Dublin Unemployed Workers' Movement, were interned apparently for leading agitation against a government scheme of forced labor for the production of turf. A sufficient number of those who mattered were outraged—the IRA and the Communists were one thing, honest Irish agitators another—and the two were released in less than a week.

Inside the Curragh, Gould not only offered Russian language classes to the bored but also the ideological temptations of communism. And he began to have some takers and, given the Curragh, some dissenters, for ultimately the Trotskyists, including Eoin McNamee (a Northerner and former IRA QMG) outnumbered the Stalinists. Somehow to them Trotsky seemed more anti-imperialist than Stalin. In any case, such discussions, not to mention conversions, were anathema to the IRA camp leadership.

In 1942 Pearse Kelly, briefly IRA C/S and member of the Northern Command, who had taken over from Leddy in an internal coup in December 1941, managed to get rid of Gould by privately appealing to Cardinal McRory. Pearse stressed the danger to the souls of IRA men exposed to ungodly communism. Gould was moved out of the Curragh, surfaced briefly in the murky world of Irish communism, and then left Ireland. The IRA volunteers, souls now safe, remained.

The splits, too, remained. Leddy's small orthodox group on one side and the majority with Kelly. A few clustered around Tadhg Lynch, a prickly independent Corkman, who defied the camp leadership by using coal when ordered to refuse it—in the closed circle of the Curragh a matter to rival the division between Stalinists and Trotskyists. And, yet again, those who sought to remain "neutral" were ostracized by everyone.

Beyond the feuds, traditional in internment camps, and the simple personal arguments, enforced proximity eroded toleration—the man in the next bunk was damned if he blew his nose and damned if he did not. And all the while the time crept by and hope for better days, undefined, faded. A few began signing out on long parole. All the IRA news from the outside was bad, rumors of splits and schisms, trials, betrayals, confessions, and futility. More gave in and signed out. The war moved away. The German-IRA connection came to naught. The Americans were in the war and Ireland still adamantly neutral. And in the Curragh, there were the traditional activities of all prison camps. There was a newspaper, *Barbed Wire,* and a sports program based on the medals and footballs sent into the camp by Padraig O'Caiomh of the GAA, an old IRA man, and concerts and dramas and one Christmas even illicit poteen.

More than all the other Curragh events, the boredom and brutality and splits, what would be remembered from the futile years would be the classes. An education committee was founded that included Gerry McCarthy, Seán O'Tuama, Seán O'Neill, Danny Gleason and others, who set up classes. There was Gould's Russian and Seamus O'Donovan's German and Mártin O'Cadhain teaching advanced and beginning Irish every day. Alack for legend, he did not teach Brendan Behan who came into the Curragh in 1944 when his classes had ended.

And there were the Curragh seminars that produced not only the odd Trotskyist but disgruntled Republicans. For example, at the beginning of November 1943, Liam Leddy was leading a study group that included O'Cadhain, notorious outside Republican circles because of his dismissal from his school-teaching position in Galway by a bishop unimpressed with his radical and Republican ideas. Within the IRA O'Cadhain had voted against the English campaign as a member of the Army Council; he felt that only military preparation was insufficient. He was voted down six to one.

O'Cadhain suggested that the Study Group might note that the IRA military effort to 1944 had not succeeded and there could be some consideration on the importance of language and cultural matters. In fact, O'Cadhain felt it might, indeed, be time to think of the future. Several of the other members of the Study Group took the agenda as a criticism of the Republican movement—a movement then all but extinct outside prison camps. They suggested a secret court to investigate the matter. There have surely been few revolutionary organizations that would feel the need for a secret court to investigate "thinking about the future."

In any case, O'Cadhain henceforth would do his thinking on his own. His classes ended and he devoted himself to studying and writing. A chair and table appeared—outward symbols of betrayal to the orthodox—and he went on to learn French and Russian and Welsh and Breton and most of all to write. Perhaps the only tangible benefit of the Curragh years was his *An Braon Broghach,* short stories written out on the deal table in a bleak hut amid sullen Republicans on the plains of Kildare.

For De Valera and the government, the tangible benefit of internment, a crucial weapon, was Irish neutrality—absolute independence from everybody including the United States. Ireland, a small nation had stood alone for a few more years in part because those who had wanted to embark on more turbulent waters had been penned in the Curragh. And, by and large, the Curragh had not been used for narrow political purposes, not filled with potential subversions or former rebels or present rivals. Few old enemies and unrepentant comrades had been locked up, no Tom Barry or Seán MacBride, only the symbols of communism and the active IRA.

Thus, a popular man like John Joe Sheehy of Kerry was snapped up but only when he became involved with the active IRA. Even Alex McCabe, an old IRA man who was tinkering with a neo-Nazi party, was interned in Cork for being "actively engaged in helping" the Germans, although soon released by Gerald Boland as too inconsequential to house. Only active members of the IRA were not inconsequential. They were not involved in any brief midsummer madness to muse over a German invasion or intricate disputations on Trotsky's role in Ireland. They, the militant gunmen of the invisible Republic, could provoke the British or bring in the Germans or tumble the fragile structure of Irish neutrality in a burst of gunfire. And so they went into the Curragh. Over a thousand IRA volunteers passed through the Irish camps and prisons and many waited out the war and their relevance.

Whatever the affront to democratic rights, Tintown and the Glasshouse performed as required, transformed the IRA militants into bored internees, squabbling over carrying coal, memorizing Irish verbs, waiting on other, distant events. Life passed them by. Careers aborted. Fiancées found other men. Families struggled along without them. Children grew up into strangers. And Dev and the State prevailed.

The IRA splintered and crumbled. Some few would help resurrect it and most would remain "Republicans" of one sort or another. The schisms of the Curragh would remain for most. The years on the plains of Kildare paid few dividends. Martin O'Cadhain had *An Braon Broghach,* but most of the others only the sour years unwillingly sacrificed for a small nation's neutrality and the ruined dream of the Republic triumphant.

By the end of the war, Ireland was set on a policy of neutrality abroad, no gun in international politics, that could not be threatened by any visible internal dissent. A few politicians had been pro-British, most in and out of the government had concurred with neutrality. The electorate had agreed and the adventurous or committed had joined the Allies without hinderance—mostly Ireland was neutral for the British. In theory this should have been an easier task when Ireland's favorite country and the home for millions who had left the island, the United States, entered the war at the end of 1941, but Washington like London failed to understand the nature of "neutrality" and increased the pressure on Dublin—to no avail. In 1945 all the pressures eased. British lack of magnanimity was transmuted from bile to nectar in Dublin. America was forgiving. Ireland's neutrality became a positive moral posture in a divided world. Ireland's violent agitators and parish gunmen had grown old and stale and irrelevant. Once again there appeared to be an end to violence on the island, since there arose the belief that even the patent injustice of partition could be eroded by agitation, political organization, and international pressure. Militant Republicanism and physical force had seemingly expired in the internment camps. The IRA would have to begin again.

Thus, it was possible to write a report for a seminar at the Center for International Affairs at Harvard on the contemporary IRA with a starting date of 1946. For a few years only a few policemen could find the IRA, led by a handful of men determined that the dream would not die. The IRA that arose from the ruins of the 1940s was, of course, not new; nothing in Ireland can be quite novel. It was, however, different in resources, aspirations, attitudes, possibilities, and constituency. Those involved, however, felt little difference and assumed that they represented, as they did, long-lived Irish forces and tides. All that needed to be done was to reorganize and begin the struggle and return the gun to politics.

Five years after the war, in 1950, the IRA had only a shadow of its former strength. The claim by the new Taoiseach (Premier) John Costello that he had taken the gun out of Irish politics seemed justified. Yet, in 1951 the IRA Army Convention ratified the decision of the Army Council to undertake in time a campaign in the North against the British, while remaining quiescent in the South.

From 1951 until the campaign opened in December 1956, the IRA concentrated on acquiring the arms and ammunition necessary to fight a guerrilla war and on training the volunteers for such operations. The most spectacular aspect of the preparations was a series of raids on British military barracks: Derry, N.I., 1951; Felstead, Essex, 1953; Armagh, N.I., June 1954; Omagh, N.I., October 1954; Arborfield, Berkshire, 1955. The impact of the raids accelerated recruitment, at least in the South, and consolidated the determination to strike. Funds flowed into the various Republican organizations but never, of course, quite as fast as they were spent. The growing political strength of Sinn Féin, infiltrated by the IRA so that it could become the civilian wing of the movement, indicated popular support, at least in the North, where in May 1955 Sinn Féin polled 154,000 votes and elected two MPs to Westminster, both prisoners captured in the Omagh raid and pledged not to take their seats. Despite a bad split in the Dublin unit and some delay, the Army Council entered the campaign with high hopes.

From the night of 11 December 1956 until 1 January 1957, the IRA held the initiative; police barracks were hit repeatedly, government property burned or destroyed, bridges dropped and roads cratered. Large areas in the western half of Northern Ireland belonged to the IRA during the long December nights. In January the Dublin government imprisoned much of the IRA leadership and tried to close the border. In the North the Unionist government, once the initial surprise had passed, undertook wide-ranging security measures, calling up special constables, arresting scores of suspects, and exerting pressure in the field. Incidents tapered off. During the summer months of 1957, little could be accomplished by the IRA because of the long hours of daylight. One ambush at Forkhill, County Fermanagh, led directly to the reopening of the Curragh Camp. Growing numbers of volunteers were interned or imprisoned in the Curragh or Crumlin Road Prison in Belfast, adding to the difficulties of the new Army Council. The campaign continued on a lower level through the second winter. By 1958 continued arrests had largely put the active leadership out of commission, and Northern police and military pressure had radically reduced the numbr of incidents.

The Dublin government, reluctant to maintain the political liability of an internment camp, began releasing men from the Curragh. By the spring of 1959, the camp was closed and judging from the number of IRA actions in the North during the third winter season, many felt that the campaign was as well. When the IRA Army Convention met, an irreconcilable split developed over differences of opinion concerning the role of the IRA leadership within the Curragh. The new Army Council had no intention of giving up the campaign, but the tide had long since turned. From 1959 to the late fall of 1961, with declining popular support, reduced membership, reduced funds, ebbing morale, and increased ineffectuality, the IRA tried to maintain the momentum of the campaign. By 1962 the campaign had clearly run its course, and the IRA formally announced that arms had been dumped and operations ended.

The IRA had once more reached rock bottom. The driving purpose of twenty years had gone. The campaign had aborted; the number of volunteers was reduced to a handful of the faithful few; the prisons were full and the coffers empty. The finances of failure produced a shrinking structure, needy dependents, and volunteers on the emigration boats. Out of the rubble, those still determined to maintain the IRA picked the most useful pieces to build a new platform. With the *raison d'être*—physical force— barred by practicalities, the IRA, while keeping the army alive, concentrated on defining the Republic. Thus, without a clear and immediate purpose, since a military campaign in the near future (perhaps even the distant future) was futile, the IRA reluctantly placed the gun on the shelf to wait for a better day.

If, as the theory runs, the IRA is simply one adjunct of the Republican Movement, then a temporary concentration on politics or publicity should not be such a searing alternative. The IRA is not in fact a branch of the Republican body but the heart, and this has, largely, been true for three generations. Sinn Féin, the political wing, *The United Irishman,* the monthly newspaper, the various youth and women's groups, temporary committees and long-lived associations exist and in theory were in 1962 facets of a single coherent whole, but in reality there was no structured, organized core to the Movement, only the authority of the IRA leadership. Most of the Republican organizations were little more than husks waiting to be filled during the glory days of success, and in the meantime existing as a result of inertia and tradition. Much of the activity of the Republican Movement was little more than a holding action—in particular the endless rounds of annual ceremonies, the Commemoration Routine, that maintain the faith in the few but seldom involved the many. The major difficulty was that most militant Irish Republicans believed that the only means to achieve a united Ireland was by physical force. When by necessity the IRA is inactive, the followers are at a loss, united as much by a distaste for compromise as by a program for the future.

In 1962 the real IRA remained largely a mystery to most in Ireland. The friends and neighbors of the few volunteers knew them; and the police, North and South, had lists and addresses and court records; but mostly few had paid attention to the Northern campaign or the reality of the militant Republican movement. For most inside Ireland and out, the IRA was irrelevant, a vestigal remnant of a romantic past. What remained, fashioned from pub ballads, patriot history, lies, exaggerations, myths, platform speeches, and school lessons, was an art work: The Irish Rebel. And along the London-Dublin-New York pub-bar-and-literary axis during this period strode the legend made real in Brendan Behan. In fact the shadow of the gunman had grown longer as the real IRA volunteer disappeared in a rising economy, an easing of national purpose, and the stark reality of a divided island. Behind the long shadow, however, there were real people who for a decade had been deeply involved in a futile effort to introduce the gun with effect into Irish politics.

7

The Shadow of the Gunman, 1969

In many of the distant and strange corners of the world, Ireland is noted not as the Emerald Isle of Saints and Scholars, but as the home of the Irish Rebel.

The long litany of patriots dead, trench coats, and Thompson guns, *The Informer*, bombs in Belfast, Brendan Behan, and the fighting Irish apparently far outweigh the Book of Kells, the seried Saints, even Patrick, Yeats, *Tipperary Far Away*, Joyce, or the High Crosses.

Certainly the resurgence of the Troubles in the North, highly photogenic, a delight to the media, and an enigma to all, has merely intensified the firmly held beliefs concerning the rebellious Irish, who as wild geese in Europe, outlaws in the Australian outback, or Fenians in America have been fighting for ages.

In Ireland, too, the gunman has cast a long shadow. Repeatedly romanticized in the singing pubs, while simultaneously imprisoned in Mountjoy by an indignant government, the contemporary rebel, admired and adhorred, is really little understood. Even the images fashioned by film directors, playwrights, or the fading memories of the devout in the Celtic diaspora clash and conflict.

For many, Brendan Behan has become the Irish Rebel incarnate. If Behan was the idealized wild Irish Rover, the broth of a lad, the obverse of the IRA coin would be the grim, implacable figure stalking the alleys of Dublin or Belfast, the gunman in the trench coat, implacable, purposeful, without humor, often without name, most assuredly without compassion.

This for a great many has become *the* IRA man, nemesis of informers, totally dedicated, apparently without past or future, certainly without family, who exists—usually during the course of a ninety-minute film or within the covers of an adventure novel—only for the mission, a superbly existential character. These gunmen in fact cast no shadow, cardboard being too thin for such purpose.

What is fascinating is that this rigorous reduction from reality—Behan was always larger than life—has produced a stock character who, dependent upon the predilictions of the observer, may be black or white, a dread avenger in a just cause or a mindless and futile hit man.

In Ireland at least the assumption would be that a truer portrait of the rebel might exist if everyone knew what Brendan was like and that *The Informer* was only a flick.

The Irish Revolutionary Patriot Game has over the course of two centuries produced with deadening regularity an all but unbroken series of disasters. Nevertheless, no one will speak ill of the patriot dead, no matter how dreadful the deed or incompetent the doer. Thus, the necessity to ease past failure, legitimize existing political postures, and order history in light of present needs produced the rebel-as-martyr, martyrs that fell into easily recognizable categories: the pure, the brave, and the victim.

The pure-martyr, the saint-and-scholar variant, has been the pale intellectual, very devout, self-sacrificing and often self-doomed. He seems to drift beyond this world, a revolutionary priest *manque*, absolutely dedicated beyond earthly care.

While all Irish martyrs are brave, some are romantically brave; these martyrs have adventures, live quick, bright lives that by necessity come swiftly to conclusion.

Finally, some martyrs, as well as brave and pure, appear victimized. They are the hard men who act and suffer, the inevitable foot soldiers of tragic revolution. Here the death becomes more important than the dash, or the spirit, or the deed.

There are some problems, of course, in fitting real men into idealized niches. The Founding Father of Irish Republicanism, Wolfe Tone, is certainly a martyr, but—alas—by his own hand. And what to do with Eamon De Valera, long the priest-figure of Republicanism, who not only lived but also assumed power. Excommunication was the answer of the orthodox Republicans and the ballad makers, who gave up the Legion of the Rear Guard after they backed into the Dáil. Then it has been necessary to hush up the ideas of James Connolly even in the Labour Party and repeatedly defend Sir Roger Casement's reputation, which some have suggested would bar him from his accustomed spot within the ranks of the pure. No matter, the coloring book rebel-martyrs exist. Perhaps they have persisted much too long, but for many they have become realer than real—and for others have made possible a cottage industry in ballads.

Beyond all those ballads, the medals of pub patriotism awarded well back from the firing line, are the real Irish rebels. For the contemporary rebels, a new and orthodox image of the gunman has been fashioned by those whose power and position appear threatened by rebel aspirations. Outraged at the pretensions of the "new" IRA, fearful of the future, horrified at the violence in the North, the men at the center have fashioned a new rebel—without romance, without virtue, without a past or a place in the future, a gunman without a cause. These new rebels, wantonly violent, have either no ideas or the wrong ones; are either mindless killers or red agents; but in all cases can have no impact except for the harm that comes out of the barrel of their gun.

This model, adapted in 1922 by the Free State forces from an earlier British script, had in the 1930s been accepted by the Republican Party, Fianna Fáil, of Eamon De Valera, and today is accepted by nearly all shades of established Irish political opinion. The constitution of this Rebel-without-Cause has produced a new IRA-man, either foolish or evil, addicted to alien ideas and outmoded means, a clear and present danger to decency and a democratic society. All of which, even if true, reveals very little about the rebel in qestion, but a great deal about those who are for the quiet life.

The contemporary IRA is new only in so much as any long-lived organization renews its membership. Those opposed to the ends and means of the IRA mean to indicate by the use of "new" that the present organization, whether or not descended from the old IRA, is illegitimate now that democratic means are available and force unnecessary.

It is possible to examine in some depth a segment of Republican experience in order to begin at least an IRA rebel profile. Obviously any analysis of a covert revolutionary organzation faces severe obstacles, particularly at a time when the mere opinion of a policeman that an individual belongs to the IRA is considered sufficient evidence to that effect. It is thus somewhat easier to focus on the era of the IRA Northern campaign that began with the first arms raid on the Ebrington Territorial Barracks in Derry in 1951 and concluded with the IRA public statement ending the campaign on 26 February 1962. Before 1951, the IRA was very weak indeed, still reorganizing after the debacle of the war years; while after 1962 only the unrepentant remained.

The IRA in the Campaign Years, 1951-62

In many ways this was the era of IRA purity, a secret army reduced to the faithful few, self-recruited, dedicated at a time the common wisdom agreed that Ireland had no need of the gun in politics. After the Republican adventures and schisms in the 1930s, it was also an army with minimal concern for politics, an army determined on an armed struggle. It was concerned with recruiting volunteers to rebel, not to agitate in the streets, write position papers, or for that matter defend the Nationalist areas in the North. The old tendency to focus on the Free State betrayal in the South had largely gone and the new "Troubles" in Ulster were a generation away. Thus, this IRA generation was the Irish Rebel distilled.

Distribution: A Map of the Movement

Whereas during the glory years of the Tan War the IRA could be found nearly everywhere, during the Northern campaign IRA membership was erratically distributed. Supposedly there are dotted through Ireland "good Republican areas" with parish or county traditions of support for the Movement.

Erhard Rumpf in his study of Irish Nationalism and Socialism (*Nationalismus und Sozialismus in Irland,* Hain, 1959) indicates that in the more distant past Republican support was concentrated in the poorer counties of the West, in particular Kerry. In the 1957 elections, the Republican Sinn Féin party polled approximately 23 percent in Kerry South, giving John Joe Rice a seat in the Dáil he did not take. Even in 1961 Rice polled 12 percent of the total although he lost his nonseat.

Some areas such as Leitrim or Roscommon in the West, or mid-Tyrone in the North, were at times strong, while much of the eastern province of Leinster outside Dublin was weak. These *traditions* often stretch far into the past and did not necessarily bear much relation to real reservoirs of IRA strength. Strangely enough, Donegal, part of the radical West and sharing a common border with North Ireland, never had more than twenty-five IRA men between 1951-62.

Kerry in the 1930s had been strong IRA territory where the Republican organization was a vast network of personal relations, shared prejudices, joint enemies, and parish pump politicians. It was, as one astute observer suggested, an underground Tammany Hall. After 1945 Kerry was on occasion willing to vote for Republicans, but the old infrastructure of the IRA had gone and little replaced it. Kerry still might be good Republican territory if you wanted something done in Kerry, but Dublin had not been organizing a Kerry army—nor had Kerry.

The same was much the case in other "good" areas—excellent attendence at commemorations, a residue Sinn Féin vote, and a pride in the past.

In this period, what made a strong Republican area as far as the IRA was concerned was a strong man. One solid man would make a solid area. The emigration of one man was known to end a unit, 75 percent of the sales of the *United Irishman* newspaper, close down the Sinn Féin branch and return a parish to the doldrums. Generally outside Dublin-Cork-Belfast, only a few areas had really been Republican territory, capable of replacing the solid man each decade. Local units particularly in rural areas proved hard to maintain, hard to train, and in an emergency easy to drain of their key personnel. Thus, the IRA was largely urban, not as myth would have it staffed with Mountainy men from the West.

Strength: The Size of the Rebel Universe

Any figures on total IRA membership or specific unit strength during these years are apt to be misleading. Paper strength, or parade strength, only reflects the health of the Army. For much of the time the IRA has almost always had more volunteers that GHQ or the C/O of a local unit could use. As a result, some local units simply closed down the membership at a set figure while others discouraged recruits by a variety of hurdles.

Even at its most swollen, during the summer of 1956, the membership was probably less than 1,500, perhaps well less. Usually the Dublin unit, only the romantic still called it a Brigade, contained between 20 to 25 percent of the total active parade strength of the IRA. The high point was June 1956 with approximately 220 actives. There were also solid units in Cork and Belfast, the size of the latter often determined both by GHQ policy and the degree of coercion exercised by Northern authorities. Before 1969, action tended to reduce the size of the Belfast unit and increase that of Cork or Dublin.

Parade strength in any case is no key to the vitality of the Army or its capacity to act; outside the cities a great many units existed in flux, expanding under the influence of one or two men or the excitement of the times and declining or disappearing in the face of economic pressure or boredom or inefficiency.

Many men who are not members of the Army will during an emergency give far more aid and comfort than some volunteers. These men have provided safe houses, arranged arms dumps and dug-outs, acted as couriers, and even undertaken operations simply to "help out the lads." A number of these men were, of course, former volunteers. In any case, between 1951 and 1962, the IRA universe, blurry edges and all, was quite small indeed.

Membership: The Anatomy of a Volunteer

The size of the rebel circle is really only of limited concern, for the real question is the nature of the members, and since membership was, and is, illegal, problems arise. Quantitative data on any active, covert, revolutionary movement are for obvious reasons difficult to acquire, even concerning those active in a previous generation. Still, shrewd estimates can be made on the nature of the typical IRA volunteer based on long personal contact, seemingly endless interviews, a few published sources, and private revelation. A real academic boon would be all the available police records, but the Special Branch, North and South, has ordinarily been as secretive as the IRA, which does not keep many records of any sort.

Through the efforts of Eamon Timony, formerly C/O of the IRA unit in Derry City, there exists a breakdown of age, occupation, marital status, and home county of all IRA men with long-term sentences in A-Wing, a total of ninety-five. Timony's figures tend to corroborate more scattered sources and the results of IRA interviews.

The IRA volunteer has always been a young man, for revolution is a young man's game. Usually he volunteers between the ages of 18 and 21. Timony found 19 was the average age in Derry. In the late 1940s the average age may have been a bit higher since the young men had to wait for the IRA to reorganize before they could enlist. In Crumlin Road the median age of all ninety-five prisoners was 21.4 and the average age 24.3 (table 1).

Even here it should be pointed out that of the three men over the age of 40 only one, P. Duffy (41), was with an Active Service Unit while the other two, T. O'Malley (51) and P. Collins (40), were arrested at home. During the campaign in the North, older men who had not been active for years became involved, thus raising the "normal" age level. This was particularly true of internments North and South where the average age would be much higher because both governments, making use of special powers, interned men on their past record, assuming that they would be active given the chance.

Active Service Units, made up of parade strength volunteers (not latecomers or old faithfuls), were composed almost inevitably of young men in their early twenties. In December 1956, the ages of three C/Os of flying columns, made up of volunteers from the South who moved into Northern Ireland, were 20, 22, and 24. The column that attacked an RUC

TABLE 1
Crumlin Road A-Wing: Ages

Under 18	2
18 to under 20	20
20 to under 24	37
24 to under 26	10
26 to under 28	7
28 to under 30	6
30 to under 35	8
35 to under 40	2
40 upwards	3

station at Brookeborough on 1 January 1957 was made up of volunteers between 18 and 29 (29, 28, 25, 25, 24, 22, 21, 20, 18, 18, 18, and three uncertain). One of the two IRA men killed, Seán South, was 28 and the other, Fergus O'Hanlon, was 20.

On 11 November 1957 in a small farmhouse at Edentubber just over the border in the Twenty-six Counties, five men were killed in an accidential explosion while preparing mines; four were on active service—19, 19, 26, 27—and one, not an active IRA man, supplying the safe house was 55: a typical group-age spread.

The marital status of active volunteers was simple and almost universal: few were married. In Crumlin Road A-Wing only nine out of ninety-five were married. In a country with the highest celibacy rate in the Western world (in an age span of 60 to 64, 30 percent of the Irish males had never married contrasted to 11 percent for the United States) and oldest marriage age (in 1951, 94.9 in the 20-24 age group and 76.5 in the 25-29 were unmarried), this was hardly surprising.

It was also generally accepted that active service after marriage is unwise. The C/O of Lurgan, J.B. O'Hagan (32) in 1956 refused to head his column because he was married and turned over leadership to John Kelly (20). Fragmentary evidence would indicate that IRA volunteers tended to marry at the "average" Irish age and in reasonable proportions; in fact, the Adjutant-General Charles Murphy even had the audacity to marry on the run in 1958 at the age of 28. This means that what might be called second generation activists differed little from the general Irish marital average. The only noticeable difference in the family structure of IRA men was the impact of prison after marriage in that old IRA men tended to have young children, or oddly spaced children, or simply fewer children.

The occupational profile of the IRA does not reflect that of Ireland as a whole. The most obvious difference is that in the Republic of Ireland, at that time approximately 35 percent of the labor force was directly employed on the land, and despite its industrial image Northern Ireland's agriculture accounted for 25 percent of total exports. As might be expected, there were few men with property or with a profession, but less unskilled labor than might be anticipated for a "revolutionary" army.

The closest to men of property to be found are a publican and the owner of a poultry packing business. There was one freelance journalist and a single student. The major block came from the skilled trades, a stratum that has from 1798 on given Ireland revolutionary leadership. The dearth of farmers was partly the result of the difficulty in organizing the rural areas and partly reflected the high age of many small, independent farmers. Most Irish farms were very small (69.0 percent less than 50 acres and 88.5 less than 100), forcing the male surplus, assuming the owner was married, to emigrate (table 2).

Second, the professional and managerial classes were underrepresented not only because the IRA was revolutionary but also because few of the IRA leaders were on active service. Within the Movement during the campaign, there were lawyers and teachers involved but on such a low statistical level that they did not appear among the A-Wing prisoners.

Furthermore, the dedication of the years between 18 and 25 to the activities of the IRA did not necessarily preclude a career in law or medicine, but it did complicate matters.

The IRA after 1946 had never been overly keen on absorbing students, particularly university students. They were too often part-time people and impatient of discipline, and their intellectual talents were not particularly useful to a secret army preparing a guerrilla campaign. During the political pauses, the clever and the trained were often attracted to the ideas of the Republican Movement but not necessarily into the IRA.

There are only a few exceptions to the general educational backgrounds of IRA volunteers. By law, all had finished primary school at fourteen. While two-thirds of Irish children went on to secondary or vocational school, many fewer lasted out the course through first the Intermediate and then the Leaving Certificate. The average IRA volunteer may have continued school, perhaps to the intermediate level, but most went into a trade or took a position by their late teens. University attendance in Ireland was almost entirely a middle-class affair attracting a tiny proportion of Irish young. Thus, the tiny handful of IRA men who attended a university were not out of line with the population as a whole. Most, however, had left secondary school after a couple of years, usually at a Christian Brothers school, and had begun to earn a living—just as had the vast majority of Irish boys.

TABLE 2
Crumlin Road A-Wing: Occupations

Laborers	17
Farmers	12
Clerical	9
Skilled Trades	33
Semiskilled	11
Service/Sales	9
Other	4
	95

The "average" IRA volunteer, who joined at 19, was 21, unmarried, a skilled or semiskilled worker with some secondary school or vocational training, living in a city. He was almost inevitably a Catholic, although the Republican Movement is nonsectarian and boasts Protestant ancestors and adherents. In this period, if he had been in the IRA over two years, he was considering resigning unless there was the hope of action. For any particular analytical insight there should be some indication as to why this representative rebel of a rather large class of young Irishmen is in the IRA at all, instead of spending his nights at the cinema or his Sunday afternoons at hurling.

In theory na Fianna Eireann, the Republican boy scouts, was supposed to feed new young recruits into the IRA. But as was so often the case with Republican organizations of the period, the Fianna was less effective than, say, the Christian Brothers who taught a blood and thunder, ultrapatriotic history course. Irish schools in general taught Heroes-and-Martyrs-history, which, more than any other factor, was the first contact for most volunteers with the "national" issue. While there were Republican families, family politics seldom specifically influenced the potential volunteer. Rather, it was the highly emotional history, stopping short of recent troubled history, that formed the context of the young man's questions.

Once he found that the Glorious Easter Rising of 1916 envisioned a different Ireland than the Twenty-six county "Republic," he searched deeper, suspecting fraud and hypocrisy. The fact that all the traditional Irish political parties then called, softly, for a United Ireland but took no real action rankled. A serious investigation (and a great many young Irishmen were exceptionally serious) revealed a great many nasty cracks in the facade of the contemporary "Republic" of Ireland, hawked as the final dream embodiment of the dreams of the 1916-men by the politicans.

The traditional Western suspicion of the young for their elders and the traditional Irish desire to serve in a country where a religious vocation is highly admired led some young men to investigate the Republican Movement and thus find in the IRA a secular vocation.

In a largely static and stable society, with opportunity for personal success limited during these years to the few, perhaps the IRA gave the ambitious an outlet for their energy and hidden talents in a cause without cant or hypocrisy. The dull, monotonous paycheck to paycheck routine in a society that could neither reward talent nor absorb the desire to serve was thus avoided.

There seemed, however, to be no particular characteristic, universal among the volunteers, that did not exist in Irish society in general. Once within the IRA, the volunteers often became deeply convinced of the validity of physical force, accepted no alternatives nor heeded the advice of parents, priests, or police. Above or beyond this particular tunnel-blindness to feasible alternatives, the volunteers seemed "normal" or "typical"—warm, tolerant, amusing, sullen or grim depending not on their politics but their characters. There was no total personality change, no all-encompassing conversion reflected in every idea, tone of voice, and emotional reaction.

Essentially, it has been said that in these years a young man came to the IRA for one of three reasons: (1) to get a gun and a reputation; (2) to join an army and unite the country; or (3) to mingle with the truly faithful inheritors of the past's legacy.

The potential gunman seldom lasted more than a few months in the face of an outrageous drain on his time and resources. The romantic, true believer often wearied of the discipline and opted out, but often reconciled himself and remained. The volunteer seeking an army accepted the discipline, accepted the time and effort necessary, obeyed orders and dedicated his life to the IRA, but only for so long—usually from two to three years. If no action was forthcoming, the keen edge of his desire was blunted, and he began to miss parades, to drift away, often to emigrate.

Another type of volunteer, found almost solely in the six counties of the North, was the young man who wanted "vengeance, bejesus" for the endless indignities suffered at the hands of the Orangemen. He, at times, became infected with the idealism of the Republican Movement and stayed on or, bored with an army that did not fight, quit. Most of the volunteers who stayed less than two years simply dropped out of sight, rarely shifting over to Sinn Féin, but some reappeared, particularly in the North during an emergency, as self-appointed auxiliaries, as was the case in August 1969.

Those who stayed on in the IRA after two years usually did so because there was action or an immediate prospect of action or because they were in prison and had no choice without denying their ideals. During the campaign, some would continue in the IRA even after privately making the decision to resign.

Who would opt out was difficult at the time to determine. After 1962 many of the orthodox idealists or the hard army men left, just as some of the cynical or the hedonists stayed. The fact is that sooner or later everyone leaves, for an army has no place for the aged.

After the initial weeding out process, many volunteers were dismissed for a variety of reasons ranging from inefficiency to personality clashes. Others went because of paternal pressure, economic necessity or ill-health. Most men at a certain age feel the attraction of a normal life, a regular job, a girl if not a wife, a little peace and quiet. In time the appeal becomes stronger than service in a seemingly hopeless cause. Many IRA people have also spent longer or shorter terms in prison, substantial chunks out of their lives, and on release seek private compensation, having done their part. Then with the constant arrival of new volunteers and new leaders, the veteran may find himself out of sympathy with the new direction or the new men. The Army has changed and he has not, or he has changed and the Army has not.

Those few who stay active are apparently exceptions to the rule but essential for the IRA since they supply both continuity and the new leadership. Some of each generation will remain with the IRA even if only on the Executive or "attached" to GHQ for the better part of their lives, but most of the others will gradually drift away or break with yet another generation of new leaders. These long-time activists may have invested too much time—their youth in prison, a career aborted, a family denied—to quit. Others seem driven by an internal governor that cannot be turned off by age or coercion. These few, hard men, ruthless, zealous, and completely undeterred by personal frailty, persecution, or the gallows, have always existed in Irish revolutionary politics—the real rebels, not masks nor ikons—but they are rare, fortunately for the forces of order.

Important also on the fringe of events were those whose whole life had been the IRA, whose shattered home, years in prison, menial job, all took on a glow of sacrifice; without the IRA such a man would have been a dull, middle-aged barman without prospects or importance. These men were often symbols of the past not leaders of the present, living totems of another revolutionary generation. Most were to be found within Sinn Féin or a Republican Commemorations but some remained, vaguely, within the structure of the IRA.

The Center of the Circle

Most active service volunteers, particularly those who end up in prison, where statistics can be parsed, are not necessarily unrepresentative of the central leadership of the IRA, except in age. Actually, during the campaign years of the two dozen or so important IRA figures, all but two ended in prison—four in Crunlin—or internment camps, usually in the South, and one of the exceptions was killed on active service. In any case, those IRA men who directed the campaign had certain characteristics in common with their colleagues and with most revolutionaries: a hard, single-minded, ruthless dedication to their ideals and their organization, which created an aura of power and purpose even to the uninitiated. Their power depended on the respect of the Army not on their charm, and most in power were cold, suspicious of dissent, and authoritarian by example. Some may have had a private face, genial, kind, and warm, but on duty the volunteer never saw it. Many had the capacity to generate intense loyalty—but always by example. Once that went, everything went.

Once parted from the self-discipline such responsibility entailed, they often underwent a sea change, became prey to affectation, self-doubt, and even personal ambition and private comforts. Their ideals seldom changed, even when expelled from the movement, but their capacity to act had somewhere, somehow been dissipated. Many stayed on the Executive or within Sinn Féin, but most moved on; some then led full if quiet private lives, some have achieved a modest success; some have broken completely with their past. This is true of much of the 1951-62 generation, which included three leadership periods.

The campaign was organized and initiated largely at the direction of three men, Antony Magan, who was 40 in 1957, Tomas McCurtain, also 40, and Patrick McLogan, who was in his sixties. McLogan had joined the Republican movement in 1913, McCurtain's father was the martyred Mayor of Cork, and he, like Magan, had joined in the 1930s. McCurtain had been sentenced to death during the era of the gunfights, reprieved at the lip of the gallows, and spent the bulk of the 1940s in prison. Magan had participated in the bombing campaign and had been imprisoned for five years in Britain. Under pressure in the South once the campaign began, leadership shifted to the next generation, Seán Cronin, who had joined the IRA in 1955 at the age of 32, and Charles Murphy, who had joined in 1949 and was 25 when the campaign opened.

On their arrest, Rory Brady took over as Chief of Staff in 1959 at 27, at first supported by Dave O'Connell, then 20, and later by men out of prison like Cathal Goulding who had joined the IRA as a boy in 1937.

Roughly the average age of the IRA leadership was 34, again roughly more than ten years older than the average volunteer—in effect a man of a different generation. In times of stress a young active service leader might be co-opted into authority, but more often the practice had been to rely on sleepers, men missed by the police sweep, marginal men, or old faithfuls. With their extra ten years, some spent in prison, the leadership had often married and begun their families.

The occupations of the leadership tended to move up a notch with more clerks, businessmen, and professional people. The urban shading was more pronounced, although many lived in small towns rather than Dublin or Belfast. But the hazy statistics do little to flesh out the *real* IRA leader. In general the men seem to have had little in common beyond the statistics except a dedication to the same idea.

A few were conspirators, cunning, sly, secretive to the point of obsession, true descendents of the Fenian brotherhood. Others were simple, plain men of no great scope, quiet and loyal. A few were agitators, the slum lad with a social consciousness and a rasp for a tongue, or the countryman with a hatred of injustice and a love of the land. Whatever they had in common as rebels, they were as good a cross-section of Ireland, warts and all, as anyone is likely to find.

When the Irish rebel entered the IRA, he joined an organization that structurally had sought conformity to history's patterns. The IRA did not want to be "new"—a label awarded the real new men who had betrayed the old ideals, given up the dream for seats in the Dáil, for jobbery and careers as accountants and solicitors, who had measured out the nation's need in ministerial limousines and houses in the country. The IRA saw all manner of virtues in the old ways and the old forms during the campaign years. And after the campaign years, as the 1960s moved on, few at the center had time to be concerned with reorganizing an army without a mission.

Structure

The formal organization of the IRA is delineated in the 1925 Constitution, written by Frank Aiken, then chief of staff and presently minister of external affairs in the Fianna Fáil government, accepted then by the Army Convention and rarely amended in the ensuing forty years. The most apparent feature of the Constitution is that the IRA is a democratic army with regular elections to determine the leadership. On a regional level the IRA is organized at the company, battalion, and brigade level, each unit with a C/O and appropriate staff. In reality local units are determined by local suppport and in recent years few have bothered with the elaborate formal structure. Once every year, recently every two years, delegates to an Army Convention are selected, including elected representatives from local units, the GHQ staff, the Army Council and the Army Executive. At the Army Convention a new twelve-man Army Executive is nominated and elected. The new Executive then, usually during the Convention, secretly selects an Army Council of seven, who in turn select the chief of staff, who appoints his own staff, which even in hard times includes an adjutant-general and quarter-master-general and usually has departments of intelligence, training, publicity, organization and operation, often overlapping.

For obvious reasons, during times of stress, this rather elaborate selection system and top-heavy structure goes by the wayside, permitting promotion by co-option or in desperate cases mutual self-appointment. In practice the 1925 Constitution written for a mass army has worked better than might be supposed for a small proscribed faction. First, the maintenance of the traditional structure is vital for ideological purposes, indicating for example that the IRA is a continuing body unsullied by the compromises of men like Aiken, who would deny the legitimacy of the IRA of 1969 as the successor to the "Old" IRA of the Troubles. Second, all members of the IRA are agreed that the democratic process with the Army Convention is vital for an organization composed of volunteers serving without pay and without hope of pension or privilege. Finally, although the 1925 Constitution was intended for an army of thousands, the provisions are sufficiently loose to be used by a few hundred volunteers. During the past twenty years, for example, the Army Executive had choosen most of the Army Council from its own membership, although in theory a vital part of the IRA structure seldom performs any other significant function. Usually the chief of staff and his most important GHQ people are on both the Army Council and Army Executive, thus maintaining the form and doubling up on the constitutional functions.

In reality the IRA from 1948 to 1967 has usually been dominated at any one time by one or two men. From 1948 to 1956, Chief of Staff Antony Magan ran a tight ship, relying heavily on the advice of Patrick McLogan, the grand old man of conspiracy who had joined the Irish volunteers in 1913, and Tómas McCurtain, son of the martyred mayor of Cork who on his own had gone to the lip of the gallows trap, and after 1953 Charles Murphy, a ruthless and dedicated young man who had joined the IRA in 1950. During the early years of the campaign, the reign of the three "M's" ended with the imprisonment of all but Murphy, who with Seán Cronin as chief of staff continued operation until 1959. After a split at the Army Convention in 1959, continued imprisonments, and inference from the Clan na Gael in America, two or three new young men appeared and one old one, Cathal Goulding, who had completed six years in British jails in 1959. Thus, the Dublin center, with the exception of one or two chaotic periods, was dominated by relatively few individuals. During this time, despite pressures and internal differences, the constitutional formalities were largely observed: Army Conventions were held in 1957, 1959, 1960, and 1962; the Army Council continued to meet, often with co-opted members, and appointed a chief of staff when the need arose. Thus, the comfort of conformity, the ties of tradition, and the possibility of democratic decision and dissent have more than compensated the IRA for maintaining an elaborate and outmoded formal structure (table 3).

If the formal structure of the IRA is elaborate, the actual form is not. For in practice just a few men, operating out of Dublin, have most of the responsibility and do much of the work of the Republican Movement as well as of the IRA. The Army Council makes most of the decisions, usually, but not always, following the advice of the chief of staff, and the GHQ staff tries to implement them. Thus, as is the case with many organizations run on a shoestring, the IRA is understaffed and overextended. During some

TABLE 3
Chiefs of Staff and Their Origins

Fleming	1945–46	Kerry
McGuinness	1946–47	Antrim/Belfast
Magan	1948–57	Meath
Burke	1957	Carlow
Cronin	1957–58, 1959	Kerry/New York
McGirl	1958	Leitrim
Brady	1959–61, 1962	Longford
Goulding	1961, 1962	Dublin

phases of the recent campaign, the leadership felt that this was an advantage, but at present the endless rounds and tireless pep talks erode the will, producing not swift decisions but rather exhaustion.

The postcampaign exhaustion of the IRA resulted in part because of the lure of various political possibilities for an army with limited resources. For the traditionalists these were not a menu of choices to act on events but rather a ticket to accommodation and betrayal. Ultimately, the differences on principles and tactics, priorities and heritage, the clash of personalties, even the reading of Republican history, lead to a formal split in 1969. The official majority of the IRA, as the Officials (the stickies), would move down the road of radical politics that led to putting (often reluctantly) the gun on the shelf and then to the Workers Party. The others, provisionally organized in the traditional way, became the Provisional IRA (the Provos) not unmindful of the ballot box largely prefering the Armalite.

For the informed during the 1960s, there was ample evidence of schism—one key was Cathal Goulding's move away from the traditional IRA control structure. Goulding did not want the IRA to depend on formal decisions of a small covert group. In fact he increasingly wanted no "secret army" at all. Thus, the IRA decision-making process officially expanded to larger groups—more easily manipulated. The entire process of transforming the IRA into an agitational party instead of a secret army was a long process, but one of the very first steps was away from the practices of the traditional IRA Army Council. Goulding may not have known exactly where he was going, but he knew too well where he had been. In turn the militant Republican provisionals set up an alternative secret army with all the forms of the traditional IRA: Army Executive, Army Council, chief of staff with a GHQ. Oddly, the key to the system of a democratic secret army, the regular meeting of the Army Convention, was to be largely ignored for a variety of good if not necessarily convincing reasons. The Army Convention did not meet again until October 1986. Before the split, all this was possible, even probable. In 1968 attitudes hardened essentially around the issue of politics, which had repeatedly in the past led to splits, schisms, expulsions, and heretics scampering away from the Republican high road. To everyone but Republicans, their immediate opponents and the odd observer, the future of this sceret army in 1968 led by felons squabbling in back rooms in north Dublin was not even of passing interest. The IRA was only a subject for pub ballads and historians of the Tan War.

Thus, just as 1946 had been a good and convenient starting place for a work on the modern IRA, the beginning of 1969 was a good ending place. Internally the campaign was long over and the future open to various approaches. Ireland was changing, emigration was off, contractors were building and demolishing, a new generation was on the move; the lure of swinging London, chrome-plated America, the wired-world of the consumer was everywhere to be found and debated on the television. Change was all about. Old forms and patterns were eroding; new people, a new generation, had ambitions not easily accommodated north or south, and tomorrow would not be like yesterday—it seemed certain to be a surprise-filled future.

And what of the secret army in 1969? What did the Republican past reveal—what of tomorrow?

> *Prediction is very difficult,*
> *especially the future.*
> —Niels Bohr

8

The Secret Army, 1969

The movement for an Irish Ireland, free and Gaelic, at times seems to stretch back over a thousand years into the Celtic twilight. The specific struggle for an Irish Republic had a history of nearly two centuries and even the organizational structure of the IRA is over fifty years old. A long and living revolutionary tradition is not unique, but what is peculiar to the IRA, by contrast with most revolutionary groups, is persistence in the face of failure. With a few exceptions revolutionary movements succeed or fail within a relatively brief space of time; they are transformed by power or wither away in isolation, evolve into new forms or are swallowed by old ones. When the Bretons, another oppressed Celtic people, tried during the Second World War to achieve autonomy and failed, the movement simply vanished, its leaders gone into exile, into prison, and before executioners. There was no sullen continuity; in fact, it took over twenty years for another and entirely new Breton liberation movement to appear. When the Irgun Zvai Leumi in Palestine failed to achieve a greater Israel, the movement did not continue to rely on former tactics but evolved into a parliamentary party. Some revolutionary parties, of course, live on in exile but seldom for more than a generation; some accept, albeit reluctantly, the dialogue of democracy; some eschew violence or in some manner deny their original means if not their goals; some are extirpated or betrayed. The militant Irish Republican Movement, however, has continued almost unchanged: the goal is the same, an Ireland both free and Gaelic without cant or compromise, and the means is the same, physical force. And time after time, with deadly regularity, as the means of movement have proven inadequate and the strength of the opponent or the entrenched institution and prejudices too great the IRA has failed. But the Movement, epitomized in the IRA, has nevertheless persisted and endured.

This persistence over half a century has resulted in one of the longest records of revolutionary activity available, revealing within the narrow scope of Republican ideology a broad spectrum of tactics and talents. Between 1918 and 1921, the IRA and the Dáil developed and refined practically all the techniques of the national liberation movements that were to flower during the next fifty years. Assassination in the streets, columns in the hills, "government" ministers secreted in basements and attics were not new; but the Irish mix of violence and publicity, moral force, shadow institutions, national pride, guerrilla tactics, urban violence, terror and a sense for the ethical English jugular became the example, par excellence, for subsequent rebels. Alien admiration would be given to Collins' Squad and to Tom Barry's ambushes, but more often the closest study was concentrated on the ultimate failure of the Irish revolution rather than the tactical successes. Various factions in Ireland have contended for various purposes that the revolution did in fact succeed, although it is obvious that this was not the case—not only during the Treaty negotiations but during the long floundering of the high Irish dream. To so many Irishmen, simply to break the visible connection with England was sufficient, and the judges could still wear wigs, the pound sterling circulate, the Six Counties opt out, the big houses in the country set the social standards and the parish priests the moral ones. As long as the tricolor flew over Dublin, the Rising had not been in vain. Just as this logic failed to convince the IRA, the foreign observers were determined that their next and future revolution would not fall so short, fly a new flag and dance to old tunes.

It is clear that all the long years of nominal independence have not greatly transformed Ireland, still a peripheral and exploited province of British interests, still a pale green copy of discarded London fashions and foibles, still a truncated nation not free, not united, and not Gaelic. Some contemporary Irish politicians feel that this is not so unfortunate and is in fact inevitable. Foreign critics looked to each generation of Irish radicals to correct the error of their elders: truly to break the connection, actually to achieve an Irish Republic in more than name. The IRA, usually unconcerned in alien interest, tried and failed, giving the distant observers a fresh catalog of lessons in disaster. So in the 1930s the Indians were horrified at De Valera's limitations as an anti-Imperialist: he was a "radical" revolutionary with no understanding of the reality of Imperial power, only the symbols. In the 1950s the Cypriots of EOKA were appalled at the futile tactics of the IRA. If Ireland and the IRA had since 1916 contributed nothing more to the revolutionary tradition of the world than the long, bitter log of failure, missed chances, bad luck, poor judgment, error and questionable compromises, this would still be a vein of most valuable ore—for others if not the Irish. But to dig into the history of the IRA is to uncover not only what to avoid but how to persist, to endure, to suffer disaster, and to maintain the ideals and the organization.

If Irish tactics have often been ill-chosen or ill-advised and regularly inappropriate, it has largely been as a result of a tradition from which the foreign student may even learn much but which seems to teach Irishmen little. Steeped in their own history, traditionalists to the core, Irish Republicans have largely misinterpreted the past, selected the inappropriate tactics, and applied a useless strategy. For example, not even the military disaster of 1916 convinced the IRA rank and file that open battle in the field—the line of pikes at the rising of the moon, the tricolors waving and the cannons roaring—was pure madness. The new realism of younger and less romantic men shaped novel tactics between 1918 and 1921 but offended the traditionalists despite their success. Many Irishmen had grave doubts about the squad's assassinations, about murder from a ditch, about lying for the public good, about the dead policemen, the ransacked banks and the burned houses. That the IRA persisted in the techniques that humiliated the British and provoked them to indefensible violence and then the conference room was the one big success after the moral victory of 1916. The Rising had been in the grand tradition and like all predecessors failed gloriously. The Tan War had been a new coalescence of the novel and the historic and unlike all previous blows against the Saxons had almost succeeded. The effort apparently exhausted Irish revolutionary ingenuity. That an April 1916 came but once in seven hundred years was not readily apparent. That the exact mixture used in 1921 was not necessarily universally applicable was ignored, even denied, by a generation of militant Republicans. In the one case the soul of romantic Ireland had been revived and in the other the might of the Empire had been frustrated; there was no reason why the combination could not in the future achieve the Republic. When it did not, men looked further back into the Irish tradition to select other false precedents. The Fenian dynamiters were poor ancestors to Seán Russell's volunteers in 1939, just as Barry, Breen, and O'Malley were inappropriate mentors for the volunteers in 1956. Worse than misreading history, the Irish Republicans have often transformed tactics into principles, waging the struggle on the level of techniques enshrined in the past rather than struggling on a new road to the high ground of the future. Perhaps it really did not matter one way or the other; many an alien observer dashing away with a head filled with Irish tactics and Irish techniques felt that Ireland would frustrate any rebel.

Essentially Britain was too close and Irish society too conservative for rebellion. What might work in Palestine or Cyprus or Aden had been influenced by the Irish tradition. What to avoid had been noted in India and Ghana. But the same lessons could not be applied again in Ireland. Either the magic moment had passed by 1921 or had never existed except in the imaginations of the irreconcilable Republicans. Even the glorious years from 1916 to 1921 had failed to transform Irish society. Even if by some miracle the IRA and the Irish delegation had achieved far more in 1921—a Thirty-two County Republic with guarantees for Ulster and mild ties by external association with Britain—there was not then, and there has not been since, any indication that Ireland would have been transformed—only relabeled. The judges would still have worn wigs, the pound sterling circulated, and the priests banned innovation. Ireland did, indeed, want to be a nation once again, but it did not want to discard the old peasant ways, the old respectable vices and virtues, and the new and desirable English imports in manners and morals.

The two great conserving institutions in Ireland, the puritanical and incredibly parochial Catholic Church and the more recent but equally inviolate tradition of bureaucratic government controlled by democratic means, have hardly been challenged in a century except by a few men of the most radical persuasion. Both institutions foster continuity, minimal change, appropriate conformity, the quiet life, and moral righteousness. Both are and have been accepted almost without thought by the majority of the population. One went to mass on Sunday, to the voting booth at election time, and to the government offices on business. Without the "Trinity" of priest, politicians, and permanent secretary, there would have been no comfortable Ireland with room for a few new factories, a Swiss investor or two, the eldest children, and the English tourist. Over half the century the Trinity could not make Ireland prosperous, keep home the emigrants, and inspire the creative, but there was no riot in the streets, rule by a dictator, influx of pagans, or ruin of property and propriety. For most this was sufficient. Once the Union Jack had come down, all the way, no one wanted more than frugal comfort for the poor, tax rebates for the rich, and a special position for the Church—all quite possible. No one in pomp or power worried much about the Six Counties or talked too much about emigration or acted too rashly to save the language. The stability of Ireland, allowing upward mobility to a few, access to emigration for the many, and the spiritual comforts of the Church to all, had not produced an island of saints and scholars, Gaelic and free, but certainly seemed to leave "revolution" for the odd crank who would deny due process of law, the deliberations of democracy, and the dictates of the clergy. Against this democratic stagnation, beneath a native flag in a state consecrated by the Church under the shadow of the British lion, the repeated failures of the IRA are hardly surprising, but the refusal to resign and flee as wild geese to Liverpool or Detroit or to withdraw into the Sunday papers and the race results and instead to persist is passing strange.

Despite the rigidity of the conservative institutions, the overspill of the discontented through the drain of emigration, and the official willingness to compromise with British power, the IRA has maintained an appeal to new generations. For some, after 1923, simple vengeance played a large part in Republican politics and certainly until 1938 the gaunt shadow of the Treaty colored all deliberations. The efforts of men more concerned with the ideals of social justice than the nostalgia of the pure national issue could not turn the IRA from gnawing again and again the treaty bone. As jerk by jerk De Valera pulled down the Union Jack, the visible symbol of an invisible control that barely receded, the *raison d' être* of the IRA slipped away. The pure nationalists were left with Ulster as their last card. Using Fenian bombs, Seán Russell played it in the streets of Coventry and London. The 1939 campaign led to gunfire in Dublin streets, the prison camps, and the gallows. By 1945 the IRA had been all but gutted, vengeance denied, idealism dissipated, and the Republic more distant than ever. The next generation, determined on military tactics not militant terror, looked to the example of 1921 rather than the 1880s. In the 1950s if any tactic was to work in Ulster, the Fenian bombs were surely more appropriate than guerrilla columns in the hills of Tyrone, but the IRA wanted no more gunmen or mad bombers, only an army. And so the campaign began and so it failed, but the volunteers of the IRA had acted as witness to the validity of the Republican ideal for another generation— romantic Ireland was not quite dead or gone.

Gradually, after 1923, as failure's shadow lengthened, the use of physical force grew to be increasingly more important than the ultimate aim: the campaign was more valid than the victory. There were no more blood sacrifices, but where Pearse had transformed Ireland by his example, increasingly the sacrifice of subsequent generations of Irish Republicans was as much homage to the purity of the cause as inevitable tactical losses on the certain road to the Republic. Force had become all but a principle, and when force failed the Movement was almost without other options. The years after 1962 have shown a new drift to the Left, a new search for a way out of the corner where the tactics of past generations have cornered the present. Still, despite the overwhelming evidence of public disapproval, private doubts, and the uneasy sense of marching along the wrong road back into the past, the IRA has not disbanded, has not turned to parliamentary politics, has not given up parades and route marches, has not withered away. If hardly virile, the IRA has persisted, perhaps fossilized. Perhaps the ideas of Tone are now encased in ancient amber, visible but dead. Or, perhaps, the Army is on the edge of a new viable departure to unite the whole people of Ireland through militant social action in a Republic of those of little property.

If this capacity to endure is, so far, peculiar to the IRA, the long catalog of misreading the past is, to be fair, by no means confined to the Irish. Lessons truly learned from history are rare indeed and surely as much the result of compensating errors as valid insights. To repeat the success of the past regardless of the conditions of the present is apparently as universal a failing as to repeat the failures. What had worked for Che Guevara in the mountains of Oriente Province in Cuba quite obviously was not applicable in the Andean highlands of Bolivia, and one would have thought that he, reading his own dictum, would have recognized the flawed analogy. What worked for Tom Barry in 1921 did not for Seán Cronin in 1957. What is special about the IRA is not the errors and defeats, which are legion, or the old successes, which are splendid, but the continuity, however futile such persistence may seem to the rational. Scorned or discounted, the IRA continues. Che Guevaras come and go; EOKA or FLOSY win or lose; the Irgun disappears or the Mau Mau is crushed or the Hungarian Freedom Fighters go into exile and the Algerians into office; but the IRA remained— generation after generation dedicated to Tone, to physical force, and to the ultimate Republic.

Although the Republican martyr Terence MacSwiney, himself a visible example of the proposition, suggested that those who could endure the most would ultimately succeed, this concept is as much Catholic and Celtic as it is a tenet of Irish Republicanism. For a millennium the Irish have accumulated a catalog of Saxon sins, brutalities beyond belief, massacres beyond number, vengeance under the cloak of the Crown's justice. And they have endured starvation, murder, exile, prison, privation, persecution and kept the faith. Nothing has ever truly been forgotten or forgiven and the fearful toll has been passed down from generation to generation in the hedgerow schools, in the oratory of the seditious, in the classes of the Christian Brothers and in tales by the turf fire. Not even a century in exile will mute the bitterness. In a society with a long and exacting memory, the bright quick appeal of the Irish Republic—the obverse of the Crown— made and makes a tremendous appeal: the details were as vague as the vision intense; vengeance would be assured and the Irish at last rule the land. No matter what the outcome of the Tan War, the reality would have fallen short of the ideal. Even if Ireland had been transformed as Cuba has been or a new national character created as in Israel, not all would have been satisfied. With a geographical position not unlike Cuba's and an exile population no smaller than Israel's, such a real revolution was at least theoretically possible, but from the Tan War instead of victory and the Republic came only compromise and treachery. To the catalog of Saxon sins were added new entries for yet another generation of Irish heretics. But this time too much visible had been won—an Irish flag, an Irish army, in time an Irish president speaking Irish—and the long resistance of the Irish people flagged. The people were content with half of a Republic. The Church was comfortable. The men of property were satisfied. Only the fanatics held out and they were discredited as in time the symbols of the Crown were discarded. Never, however, could the habit of centuries disappear over the course of only a few decades.

The residue revolutionary tradition was largely a husk, but one repeatedly filled by the youth of another generation unaware of their elders' hypocrisy. This legend of persecution dotted by the bright examples of martyrs and patriots created a frame of reference for dedicated young men. The young Irishman lives within a society that admires a religious vocation beyond all price, which applauds denial and lauds puritanical dedication. In the Republican Movement the two seemingly opposing traditions, one of the revolution and physical force and the other of pious and puritanical service, combine into a secular vocation. That the revolutionary tradition is largely a myth parroted by politicians who have no longer any love of the gun and that the hierarchy has never loved a rebel, even a devout one, matters little. Certain of a true cause, possessed of the moral justification for the use of force, intimate with the long tradition of the struggle, comfortable in the company of proud men, an IRA volunteer often lives a life not so much of denial as dedication, a laic pilgrim on the road to the Republic, a knight templar justified in the use of his sword. This atmosphere of sanctity and violence is alien to the Saxon world, where political "crime" is a mad act of men and revolution finds a place only in the history book. Other societies are not so inclined and may create or endure blood feuds, institutionalized assassination, repeated coups, or vigilante justice. But almost nowhere, until recently, except Ireland are the long-lived pressures toward a violent vocation in a vain cause so persuasive.

Increasingly it would appear that the factors that produce an Irish volunteer although very clearly within an Irish tradition and molded by Irish institutions may have parallel forms elsewhere. Increasingly throughout the world young men are infected with the virulent bacillus of pure nationalism or alienated by the prim and dishonest compromises of their elders or disgusted with a system based on lies and habit. Like the Irish volunteer they are increasingly willing to strike, somewhere, somehow, the first blow. Perhaps the Irish example is totally insular and the factors involved purely parochial. Perhaps the static Irish society has shut in men without hope of economic success or social mobility. Perhaps the peculiar ethical atmosphere of service or the tempting voices of the Celtic past have kept the IRA alive where a similar atmosphere or like voices would fail in Paris or Cairo. Yet there has always been a revolutionary tradition valid for all rebels. Robespierre and Castro and Sorel, the Red Flag and the Black, the Tree of Liberty and the Blood of Patriots are there to be plucked and worn. A man need not have bog on his boots to be enriched by Tone's example. Any rebel can strike within a tradition. It was unnecessary for L'Ouverture to have a white skin to be a truer son of the revolution than his French opponents. If a tradition of revolt can exist for all, no matter what the litany, if a desire to serve gods other than those found in the market places or the ivory towers, if violence in a just cause is just, then as always, everywhere revolution is possible. But until a generation of rebels accepts the Irish example that to endure is sufficient, to act with only faint hope of success is an adequate reward, then as always the quick bright flame of revolt will gutter out or light a victory soon to be wrapped in red tape and the correspondence of clerks. Meanwhile, the IRA persists.

The IRA grown stale with little relevance to the tranquil new Ireland of glass buildings, radical priests on television, and the old emigration may well gut out in a squabble of the bitter and unrepentant, grown too few and too faithful to the dead. Some few men seem ordained to live lives of open revolt, discontent with order, blind to rational alternatives. At the right moment in the right place they combined with others to inspire still more to strike. For a few, from time to time and from place to place, the very act of rebellion seems their only natural environment, the barricades their only real niche. Fortunately for order, the vocation of the rebel is erratically distributed and open to cure by aging; however, if the example of institutionalizing the revolutionary capacity over several generations developed by the IRA could be exported to more volatile societies, the antibiotics of conservatism might be sorely pressed. Ireland, however, appears immune, possibly because of constant exposure to the limited threat of the IRA.

Whatever the future hold for the IRA, the long years of failure have been exploited by others elsewhere. If Tone's Republic does not yet exist in Ireland, his advocates have sown far fields. If the IRA has had few victories to cherish, perhaps the volunteers in a small way share those of EOKA or the FLN. In that mysterious brotherhood of revolutionaries, the IRA volunteer, futile or no, has a reserved seat, perhaps not in the front row but in a prominent position. If the IRA's capacity to endure has not as yet proven exportable, the forces of stability in fragile societies can breathe easier. In Ireland, too, the long years have not gone unnoticed for Republican ideas have fertilized Irish life even while the sower was denied. Even in the last lonely years, with horizons narrowed to a desperate guerrilla campaign, the IRA testified to the vitality of Tone's appeal and the failure of the powerful to secure the Republic. The day of the gun may, indeed, be gone as the cautious have insisted for years and with it the IRA, but the last fifty years have given ample evidence of the vitality of the Republican Movement, annually consigned to the boneyard of Irish history and annually appearing before Tone's grave to renew dedication to the invisible Republic. There, even today, the small band of persistent men on the perimeter of Europe, on the edge of events, create for that one summer's day an atmosphere of hope, of possibility, of pure dedication. At least in these men's eyes, Ireland unfree shall never be at peace, nor shall they, at least for this generation.

PART III
The Ulster Troubles Since 1969: Old Myths, Old Realities, and Alien Perspectives

> *Killing a man is murder*
> *Unless you do it to the sound*
> *of trumpets.*
> —Voltaire

Ireland in 1969 was apparently fated to spend the rest of the century living amid interesting times. There was no surprise-free future for those of the secret army gathered before Tone's grave in June 1968. The volunteers and veterans would soon go various ways, often into opposing secret armies; their lives disrupted, sacrificed, spent, or wasted in the pursuit of the Republic. A few names would become well known, appearing nightly on the television news not just in Dublin or Belfast but also in New York and Rome and Paris. Some would drift away, but never again would the army lack for volunteers or official opponents or alien observers.

By the end of 1969, the Province of Northern Ireland had become a nexus of turmoil. Each new year seemed to find the level of violence higher, the number of dead greater, the alienation and anguish deeper. Finally, after a decade of rioting, insurrection and reform, random murder and spectacular assassinations, new ballads, new history, one-hour television spectaculars and the arrival of droves of analysts and speculators in theories of violence, the Troubles became institutionalized. The level of violence was managed and monitored by the security forces and maintained by the IRA; the Unionists perpetually hovered on the edge of a pogrom, and the governments of Dublin and London sought only the quiet life and a return to politics without the gun. On distant maps in bureaucrats' offices, on the walls of university classrooms and newspaper offices, at the back of volumns on terror and war, Ulster was circled red, a crisis point. Some years the circles might be made thick with greasy wax crayon and others a simple check. But Ulster, Ireland (the Troubles), was always on the butcher's list— last year no surprise, this year no surprise, next year no surprise.

In 1969 the surprises began. A few were surprised that the campaign for civil rights in a province where injustice had been institutionalized had taken so long. Those who took to the streets were often surprised at the depth of anger toward the establishment, the unbridled determination to smash provocation. In turn the threatened were surprised that anyone would dare strike openly at the system. The British were surprised at the Irish turmoil out of an Ulster largely quiescent for fifty years. And Dublin was surprised—in some quarters pleasantly, in others less so—that partitioned Ireland had become an issue. As events swept from one crisis to the next, from one protest to the next, from repeated threats (some made good) to various initiatives (few made real), all, even those responsible, were surprised at the descent into violence. No one had really foreseen chaos, murder, and turmoil. Many political Republicans, in and out of the IRA, had been attracted to the potential if not the principles of civil disobedience. Others, the hard men, those truly dedicated to physical force had little time for nonviolence, civic protest, concessions, or compromise; they would wait until the gun could be taken off the shelf. Increasingly a few of the Northerners, distrusting the politicals at IRA-GHQ in Dublin, made their own plans, sent their own agents across to the American diaspora, and prepared for the inevitable. And the inevitable did come. The disorder escalated; the "politicals" went their own way, and the orthodox found, as they had hoped, the gun returned to politics.

From a distance it appeared remarkable that so few noticed that Ulster was not so much slipping toward insurrection as being pushed. And for that matter, the ubiquitous television camera seemed to be missing the extent of that insurrection: Within the bounds of the United Kingdom, a premier democracy supposedly run by decent men with honest efficiency, an open and armed rebellion with long historical roots, ruthless leadership, and specific rational goals was underway. In 1970 and 1971 every counter of violence clicked higher. Numbers, if nothing else, indicated real trouble, new Ulster Toubles that had not, like Topsy, just grown. For much of the century the world's rebels had sought to define for application the necessary conditions of revolution. And suddenly, with no one noticing that old secret army out of Ireland's past, composed of men of no property and little formal education, an army scant on theory and well versed in practice had arisen in the mean Belfast streets and the scruffy hills of the countryside. Few noticed at first. The politicians proposed change; the radicals analyzed historical tides; and the security forces acted out their lesson plans from other rebellions. By the end of 1971, the Troubles had come to stay; there was a war, not exactly like the Tan War and not exactly like any other war, an Irish war, particular, special, and soon spectacular—a surprise to all but a few.

9

The Escalation of Insurgency, 1969-71

There exists a substantial body of revolutionary analysis focused on those elusive objective conditions that permit rebels to rise with some hope of success. There is, of course, no more a general consensus on how to begin an insurrection than on how to prevent one. At one extreme there exist the more simple-minded adherents of Régis Debray who have suggested that a small band of the brave, a *foco,* may alone spark an insurrection against an oppressive regime. At the other are those reluctant rebels who insist on so extensive a roster of assets that the moment to rise continues to recede into the distant future. Still, within the middle ground, conditions have sufficiently encouraged some so that, possessed of a just cause and hopeful of ultimate victory, the armed struggle has been launched. As a result in southern Africa and Latin America, on Mindanao and in the Basque country of Spain, there are insurrections under different banners. Some appear close to victory and others on the verge of disaster; a few are little more than the disorderly residue of past hopes and others scarcely begun. For all a crucial question remains how to escalate the initial thrust. An insurrection may begin as the act of an urban conspiracy, spring from the operations of a rural *foco,* evolve out of the spontaneous rising of the masses, but unless the moment is ripe any insurrection can flicker out in the recriminations of exiles or be interned with the dead. And, perhaps, no set of potential rebels have had as much experience and as little luck in identifying the moment to strike as the Irish. Yet the news from Northern Ireland indicates that this time they must be doing something right—or the British something wrong.

In Ireland some would trace resistance to British domination back to the eleventh century—eight hundred years of sporadic failure, employing strategies from civic petition to assassination. In this long struggle for an Irish nation, both free and Gaelic, the tradition of physical force rather than recourse to conventional politics or civil disobedience has been a prominent but by no means dominant factor. In the 1790s Theobald Wolfe Tone wedded the concept of physical force to the ideas of the French Revolution in order to subvert the authority of the British crown. To break the British connection, he sought to unite the whole people of Ireland, to substitute the common name of Irishmen in place of the denominations of Protestant, Catholic, and Dissenter. In 1798 his Rising failed, but out of his example sprang the Irish Republican Movement. The present IRA has specific organizational ancestors stretching back to 1848 and is, in fact, the oldest of all active revolutionary movements, and possessed of an almost unbroken record of failure.

In 1962 the Northern campaign despite some initial success finally dwindled to a close leaving the IRA in vast disarray, apparently at last discredited in Irish eyes. The faithful few with the gun on the shelf began to investigate the prospects of political agitation, even participation in those elections so long ignored. Romantic Ireland—at last—appeared dead and gone. By 1969 IRA volunteers had become deeply involved in the Northern civil rights campaign, and the idea of physical force became less appealing.

Two years later Northern Ireland was in the grip of violence unequaled since the Tan War. As early as February 1971, after serious rioting in Belfast, the Northern Prime Minister Chichester-Clark announced on television that Northern Ireland was at war with the Irish Republican Army Provisionals. After the introduction of internment of suspects without trial in August, there was ample evidence that Chichester-Clark was not far wrong. Between August 9 and December 1, thirty British soldiers, eleven members of the Royal Ulster Constabulary and the Ulster Defense Regiment, and seventy-three civilians were killed. IRA bombing operations destroyed whole urban districts. Belfast and Derry, bombed out and smoldering, looked like targets of aerial attack. In the countryside there were frequent ambushes, and the roads were mined. Between September and November, IRA snipers fired across the border on the British Army in 243 incidents. Catholic housing estates in Derry and Belfast became no-go zones barricaded against security forces, ruled by the IRA. Until December British army spokesmen remained optimistic. Then the Provisional IRA carried out thirty simultaneous bombing operations across the province. On December 15, British Home Secretary Reginald Maudling noted in Belfast that the IRA "could not be defeated, not completely eliminated, but have their violence reduced to an acceptable level."[1]

Less than three years before the Provisional IRA had not existed. The entire Irish Republic Movement in the North then appeared to be a few hundred agitators swept along in the civil-rights campaign; the IRA arsenal in Belfast consisted of twenty-two guns of various makes and models. Obviously *something* had happened, and if the Irish experience in escalating an insurgency could be exported, the forces of order elsewhere might well rest uneasily.

To the English, and in fact to a good many Irishmen, Northern Ireland had always been a mysterious and often rather unpleasant place. Settled in the seventeenth century by Protestants planted on land seized from disloyal Catholics, the new Loyalist society remained, if not always quite loyal, at least alien to the indigenous Irish. Fearful of Catholic retaliation, the new Ulstermen remained loyal to the Protestant crown: their great holiday remains the anniversary of Protestant William's victory over Catholic James at the Battle of the Boyne in 1694, the Glorious Twelfth of July. Such Protestant successes are celebrated with vast parades, patriotic bands, the thump of huge drums and triumphant banners, all organized by various Orange Masonic lodges. Only in 1798, when the interest of the Protestant dissenters, alienated from the established Church of England, converged with those of their Catholic neighbors—both men of no property—could sectarian differences be overcome. And Tone's Rising failed. The Protestants, all varieties, were co-opted by the expanding Orange lodges and subsequently resisted all Republican blandishments. The two communities grew further apart, isolated and mutually suspicious, heirs to a different heritage, students at different schools. Two societies began to emerge in Ulster, outwardly similar but with different ideals and institutions where men walked on the same streets as strangers, played different games on different days, sang different songs. Peace between the two was uneasily maintained, each took care of its own and feared the other. Sectarian riots were not uncommon and community cooperation rare.

During the long struggle for Irish home rule, the Protestants remained fiercely loyal, adamantly opposed to concessions. Their determination to avoid absorption into a Catholic Irish Free State had been rewarded in 1921 with the creation of a regional parliament outside Belfast at Stormont and control of six of Ulster's nine counties. Northern Ireland, where Protestants outnumbered Catholics two to one, remained part of the United Kingdom. Fearful of the larger Irish state to the south, fearful of the minority Catholic population of Ulster, the majority ruled with outward arrogance, determined to maintain their privileges and their way of life. As one Loyalist spokesman indiscreetly admitted, Northern Ireland was a Protestant state for a Protestant people. The Protestant establishment, the Unionist Party within Stormont and the Orange Order without, suspected their minority population to be disloyal, agents of Rome, advocates of the IRA. Thus, the situation of the Catholics worsened. For a united Ireland, ruled from London before 1921, offered certain safeguards that a Northern Ireland ruled by Stormont did not. And for nearly fifty years there was no response to minority complaints; in fact, the litanty of grievances grew.

These grievances—discrimination in housing and jobs, gerry-mandered voting districts and coercive legislation enforced by the largely Protestant

Royal Ulster Constabulary backed by the B-Specials—were intensified by the repeated symbolic humiliations of the great Orange parades. Of course, the minority responded in kind where possible: jobs to their own and commemorations of Irish victories over British imperialism. And so the two communities lived separate fearful lives, reacting to each other in slogans—*No Pope Here* and *Up the Republic*—and self-fulfilling prophecies. The first real challenge to the Stormont system, other than the various abortive IRA campaigns, came after 1967 when a civil-rights movement dominated by a new young generation demanded for the minority the same rights open to all British citizens. In Orange eyes civil rights meant Catholic rights and those "rights" nothing more than the thin edge of the wedge of subversion. Consequently, the establishment tended to react first with scorn and then truculent violence. Since most of the grievances seemed valid and the reaction of the Northern Ireland authorities unsavory, there was considerable sympathy for the demonstrators both in Britain and elsewhere. The minority population, increasingly feeling emboldened, joined demonstrations at some risk. There was risk because Protestant militants provoked by "treason" reacted violently. And it appeared that the forces of order—the police—intended to break the law by beating down those demonstrating for a change. The credibility of the Stormont regime began to erode despite the efforts of Prime Minister Terence O'Neill to portray a moderate and decent image. As the civil-rights movement gained momentum so did Protestant determination not to give an inch. The police appeared unable and in many cases unwilling to protect the demonstrators. On August 12, 1969, an Orange parade provoked an escalating riot that ripped apart the city as the Catholic district of Bogside repulsed police charges. Rioting spread to Belfast where on the fourteenth, six people were shot to death. Protestant mobs seemed about to smash into Catholic districts. Firing had become general, and civil war seemed possible. On the fifteenth, British troops moved into Belfast.

Before the arrival of the British army on August 15, the Catholics of Belfast had assumed that the IRA could defend them. No such armed underground army existed except in the popular imagination. Several of the retired volunteers of the previous generation rushed to the Dublin GHQ seeking arms and reinforcements only to find that there was nothing to be had. Many Irish Republicans had grave doubts about the new shift to radical politics, but to find that the IRA was an army without arms completed their alienation. In Belfast they formed a Northern Command and uneasily existed alongside the Official IRA unit for several months, but a break was almost inevitable. At the 1969 IRA Convention, backed by the like-minded elsewhere, they withdrew to form a Provisional IRA—the Provos—and were later joined by a breakaway Sinn Fein, the political arm of the Republican Movement, completing the split. At the beginning of 1970, there were only a few hundred Provos, and their overwhelming concern was with the acquisition of arms in order to defend the Catholics of the North. No one was opposed to the presence of the British army, rather the contrary, but no one wanted to be caught defenseless again; one August 1969 was enough.

The Labour government of Harold Wilson, too, felt one August 1969 was more than sufficient. The Irish crisis, however, could not be wound down solely by the British army mounting a domestic peacekeeping operation. The Catholic grievances were seen as legitimate, and London recognized that the minority was no longer willing to tolerate institutionalized injustice when a means to reform in the civil-rights campaign existed. There could be no orderly future, despite Stormont's reluctance and militant Protestant fear, without extensive reforms. British priorities, then, were first to keep the peace and thus cool the tensions between the two communities, so that, second, reforms could be fashioned by the appropriate institutions, at, third, a pace that would satisfy the minority without enraging the majority. Clearly the cabinet knew little of Irish matters; few understood the underlying fears and fantasies of the two communities. Home Secretary James Callaghan began to interest himself in devising an Irish accommodation, but there was little sense of urgency in London and little realization of how intractable the Irish crisis was. The result was drift.

The reluctance of London to impose immediate and radical reforms with or without the consent of Stormont meant that in Catholic eyes the only legitimate authority remained the British army. The police, the courts, the prisons, the entire Stormont security system had been discredited. Large Catholic districts had no visible sign of order but the British army—and that army gradually became alienated from the minority. Given the attitudes and loyalties of the two Ulster communities, any neutral force inserted between them would have faced severe trials. Obviously the majority regulated by the constitutional provincial forces of law and order avowing loyalty to Britain and flying the Union Jack caused fewer troubles. They had no grievances that needed redress nor a desire for change. There were some confrontations with the British army but these were patched up. Rather, it was the minority that tended to cause "problems," and when these problems resulted in violent confrontations, the individual troops gradually perceived *them* as disloyal, dangerous, and finally in terms little different from those of the majority. The British army tried very hard to be evenhanded but increasingly one hand lay more heavily on the minority. Given the clash of historic loyalties, the use of British symbols for majority purposes, and the existence of a legitimate provincial government, the erosion of British army neutrality was probably inevitable. If the troops were not going to be replaced by the police, and this could not happen without a political arrangement, then time was against them. A good rule is to send the army in quickly and in force and get them out equally quickly. This was not done. In London there seemed no realization that there was a real if undefinable time limit before army credit ran out.

Under the best of circumstances that limit might have been extended for a year or two; however, Ireland often tends to bring out the worst in the British. The peculiar thing about the British army in Ulster was that the challenge brought out the best professionally. The army introduced a carefully conceived tactical response to provocation that had been honed and elaborated over a generation of experience with insurrection and rebellion. The army commanders saw—and were allowed to see by London—its mission as the imposition of order. And despite various institutional and political restraints on army tactics, this mission was pursued with vigor, with the most disastrous results. The military response to provocation had a disproportionate effect simply because it appeared so harsh. Thus, the British tactics were effective in producing local order but assured that there would be subsequent disorder. In April 1970, for example, during a quiet time in Belfast, a group of young men at the edge of the Catholic Ballymurphy housing estate began to stone a passing Orange parade. Orange parades passed as close to "Fenian" areas as possible in a constant game of challenge and response. To control the rowdy crowd of 400, some 70 Royal Scots arrived backed by Saracen armored cars. The army rushed in and cleared the area using CS gas, a relatively moderate response to disorder. The army did not seem to realize how radicalizing CS gas could be drifting through "innocent" houses; CS gas did more for the Provos than all the legends of heroes and all the patriot graves. Slowly, but almost inevitably, in 1970 the new military order began to decay.

There might still have been time for an effective British initiative. Callaghan was reported ready to junk Stormont and impose direct rule, but any such move would have to wait until after the general elections in June. The unexpected result of the elections was a Conservative cabinet under Ted Heath. Allied to the Unionist establishment in Ulster, the new prime minister had no intention of taking drastic steps in Northern Ireland, where matters seemed to be grumbling along. In any case, his appointment of Reginald Maudling as home secretary instead of his shadow minister Quintin Hogg meant that the new minister knew little of Ireland. Maudling by wont approached difficult problems with caution, with languor some would say. Since there was neither an easy nor an obvious accommodation in sight for Ulster, Maudling tended to drift.

Almost at once the price of drift became somewhat clearer. In Belfast an

Orange parade was permitted by mistake to follow a provocative route that security forces felt was the least dangerous alternative. Not unexpectedly on June 27, rioting began on the edge of the Catholic Ardoyne; three Protestants were killed and rioting became general throughout the city. That night a Protestant crowd attacked St. Matthew's Church in the isolated Catholic district of the Short Strand across the River Lagan. With riots throughout the city, the British army was stretched too thin to intervene. The Provos defended the church, four Protestants were shot and killed. For many Catholics the British army's absence at the Short Strand was ominous. The British commander, Lieutenant General Sir Ian Freeland, for different reasons, also felt the situation ominous: he had too few troops. London would have to do something. Maudling flew over, still devoid of experience or ideas, and, as so many others before him, left Ulster appalled: "What a bloody awful place."[2] Nothing was done.

The next week was even more "awful" for the British. On July 3, British security forces made a successful arms swoop on an Official IRA dump in the Lower Falls in Belfast. On their way out of the warren of little streets, the soldiers were surrounded by a crowd still angry at the betrayal of the Short Strand the previous weekend. Standard operating procedure was to stand firm. Reinforcements were sent in to extricate the first lot and were surrounded in turn. The crowd grew larger and uglier. Communications collapsed in a welter of confusion; no one in command knew what was going on in the Lower Falls except that the whole area was in an uproar, and British troops couldn't get in or out. Stoning began. CS gas was used. Barricades began to go up. Freeland began to cordon off the entire area. The Official IRA decided to take on the army. Snipers opened up on the British when they attempted to penetrate beyond the cordon. Firing became general. A curfew was imposed that lasted thirty-five hours until Sunday morning. By then the British had swept the Lower Falls clear of resistance. Four civilians were dead—none an IRA man—and twenty thousand alienated. To cap the best of a bad job, in a disastrous public-relations ploy, the army then drove two delighted Unionist cabinet ministers about the "pacified" Falls. Between June 27 and July 5, the British army had quietly passed beyond the time limit; after that began the long slide to open insurgency as recruiting into both IRAs soared.

During the period from July 1970 until January 1971, when Provo strength in Belfast probably passed one thousand and was somewhat less than that in the rest of the province, the major concern of the leadership was the creation of a satisfactory defense. No one wanted to provoke either the Protestants or the British army. In fact, at times Provo units cooperated with British officers to limit the never-ending disturbances, rock throwing and parade baiting. As Provo strength increased and with it effective control of the Catholic districts, the more ambitious began to recognize the advantages in fomenting a sufficient level of violence so that the British army response would solidify Provo support. It was simply a matter of time and luck before a confrontation would occur that would raise the level of violence another peg.

In January during riots and the inevitable house-to-house sweep through the Ballymurphy housing estate, a British soldier was shot and wounded by a Provo gunman. During serious rioting in the Clonard early in February, eight British soldiers were hit with gunfire. The inevitable came on February 6 when the first British soldier was killed. The next morning the Stormont prime minister announced on television that Northern Ireland was at war with the Irish Republican Army Provisionals—a typical Ulster self-fulfilling prophecy. Within a month defensive sniping had given way to gunmen seeking targets of opportunity and the bomb was introduced. Few contended that the bombing was defensive: thirty-seven explosions in April, forty-seven in May, fifty in June. Stormont, London, and the British army all felt something must be done. The bombs were going off once or twice a day. Sniping was continuous. Military movement in most Catholic areas was nearly impossible without a large buildup and the use of armor. Between April and August, four British soldiers had been killed and twenty-nine wounded, over one hundred civilians had been injured. Civil order and civilian morale seemed about to collapse.

Still, viewed as an insurgency, the level of violence remained relatively low. The core Provo areas were the urban Catholic districts in Belfast and Derry where the population had already felt the brunt of Protestant wrath and the British army. A substantial proportion of the civil-rights people and the anti-Unionist political leadership hoped for swift reforms that would force the Provos to wind down their aggressive operations. The response of the British cabinet, however, was to seek order before changing the laws. The Stormont government insisted that the most effective way to choke off the Provos and restore order was to introduce internment of suspects as permitted by the Special Powers Act of 1922. The army, so far unable to keep the peace, could then impose a peace. What the British army wanted was an effective internment sweep that would in fact cripple the IRA. Given the lamentable state of existing intelligence, this was nearly impossible, and the British commanders so informed the cabinet in London. What Stormont wanted was a "victory"—a public humiliation of the disloyal minority rather than a rigorous police operation. Given British army cooperation, this was quite possible, for all that need be done was intern several hundred Catholic Republicans or agitators.

In London the British government failed to realize that the symbolic nature of internment would be all too clear to the Catholic minority who had no intention of being humiliated by the British army for the benefit of the Orangemen. Having erred by doing nothing, the cabinet then erred by doing something: authorizing the internment of several hundred suspects, almost all Catholic. As a security measure the operation was a disaster; very few active IRA people were picked up, although the British army did the best it could. On August 13, four days after the first sweep, Brigadier Marston Tickelly met the the press to explain how the IRA had been "virtually" destroyed. British credibility was being destroyed only a few streets away where the Provo C/O of Belfast, Joe Cahill, was holding his own fully attended press conference. As a symbolic victory for the majority, it was an equal disaster. Stormont's credit in London had been destroyed; instead of humiliation, the minority had all but risen in arms; instead of ending violence, internment escalated the Provo campaign. And finally as a British policy, no worse initiative could be imagined since world opinion immediately recognized the sectarian nature of the exercise. Internment appeared a vindictive weapon of an arrogant government that had chosen bigoted coercion over necessary concession and had apparently lost the opportunity to find a relatively comfortable accommodation for internment. As a result, they had not crushed the Provos but unleashed them.

In August there were over one hundred bomb explosions. Rifle and submachine gun fire was general. The IRA no-go zones were created. And thirty-five people were killed. Throughout the autumn of 1971, the level of violence rose. The Provo campaign, backed by a civil-disobedience rate and rent strike, reached a level comparable to the glory days of the Tan War. By December even the most sanguine accepted that by any definition there was an insurrection in Northern Ireland. There would be further British errors and blunders that would help to maintain Provo momentum during much of 1972, but by the end of 1971, the factors that had permitted or encouraged the escalation of insurgency had been revealed.

The crucial British blunder was to let matters drift in hopes that a rigorous intervention from London would not be necessary. This encouraged Stormont to give too little, too late, continually alienating the Catholic minority. After August 1969, the minority all but withdrew its consent to be governed. Without legitimacy or the capacity to maintain order, Stormont had to turn to London. The task of maintaining order as the legitimate representative of the British government fell to an army whose attitudes, postures and policies in time alienated the minority and encouraged the Provos. It would be too facile to suggest that a quick decision in 1969 or 1970 sufficiently far-reaching to satisfy the minority and sufficiently imposed to discourage majority opposition would have saved the day; the British have never had very good luck in Ireland even when doing the decent thing. And it was surely bad luck for an Irish accommodation that Labour lost office and Callaghan could not try out direct rule in 1970. Perhaps this was not in the cards either, for politicians in opposition always recall their decisive intentions with penetrating hindsight. In any case, there was no decision. The army, left to its own devices, by August 1970 had slipped into growing disrepute in Catholic eyes, first an oppressor and then a Provo target. Then the British cabinet opted to impose a demonstrably sectarian measure on a restive people who had the means in the IRAs to resist.

The means to resist are hardly created overnight any more than is the will to do so. If there were no Provos in August 1969, conditions had somehow become ripe for their birth and growth. To the alien eye the potential for insurrection had existed in Northern Ireland for at least fifty years, yet there had been no serious challenge to authority. All the IRA efforts had aborted, but any future rebels could pick up the Republican legacy. Thus, the rebels against the Crown would have three ready-made assets: an inspiring revolutionary tradition that granted legitimacy, authorized an army without banners; a demonstrably viable alternative to the institutionalized sectarian injustice of the Northern Ireland establishment in Tone's Republic; and an organizational core of trained and zealous men to direct any rebellion. This tradition, the Republican alternative, and the band of IRA zealots had existed for fifty years without serious effect until the peculiar combination of circumstances arose in 1969-70. At long last the objective conditions favored the rebels.

In qualitative terms the civil-rights campaign after 1967 gradually lowered the minority's capacity to tolerate further oppression; the question of a united Ireland aside, the minority wanted fair play. Many thus risked more by taking to the streets, and support for them grew among those who stayed home. For the first time the Ulster security forces could not maintain order or the privileges of the establishment by means that would satisfy the British cabinet or more important the fearful Protestants. The result was the Derry-Belfast riots in August 1969 that created a need for a minority defense that the British army emotionally could not fill. In filling the vacuum as Catholic defenders, the Provos had as a goal not simply the establishment of a safe ghetto for comfortable Catholics but a united Irish Republic that in the long run was the only way to guarantee peace with justice. Once the events of the summer of 1970 transformed the British army into a threat, the Catholic minority increasingly had to depend on the IRA for defense; in fact, the Provo growth was almost exactly proportional to the decay of British army neutrality as perceived by the Catholics. By 1971 the Catholic community could not repudiate the Provos without losing their only sure defense. This made possible an increase in offensive operations that, of course, provoked further British army retaliation. Not until the use of internment, however, could the Provos be certain that the people would support a campaign as much out of conviction as from fear. After August 1971, there was by anyone's definition a full-scale insurgency that then faced the British with the challenge of deescalation, another matter altogether. By then the Provos were at the crest of the tide in Irish affairs, for which they were only marginally responsible but in which they had recognized the course toward if not to Tone's Republic.

An insurrection is recourse to the armed struggle by a substantial number of the people to achieve aspirations that cannot be conceded but can be resisted by the existing regime. An enfeebled regime will simply collapse while effective authority may crush the insurrection. All insurrections are special cases and certainly the Northern Ireland example as special as any. Yet surely certain aspects of the genre may be dissected from a single example. In Ireland there has been recourse to the armed struggle in the name of an Irish Republic that London could not envision within the United Kingdom, so that a major British response has been force. This lethal asymmetrical dialogue between order and rebellion in Ireland and elsewhere has as the prize the toleration, perhaps even the support, of the mass of the people: in Ireland the Catholic minority has become the foundation for the Provisional IRA, a special case. Almost always the forces of order have the advantage: most people are for the easy life, few care to sacrifice in the name of change without the assurance of victory, but many will tolerate a remarkably long train of abuses. Consequently, to create an insurrectional base, the cause must be most attractive, the imposition of order by authority most disagreeable, and the prospects of success promising. Some men will always rise on command, see the third month as the ninth, pursue the vocation of the rebel, but few will follow. Such rebels may make a *coup,* the few snatching the authority from the unexpectedly feeble as the Free Officers did in Egypt in 1952, or achieve a glorious failure, the Easter Rising of 1916. An insurrection, however, requires a mass following alienated from authority.

To marshal the masses there must be perceived decay in the legitimacy of authority, a real and pragmatic advantage for the many in taking up arms, and a talented and ruthless leadership capable of elaborating their own assets and exploiting their opponents' errors. In Ireland, Stormont in Catholic eyes had always been illegitimate but capable of exerting authority so an IRA campaign although endangering the minority could be endured but without hope. In 1969 the general challenge to authority, supported with great enthusiasm by most of the minority, had gone so far that retreat was no longer possible and a stubborn determination to hold fast prevalent. There was the need for the IRA as a legitimate defender. The Provos had gradually recognized the opportunity to strike, exploiting the people's fears, depending on their new militancy and evoking their historic loyalties. The British in failing to grasp the nettle of rigorous reform, putting off for the morrow what might best have been done yesterday, encouraged the fatal confluence of Catholic pragmatism and Republican aspiration, and still worse sought recourse in internment, an option that proved both brutal and inefficient—a disastrous combination.

The Provos' capacity to combine pragmatism, patriotism, and ruthlessness has often been neglected by potential rebels who have been inclined to import their options. Broad theories wrapped in inspiring revolutionary rhetoric coupled with a quick course in battle techniques have led to many an abortive revolt. Thus, a Che Guevara brought a Cuban formula to Bolivian Indians hopeful that the techniques of the *foco* would prove effective: idealistic, alien and unknown, he had little impact in Bolivia. In Ethiopia the Eritrean Liberation Front within the combat zones ultimately discarded a nonsectarian "revolutionary" appeal to depend on the Islamic loyalties and tribal habits of the nomadic *shifta*. As has been the case in Ireland, common sense and recourse to the loyalties of the past may prove more effective incubators than elegant ideological analysis.

Once the bombs began and the film crews arrived, there followed a rush for explanations, a not unreasonable desire to make sense of a violence-zone only vaguely known even to those concerned in Dublin and London. Elsewhere in the world there arose, often without apparent cause and rarely with warning, a great wave of disorder: new fanatics shot down innocents; student anarchists held the center of Paris; freedom fighters sought the liberation of unknown nations; gunmen arrived in European capitals. Many felt a time of terror had arrived as well. In this noise and clamor of gunmen, the old Irish Troubles had to compete for media attention, for analytical interest, and for a place in the new terror arena. Most observers were inundated with examples, swamped by cases. Innocent of historical precedent and appalled by the politics of atrocity, many were content to lump the IRA with the other cells of the fanatical, the Unionists killers with lynch mobs, and the British army with villains or heroes dependent on ideological posture. Within Ireland, of course, the violence was unusual, an aberration of the present; the Irish to the Irish were not prone to terror, congenial to violence, nor creatures of a bloody history.

There were available lists of casualties or operations or election returns, speeches and declarations and proclamations from the dock; Ulster was swamped with violent details. Above and often far beyond these flew the ideological banners of explanation, raised in faith without special reference to the quite unpleasant, real world along the Shankhill or in the hills of South Armagh. They offered class war, religious conflict, relative deprevation, imperialism or communism or Catholicism, original sin or societal injustice as models, explanations, outlines, or paradigms.

There existed, then, a detailed chronology, a chronicle of events that could skip the murderous forays of the Protestant militants who, for some time, flew no banner, engendered no apologists, and broadcast no programs. And there existed all those under ideological banners, the apologists for the decent Dublin center or the elected and democratic government at Westminster or the forces of the invisible Republic or the risen proletariat—Catholic chapel only. There was not much in the middle about the ways and means of violence. What were the dreadful tactics, the military brutality, the random bombings supposed to achieve tactically, and how were the murders to be fashioned into a strategy to capture the future? Quite often it seemed that those who could give detailed rationalizations for Ulster did not act on events but only before audiences of the like-minded: at worse, potty Colonel Blimps or trendy Trotskyite students, at best, anguished elected politicians or lead writers on concerned elite papers. There seemed a need, at least for distant audiences, to treat the ways and means of violence, the strategy and tactics of the involved, without recourse to the model of the moment.

Notes

1. *Sunday Times* Insight Team, *Ulster* (Harmondsworth, Middlesex, 1972), p. 309.
2. *Ulster,* p. 213.

10

Strategy, Tactics, and Terror, 1969-74

Since 1969 Ireland has been gripped by murder in the streets of Belfast, bombs in supermarkets, ritual riots, and random murder. Neither elegant position papers nor historical rationalizations nor moral justification can hide this slaughter of the innocents. Yet despite the record of terrible deeds and ruthless brutality, Ireland admits to no "terrorists." The gunmen, whether or not they wear uniforms, act within a tradition. They are legitimated by legend, habit, and an act of Parliament. The Paras, the Prods, and the Provos may call each other terrorists, but they are not terrorists in their own eyes. From their point of view their strategy, tactics, intentions, and perceptions are perfectly justifiable. In a sense, these rather ordinary men and women have become locked in a historical process that defies easy academic definition or comfortable categorization by those who have never been subject to institutional injustice, the threat of alien occupation, or the danger of murder perpetrated from a ditch.

Northern Ireland is a small, intensive country. Even the weapons are small—a .50 caliber machine gun is rarely used. The bombs may be cleverly put together, but they are usually fashioned by amateurs and are years behind the times. Killing in Ireland is done by hand, one or two at a time, and almost as many deaths result from incompetence as from malice.

The explanation of the real meaning of the new Irish Troubles soon produced various and often contradictory theories. The violence could be viewed as a religious war in a province in which the issues of the Reformation remained alive, or as a tribal confrontation by peoples who looked alike but went to different churches, had different myths, sang different songs, and who, from the cradle, were taught to suspect each other. There were those who saw Northern Ireland as a postimperial colony or as the prize sought by capitalists manipulating the working class with religious symbols. The Irish Republican movement saw the unfailing source of Ireland's woes in the British occupation of the six counties of Ulster. The Protestant Orangemen saw "civil rights" as a disguised attempt by the IRA to create a united Catholic Ireland. Outside the province, sympathy went to those who sought civil rights. The young, dynamic university students,

148

especially Bernadette Devlin, elected to Parliament at Westminster at the age of 20, could in the welter of strange historical references, ancient feuds, and unfamiliar myths, be recognized as decent. The closer the observer came, however, the more difficult it became to distinguish between the forces of justice and those of bigotry, the past and the future, and the advocates of nonviolence and the gunmen. For most, over the next five years, Ireland would continue to remain a distressful country where armies without banners bombed and murdered in back lanes. Novel political institutions rose and fell, and parties and programs disappeared over night. Neither British political magic nor recourse to the less savory strategems of Perfidious Albion could effect any significant change. In five years, at one time or another, the province had become a proving ground for every sort of violence short of conventional war—torture, assassination, car bombs, mutilation, random murder, and eventually the export of bombs to London and Manchester and Dublin, where explosions killed those often innocent of any knowledge of the Northern Ireland issue. The Provos provoked the British army into repressive measures that guaranteed their own base and permitted an IRA offensive campaign of liberation.

After July 1972, the British sought to fashion new and moderate political institutions in Ireland and crush the Provos. The Official IRA had gone over to "the defensive." The Protestants, horrified by the end of Stormont and unsatisfied with the level of repression, created their own paramilitary forces and began an almost spontaneous campaign of vengeance against the disloyal Catholics. This Protestant militancy, which spawned a welter of groups—the Ulster Volunteer Force (UVF), the Vanguard movement, the Workers' Councils, the Red Hand Commandos—in a way horrified observers less than the revelations that the supposedly civilized British army had been accused of torture, murder, and provocation. There could be no evading the fact that, in January 1972, during a rally in Derry, British paratroopers had shot and killed thirteen Irishmen, none of whom had weapons or belonged to the IRA. In fact, no one who went about Northern Ireland with a gun under any auspices had kept a clean copybook.

During the five violent years of the Irish crisis, none of the participants advocated the use of "terror" or admitted that their strategies, much less their tactics, could be so categorized. The various political parties, of course, had no registered gunmen, but the politicians, if they did not urge violence, often seemed to tolerate it. The security forces, of course, simply performed their legal duties. British army interrogation could not be called torture, according to the official investigation, because the soldiers did not enjoy giving pain. The Provisional IRA bombs that killed innocent civilians were regrettable, for warning had been given. The assassination of politicians or soldiers or informers by the Official IRA was simply one facet of revolutionary politics by the people's army of defense. A bomb in the Tower of London, detonated without warning amid a crowd of tourists, became an act of war. The rising toll of civilians gunned down in the streets by British soldiers—suspects who turned out to be priests, children, a deaf-mute—was discounted by official spokesmen—deplorable but unavoidable, and certainly not a matter of policy or even faulty training. And, as for the Protestants, the random murder of "them"—the Mickies, Fenians, papists—by the Ulster Volunteer Force or the Red Hand Commandos was a justifiable act of revenge against traitors, an act that would discipline the unruly minority, prevent IRA operations, and protect the Protestant way of life from papal interference. Each group, however, agreed that their enemies had been guilty of recourse to terror. For those involved, it was one of the few areas of agreement.

Today there is a general consensus by the uninvolved on several matters. First, the present troubles have roots deep in the Irish past, some have in fact traced their roots to the Anglo-Norman invasions of the eleventh century. Second, in a maze of complex issues and conflicting priorities, few of those involved have emerged spotless. The Protestant militants are unsavory at best. British officialdom has been hypocritical and the security forces biased and crude. The Irish Republicans have proved as ruthless as they are narrow-minded. The Dublin government has been inept and the Nationalist politicans self-serving. Few have retained their innocence or kept their reputation. Third, while violence has changed much, it has solved nothing. To seek a fourth point—that all, or none, of the participants could be labeled terrorists—would be a sticky point for many. It would be wiser to examine the question of strategy and tactics, perception and reality, without applying the terrorist tag.

The British Army

On August 15, 1969, the British cabinet committed the army to maintain order in the streets, prevent further riots, and keep the peace. Intended to supplement the police, the army largely replaced them, accepting the burden of maintaining order with the aid of the RUC. Welcomed particularly in the Catholic districts, where the minority feared that their own feeble defenses would collapse under the pressure of the Orange mobs, no one believed that the Protestant RUC, or B–Specials, would intervene effectively. The Catholics, for their purposes, had ample evidence that the only difference between the police B–Specials and the Orange mobs was that the former were better armed—and the RUC was little better. In effect, the Catholics believed that the police had inspired, or at least tolerated, disorder. They assumed that the British army would pursue an evenhanded policy. Consequently, the soldiers were welcomed with relief and enthusiasm in the Bogside and on the Falls.

Several factors began to erode the Anglo-Irish honeymoon. First, the British army, ignorant of Irish matters, discovered two "tribes." One professed loyalty to Britain, flew the Union Jack, wanted no change in the status quo, and was led by articulate and intelligent men who often held official positions. The other proved poorer, a bit scruffy, often lived in housing estates or marginal slums, was Irish not British, often flew the Tricolor, wanted instant change, and was often led by self-appointed spokesmen warped by deep grievances. Obviously, it was easier to identify with the Loyalists, who had familiar symbols if odd habits. Also, while neither side trusted any outsider, including the British army, the Loyalists could depend on existing and legal institutions—their police, their prisons, their courts—to defend them, while the Nationalists, long victims of those institutions, increasingly turned for protection to the IRA as a neighborhood militia—just in case. Neither IRA at this time had the slightest interest in any military program except self-defense and did not even have the capacity for that, but the British army could hardly look with favor upon the creation of secret, underground armies officially dedicated to their expulsion. Finally, no army, even when properly trained in peace-keeping, is a police force. The military response to disorder and provocation is almost always far harsher and far more extensive than that which the police would consider appropriate.

In Northern Ireland, after the autumn of 1969, when the British army intervened between the two "tribes" to restrict or end ritual violence and mute spontaneous confrontations, there was a tendency to follow accepted military procedures and go in heavily. Since, after interposition, the British army found the provocation to be coming on the average from the Nationalists, a tendency arose to apply the techniques of repression more readily against them. More than anything else, the massing of troops, the arrival of armor and the paraphernalia of war, and the indiscriminate use of CS gas in response to teenage rock throwing gradually transformed the image of the army in Nationalist eyes. The British army was seen as alien, an institution not unlike the RUC, dedicated to maintaining an odious system. Such a shift in perception proved to be an incalculable asset to the two IRAs busily recruiting local defenders, but with an eye on a future campaign.

The army thus faced a decaying situation, particularly dangerous because within one tribe was the germ of a revolutionary movement— disciplined, trained, experienced, dedicated, and eager to exploit further disorder. The IRA leaders were not simply local defenders thrown up after the riots. The British army's position worsened because London did not dismantle the Stormont system and pushed reforms that had little impact in the Nationalist ghettos. Without a political initiative to undermine these grievances, the British army had to stay in place, alienating the minority through recourse to tactics that encouraged the further growth of the IRA, whose leaders began to provoke further British repression. Given all, from August 1969 until the beginning of 1971, the British army had a long run, kept the peace, acquired some knowledge of the local scene, and maintained discipline under provocation. There had been no outrageous incident and no scandal—only the slow erosion of Nationalist trust and the ominous growth of the IRA. The British army had tactics but no "strategy," for the civilian government in London had to fashion a political initiative that would satisfy the minority without unleashing majority violence. In the meantime, the British army intended to maintain order by the techniques and tactics of the manual, a manual that was more fitted for use in an urban guerrilla campaign than in peacekeeping. The Nationalist distaste for these orthodox tactics would in 1971 produce conditions that would narrowly limit London's strategic choices. By then the British army's tactics would create conditions that would encourage a real Provo insurgency—bullets instead of bottles.

The Provisional Irish Republican Army

The Provo Army Council, while not unmindful of the experiences of others, felt little call to fashion its revolutionary strategy from alien cloth. Irish experience extended over several hundred years and could be grounded in the largely successful Tan War. The first and most important step for Northern Ireland was to provoke the British security forces into a repression that would alienate the Nationalist population. This task was greatly facilitated by the tendency of the British army to view its task in similar terms of antiinsurgency and to make use of historical analogies, such as Cyprus, South Arabia, and Palestine. Then, when the Provos' offensive campaign began sniping and bombing, the IRA strategy was to make Northern Ireland ungovernable while simultaneously eroding the desire of the British public to support continued repression. During the halcyon days of 1971 and 1972, when IRA volunteers were bombing the centers of Belfast and Derry, the Provo Army Council was inclined to think that the British government would concede as a result of the level of pressure alone. The Provos did not quite plan to win in the field but did anticipate a British military withdrawal, because the cost to stay would be too great—the Provo Army Council knew exactly how many British soldiers had been killed in South Arabia before the British army evacuated in 1967. When there was no British evacuation from Northern Ireland, even when the toll rose above that of South Arabia, but rather a decline in Provo capacity, the campaign was continued with the expectation that in a war of attrition the British public would tire first. One of the means to encourage such exhaustion was to open a second bombing front in Britain. Hundreds of bombs have been planted—small and large, symbolic, specific, and random, in the Tower of London, soldiers' clubs, Harrods' department store, shops, and tube stations. The bombing in Britain has not been particularly intense, but it has been persistent. The Provos thus felt that the military campaign, largely directed against the security forces in Northern Ireland, coupled with the British bombs, would in time convince the British public that the advantages of holding on to the six counties were minimal. In the process of a campaign of attrition, the Provos realized that if the British public were horrified, disgusted, and appalled at the "mindless Provo violence," then the prospects of evacuation would be greater.

While individuals, recognizing the pragmatic aspects of bombs, were willing to kill the innocent without warning, the Provo Army Council had always opposed operations against the innocent, advocated military operations, and insisted on bomb warnings. This warning policy had not been uniformly extended to Great Britain, and in mid-November 1974, Dave O'Connell, spokesman for the Provo Army Council, indicated that, in the case of economic and military targets, no warning would be given. There was, in fact, a warning just before the Birmingham bomb that killed seventeen people in two pubs exploded. Mistakes have clearly been made: an army bus was bombed, but soldiers' dependents were killed; car bomb warnings were given too late; and civilians were killed in cross-fire. Objectively, each of these accidents increased British disgust with the entire Irish involvement. So too did the assassination by the Provo Belfast Brigade on Army Council orders of two justices, both highly respected, both relatively moderate, one Catholic and one Protestant. Whether any but the Provos would consider the judiciary to be a legitimate target, there was no doubt that the killings produced widespread, outraged indignation and disgust. Whether this disgust could be translated into a net Provo gain remained uncertain, as the British public seemed equally disgusted with the lack of Protestant gratitude.

At the end of 1974, the Provos still intended to continue their war of attrition, for to call a halt would all but ensure that the capacity to act on events would disappear and any future return to guerrilla war would be very difficult. This war of attrition could not really erode the capacity of the security forces to respond, nor, probably, could new and violent Provo tactics provoke the British army into counterterror. Thus, the victim of Provo violence, whether an innocent civilian or a "legitimate" paratrooper, was not the target. The target was British public opinion. In time, the

British public, disgusted with the violence and exhausted by the pointless sacrifices for the ungrateful Irish, would demand a British evacuation that at the very least would save the lives of British soldiers, not to mention a good deal of money. The Provos felt that their strategy, adjusted to reality, was sound and their tactics, limited only by logistical problems and the erosion of the trained volunteer, were effective. As for the legitimacy of the campaign that killed the innocent and, so said many, risked civil war in the North, the IRA has always claimed the moral right to seek the Republic, denied the pretentions of the Dublin government, and presented tenuous legal arguments for its own continued existence. And if it is regularly denied in public and at the polls, there is evidence that many Irish Nationalists, both in the North and in the South, tolerate its presence, understand its motives, doubt its means, yet recognize its self-declared mandate.

The Official Irish Republican Army

Of all the groups involved in the Irish Troubles, perhaps none has given as long and as thoughtful consideration to the fashioning of an appropriate and evolving strategy, the selection of relevant tactics, and the relation of political and military priorities as the Official IRA. The Officials scorn the simple-minded "pure" military strategy of the Provos and the parochial ward politics of the Nationalist politicians. They are appalled by the poorly articulated, highly emotional response of the militant Loyalist working class, which the Officials feel should be a natural ally but which has been manipulated for capitalist gain. They recognize the British army as a faulty tool doomed to refining "military" tactics without strategic political relevance. Nor is the Official IRA without talent—it could probably supply a front bench equal to any in Ireland. The end result of this Official exercise, however, can in retrospect be seen to be an appalling mix of revolutionary models inappropriate for Ireland—rhetoric without substance, rationalization passing as analysis, dreadful blunders in the field, and spontaneous decisions that often reveal an emotive response little different from that of the Loyalist militants in a direction indistinguishable from that of the Provos.

The early, tortuous Official attempts to apply theoretical Marxist models of revolutionary stages (a "democratic" Stormont as a necessary stage) simply collapsed under their own weight when Northern events outran theory. Holding fast to old Republican conventions and assured by revolutionary colleagues elsewhere, the Officials believed in the ultimate collapse of working-class prejudice in Northern Ireland. The Officials insist that the Protestant working class has been deluded by British capitalism and will eventually recognize the necessity for class solidarity. The deluded Protestants, despite occasional whimpers of interest, have failed to act as programed by the Officials over a period of five years. The hope remains, however, occasionally fed by contacts and overtures. In any case, coupled with this class analysis came the contradictory impulse to defend "our" people—obviously Catholic, albeit often working-class. It was thus a tremendous relief to many Officials when, under Provo provocation, the British army—the traditional foe, the tool of the bosses in London, and the protector of the Stormont puppets—became the prime enemy during 1971. During the Officials' campaign against the army, before the self-imposed truce in May 1972, both ideology and sentiment were served. Other Official ventures, no matter how closely reasoned, hardly seemed to be cunningly crafted "political" operations, but were rather raw vengeance coupled with incompetence. The assassination attempt on John Taylor, a member of Stormont, failed, while amateur panic resulted in the "assassination" of Senator Barnhill. In response to Bloody Sunday in Derry, when the British killed thirteen demonstrators, the Officials threatened vengeance in like numbers—hardly a Marxist-Leninist tactic—but their bomb at the Aldershot regimental headquarters of the paratroops killed cleaning women and a Catholic priest to boot. Stripped of revolutionary verbiage, this was at worst vengeance and at best intimidation. Thus, even when Official analysis appears to be in phase with Northern Irish reality, Official operations occasionally raise doubts about the depth of any ideological commitment.

By May 1972, for a variety of reasons and at the end of several dubious operations, the Officials decided that futher offensive attacks would be self-defeating. IRA attacks simply alienated the Protestant working class. The Provos' bombs were sectarian. The Officials would only defend the people, but even defensive actions not tied to the conversion of the masses to Official principles could only save lives and not prepare for revolution and a new Ireland. The Officials' military truce, occasionally ignored for local reasons or as a result of official exceptions, continued, as did political agitation. There were in 1973 and 1974 sufficient hints that the increasingly militant Protestant working class might just consider an alliance to maintain hope in a workers' revolution. There was only limited evidence at the polls, particularly in the south, that there was a swing to the Officials, and the strains caused by the continued Provo campaign while the Officials practiced restraint resulted in internal dissent and the expulsion of the advocates of greater militancy. In sum, over five years, the Officials' strategy proved to be a mixture of Republican and orthodox revolutionary ideas that often failed as a guide to action, a tactical incompetence and indiscipline that frustrated strategic intentions, and a faith in the call of class that has yet to be answered.

Protestant Militants

Almost from the moment that it became clear that the civil rights movement was more than a wee ripple in 1968, the Loyalist response was swift, harsh, and traditional. Inspired by inflammatory oratory and without the need for excessive organization, the self-appointed defenders of the system came down hard with the boot. When this proved ineffectual, the agencies of the state often made abundantly clear their marginal interest in protecting the protesters from physical violence. In fact, it became difficult to distinguish—and properly so—the formal and the informal defenders of the system inasmuch as the order imposed by the agencies of the Stormont state equaled oppression in the eyes of the demonstrators. Derry in August 1969 became a battlefield for the aggressive police and the unintimidated Nationalist minority.

With the arrival of the British army—"their" British army in Loyalist eyes—there was no longer an immediate need for an aggressive, if informal, defense of the Stormont system. Only when the British army truly attempted to act as a peacekeeping force rather than as a surrogate of the Stormont system did the Loyalists react—and with violence—coming out into the streets for nightlong clashes with the soliders. From late 1969 to the beginning of the shooting war between the Provos and the British army in February 1971 and to internment in August 1971, the traditional, ritual humiliation of "them," the Protestants assumed that order would be imposed by the British army. The Stormont systems, with the odd concession to placate London, would be retained, and the comfortable past would return. It did not. The Provo-Official IRA campaign did not wane but escalated. By December 1971, the Conservative minister of home affairs, after a whirlwind visit to Northern Ireland, could hope only for a tolerable level of violence. Bloody Sunday in Derry made it very difficult for the Dublin government to close down the IRA in the south and attracted swarms of foreign journalists. There was a growing Loyalist unease that not only were the Provos not about to be humiliated but they were actually on the crest of a wave. The British, unable to impose order, might actually concede to the bombers. And this, indeed, proved to be the case.

In March 1972, Stormont was promulgated. The Loyalists felt betrayed. The papist Provos had bombed away their birthright. In July it was discovered that the Provos had even bombed their way to the bargaining table, meeting with a British minister outside of London. Violence had paid. The Loyalists took note and began organizing. Hurriedly, a variety of "leaders," arising out of the disarray of the Stormont system or up from the mean streets of East Belfast, began to compete in the Loyalist marketplace. The most militantly fashioned paramilitary groups had prepared informally and secretly to wreak vengance on "them." Overnight the Belfast Tartan street gangs became Loyalist defenders, while older and cruder men fashioned instant commando units or local battalions from the lads down the lane. The politicians sought to capture the center or sweep up the Right, harness working-class energy in the new Vanguard movement or devise a new formula like direct rule, that would appeal to all. The old monolithic Unionist Party collapsed into those who supported the new power-sharing assembly and those who looked to the past or to a different future. Seemingly at every opportunity, the Protestant population drifted to the Right, away from concession. All the while the Loyalist gunmen went right on killing in a campaign so disorganized that the murders went unrecognized. There was no Loyalist desire to rationalize the random murders with an elegant ideology or a foundation of moral justification.

The British attempt to build a middle ground on which to plant the new assembly, thus eroding IRA strength and lessening Loyalist anguish, faltered as the center dissolved. The assembly collapsed when the Protestant workingmen organized a general strike; a strike that the cabinet in London, apparently on the advice of the British army, reluctantly refused to break with force. The tactics of the general strike, enforced by militant gunmen, in no way interrupted the random murders—killing that, when recognized, resulted in a cycle of vengeance by Catholic gunmen uninterested in the restraints of Republican ideology. On their part, the Loyalist gunmen, unable to depend on the government in London, the British army, the old Unionist leadership, or the new political prophets out of the middle class, relied on the gun, held fast to the old slogans, recognized the enemy as "them," and maintained with minimal thought and negligible organization a murder campaign. Tactics were for the Loyalist gunman strategy.

The Counterinsurgent—The British Army

In the study of political violence, the inclusion of authorized force employed by the security agencies of the state has often been neglected. This has particularly been true with advanced, highly legitimate, democratic regimes, for the assumption by the comfortable has been that state recourse to counterterror—torture in the basement or the murder of prisoners—has largely been limited to either authoritarian states or insecure regimes in the underdeveloped world. Police brutality, for example, is, for those who have not been brutalized, a political slogan. When this assumption proves false, public opinion is scandalized at the "exception"—My Lai or torture in Algeria. War—and irregular war in particular—is always a brutal business, and that the rebels have adopted means often defined as illicit by those in authority should not really come as a surprise. Again the assumption has been that the truly frustrated are the rebels—the terrorist guerrillas—not the security forces. Yet it is the very irregular nature of the war that is apt to frustrate the security forces into mimicking what they perceive as rebel willingness to use any means, however illicit. When the security forces are found out by those with qualms, by journalists, or by their own excesses, the public in Britain or France or the United States is assured that such lapses are exceptions that are in no way related to the accepted tactics of war. And somehow it is the special, individual nature of such aberrations that horrifies. Strategic carpet bombing, even Hiroshima, can be explained to the public's satisfaction more easily than one dead child in an Asian ditch. And insurrections produce murders in ditches as a matter of course.

In the case of Northern Ireland, the British public has assumed that any lapse from appropriate legal behavior by the security forces is rare and is then only the result of outrageous provocation and is always vastly exaggerated by "the terrorists." Everyone knows that the British soldier is under severe restraint in the north, must account for his actions and for any shots fired, and has a special card listing the rules. The British army, furthermore, has shown more restraint than any other force would have in a similar situation, as the record has indicated in Palestine, Aden, and Malaya. This is, however, faint comfort for the "exceptional" victim. In the recent Irish experience, what cannot be avoided, even by Anglophiles, is the systematic use of military force beyond that conventionally employed by any police force to maintain order and in ways not congenial to disinterested public opinion. This excludes the various "legal" problems surrounding the use of extraordinary powers to arrest, detain, ban, fine, question, and imprison without trial—to in fact pass laws that permit the normal canons of law to be set aside because of the needs of the moment. To be snatched from one's bed without explanation, questioned for days, verbally threatened, interned again without explanation for years while one's family is harassed by repeated searches, however unpleasant, falls only on the margin of the authorized use of state violence. When a suspect is tortured, a wanted man murdered in the street, an "illegal" crowd machine-gunned, or a captive killed, either as a matter of policy or without penalty, then the agencies of the state have gone beyond the conventions of democratically controlled security forces. In Northern Ireland, British security forces have overstepped that bound, whether it be systematically, erratically, or inevitably.

The British army has seen and been allowed to see as a primary mission the defeat of the Provos—Irish terrorists engaged in an urban guerrilla war with British soldiers as their prime target. In following the evolving British military doctrine fashioned to respond to Provo tactics and Provo assets,

British units have transformed the original peacekeeping mission into a low-intensity war more congenial to army doctrine. The result, perhaps inevitably, has been a high level of military violence despite avowed efforts to restrict individual initiative, limit wild firing, and control spontaneous brutality. For the vulnerable, the efforts have not been particularly impressive. Over fifty civilians, for example, have been killed by error. Many of these "accidents" were reported first as deaths of suspects until eyewitness accounts indicated the contrary. The single most distressing such incident, Bloody Sunday in Derry, revealed that efforts had been made to plant weapons on the dead, and the ultimate British investigatory report by the chief justice of England, Lord Widgery, despite his vast credulity, could not quite clear the British army. The security forces had somehow killed thirteen innocent people by mistake. The weight of the evidence since 1971 is that, despite real efforts to restrict the men in the field, a remarkable number of innocent civilians have been killed in error. The Nationalist population, justifiably alarmed, has been fearful that this might be a consciously crafted British campaign to intimidate them.

Such an assumption seems more logical to the threatened not only because of the discovery of British soldiers in civilian clothes hiding in ambush positions waiting for "suspects," but also because of the evidence of brutality surrounding the initiation of internment in August 1971. The British deep-interrogation process differed from torture only in that the soldiers involved did not enjoy inflicting pain, according to the official published British investigation. That sophisticated psychological techniques were coupled with pain has been demonstrated, and that, unlike "accidental" shootings, was demonstrably official army policy. The distinction between the interrogator liking or not liking his work was lost on those involved, Nationalist opinion, and disinterested observers. That deep interrogation has been suspended so that those questioned as suspected "terrorists" are now far less likely to be brutalized and that torture in any case is not to the British advantage may be true, but again the threatened feel that the new restraint of the British army could be only momentary, retained through the fear of future exposure. And in any case, spontaneous, ruthless brutality continues when suspects are arrested or stopped during searches and sweeps. Rubber bullets hit too many women and old men. The toll of civilians who have been shot by mistake grows. The rumors of British assassination squads find many takers.

What is clear is that the low intensity campaign waged under British military doctrine has stretched the bounds of the permissible, at least for operations within the United Kingdom that are readily visible on the evening news. Way off in Aden or Kenya, the army may have justified its reputation for restraint, but under the television cameras in Northern

Ireland, the security forces have demonstrated that their actions are difficult to reconcile with the pronounced ideals of British society. For much of the British public, which is convinced that other armies would be more dreadful and that the IRA provocation has been unbearable, the lapses, even if systematic, have been easy to excuse. In the heel of the hunt, counterinsurgency is a brutal business, and while the security forces may not be waging a campaign of terror against the Provos, they have still terrified the innocent without intimidating the guilty.

The Urban Guerrilla—The Provisional IRA

That the Provos are guilty of terrible deeds has become axiomatic and, even within Republican circles, produces only painful rationalizations that it cannot be denied that the innocent must pay a price for Irish freedom, willingly or not. The tactics and techniques of the traditional rural guerrilla have, over the years, been gradually legitimized. In theory, uniforms are worn, prisoners taken, torture eschewed, and civilians respected. In practice, irregular rural wars tend to lead to irregular practices by both the guerrillas and their opponents. In the countryside, as often as not, uniforms are discarded or ignored, and torture is defended by elegant rationalizations or resorted to at the first opportunity. Civilians are assassinated, carpet-bombed, and shot as suspects or informers. Prisoners are not taken. Still, relatively speaking, the distinction between civilians and combatants, military operations and open murder—the limits of violence—are recognized, if occasionally with reluctance. Rural guerrilla war is more or less a conventional form of violent confrontation. Such insurrections may be unconventional in form, but they are clearly military in intent. The same partial legitimacy is not as clear with urban guerrilla war, and despite the scenic and apparently rural setting of Northern Ireland, there is very little jungle in which to hide guerrilla operations. IRA operations in the countryside are not very different from those in Belfast or Derry. Whatever the traditional limits of rural guerrilla warfare, they barely apply in Northern Ireland.

The Provos only rarely wear their "uniforms," consisting of combat jackets and black berets and then only in the no-go zones of Derry and Belfast or at commemorations in the south. Bombing operations are regularly and overwhelmingly directed at economic targets (shops, garages, and hotels) rather than at military targets, with the not unexpected loss of civilian life. Improved British security has even forced the introduction of the proxy car bomb, with which the driver is forced to protect his hostage family by taking the vehicle to its target. Informers, off-duty policemen, soldiers on leave, strikebreakers, and suspected Protestant vigilantes become "legitimate" targets for Provo volunteers. Women who collaborate with the British are tarred and feathered. Men who are judged criminal are shot in the kneecap when they refuse to reform. All this is official IRA policy. For some less discriminating volunteers or simple lads down the lane, any Protestant or any "suspect" becomes a victim in an atmosphere of moral decay and wanton murder. In the spiral of what theoretically passes as low-intensity war, with Provo ambushes in crowded streets, bombs detonating without warning, the assassination of judges, bank robberies for the cause, and hooded bodies shot in the neck, only the most determined can detect the limits on Provo violence or the bounds of urban guerrilla war.

The Provos do, of course, have bounds. It is policy to give bomb warnings—at least in Northern Ireland—so that not too many innocent civilians will involuntarily have to pay a price for Irish freedom. Others in the north or in Britain, as unofficial participants in the bombing campaign, have felt no compunction about denying a warning to the enemy, but Provo policy remains the same. From the Birmingham bomb that killed seventeen people, a Provo bomb, it is clear that the IRA technical capacity to deliver an effective warning has remained the same—doubtful. Certain targets are avoided as well—not only hospitals and the like but crucial "Protestant" targets such as the shipyards of Belfast, for these would be sectarian operations and certainly ensure Protestant retaliation. More symbolic sectarian targets have been bombed, in particular the towering statue of the Hero of the Londonderry Siege, which has been destroyed. The Provos have also largely avoided certain currently fashionable tactics, such as kidnapping, hijacking, asassinations in Britain, and certain strategic options; there are no operations in Southern Ireland. It is also Army Council policy to opt for the military target if possible, but this has hardly been obvious except in the repeated urban snipes and rural ambushes. Even when the target is a soldier, too often he is off duty and lured into a trap or killed by a mine or shot in the back, so that the means seems as illicit as the act.

The fact that the Provos attempt, as a matter of policy, to limit their military activities to those that are easily recognized as unconventional but within the guerrilla tradition can hardly convince the skeptic examining the evidence of the past four years. It may be that urban guerrillas, including Provos, are by nature violent, brutal, immune to humane considerations, willing if not eager to risk civilian lives, cunning, and callous. But in Northern Ireland the Army Council restraints and limitations imposed on the volunteers as a matter of policy have often been counterproductive and have permitted the war of attrition to drag on when an intensive dose of the horrors might have disgusted the British into withdrawal or counterterror.

Certainly the long, drawn-out dose has currently disgusted much of the British public and created an atmosphere in which evacuation has become a real possibility. In any case, the Provos do not see their actions as a campaign of terror. They intend not to intimidate either the Protestant population or the British army, but to create disorder and chaos, to force the British taxpayer to underwrite the destruction, and to affect British public opinion. That a great many people in Northern Ireland are terrified can hardly be denied, but the Provos, recognizing the results of the IRA bombing campaign in Britain of 1938–41 and the Blitz, accept that the British public cannot be coerced or terrorized.

At present, the Army Council is disappointed that the level of 1971–72 cannot at least be maintained with present equipment, but feel sure that the campaign of attrition can be continued and perhaps widened in Britain with more bombs. That innocent people are killed and blunders made are part of wars of liberation, and as far as the Provos can see neither the British army nor the Protestant vigilantes have shown much restraint. Still in all, despite the logical Provo strategy and predictable rationalizations, despite the recognized desire of the Provo Army Council to pursue a military campaign, many observers are convinced that the Provos are no more than bloodthirsty murderers who are incapable of thinking beyond the next bomb and so incompetent that more volunteers kill themselves than are killed by the British. Their "military" campaign has left a ruined province and a toll of innocent victims, has destroyed the political center, and contains only the promise that sectarian and intercommunal violence will escalate, perhaps into a general civil war beyond even the capacity of the British army to monitor. The critics of the Provos feel that not only are the means horrid but also the aim—a united Ireland.

The Armed Agitator—The Official IRA

The most articulate and knowledgeable critics of the Provos' pretentsions can be found within the ranks of the Official IRA. After all the shifts and turns of Official analysis and after deeds as bloodthirsty, horrid, and incompetent as those of the Provos, the present position of the movement stresses the political aspects of the crisis far more than the military possibilities. Putting aside the Provos' political aspiration—a four-province, federated Ireland of workers and small farmers as window dressing for more bombs—the Officials fear that continued violence, even directed against the British army, will further alienate the Protestant working class. By mid-1974, this was particularly galling because there were signs that the Protestants were turning from the old symbols toward a new class solidarity. The spontaneous general strike with a leadership emerging from those involved was impressive not simply for the Protestants' capacity to prevent an imposed British "solution" but for their demonstration of class solidarity without the need for elite leadership. There were even talks with the Ulster Workers' Council and Official Sinn Féin representatives. All this might be a long way from the Officials' ultimate goal, which includes a united Irish Republic, but did give hope that the Belfast working class could at least begin a dialogue about its own future. Thus, the Provo bombs only weakened class ties and led to demands for vengeance that, when effected, produced, even in official volunteers, a demand to continue the cycle. More distressing, when the Officials got in the way of the Provo-British army war, the volunteers were even less interested in showing restraint in regard to the occupying power. The Army Council's insistence that the Official IRA volunteer was an armed agitator, a member of a people's army, and a defender of life on the one hand and an advocate of revolution on the other might sound splendid at Gardner Place in Dublin, but many of the lads off the Falls wanted action. In the past, under provocation or as a result of policy, the Dublin center had initiated operations that had satisfied this urge to act even when the act had proved difficult to explain ideologically. Also, in the past, Official volunteers had not waited for the good word from Dublin.

By 1974, then, putting aside the Officials' pretensions of being the army of the people with a right to act for all the Irish people, the position of the Official Republican movement had evolved into a revolutionary, political posture with a detailed if idealistic program, with a searching if optimistic Socialist analysis of the Northern Ireland situation, and with the gun as only a last resort. Over the course of the preceding five years, however, the Officials had been involved in a variety of operations—some of which had been authorized only by a bare majority and were soon the subject of serious recrimination—that had placed the gun in the forefront of policy. What tended to differ about Official operations—and the distinction is by no means clear—is that while the Provos waged a "campaign," Official operations, however brutal, had been tied to specific events or existing political conditions. Officials tended to see movement, change, new options, and a dynamic political process, while Provos viewed events through traditional Republican glasses and hence produced traditional Republican answers: physical force will break the connection with England and there will be a new Ireland. The Officials scrambled to find the endless stages of political development in order to exploit the moment. That many of these "exploits" proved disastrous—the botched assassination attempt on Taylor, the unintended death of Senator Barnhill, the murder of a local Derry soldier home on leave from the British army, the Aldershot explosion—and that many were initiated locally in competition with the Provos has been obvious if not always admitted at Gardner Place. If Official analysis is now more rigorous and related more closely to Irish reality than to distant dialectics, if Official operations are now more politically fashioned and rigorously controlled, there are many who can easily recall the past blunders. And, more than anything else, the Officials' gun, when it is to be used, will be used in the name of working-class unity and with the belief that Protestants will in time opt for class interests. Scientific analysis aside, this is a proposition that many cannot support, and hence the elaborate Official rationalization for the revolutionary use of violence seems to some to be as simple-minded as the Provo exercise. In any case, the Officials' course record differs from that of the Provos more in degree than in kind.

The Sectarian Vigilante—The Protestant Loyalist

The Loyalist gunman in the Red Hand Commandos or the Ulster Volunteer Force certainly can see little difference between the Provos and the Officials. Both organizations, except for the odd showpiece Protestant, are wholly Catholic and dedicated to the establishment of a united Ireland that would be dominated by Catholics, who have always been manipulated by the hierarchy. The twenty-six-county Irish Republic has a "Roman Catholic" constitution, and there has been ample evidence that the Church has intervened in politics, which has not even been denied in Dublin. Any thirty-two-county Ireland, then, would be ruled by Rome. Objectively, no matter what they say or think, IRA gunmen are papal outriders. The entire rhetoric of the Loyalist-Protestant-Orange establishment, whether found in the speeches at Stormont or on the walls of the Shankhill in Belfast, has stressed defense of their way of life—"Not an Inch," "No Surrender." Since the entire Stormont system was fashioned to maintain Protestant domination within the six counties, there was little need for an unofficial defense. Why bother with a posse when the B-Special police militia could do as well? Why intimidate Catholic voters when the voting system was rigged? Why organize to oppose an IRA campaign when the province of Northern Ireland had paramilitary police and the British army on call? Thus, the monolithic Protestant community, united in the Orange lodges, controlling the Stormont state, and tied to Britain, could defend their own without recourse to covert violence. In fact, during the IRA campaign between 1956 and 1962, Stormont seldom had to call on the British army—the RUC and B-Specials did the job.

The Protestant monolith began to show signs of stress after 1962 when the premiers at Stormont and Dublin exchanged visits and proper people began talking of bridge building. Whatever the economic and social advantages of a rapprochement, the stern Loyalists saw none. A sign of the times was the creation of a new UVF under Gusty Spence, a little band of bigots whose "armed struggle" consisted of a miserable shooting in a Belfast side street of men innocent of anything but their faith. There was general indignation and no further unofficial violence until the beginning of the civil-rights campaign. Then counterdemonstrations, led by various self-appointed leaders like the Reverend Ian Paisley, and the partisanship of the police did not have the traditional effect—even worse, members of the Unionist leadership in Stormont began making reform noises with a weather eye toward Westminster. The riots of August 1969 and the arrival of the British army reassured some of the militants so that Protestant violence was sporadic, spontaneous (at times even directed against the British army), and traditional in form—riots, arson, and screaming mobs. When the Unionist premier Terence O'Neill appeared to be too moderate, a few bombs and some political infighting produced a change, but it soon became apparent that it was not one for the better. The politicans seemed too interested in British opinion, and the British army seemed too restrained in dealing with the Mickies. The last conventional response of the old system came with the introduction of internment in August 1971, and that produced war, not repression. As the months passed and the IRA campaign escalated, the militants lost faith in the British army. There followed one blow after another, until Stormont disappeared in March 1972.

Over the next two years, the various Loyalist schisms, splinters, alliances, and alignments became far too complex for distant observers. Conventional politicians attempted to form parties, fronts, or umbrella organizations that would direct fear and anguish into the appropriate channels. Britain tried to devise formulas or institutions that would again permit conventional politics and incorporate reforms from the discarded system. All the right people in London, Dublin, and the North urged moderation and restraint and pointed to the dangers of polarization. All this movement passed over the heads of the hard men in the back lanes of East Belfast or along the Shankhill. If Britain, the British army, the Unionist politicians, and the RUC would not or could not defend the system, then they would.

A variety of uncertain and often ephemeral groups clustered around one man or one area emerged. The most famous and the only one with even a fragment of continuity was the UVF. The original anti-Home Rule militants had organized the UVF in 1914, and Gusty Spence appropriated the title for his little group. Spence, while out on parole, was "kidnapped" and briefly rejoined the new UVF, oddly enough bringing with him some of the discipline, organization, and ideals of the IRA volunteers he had met in prison. Essentially the UVF and most of the other defenders were small, ill-formed bands of vigilantes, sometimes with elegant titles and formal meetings, other times with nothing but three men, a lifted car, a couple of guns, and the desire to knock off a Fenian. Over two years, various groups arose, merged, melted, and disappeared. In some areas the "defenders" went into rackets; in others serious efforts were made to link up all the vigilante groups. The politicians saw the potential danger of armed bands of men of no property roaming the streets and established their own paramilitary organizations. The main impact of the new militancy was the campaign of random assassination of Fenians, largely limited to Catholic males who stumbled into the wrong streets, worked in the wrong areas, or simply presented a target of opportunity to a cruising carload of armed defenders.

The purpose, if the killers could have articulated it, was simple and crude and might even in time have become effective—the Catholics would be punished for past errors, intimidated from future ambition, and, if need be, driven from the province. Since all Catholics were guilty of disloyalty, all were legitimate targets. Efforts to concentrate on the specifically guilty—Provos or Officials—were crude, ineffectual, or abortive. Almost no IRA man was a victim, even though the total number of victims in two years was well over 200. The campaign waged by crude men, often cruel and unsavory, attracted few idealists or politicians. Occasionally there would be anonymous explanatory leaflets, but few of those involved had the time or the interest to read reasoned statements. The militants could and did supply volunteers for a few more elegant exercises in violence. Thus, the cunningly timed car bombs in Dublin in 1972 assured that harder Irish security laws would be passed. Another bombing operation in the spring of 1974 that had been timed to kill pedestrians in Dublin and Monaghan was also intended to affect Dublin policy. In both cases, there were those who thought that the bombers had been used, perhaps even by the British army. While there had been "operations" in the Irish Republic by the UVF and others, the two major bombing operations appeared atypical. A typical UVF operation consisted of a burst of machine-gun fire through the window of a Catholic pub—hardly elegant, but effective.

The dubious battle against the Fenians spread from the mean streets of Belfast to other towns and finally to the countryside. There can be no firm numbers, but the death total had risen to about 250 and during the autumn of 1974 showed no signs of easing off. The Protestant militants, however, did not see themselves as murderers and terrorists: "The world is condemning us as murderers—we call ourselves patriots. We are fighting for Ulster's freedom." There are no motiveless murders, according to militant spokesmen, because if the background of the victim is examined, "Republican connections" can be found. With the odd exception, such rationalizations (and many Protestant gunmen don't bother) are hardly convincing. What is clear is that the murders are not motiveless and that vengeance and intimidation are unpleasant, particularly when the victim is randomly chosen. The victims are chosen, if indiscriminately, from the pool of the disloyal—male Catholics—all, even if unwittingly, traitors and potential "Republicans."

The assassination campaign of the militants has deep roots, building on a tradition of pogroms, riots, authorized arson, and tolerated violence against the Fenians. For over a century Belfast has had repeated riots, and for over a century the respectable Protestant community has "understood" the anxiety of "their" working class when threatened by Catholic domination. With the presence of the British army limiting the traditional riotous pogrom, the militants had simply shifted tactics and extended the time scale. The killings may indeed have the desired effect of intimidating the Catholic population, coercing a mass emigration to the south, eroding the IRA base and thus saving the Loyalist way of life.

The burden of the present argument is that the definitional question of what is terror very much concerns the legitimacy of political violence. In the Irish case, none of those who have had recourse to force perceive their actions as illicit—illegal yes, but illicit no—and none advocate the use of terror. They are not murderers, but soldiers or volunteers, patriots or revolutionaries. Many would accept that they have made mistakes, that there have been excesses, but it is the others who have used systematic terror. Their own strategy and tactics, while open to misinterpretation, are sound, viable, and, given the situation, within permissible limits. The Protestant gunmen may choose random victims, but they do not set bombs that maim women and children. The British soldiers may use excessive force in interrogation or shoot civilians by mistake, but they do not murder from a ditch or booby-trap bodies. The IRA volunteers may execute an informer, but they do not drop screaming prisoners from a helicopter or shoot their next-door neighbor simply because he goes to a different church. What becomes clear is that all the violent actors in the Irish crisis respond to events within a clearly defined, historical tradition that to them—and often to them alone—legitimizes their tactics and determines their strategy.

The organization most readily visible as legitimate is the British army, which is licensed to kill within certain bounds by a recognized state. To a large degree even the IRA accepts the validity of that license and so defines "army terror" as those acts performed beyond the conventional limits. And for the Irish, like many other rebels before them, it is the British hypocrisy in denying any transgressions—torture without pleasure, murder by mistake—that so enrages them. If it were another army, not based on the admired British ideals, there would be less distaste; but the Irish, at least, have experienced hundreds of years of vengeance disguised as Crown justice. In any case, hypocrisy aside, the British army has crossed its own limits, not so much as a matter of policy but rather because there has been a systematic reluctance to punish the "guilty," thus encouraging subsequent transgressions.

Of all those involved, surely the assassination campaign of the Loyalist gunmen falls completely outside of conventional bounds. Yet the vigilante is hardly novel, even if the choice of random victims has had fewer takers. Given their record, it is small wonder that the Protestants fear "them," assume that all will be disloyal, and, if not disciplined, will strike back at the system. Thus, the Protestant community has regularly permitted or encouraged violent onslaughts on "them" in defense of the established system. In Northern Ireland, particularly in Belfast, the pogrom had almost been institutionalized as a means of control, and even with the establishment of the Stormont system in 1921, extralegal violence was not entirely eschewed. Thus, the Red Hand Commando is a patriot to his neighbors even when arrested by the RUC for a "motiveless" murder, for his neighbors and the RUC know the motive even if they do not know the victim's name.

While the British army is not unduly troubled by problems of legitimacy and the question seldom concerns the UVF, the Republican movement has a highly complex historical and legal justification for the use of the gun, institutional restrictions on tactics, and a continuing concern with the issue. Ireland is a moral country and there must be a sound justification for political murder, no matter what the goal, if the volunteer is not to have a troubled mind and the public witthdraw toleration. There are legal reasons why the present IRA, Provo or Official, depending on one's interpretation, can claim to be the real army of the Republic, authorized by the Second Dáil, while the "Free State Army" was a child of an illegal Dáil. This is too arcane for most volunteers and the public at large. For a great many years, every Irish politican has publicly proclaimed the end of partition a goal and a united Ireland the grail of hundreds of years of struggle. Privately their views vary and, patently, beyond oratory the Dublin governments have done little. For fifty years, history as taught in a great many schools in Ireland has been a serious factor in persuading many young men to continue the struggle. And less visible but more real has been the collective memory of repression and struggle, a doubt about the moral authority of the state, and an admiration of those who resist. Even the establishment of an Irish state has not eroded the love of a rebel. Although few will vote for trouble or want his own involved, a general toleration exists. Recent events often encouraged this tendency because so many in Ireland see the IRA as the only viable defender of the Northern Catholics. Consequently, the IRA volunteer can be assured of the toleration of many, the support of some, but, most important, the comfort of a very long tradition that insists that his actions are legitimate, his goals those of the nation, and his ideals those of the people. His army may not have banners, but it is an army, not a vigilante mob; his army may not have uniforms, but it fights for the Irish people, not to maintain a British colony.

In sum, all the actors feel legitimate, and all act within a tradition that authorizes their strategies and limits their tactics. Each is a patriot, none a murderer. All are rational, some even reasonable, their course, if single-minded, set from a partially understood past toward a specific if improbable goal. As with most other lethal political questions, the ground has been strewn with myths, special pleading, fine slogans, and elegant rationalizations. The distant observer may select from the lot, but the burden here is relatively simple. Even if the perceptions of those involved differ from those of the alien eye, the gunmen are not mindless, and their strategies and tactics are shaped by tradition and policy.

In fact, one of the concerns of contemporary political scientists that seemed to only marginally touch the Ulster Troubles has been that of legitimacy. In Ireland, of course, this aspect of politics has a long and troubled history. Who has the right to speak for Ireland? And, then, who the right to govern it? Outside, beyond the island, there are academic questions of elites and divided nations, support and ethnic schism, inequality and social order. And in the arena of action, it is rare to uncover a gunman that is not a patriot, a rebel without a legitimate cause, a killer beyond the trumpet's echo. Some contemporary gunmen (terrorists to the threatened) seek nations that never were (South Molucca or Croatia), struggle for a fettered mass bemused by capitalist consumer opiates (television, fast cars, and council houses), fight for the old gods of Franco Spain or Fascist Italy, or seek simple vengeance or history's verdict rewritten. Ireland knows almost all of them, even if the advocates of ideological crusades have been few and feeble—the Blue Shirts dispatched to Spain and the advocates of the Red Flag ignored and futile.

In Ireland the faithful Republicans, uncompromising, pure, beyond concession in matters of principle, have never conceded their right to speak for the nation. Eamon De Valera needed only to look into his own heart to know the desires of the Irish people, and to act on them even when the people's representatives opposed him. No one, whether elected or not, had the right to draw a line to a nation's march. So with or without the shaky scaffolding of legal arguments, the support of shards of old Dáils, the skilled reading of historical tea leaves, the real Republicans for over a century have built on their rock of legitimacy. And for those conventional representatives of the Irish people, North and South, serving a nation or a province made manifest at the polls, responsible for law and order, justice, day-to-day accounts, the getting and spending, nothing is more outrageous than the pretensions of the gunmen. The IRA Army Council speaks for the movement and the movement for Ireland; the volunteer kills with historical precedence and present authorization. And such a volunteer is not limited to Ireland but is everywhere to be found, moving to the trill of those invisible trumpets, not to murder, but to justified operations in the service of a secret army. Some of those armies are founded on the oppression of all classes, some on the ruin of a great world view or the future salvation for the faithful; most, however, are dedicated to a nation denied. Most are filled with volunteers, idealists armed with a legitimate cause, permitted violent dissent against present injustices. The Irish experience has a general echo, the Irish gunmen distant shadows.

11

Men with Guns:
The Legitimacy of Violent Dissent

Europe, East and West, has not seen a boundary change in thirty years, and, unlike the generation of stability after the unification of Germany and Italy, there are no serious irredentist claims. Not only have the boundaries been static but also to a very large extent so have the state institutions. Efforts to modify by various means the Eastern Marxist regimes failed in Poland and Germany without recourse to the direct Soviet military intervention that proved necessary in Hungary and Czechoslovakia. In Greece there has been the interregnum of the colonels, while Portugal and Spain have moved from authoritarianism toward democracy. Elsewhere, except for the emergency of the De Gaulle Republic, European institutions have been unchallenged, and, quite often, even in the West, a single party has dominated the political processes.

As a general rule the opportunity for men with guns to murder for the cause does not exist in efficient, brutal, authoritarian states. The swift and adamant repression by the threatened center—and the absolute acceptance that maximum coercion will be used—dissuade even the most frustrated and the most ambitious. In Eastern Europe the challenges to authority—essentially Soviet control—have arisen spontaneously. Budapest in 1956 was not the end result of a conspiracy or an urban guerilla campaign; there were no gunmen involved in Polish demonstrations or in the government offices of Prague. Only in Yugoslavia, where a relatively open internal society on top of old ethnic flaw lines, might there now be room for the gunmen. Certainly the Croatian diaspora has sought to bring the struggle into the homeland but have been more visible and more effective elsewhere in employing the techniques of spectacular terror in hijackings, assassinations, and escapes. For Eastern Europe, then, the operative word has been effective; ineffectual repression, the end product of incompetence or the restraints of the democratic society or failing of will or talent, permits armed dissent while brutal, ineffectual repression encourages it. At the present time, then, all that exists in the East is a distant potential, perhaps not so distant in Yugoslavia, but as yet invisible to most observers. Some of the pressures of bloc conformity have been eased and with them the tensions that endanger the existing regimes. In very slight diversity there is strength and hence stability.

Rather the reverse seems to have been the direction of events in Western Europe. There the three decades have been a tide toward interdependency. The outward symbols have been the creation of various regional political, military, and economic institutions—the EEC, the European Parliament, Euratom, and NATO. These formal structures largely reflect the gradual and as yet imperfect creation of Europeans—those with French nationality who work in London for Royal-Dutch Shell, wear Italian shoes, drive German automobiles, and holiday in Sweden. There remain, of course, vast national-bound differences, not the least being language. But the trend, definitely and irreversibly, has been the erosion of splendid isolation, the fashioning of Western European institutions, and the rise of a single, postindustrial, style of life. Europe is, of course, still pocked with regional habits, parochical concerns, and those by-passed by the new consumer society. The assumption of most, however, has been that national differences will continue to decay, that Western Europe will incrementally move toward a unity retaining ample diversity to satisfy local values and the American tourist. Tomorrow will be like yesterday.

Continuity does not necessarily mean stability and, for Europeans with unsatisfied national aspirations, does not even bestow legitimacy. There are those who see the present European state system—especially its economic success and stability—as institutionalized tyranny that denies just national aspirations or the appropriate form of government or even the inevitable triumph of a liberated proletariat. Simply *because* the system is effective and stable and appears beyond serious challenge, those who dissent have become desperate. Few believe, as did those with unsatisfied desires in 1875 or 1895, that sooner or later a European war will shatter the old molds. After 1870 the French anticipated, sooner or later, conditions that would permit the return of Alsace and Lorraine, and the revolutionary anarchists a capitalist war that would sap the system. The Greeks awaited the collapse of Turkey, the Serbs the fall of the Austrian-Hungarian Empire, the Poles some transformation that would free Warsaw. Violent change was not only desirable but also probable. In 1977 a war in Europe, in an area of uneasy detente, under the shadow of a possible nuclear confrontation between the two great powers, while hardly unthinkable appeared first unlikely and second a certain disaster for all. If an interstate war as a *deus ex machina* of change cannot seriously be envisaged, then those who dispute the present order must seek other means. Because the tides of interdependency run swiftly, they must do so *now* rather than at some future moment when the appropriate objective revolutionary conditions exist. Thus, at the very time that most observers in the new Europe recognized the direction of history, the end of parochial nationalism and violent politics based on universalism or particularism—a new generation of revolutionaries have appeared. Under various strange devices they deny the legitimacy of the new order, speak in the names of peoples, classes, and nations either long ignored or thought long satisfied.

Ethnic Separatism

With few exceptions, those who seek to liberate nations unnoticed except by specialists and antiquarians accept that the tides are against them. In ten years or twenty the language will be lost, the young will have migrated to the Saar, the old farmers and old ways will have died out and the houses bought up by Dutch businessmen for vacation villas. One need only go to the West of Ireland to see the ruined stone hovels of a peasant population now living in a Celtic diaspora—Boston or Liverpool or Sydney. They now speak English and are lost to a nation that is but a pale copy of London fashions, a park for tourists, a site for branch offices. It is not romantic Ireland that is dead and gone but a vital, living people with their own language, with their own ways, but with no control over their future. And everywhere on the periphery of Europe the process continues to the anguish of the Basques or Corsicans or Welsh. Consequently, the submerged nations have been breeding grounds for separatist movements, some little more than folklore societies, others engaged in national liberation struggles by recourse to guerrilla warfare. To a greater or lesser extent all the separatists deny the legitimacy, if recognizing the capacity, of the center, no matter that at the center is a democratic government, no matter that at the periphery is a "nation" that has been submerged for centuries. All want a devolution of authority, if no more significant than support for regional differences, even the "right" to name children in Breton rather than choose a "French" name from an authorized list. Some, however, want to fashion an independent nation—a Basque Republic.

The separatists, in nearly every case, form a triangle. At the bottom nearly everyone wants to emphasize the special differences (in dress or habits or tongue) if it is to local advantage, that is, helps the tourist trade or neighborhood pride. Often submerged nations on the periphery have been scorned—their dress or habits or tongue decried from the capital as crude, obscure, the outward symbols of those left behind who in time would give up Gaelic for English, Catalan for Spanish, put away "peasant" clothes and live like the others. Thus, a first step in separatism is the creation of pride, a new national commitment to counteract the lures of the center. And the center offers tangible societal advancement, incorporation into the universalist future, prizes of the pocket and place in preferment. Thus, a national literature must be discovered or created and distributed; national sports and games must be introduced and imposed, the national language lauded and used, and the old symbols imbued with new meaning. The pragmatist, however, must be convinced that Basque or Irish has a value that Spanish or English does not, that speaking Welsh will not assure an economic penalty in an English world. Obviously all of this is a slow process. This old nationalism, eroded by the charms of the modern world, often resides in the most pragmatic or rural populations that have retained the old ways and tongue by necessity, not choice. Even with all the resources of the state and the use of coercion, the Irish government has not been able to revive the Irish language as a living tongue. The Catalans or the Basques, therefore, have ample evidence that devolution can come too late, that the central language has incalculable drawing power, that the time to act is now. Thus, further up the triangle are those who want simply to be different and to encourage that difference and to possess the power to protect that difference. They advocate regional authority, control over the existing assets, the devolution of real power from the center as a right. Thus, the Scottish Nationalists include both those who simply want to be different and those who have formed a particular separatist political party to seek devolution of political and economic power by democratic means. In this they followed part of the Irish pattern of agitating for Home Rule within the parliamentary system and as yet, unlike the Irish, have not produced those who advocate recourse to violence, civil disobedience, mass protests, boycotts and assassinations, or any mix of such tactics. In fact, as one moves toward the peak of the separatist pyramid, those fewer and fewer want more and more—a Welsh Republic, not some squalid little regional council conceded grudgingly from Westminster. And they are willing, as their aspirations become more extreme, to seek more extreme means than the system will tolerate: symbolic Breton bombs in Paris, a shot fired at the French Foreign Legion in Corsica, and ultimately an armed struggle waged with limited resources and irregular tactics. These, the nationalist rebels, have always been few, certainly in the beginning when someone, someplace must strike the first blow. They speak, however, for the nation—a nation that need not be polled for they need look only into their own hearts to know the desires of the people.

These separatists claim for themselves the authority of an inchoate nation, repressed through the years by alien conquerors. Once the submerged nation is liberated, many of the inherent problems (e.g., a decaying economy, emigration, a decay in the cultural and linguistic heritage, and the importation of foreign foibles) will be solved, usually by the introduction of some form of socialist equalitarianism and the redistribution of the national assets, the end of manipulation from the center and the appropriate exploitation of national resources. In some cases (e.g., Scotland) such a program, now advocated by a minority, has a basis in reality, but in any case the problem facing the militant separatists is to convert the skeptical—or at least secure their toleration—and to fashion a counterstate, a shadow institution draped in historical legitimacy.

Ireland

In Ireland in 1969-70 the Provisional Irish Republican Army evolved out of a split within the Irish Republican movement. The Provisionals sought and still seek to establish in all thirty-two counties of Ireland a small farmers' and workers' government—an aspiration that would remove the six counties of the North from the United Kingdom and replace the Republican government in Dublin with an all-Ireland successor. The Provisionals are thus opposed by Westminster, by Dublin, and by whatever regional government might exist in the North. This is particularly so, for the prime means the Provisional IRA has used in attempting to "break the connection with England" has been physical force—guerrilla warfare: rural ambushes, letter bombs, assassinations, extortion, theft, sabotage, arson. The whole spectrum of tactics of irregular warfare has been employed not only in the North but also in English cities. In Dublin, as well as London, the Provisionals are scorned as terrorists, unsavory murderers whose claim to represent anyone but themselves is ridiculous. The Provisionals speak for no one. No one respectable in Britain or Ireland recognizes their claims and postures. Their "military" campaign is brutal, murderous, and counterproductive. Their talent is minimal; their future lies in prison or in conversion to reason and the claims of legitimacy authority. The position was made quite clear over fifty years ago by the then Irish Minister of Justice, Kevin O'Higgins:

> We will not have two governments in this country, and we will not have two armies in this country. If people have a creed to preach, a message to expound, they can go before their fellow-citizens and preach and expound it. But let the appeal be to the mind, to reason rather than to physical fear. They cannot have it both ways. They cannot have the platform and the bomb. [*Dail Debates,* Vol. X, col. 280]

In 1923 O'Higgins was speaking to those who belonged to a movement (the IRA) that could trace its organizational roots back to 1849 and the Irish Republican Brotherhood and beyond that to the example of Wolfe Tone, who in 1798 merged the ideals of the French revolution with those of Irish nationalism. The men of physical force, disdaining electoral means or even riotous protest, sought again and again to break the connection. After each adventure there seemed fewer of the faithful and fewer remaining chances to use physical force.

When the civil rights campaigns of 1968-69 in Northern Ireland sparked sectarian violence, the IRA was too weak to play any significant role as a defender of the Nationalist population. The result was the split that produced the Provisionals—the classic descendents of the men of physical force who had found a new role and a new popularity in the North, new toleration by some in the Fianna Fáil government in the South, and a new source of aid and comfort in the Irish diaspora. By 1971 their new campaign was underway, tolerated by the Nationalist population, angered by the British army's apparent bias against them. The next year saw Bloody Sunday in Derry, the end of the Northern Ireland Parliament, talks between the Provisionals and British cabinet officers, a truce, renewed violence, and the beginning of a five-year campaign of attrition.

During this time the Provisionals' position remained that they represented the ideals of the Irish nation, that Britain was an alien, occupying power, that the Dublin parliament was a pawn of the British, that any Northern assembly was equally illegitimate, and that only all the Irish people, North and South, had the right to decide the institutions of the nation. Ireland was occupied by an imperialist British army in the six counties in the North and their Irish allies in the South. Outside the Republican movement few took these pretensions very seriously; most, however, took the Provisionals very seriously. They had a veto power over any political initiative in the North and the capacity to cause untold harm in the South. And no matter how unsavory their military campaign might become they could not quite be disowned by the Northern minority who feared that someday the Protestant majority might turn on them using the security institutions of the Province. If such an attack were tolerated by London and unhindered by the Dublin government, doomsday would come. Thus, there had to be some Provisional defenders on the ground. So the IRA was tolerated by many, North and South, whose fear of doomsday was greater than their loathing of IRA violence. And the Provisional IRA did in fact have real assets as well.

Traditional Legitimacy

The foundation that permits the operation of the Irish Republican movement has quite literally been centuries in the making and cannot readily be eroded by right reason or by the grating of a new reality. The Republicans have been strengthened by nearly two centuries of uncompromising efforts to break the British connection. They have claimed, and their claims until recently have seldom been denied by those seeking office,

that the Republican revolutionary tradition has been largely responsible
for what freedom Ireland has gained—that violence works. This legacy of
patriots has been accepted in Ireland as real history, not myth or legend.
Those who would deny the benefits accrued through an armed struggle,
balance politics, agitation, and concession against physical force, have until recently been in a minority. Even today a great many of the Irish read
their past as a long confrontation with British power and accept the present
IRA as, deserving or no, heirs to a heritage of struggle. Almost all the
effective symbols of the state, almost all the most gripping patriotic myths,
almost all of the stuff of history so authorizes this legitimacy.

When at the funeral of a fallen volunteer, the Provisional IRA march
slowly to the wail of pipes, impassive under black berets, awaiting the final
volley over the grave of another patriot and martyr, there is a moment of
deep emotion. No one believes for a moment that Fianna Fáil is truly a
"Republican" party and all that this means in Ireland; no one feels very
deeply about an Irish army parade or the opening of the Dáil. For over fifty
years the elected politicians have employed the Republican rhetoric,
praised the old heroes, advocated their goals, and accepted their means.
After all, De Valera's new 1937 Constitution insisted that Dublin's writ
should run over all thirty-two counties. No one seeking office wanted to
draw the bounds to the nation. Most of all, no one wanted to point out the
distressing impact of incorporating a million Protestants into a system that
worked quite nicely for the Church, the men of some property, the existing
parties and institutions.

So, for almost all the history of the state there was no dissent on the
"national issue." The various efforts of the major Irish parties to defuse the
Republican bomb in no way tampered with Republican ideals and in no
sense created a parallel rhetoric. In fact, the strongest single attraction of
the Republican movement increasingly became the obvious hypocrisy of
the legitimate institutions. Men who cried havoc on the platform were all
too content to concentrate on getting a penny more on milk. Politicians
who served in the "official" Republican party were all too willing to jail and
intern those who sought to turn oratory into action. Thus, a Republican
commemoration is real; a real young man is dead; the flag on his coffin is
not just a banner; the volley over his grave is not just a sordid ritual but a
reward and a promise. The state has been left without the rites of legitimacy—five decades of overt hypocrisy have allowed these assets to slip
into militant hands. And emotive ritual dramas cannot be easily repossessed or new ones easily created.

The Old Ideals

What the IRA ritual summons forth in public is an attitude toward
history and toward existing institutions. For a great many of the Irish, all

with long and exacting memories, there has seldom been an intimate connection between justice and law, law and order. The agencies of order were often considered, justly, as imposed; the laws constructed to preserve others' privileges, and the Crown's justice no more than mean self-interest. Forbidden their religion, paupers in a green land, denied education, advancement or common decency, few could see a communality of interest with the Ascendency landlords, with the agencies of the Crown, with *them*. Laws were to be evaded or changed, not obeyed. Opposition, silent or violent, was the only legitimate means of change. Concession, compromise, changing times, prosperity, or prospects did indeed erode this posture. But in the South basically an abiding suspicion remains. No one, of course, really considers the Irish uniformed police as agents of the Crown or as plots to evade democratically elected laws. In the North, injustice was, and many feel still is, institutionalized. "Political crime" truly exists in Ireland, and the IRA, whether engaged in train robbery in the South or random bombing in the North, can continue to feed on a considerable pool not so much of sympathy—certainly not lately—but rather toleration. The informer, no matter how highly motivated by democratic ideals, by loyalty to the state, remains hateful. Thus Ireland, really a most law-abiding state, still is populated by those whose dedication to democracy, to the proposition that now law and justice are truly linked, still somehow, cannot easily betray those Dublin calls "men of violence." And most especially so, when over the past decade at times the only defender of the embattled Northern minority has been the volunteers of the IRA. No matter how brutal or unsavory the IRA may appear, they at least are *there*. This by no means indicates that all the Irish tolerate the IRA, only that the habits of the past coupled with the situation in the North create an ambivalence.

A New Role

It is in fact the events in the North that give the present IRA a legitimacy related neither to the old rituals nor the old attitudes. Once the civil rights movement had engendered a Protestant backlash, very few in the South trusted the police or the British army to defend—effectively, or in time, or perhaps at all—the Northern minority. The "Republican" Fianna Fáil had opted to stand back. The victory of the opponents in 1973 did bring to the fore those who at last, if haltingly, in public denied the historical aspirations of the Nationalists. There was no longer an inalienable right to unity, and increasingly there was no longer any interest in a unity that would cause chaos and undesired change, North and South. If civil war came to the North—and surely the victims would be the outnumbered minority—then Dublin would, could, do nothing. That very few people *really* wanted a united Ireland, that very few in the South would benefit by a united country and many might suffer, that without harsh sacrifices no Dublin government would be capable of acting on Northern events, all might be true. But the desertion of the Northern Catholic population, whether logical or inevitable, caused grave concern and some guilt. Thus, *at least* the IRA was there, doing something, holding a thin line. If the IRA were hounded and crushed, what then?

So the IRA has three factors to exploit: possession of living historical rituals that grant legitimacy of a long tradition, the reluctance of the population to betray those who advocate the old ideals of the people, and a position as Catholic defenders in the North. It would appear that certainly the first two and perhaps the last are wasting assets. Yet old ways and old dreams change—but slowly. There is a charm about myths that the new realities of the democratic state cannot quickly or easily erode. Fifty years of political cant are not suddenly discarded; there are years of debts yet to fall due. New rituals and myths cannot be fashioned at will, new attitudes summoned up by emergency legislation, and old responsibilities discarded in the name of practicality. Ireland has not always been a very practical country, has often preferred the old myths to the new realities, and still can be touched by the old dreams made manifest in the old ways.

The Irish case is special, most cases are, but the ideological pretensions are similar to those found elsewhere. The movement speaks for the nation, no matter how often the nation denies them at the ballot box, and for a higher and more compelling authority—the people. And the movement, being pure and unwavering, beyond cant or compromise, holds true to the national ideals without the need to mess in the day-to-day political process of compromise and manuever and the corruption of high purpose. Possessed of the truth, the movement also demands the moral right to resort to physical force—more important in Ireland than elsewhere—to oppose the oppressor who can "only thus" be defeated. Politics, like prostitution, is alluring but corrupting. Only an armed struggle will win the nation. Presently in Europe small groups of patriots in submerged nations have accepted many of these assumptions, speak for old nations, if in recent revolutionary rhetoric, and call for violence in the people's name. Far larger groups in these submerged nations deny the gunmen's presumptions, but in turn share some, and occasionally all, of their aspirations. And toleration for the guerrilla is sufficient in the Basque country now, perhaps in Wales or Scotland tomorrow.

The greatest risk of disorder arising from ethnic separatism exists where a real rather than an imaginary community exists with a different religion or a different language and always a different heritage. If there can be a Maldive Island Republic, why not a Basque Republic or a Free Scotland?

Elsewhere on the European periphery, the advocates of a Free Sardinia or a Bavarian Republic seem unlikely to appear or to fashion an alternative nation. Sicilians want more from the Italian system rather than separation. There are, as well, in Europe little noted pools of ethnic isolation quite without historical legitimacy or present national aspirations: Turks in Germany, Algerians in France, South Moluccans in the Netherlands. As time passes they come to live in two worlds, being part of neither, increasingly alien to the Turkish village or the Spice Islands, yet not German and not Dutch. Again it seems more likely that their aspirations will be toward absorption—as yet an alien option in much of Western Europe. The Portuguese colonialists or the French Algerians are easy to manage, coming back to a "home" they never knew, disgruntled and often violent; in time they can be melded in the homeland. The "foreign" workers and their families are another and more difficult matter—as a new generation of South Moluccans demonstrated. In any case, so far their aspirations do not reflect on inchoate ethnic legitimacy but rather interest in a better deal. The real alternative legitimacies remain those of the Catalans or Bretons or Scots. There, without the greatest of care, the inevitable process of devolution may lead to the violence of the Basque country or Ulster when the old myths clash with new realities.

In the academic concern with myths and realities, the nature of legitimacy, and the problems and probes of analysis, it is easy to forget that the subject is real. There are actual people concerned, those with dearly held ideals and ideas who, too, have addresses, school friends, daily rounds, bad habits, and often regular jobs. In the ballads and legends, the IRA seems filled with romantic gunmen, foolish patriots, martyrs determined on blood sacrifice. The IRA volunteer appears with dreary regularity in new thrillers, bad films, and, of course, in the pages of terrorist typologies or revolutionary texts. The myths have pretty well snuffed out the facts across the spectrum of sad songs crooned in safe snugs and the clinical display of numbers, charts, and graphs in university seminars.

While the IRA volunteer is different from his apolitical friends or old classmates, he is hardly, in real life, the stuff of legends. A few in various fields have surely consciously used their art to serve their cause—Dylan Thomas as Poet, Brendan Behan as Irish rebel, and Salvador Dali as surreal painter—but with a cost. The IRA, however, offers a mission, a sacrifice, rigid discipline, not a role. There *are* hard men but no typical gunmen, few martyrs-in-waiting, not even a merry plow boy. Still, it is possible to depict the real people behind the fancy titles of the secret army and the nature of most volunteers. There are no great surprises. In particular no one, teacher, parent or friend, seems to be able to determine who will go into the IRA, who will opt for Liverpool or London, who will stay home in the narrow lanes of Ulster violence, living what passes as a normal life.

The IRA volunteer is not much different, in fact often quite like his opposite in the British army: a working-class male, moderately ambitious, slightly romantic, a bit of an idealist, in need of discipline and excitement. For him, however, no promise of promotion or pension, no uniform, no assured monthly wage, fringe benefits, or open bugle call. Service in the invisible army of the Republic pays wages in pain, imprisonment, wasted years, and terror. Time and tenure may erode both ideals and romance, excitement palls, discipline deadens, and ambition leads only to responsibility for failure and spilled blood. Purity may go, dribbled away along with years in prison or on the run or in the dreary rounds of routine. Still, there are always new volunteers, who mostly know the map ahead; it has been a long time since the IRA was thought romantic along the Falls or in the bandit country on the border. Others may sing of hunger strikes, prison escapes, or the rattle of a Thompson gun. But most volunteers sign on to a small, dreary, deadly underground army, financed by bank robberies, armed out of the diaspora (poorly and rarely), led by those determined on persistence as much as victory, dedicated if need be to suffering—an army that would have few takers except in Ulster. So behind the shadows of the gunmen, and the community of Irish rebels, the martyrs and patriot bombers are real people particularly organized to persist in a real, if low-intensity war.

In 1969, after the riots in Derry and Belfast, for the discarded men of physical force, for Republicans who had doubted the new radical directions, and for a great many apolitical young people alienated by institutionalized injustice and threatened by Loyalist mobs and the Protestant paramilitary RUC, the time had come for a different IRA leadership. It was clear, however, that unlike similar crises in the past, the present leadership controlled the machinery of Sinn Féin and the IRA. While an attempt would be made to take over the IRA reins by a democratic vote, an increasing number of the traditional Republicans began to prepare for the inevitable split. Emissaries were sent to the United States to round up money and arms shipments. Old contacts throughout the country were renewed. Overtures from members of the Fianna Fáil government in Dublin were entertained. Traditional Fianna Fáil people felt they could protect "their" Nationalists in the North with an IRA proxy and simultaneously isolate the new IRA radicals. In 1969 in Dublin, the IRA Convention met and split on the issue of whether Sinn Féin representatives should take their seats in the puppet governments in Leinster House and Stormont. The official line of ending abstention was accepted by thirty-nine votes to twelve. The losers withdrew on the matter of moral principle and formed the Provisional Army Council declaring "our allegiance to the 32-County Irish Republic proclaimed at Easter 1916." Sinn Féin split in January 1970 and not for the first time there were two Republican movements—not to mention the Republican Fianna Fáil government.

The new Provisional organization, claiming to be the only true heir to Republican tradition, maintained the traditional IRA structure. The IRA is organized on a geographic basis with sections, companies, battalions, and brigades; although not until recruiting soared in 1970-71 did volunteers fill up the appropriate slots. Regularly, often each year, the various units elect representatives to an Army Convention that will decide on matters of policy and elect a leadership. The Convention votes on an Executive, usually eleven men, who, meeting in secret, elect a seven-man Army Council, which then appoints a chief of staff who selects an adjutant-general, a quarter-master general, intelligence director, and other functional staff members. In hard times and at first when the Provisionals— soon called the Provos—began, many of these positions were filled by the same people. Outside the IRA, again with overlapping memberships, are other organizations (the legal political party Sinn Féin, a women's organization, Republican boy scouts, supporters of prisoners' dependents, newspapers, support groups abroad), all dominated by the IRA Army Council even though legally or technically independent.

Since the foundation of the Provisionals in 1968-69, the organization has largely been dominated by Northerners as commanders or military active volunteers. Quite simply it is impossible for a Kerryman or a Dubliner to open his mouth in Belfast or Derry without being recognized; in fact an American accent is less alien in that it could be a New York cousin. And since the action has largely been in the North, there was little the eager Kerry or Dublin volunteer could do but train and wait on standby. The Provos' ranks in the North were flooded as the security situation deteriorated and the prospect for real action increased. With few exceptions, the volunteers were young men—and women—between the ages of 16 and 26, mostly 18 and 21, school dropouts with limited skills, either unemployed or with scanty employment records. Unmarried, without responsibilities, they were attracted by the lure of the gun, the romance of the IRA, the chance of action and reputation and the obvious need to defend their own. These were insufficient reasons from the point of view of the leadership. Hence, at first the volunteers were bored in ideological recruit classes fashioned to turn away the romantic and impatient and to indoctrinate the dedicated and determined. Upon graduation into the IRA, the volunteer was usually assigned to an active service unit in his or her neighborhood. Some learned special skills, bomb-making or communications, and some moved into leadership positions, often very rapidly. For the Provos this was the new generation, the Class of 1969.

In some areas of rural Northern Ireland, like South Armagh or Mid-Tyrone, the Provos in a classical manner dominated the countryside. In Belfast and Derry there were no-go zones, first informally and then as the campaign developed formally, where British security forces did not venture. And by 1971 the Provos were waging a classical armed struggle against the British army and the RUC so intense that Home Minister Reginald Maudling on December 15 could only foresee a situation where the IRA would "not be defeated, not completely eliminated, but have their violence reduced to an acceptable level." In 1972 the violence escalated. The British shot and killed thirteen civilians on Bloody Sunday in Derry—a "Butcher's Dozen." Stormont was prorogued in March. In July the leadership of the Provos secretly met in England with the British ministerial team on Northern Ireland. They and their volunteers had bombed down Stormont and their way to the negotiation table.

Essentially, the provisional leadership represents three distinct Republican generations: the men of the 1940s, many from the North, whose careers and memories stretched back to the English bombing campaign and the schisms and divisions of the 1930s; the men of the 1950s, who were largely self-recruited and often from the south, columns having been sent north into the six-counties; and finally, the new volunteers originally motivated by the threat of a Loyalist pogrom and alienated by a "Protestant State for a Protestant people." At first the Provos tended to cluster around the local Republican leaders who were in 1968-69 collecting arms and reorganizing even before the threat to the Nationalist population became abundantly clear. In some Nationalist areas without a Republican heritage, there were no old Republicans so that new leaders appeared from the new volunteers and often disappeared quickly as well.

Among the men of the 1940s in the north, one of the most prominent, and visible, was Joe Cahill, who succeeded Billy McKee in March 1971 as C/O of the Belfast Brigade. It was on 13 August 1971, after Brigadier Marston Tickell had called a press conference to explain that internment begun on August 9 had "virtually defeated" the IRA, that Cahill simultaneously, a few hundred yards away, held a press conference to explain that the Provos were alive and well. Cahill was in many ways a typical Belfast Republican. A man of no property in the contracting business, he had been in and out of prison and internment camps during all the crisis times and had once been under sentence of death for shooting a policeman. Small, bald, a gnome of a man, simply dressed with a porkpie hat to hand, he could not be said to have the superficial appearance that might be expected in the commander of an urban guerilla force that had brought war to the United

Kingdom, but once seen, he was never forgotten. In 1971 Cahill was moved to Dublin as quarter-master general in charge of procuring arms, and was replaced by Seamus Twomey, another 1940s man, who was a bookmaker's agent. Larger than Cahill, avuncular, with horn-rimmed glasses and a quiet manner, he was as unremarkable as Cahill was unforgettable. All three, McKee, Cahill, and Twomey, however, were typical Belfast Republicans, working class, parochial in experience, deeply immersed in Republic history and legend, knowledgeable and with the most profound, if narrow, convictions. Hard men, they had always believed in physical force, seldom shown any concern even with Sinn Féin political activities, and in 1969 had rushed back when the new troubles began. Over the next ten years all three would either be in prison or on active service. Cahill on the GHQ and Twomey as chief of staff served while McKee was in prison. By 1980 McKee and Cahill were still active and Twomey was once more in a southern prison after a remarkable Provo helicopter escape from Mountjoy jail. In the country in Crossmaglen or Pomeroy or the little towns, the men would too be typical of their own small farmers, shopkeepers, and unemployed, united with the hard men from the Falls or the Short Strand in Belfast in the absolute depth of their Republican convictions.

The 1950s generation, Republican convictions aside, tended to be somewhat less parochial and had by 1969 become somewhat more successful although still men of no property. When the Provos were organized in 1968 by men from the North, they had wanted as chief of staff someone from the Dublin establishment. The IRA was dominated by Cathal Goulding, painting contractor, Dublin radical, friend of Brendan Behan, a life-long IRA man who had been interned in the 1940s in Ireland and imprisoned in Great Britain for an arms raid in the 1950s; and Séan Garland who fought in the northern campaign and was wounded in an attack on a northern police barracks that became legend. Goulding, Garland, Mick Ryan, and Seamus Costello of the 1950s, in fact all but one of the Dublin center, remained loyal to the new direction and new ideas. So the Northerners co-opted Séan MacStiofáin, IRA director of intelligence, to underscore the legitimacy of the Provisionals. The new chief of staff, once John Stephenson, had an English father and a Belfast mother, converted to Catholicism as a child, and then stressed his Irish background. Joining the IRA in England he was arrested and imprisoned along with Goulding for the failed arms raid. There he became more Irish than the Irish, learning not only his adopted history but his new language. Transmuted first to Séan Stephenson and then Séan MacStiofáin, he made a career within the language movement—and stayed with the IRA. Tall, dark, solid, impressive, he somehow lacked Irish charm. In his porkpie hat, followed by bodyguards, as Séan Mac of the Provos, he emanated an atmosphere of cold power and purpose.

But he was not simply a gunman's gunman; he read widely and saw a different world from his older Belfast colleagues—but his Republican ideals and convictions were no broader. He might have read Grivas and Mao but he was at home with his own.

Two other prominent Republicans of the 1950s emerged within the Provos. Both had been involved in the raids on the North and one, Dave O'Connell, had been badly wounded, captured and imprisoned in Crumlin Road jail, Belfast. At the end of the campaign, on his release, O'Connell, another man of no property, made a late career change and became a vocational schoolteacher, no small accomplishment since he began with nothing and had a prison record. But he was reluctant to take any prominent part in the political activities after 1962 or accept the new direction. The other, Rory Brady, a schoolteacher in Roscommon, was one of the few university-educated volunteers of his generation. From the Midlands he continued to play an important role in Sinn Féin and other Republican activities. While much of the new direction appeared promising, his Republican ideas were profoundly traditional—particularly on the matter of abstention. Like his colleagues of the 1950s he was not a man of one lane or a single village, he was broader, better-educated, and tactically flexible. He became president of the Provisional Sinn Féin. O'Connell, who was tall, striking, the very idealized portrait of an Irish gunman, served the Provos in a variety of positions. Visibly in Sinn Féin, he was seen by the press as the Provos' political director. Together with MacStiofáin, who was eased out of the movement when he came off a hunger and thirst strike while in prison, O'Connell and Brady currently have similar roles. While personally quite different from one another, the three men are all austere, absolutely committed, often tunnel-blind to alternatives. They share with the men from Belfast the same mind-set but in a broader and more flexible framework.

The new Northern generation represents its own even more clearly than the men of the 1950s, who had been self-selected during a time of little action. In 1970 it seemed as if every Nationalist in the North wanted to sign up: unemployed dropouts, construction workers, university students, teachers, butchers' assistants, pub owners and postmen. Largely in the Nationalist population in the North, there are a disproportionate number of unemployed or under-employed men in the construction trade, women in the linen industry or shop assistants, and few wealthy landowners or bankers. Thus, all sorts and conditions came into the Provos from university graduates to hotel porters, but few bankers or industrialists. Many were weeded out. Others with varying talents rose swiftly. Irregular armies give an opportunity of advancement to those with courage, dedication, ambition, potential but without specific training. Thus in Derry, without a real

Republican heritage, there were lots of volunteers but no successful C/O until a young recruit was given the job. Martin MacGuinness at age 20 was tall, slender, with curly red hair and freckles, the Irish lad down the lane. He was also the kind of promising young man who might have been head boy at school. For him, as for so many Republicans, slogans were revealed truth, sacrifice essential, discipline inviolate. He was the ideal IRA volunteer and led by example. Admired by his friends and neighbors, followed by his fellows, he ran Derry until withdrawal across the border was necessary when the British army closed down the no-go zones.

The Provo-British meeting in July 1972 gives some indication of the composition of the IRA leadership: MacStiofáin, O'Connell, Twomey, McGuinness, together with two others of his 1969 generation from Belfast, Ivor Bell, Gerry Adams, and Myles Shevlin, a solicitor of the 1950s generation representing Sinn Féin instead of Brady. Some of the old, some of the new, and mostly Northerners held the key positions.

To a degree the jury is still out on the present generation of Republicans, for quantitative research on an active revolutionary organization presents certain problems. While the secret army of the Provos today is not absolutely secret, it is certainly less forthcoming than the IRA in the 1960s or, for that matter, the Provos of MacStiofáin. It is not a matter of public record who serves on Army Council, is chief of staff or C/O of Belfast or who belongs to the new cell structure introduced in December 1977. But from what is known about the visible leadership, from the published details of arrests, trials, and internments, from hints and guesses, the general profile remains much as indicated. The Provos, especially in the North, are representative of their constituency on one hand and of typical covert military organizations on the other. It is a working-class organization screwed into threatened Nationalist ghettos or strong country areas. The active service volunteer in the Provisional IRA is in many ways—economic, social, personal—the counterpart of his opponent in the British paratroopers except that he or she is intensely political and, unlike the enlisted soldier, capable of rising to the top of the movement. And the top of the movement, like the bottom, is working-class in character, from time to time sprinkled with those of recent success and the occasional university graduate. The Army Council represents a Northern constituency where few Nationalists are upper middle-class or professional.

Just such a profile has remained remarkably stable since the Second World War, for after all revolution is a young man's game that seldom attracts the comfortable and successful. The IRA in 1918–21 *did* include all classes and kinds, but then the struggle was a total national resistance and the IRA, too, represented an entire national constituency excluding only the Protestant loyalists, just as, say, the French resistance in 1944 excluded the collaborationists. In the case of the 1950s generation, the average IRA active service volunteer of the 1950s had joined at 19, was 21, unmarried, a skilled or semi-skilled worker with some secondary school or vocational training, living in a city. The situation in Belfast in 1977 was much the same and, with the exception of occupation, equally so in the country.

The leaders of the movement are obviously older. They are more likely to be married, to have pursued, often successfully, a career of sorts—say a plumbing contractor or a schoolteacher or a travel agent. Tall or short, congenial or taciturn, they all share a special approach to the national question; all, even the most political, are men of physical force. And give or take a few, they and their volunteers are a working-class movement, dependent on the Nationalist base in Northern Ireland, consisting of only 500,000, for their new generation of volunteers, a generation they anticipate no difficulty in attracting. It will be a generation that will, like their predecessors, possess no property and will know for certain the unfailing cause of Ireland's ills, the means to end them, and be unwavering in support of the ultimate goal of the movement, the Republic.

12

Revolts Against the British Crown

The goal of the IRA is particular, the volunteers special, the arena unique. There are roots difficult to unearth without killing, battles hard to compare, a display of specifics, and always the need for exception. Ireland is singular surely, but in the menu of revolutionary movements all items must share some factors and a few be similar. At least this does not seem unreasonable to any but those totally emersed in singularity. The IRA has since inception been dedicated to breaking the connection with England— "the never-failing source of all our political evils"—and hence it does not seem unreasonable to approach other rebels against the British Crown who seek through physical force to break that connection. At the very least, no matter how various the rebels, how special the battleground, or how particular the conditions of revolt, the British should in some part—in large part—respond as is their wont. Before the Irish events from 1916–23, the only open revolt against Britain had been over a century before in America. But after the Second World War, an era of imperial dissolution opened, and there were a flurry of examples within a generation, culminating with the collapse of Ulster into insurrection.

For those concerned with Ireland, often too concerned for parsing other arenas, there should be a concern with the nature of the British response: Was, or is, London predictable? Those who led revolts against the Crown came from the most diverse backgrounds—the Greek regular army, Eastern European revolutionary Zionism, the uplands of South Arabia, East African reservations, Asian communism—often were only marginally aware of the nature of Perfidious Albion. They truly began their revolution from the first toss of the dice, limited in historical experience, limited in real exposure to the British, and like all rebels, very limited in assets. Their experience, essentially at the end of colonialism, was, perhaps is in part relevant to Ulster events. Certainly some within the IRA thought it very relevant: MacStiofáin knew the number of British troops killed in South Arabia and read Kitson on low-intensity war. Certainly those who saw the conflict as largely imperial accepted similarities that should have offered rebel options. As always, of course, the Army Council of the IRA went its own special way, more emboldened by British imperial events than enlightened.

Thus, it seems profitable for analytical purposes, to examine first the results of an investigation into the British response to insurgency and then the Irish experience. To generalize from the first to second is quite possible; however, to move from the Irish case, founded on particulars but not unlike others, to insights into the nature of revolutionary insurgency in general is no small matter. To do so (generalize from the special) has been an enormously dangerous task for practitioners of rebellion. The streets of Vienna were once littered with the bodies of those who believed in the Leninist tenets of urban proletariat insurrection and the hills of Spain covered with the bodies of anarchists who organized war according to proper principle. A generation in Latin America burned out trying to apply lessons improperly learned from Castro in Cuba, culminating in Che's futile, doomed mission, the squalid, bloody coda to the clash of theory and practice. What, then, is reassuring about British experience and the Irish case is that there are generalizations valid in the past. What, then, is not so reassuring for the Irish rebel is that after the end of an empire these responses to events no longer seem relevant. The Irish case proved the rule, but because Ulster is a special and different example, beyond empire, and not simply a colonial conflict (however intense), the tides of history moved on. There have been new stages, different roles and rules and realities; the old responses have faltered; the old rebel tactics and stratagems have grown irrelevant. The keys to the kingdom, the Republic, now no longer fit the lock. Perhaps they never did; perhaps the other colonial rebels were too different. Certainly the British in the last decade have refused the old part. And yet, for the innovative, steeped in the special, the generation of British experience could offer an opening into the future. And still, most theorists end not in the Winter Palace or the Knesset but sprawled on a hillside shot down. But the ultimate realists end sweeping the bush for the guerrilla of the moment, the rebel on today's list.

In January 1944, an illicit proclamation began circulating in the British Mandate of Palestine. This declaration of a Jewish revolt by Irgun Zvai Leumi was to be a harbinger of a generation of imperial insurrection, the first scene in the final act of the Empire. In 1944 an "armed struggle" by a small, "military" arm of the schismatic Zionist Revisionist Movement neither impressed nor particularly concerned the British. A vast world war was underway, in part directed against the Zionists' most dedicated enemy, Adolph Hitler. All the orthodox Zionists opposed the antics of the little group of zealots in the Mandate, a minority of a minority that frightened no one. What was surprising to the British was that an open revolt, however ineffectual, had been launched by these fanatical Jews against their old "ally"; the British were shocked, outraged, and indignant at the pretensions of a gang of terrorists who were without legitimacy or popular support. No matter what the British moral response, the tiny revolt escalated year by year into a massive emergency that drew in tens of thousands of British troops, ate up precious sterling balances, alienated old friends, even the Arabs, and ultimately engendered profound disgust on the part of the British public. In pique and desperation the British sought recourse in the United Nations, finally evacuating the Mandate in general disarray in 1948. By then the armed struggle of the Irgun Zvai Leumi had become a classic model. Under Menachem Begin, the Irgun had devised a strategy that became a paradigm for imperial revolt; a means had been discovered for the weak to lever out the strong—or so it seemed to some.

Prior to 1944, the British Empire had been exposed to two serious experiences of national revolt. In America in 1776, the rebels, benefiting from distance and a major ally, created alternative institutions and defended them by conventional military means. Learning in part their lesson, the British during the nineteenth century slowly evolved a counter strategy to rebellion by those sufficiently mature for self-government: the devolution or gradual transfer of power to newly created dominions. This technique by the twentieth century had been refined into the Commonwealth strategy, immediately effective in the English-speaking Dominions and potentially applicable elsewhere. By then, however, an alternative rebel strategy had been devised by the Irish, who by the application of an entire spectrum of techniques and tactics had for hundreds of years engaged in an effort to create an Irish Ireland. The Irish experience, rather than the distant American, became a primer for potential rebels elsewhere in the empire who did not consider themselves candidates for the Commonwealth Strategy.

In 1916 a traditional "rising" wracked Dublin. This Easter Rising, however, as had all others, collapsed into mere bitterness and recrimination. Beginning in 1918, a more thoughtful attempt was launched by a younger generation. They attempted to create an Irish Republic, free and Gaelic, by coupling irregular war led by an underground Irish Republican Army with the creation of an alternative governmental institution. The subsequent British repression could prohibit the Republican institution from functioning, but could not crush the IRA "terrorists"—in fact the increasingly stringent measures taken against the IRA became distasteful to the British public. In time the British found a means of compromising the issues with a formula that created the Irish Free State in twenty-six counties; a loyal, largely Protestant enclave in six counties of Ulster; and a guarantee of British bases and economics interests. In Britain the Irish Treaty was viewed as a splendid, if unique, exercise in the accommodation of national aspiration—a judicious application of a strategy of devolution.

The Irish strategy of revolt, even if not emulated in the other parts of the Empire, was not forgotten. Few potential Nationalist rebel groups could hope for the likes of a George Washington, but all could in a pinch manage murder from a ditch.

By and large, however, it was not the combination of terror, British hypocrisy, shadow institutions, international propaganda, guerrillas in the hills, the exhausted imperial machine, and the war-weary population that potential rebels studied. The real key to national liberation appeared to be in India where Mahatma Gandhi and Jawaharlal Nehru fashioned a mass movement based on a disciplined, nonviolent campaign of civil disobedience. The leaders of the Indian Congress Movement were convinced that once the masses were motivated, disciplined, and determined, the British would have no choice but to rule by the most brutal and self-destructive force or concede. And they suspected that the force to coerce four hundred thousand people did not exist, even if British had the will to employ it, which that nation probably did not. In 1942, in the midst of the war, London had in effect promised independence to the Congress leaders. For many Nationalists the Indian strategy seemed to offer the most, for it neatly fit into the British Commonwealth strategy, peacefully demanding what should be cheerfully granted, avoiding the risks of open revolt by the weak, and offering a means to mold the future nation through disciplined political activities.

At the end of the war, there were two major Nationalist strategies within the British Empire: leverage based on armed struggle of attrition, as in the Irish-Irgun option; and the Indian model, dependent on civil disobedience on a vast scale by a diciplined mass party. At the time, the strategies of the orthodox revolutionaries (the rush by the urban proletariat to the Marxist-Leninist barricades and the distant experience of Mao Tse-tung in rural China) appeared alien to imperial experience. In the course of the next generation, the British Empire would disappear—a massive act of devolution that for the most part passed peacefully. The Indian strategy was applied in all sorts of odd corners of the world and with some exceptions became the conventional means to power, however much the process might have been accelerated by open revolt elsewhere. After the Indian sucess it very soon became clear that even in less mature colonies like the Gold Coast, progress was possible. There, Kwame Nkrumah effected the independence of Ghana by adapting similar methods that, though less disciplined and more disruptive, were in time equally valid.

There were exceptions. For varying reasons the process of devolution did not always run smoothly. The Malayan Communist Party (MCP) launched a guerrilla war using the strategy of Mao Tse-tung and the enthusiasm and ambitions of the local Chinese community. In Kenya the Kikuyu, outraged by colonial policies and the "theft" of their land, attempted to combine the politics of agitation led by the Kenya African Union with the terror of tribal violence loosely organized as the Mau Mau. In Egypt the various political factions sponsored fedayeen raids into the Canal Zone to coerce British concessions. In Cyprus Colonel George Grivas organized a resistance movement, EOKA, and in collaboration with Archbishop Makarios sought unsuccessfully to achieve union (*Enosis*) with Greece. In South Arabia the militant Arab nationalists, emboldened by the direction of events after 1956, launched an armed struggle, certain that Britain's moment in the Middle East had passed. And in 1967 after the British departure, the triumphant National Liberation Front (NLF) established the new People's Republic of South Yemen. There were as well other rebellions, disorders, and continued imperial responsibilities that found British troops active in Borneo, Oman, and Ulster, but, the Gold Coast aside, the major imperial emergencies faced by the British were Malaya, Kenya, Crpyus, South Arabia, and in a special way Egypt. All were very different indeed—the Malay Communists had recourse to the strategy of Mao and the Mau Mau to atavistic tribal custom—and yet the British response became a pattern sufficiently predictable to be negatable at small rebel risk, a pattern so fixed that even after the end of imperial insurrections the response in Northern Ireland in the 1970s to renewed violence by the IRA appeared to come from the same imperial mold.

That the Commonwealth strategy did not work everywhere was mainly, the British assumed, because the imperial power was faced with the thankless responsibilities of adjusting conflicting claims (for example, those of the Arabs and the Jews or the Greeks and the Turks) or eliminating unrepresentative claimants (the Communists in Malaya or the Mau Mau in Kenya). In any case those gunmen and terrorists who sought power outside the Commonwealth route were considered to be without legitimacy. Thus for the British, a revolt opens not with bombs but with the unexpected surfacing of a conflict over legitimacy, a conflict that in most cases has a long and troubled history, a history cherished by the rebel and ignored or denied by the British.

The immediate British reaction to the rebels' aspirations, no matter what the circumstances, is outraged indignation. The rebel is an alien and evil man, motivated by personal ambitions, often deluded by an imported ideology, who uses terror to acquire support—a man outside the law, outside common decency, outside reason. The full majesty of historically recognized, internationally accepted, *legitimate* authority is turned on the little band of assassins. In the long run rebel legitimacy can only be won by force—or by concession. Some of these illegitmate claimants could, as had been the case with the Irish in 1921, be co-opted by means of an adjusted

Commonwealth strategy, but in some cases there was nothing for it but repression. After 1944 in some foreign corner or another, regularly to their surprise, the British had to confront an insurgency campaign led by indigestible rebels. British colonial officials, career officers, and policemen might, if they were keen, serve in several emergencies. Some reappear a little futher up the ladder in each new campaign, a little greyer, a little wiser, like spirits of revolts past. The British knew and continued to have their knowledge reinforced of the dangers and costs of such revolts and the means to avoid the worst problems. From their exposure the British learned the tactics of anti-insurgency, the cost of an emergency, the importance of political concessions, and the means to manipulate the Commonwealth strategy. The Cabinet of whatever composition knew the cost of staying or getting out. Still, caught every time by surprise when a revolt did begin, the British continued to be shocked, outraged, indignant.

Only rarely did the authorities, either on the spot or in London, foresee the possibility of an armed revolt. Conditions that the potential rebels felt were intolerable, that created deep frustration, and that could not be ameliorated except through violence, did not so appear to the British. In many cases the British could not conceive of priorities different from their own.

In Palestine the British simply did not understand the impact of the Holocaust, the depth of Jewish agony, nor could they credit the charge of genocide made against them. In the Gold Coast the motive of the mob (political power) went far beyond the usual bread-and-butter issues of colonial politics. The British had simply not dreamed that such factors would appear in the colony for decades. In Malaya the revolt by the MCP was launched not from the depths of despair as in Palestine, but from the high ground of ideological certainty—native Chinses ambition in Malaya hued over with a vision of a Communist future. In this case the British were surprised less at the MCP's aspirations than at the mere fact that it dared to revolt. In Kenya the European settlers and local observes had *feared* a revolt but had not anticipated one. Thus, despite policies after mid-1952 that almost insured a Kikuyu "revolt" would take place, there was still surprise at the extent of Kikuyu alienation in Nairobi, while in London the new emergency had been quite unanticipated. Long after the Cypriot emergency was over, British spokesmen of various hues insisted that *Enosis* was and always had been an artificial issue exploited by agitators. By so refusing even to consider the matter, the British, knowing what the Greeks *really* wanted, had set a boundary to nationalism that someone, sooner or later, would cross—as Grivas did to British surprise. By the time of the South Arabian misadventures, Britain should have been beyond surprise at the ambitions of radical Arabs. But even though Radio Cairo reached into the hills of Dhala, the British still hoped that the old ways and old forms would work with the new Arabs and were surprised and indignant when they did not.

The British difficulty in perception was a fault hardly limited to the British, since surprise had long played a commanding role in military and political affairs. In some cases the potential rebel intended to take up arms no matter what accommodation was offered, but there at least the British might have been forearmed. Even if the rebels did in fact represent alien strains within the Empire, there remains the possibility that a more perceptive eye would have uncovered the pattern of frustration and suggested an alternative to repression. It is, to be fair, difficult to see how London heeding Casandra could or would have acted much differently in most cases. The rebels largely felt impelled to revolt, for a nonviolent dialogue no longer offered them anything. In Palestine the whole direction of British Middle East policies since 1939 largely precluded undue concessions to the Zionists, and for the men of the Irgun no concession, however generous, would have done. In Malaya the MCP's conviction that victory was certain and any course but armed struggle was dangerous would probably have remained no matter what the British did or did not do. In Kenya, at least a realization of the nature of the most immediate Kikuyu grievances might have allowed time for a Gold Coast dialogue to evolve; then again, given the settlers' attitudes, perhaps the necessary concessions were out of the question at the time. In Cyprus the British might have taken *Enosis* seriously so in any case to point out the international complications that might ensure and the rigid requirements of British security—but would the patriots have listened? And surely no concession would have swerved the Arabs in Cairo and Aden from their allotted courses. Almost nowhere then, except perhaps Kenya, could a dash of prescience have greatly altered the situation, for the rebels wanted to rise in arms for purposes quite beyond the capacity of the British to concede.

In most cases the closer the individual was to the scene of the action on the eve of the trouble, the more likely the chance of error and the failure to perceive change. Often those who knew the most saw the least. The-man-who-knew-the-natives often missed the impact of modernization or the influence of new ideas. Often he had learned his job and his knowledge of the natives on the spot, acquiring the rare and esoteric languages of the bush, absorbing detailed and extensive anthropological data, fashioning a career on extended tours. Some of the "natives" in Tel Aviv or Nicosia, however, were quite different from the stereotyped impressions gained by colonial experts in their previous experiences. Elsewhere, the attractions of education and the appeal of Western technology wrought swift changes: they stirred quite "unnative" ambitions, tilting the familiar into new and not always visible patterns without ever showing the British on the spot a new face. And when the face did appear above ill-fitting white collar and obscure school tie, few realized just how profound the change and how limited the old means of control. Even when that control crumbled, there was only limited understanding of what had gone wrong, that the natives had given up the effort to take part in a dialogue with the deaf, and had sought recourse with bombs.

In carrying on the imperial dialogue in many places, the British had been talking without listening, looking at events without seeing. As the years passed, the discontent turned to the more lethal dialogue, a strategy that inevitably came as a surprise to the British. Mass nonviolence, the politics of confrontation, the tactics of direct action, first in Asia and then in Africa, not only surprised the British but also caught their attention. The British monologue died down and the new native voices of the Gold Coast or Egypt could be heard. If the means of interrupting the British mono-logue appeared illegitimate (e.g., Mau Mau oathings or Grivas's bombs), or if the time to attract British attention was too short (Palestine in 1944), or if the rebels did not care to talk, which was mostly the case, then Britain would be surprised at the new form of communication—a revolt by the natives no one ever knew.

After surprise at the new lethal dialogue came shock that rebels would seek recourse to violence when means of accommodation abounded, when the expressed grievances were not legitimate and when the mass of decent people disapproved. Without exception the first analysis on the spot and then in London was that the revolt was the work of a tiny disgruntled minority, dependent on support achieved by coercion or intimidation or violence.

This British analysis was almost always in part correct, for revolts, cer-tainly at the beginning, are the work of a tiny handful of men acting in the name of the masses who, of course, can hardly be polled. The Irgun, EOKA, the Egyptian fedayeen, and the South Yemen NLF were tiny in gross numbers and remained so until the end. The British approach was that because the revolutionary organization was small it was also unrepre-sentative. And this, too, was often true. The emergency in Kenya was as much a Kikuyu civil war as an armed insurrection and hardly involved most of the other Kenya Africans. The Irgun were a self-confessed minority in a Jewish community that in turn was a minority in the Palestine Man-date. The Communist in the jungles of Malaya was tied to less than a majority of the Chinese, who were again a minority in the colony. Most revolutionary movements, where reasonable estimate is possible, always have been led by a tiny minority, actively, even passively, supported by less than a substantial majority. Often the rebels must coerce or eliminate the loyalists. In South Arabia, for example, more Arabs were killed by the rebels than by British security forces, Thus, the British were quite right: the rebels were a minority with limited active support and probably limited support of any kind. The British noted too, if reluctantly, that some support must exist, for information and intelligence about the rebels proved difficult to acquire, and public expression of gratitude for British counterinsurgency efforts was limited.

The obvious conclusion was that the minority was intimidating the majority. That rebel support must be the result of intimidation does not, however, logically follow. Many Jews in Palestine, for example, did not approve of the Irgun's campaign but would not oppose it. They wanted to be neither informer nor advocate. Much the same was the case with the Greek Cypriots, where many who preferred the quiet life would not oppose EOKA. In fact much if not all the mass always seems to tend toward the quiet life. Given a chance they would vote for a truce or a pause; given no chance they permit the rebels to sacrifice for a higher national "purpose" beyond the ballot box. This neutrality, a slightly biased neutrality, however, is all that a rebel needs. A government needs more. For if the rebel continues to exist, he may in time win—while a government must govern, must win outright, must restore order and hence law. The British problem was to woo the vast apolitical audience, an audience that was often only marginally interested.

The British assumed that only through force could the rebels achieve toleration. This often was the case: neither EOKA nor the Malayan Communists nor the Kikuyu pretended otherwise than that they were executing traitors and informers. Thus, the British assumed that at heart the population supported them and not the rebels. This attitude on the part of the British was not counterpropaganda but an article of faith. The British believed and so acted. Trust is maintained in the "real" people, and outrageous risks are taken because of this trust. In Nicosia the valet slipping a bomb under the bed of Field Marshal Sir John Harding, the military governor, was by no means a unique betrayal of that trust; there were repeated betrayals. Everywhere from Malaya to Aden, the potentially disloyal servants were kept, often to the last day and the ultimate betrayal. Even the frantic settlers in Kenya wanted to kill every Kikuyu but their own. Since British authority, then, is legitimate, all good men and true will rally about in opposition to the illicit pretenders—unless so prevented by violence. And the rebels are violent, illegitimate men who at best can count on the dubious virtue of certification from a recognized revolutionary center in Cairo or Moscow or from a greedy regime in Athens.

The British had to stand for something as well as to oppose sin. The simple legitimacy of being first in possession of power is insufficient once the old dialogue has broken down an the violence begun. To stand behind the banners of imperialism and the primacy of the British was synonymous with order, decency, fair play, good government, civilization, justice, law, and occasionally Christianity. And, of course, this was true. What Britain did not stand for was immediate independence and native interests over those of Britain. This was the rebel program—everything for us now—and it had great charm. For the British to insist that immediate independence would be disastrous and that Britain could do more for the natives than they could do for themselves would not go over well. Whatever Britain's position on self-determination, now or later or never, the rebels had to be depicted as men who would use proud slogans for low purpose or wave the national banner while selling the nation abroad to alien ideologies. The rebels were thus not nationalists but illegitimate pretenders to power that they intended to misuse—men who had passed from the stage of foolishness into knavery and criminal knavery at that.

If the revolt is absolutely illegitimate, totally without moral justification, led by men without scruple or decency, then it is obviously both easier to oppose and harder to ignore, and almost impossible to compromise. In all consciousness, it is difficult to take tea with a terrorist or accept a criminal into the palace; much more important, however, it is far more tempting to seek out and destroy evil. From the first the leadership of the revolt is defined not simply as evil but as alien. And the more appropriate the label the more likely that the establishment of order will be pursued with maximum force. And the "cause" that led to the open revolt has also been perceived by the British as alien, spurious. If not exactly spurious, the rebel causes over the past thirty years have certainly been indigestible. While some nationalists needed and accepted the slow process of institution-building within the Empire and accepted the British Westminster model (whether appropriate or not), the rebels did not.

The most alien of all enemies of Empire were the Mau Mau, atavistic descendants into savagery, absolutely illegitimate in political terms. The toll of Mau Mau killed, the mass detentions, resettlements, and imprisonment could all the more easily be undertaken in light of the horror of the Mau Mau oath and the brutality of their massacres. No one seemed particularly surprised that over 1000 Mau Mau were executed in contrast to only eight members of the Irgun during that Palestine emergency. It was, no matter what the provocation, *hard* for the British to kill Jews. Much the same was true in Cyprus, where the British were fond of the Greeks and deeply frustrated that EOKA could not see where their struggle for *Enosis* was leading. The British were not fond of the Chinese Communists in Malaya—an international conspiracy of an alien ethnic group that threatened British security and the future of Malayan development. The MCP therefore was absolutely illegitimate. The Chinese were not mad, as were the Mau Mau, but they had been converted to an alien ideology. So, too, in Malaya there were the detentions and arrests on a vast scale, deprogramming camps, the wholesale movement of populations, and the huge toll of dead terrorists, executed or killed in the jungle sweeps. The more effective the British were in defining the rebel as alien (and if as a rebel you start by being a Kikuyu instead of a Greek the process is simpler), the more likely the authorities were to see a polarized conflict as without solution and without a need for excess compassion. Rigorous repression thus became the order of the day.

Naturally once this policy of repression begins to show results, a reversal to allow for accommodation becomes difficult, since such a reversal requires a lengthy process of redefining and reconsidering. In the Gold Coast the Watson commission investigating the disturbances of 1948 produced a report that depicted Nkrumah as imbued with a pure Communist ideology blurred only somewhat by political experience. A red knave with a black skin quite obviously would not be the man for the future. There was in the Gold Coast sufficient leeway for Nkrumah to apply the Indian strategy, adapted for African use, and most important there were British officials in Accra and London who recognized what he was doing. In Kenya, even in 1960, Kenyatta was still the leader of darkness and death to Governor Sir Patrick Renison. In two more years Kenyatta would be a senior minister serving in a African administration presided over by the same governor. The process of turning Kenyatta, a man "definitely guilty" of leading a murderous cult, into the doyen of the new African statesmen took not only time but also the pressure of expediency—still it was done. Nor if the nationalists in South Arabia had played the game is there much doubt that the Arab terrorists, thugs and pawns of Egypt, could have been transmuted into candidates for the Commonwealth conference. It is not a process without pain, for many persist in seeing yesterday's villain behind today's glory. Through practice and experience, however, the British could reverse the policy of alienation.

At the time of the revolt, if the rebel is alien, the alternatives appear exacting: crush the revolt or evacuate. Both the Mau Mau and the MCP were crushed and remained in British eyes primitive tribesmen and pawns of communism. In South Arabia the British managed only a semblance of devolution in a last-minute agreement at Geneva; in effect, London threw the keys over the wall and evacuated, leaving a long line of Arab friends who had been led up the garden path. In Cyprus the Commonwealth strategy finally came to the rescue. In Egypt a typical treaty solution in 1954 led only to the Suez invasion of 1956, the last violent hurrah of Empire. In Palestine, as in South Arabia, the British scuttled, but under the auspices of the United Nations. Still, two clear wins, two clear losses, and two revolts accommodated is not a bad show for either the military or the diplomats.

Even when facing what appeared alien, unrepresentative, and illegitimate power-grabs, the British did not rely on coercion alone. Experience had revealed to all that terror could best be countered by political maneuvers. Thus if the rebels were not *too* alien (e.g., the Irgun, EOKA, and Arab nationalists in Aden), then the British sought a political option to involve the forces concerned. Such a political strategy might exclude compromise with the rebels but might produce an accommodation that the rebels would accept, as was the case with Cyprus. Even in Malaya and Kenya, parallel political programs were launched to erode the support of the rebels, even while the existence of such "support" was officially denied. It was, of course, easier to reach an accommodation, no matter what sort, when the perceived level of rebel violence was low. The Mau Mau violence level was perceived as frightful, which in the number of European casualties it was not, while the fedayeen attacks and the subsequent burning of Cairo were labeled as traditional Egyptian trouble-making and easily discounted at the bargaining table. In almost all cases, alien rebel or no, the British sought a small bit of uneven middle ground even when the aspirations of the rebels endangered crucial British interests or seemed beyond any rational accommodation.

British colonial strategy, then, was to open and maintain a dialogue, unless caught by surprise. Then, if the rebels were too alien to be co-opted, Britain would fight it out. Simultaneously, Britain might grant parallel concessions (e.g., self government to the loyal natives). The tactics Britain used to balance concession with coercion varied greatly and were often the result of independent initiatives, contingency factors, and contradictory impulses. Britain never had an overall book of colonial tactics. The British on the military side devised after long experience a basic approach to both urban and rural insurrection that, properly applied, went far to reduce to manageable proportions the level of violence. As long as a few men were determined on liberty or death, there would be some trouble, but the British experience indicated that such trouble could be narrowly limited if the Cabinet wanted to wait long enough, invest enough in repression, and cooperate in devising parallel political solutions. If not, all the military efforts would abort.

Military tactics in the field, refined over a generation in the hands of officers and men who often had differing experiences in counterinsurgency, could be learned and in the long run could be largely effective, but only if used in a cunningly prescribed political formula. Military operations in a political vacuum only created a more efficient rebel playing up to the challenge. British military tactics were, therefore, of little use unless political conditions were factored into the formula. Since the political conditions in each case were quite special, the ultimate formula, adjusted to the various regional unknowns, was in each revolt different.

British political tactics in pursuing a strategy of devolution, even in the midst of open revolt, varied vastly and could be quite flexible. Naturally a basic principle was to isolate and if possible ignore the rebels. This meant keeping out international investigators, ignoring United Nations resolutions, and turning back efforts to broaden the crisis. The British, however, if there was advantage, had not the slightest compunction in switching gears. Until Grivas's bombs went off, Cyprus was an internal matter. Almost immediately after the reverberations of the EOKA bombs, there was suddenly a London Tripartite Conference: Cyprus had become an international matter, at least to the degree that Ankara had a veto over Greek ambitions. Palestine, too, in time became an international problem before the United Nations, although the British withdrew rather than effect an international solution not to their own advantage. And when all else failed in South Arabia, London snatched at the United Nations straw in hopes that one more committee might produce results. There were, then, few hard-and-fast rules in the use of political tactics.

The British continued to devise a variety of approaches to each crisis that might support a return to order: constitutions, commissions, royal visits, aid and development, promises, and programs. All were used, not so much indiscriminately but as part of the uncertain dialogue. Some of the offers might appear to be positive steps, some might actually be so, some might lead to further devolution, but all played a vital role in forcing the pace. Year in and year out, the British divided and conquered, united and ruled, found old ways out of new corners and the reverse. Tactically, the political initiatives in colonial matters were inventive, creative, and often effective. That there were so few revolts and that those so often led to accommodation attest to British political acumen. The British did stumble on occasion, but still there was enough of that graceful swiftness of foot, so admired and so feared by the lesser breeds, to giver evidence that there was life yet in Prefidious Albion.

British political responses to colonial insurgency were often complicated by British strategic interest—although seldom by economic factors. London often had to pick up the chits for the strategists, maintaining possession of the odd bit of real estate the generals needed. Essentially on this level the military laid down that the cost of maintaining a strategic position was worth the price in colonial turmoil. As long as the Cabinet bought the premise, the ground for political maneuver was limited. The criticism that this turmoil negated the strategic value of the colony in question long remained an article of faith with many imperial critics.

Whether or not Britain needed Aden in 1965, Cyprus in 1957, or the Suez Canal in 1952 is perhaps problematic. What is quite clear is that the cost of repression, high or low, can also pay dividends. An occupier with sufficient power can put down resistance or contain insurrection and continue to use any base—as the British proved in Cyprus in 1956. Totting up the real cost is much more subtle, however, than satisfying the generals' demands for a fortress. In any event as the generation of devolution progressed, the review of value received indicated that often the strategic content was less vital than the generals assumed and the room for political maneuver broader; even outright evacuation proved in some cases no longer a strategic disaster. Increasingly, too, those in power felt that British economic interests would be as well or better maintained with an indirect presence. Some more pragmatic capitalists had their doubts in certain countries, but hardly anyone wanted to stand up and be counted as an opponent of devolution solely because British profits might suffer. Thus by the late 1960s, neither strategic nor economic interests greatly impeded the rush to dismantle the Empire.

Just as in the case of the political response by the politicians, so had there been a patterned military response on the part of the British army. The first was an avid desire that the political strategy devised in London be forthright, rigorous, and orchestrated with the local military effort. At times, of course, as noted, the military's own definition of British strategic needs (for example, the whole island of Cyprus as a military base) determined to a large extent the bounds of political action. The military recognized, however, that those bounds were limned in London on advice—not as a result of the direction—of the General Staff. Beginning with the Palestine experience of drift and scuttle, the British army recognized and was sensitive to both the political aspects of revolt and to the ultimate power of the Cabinet. Second, if possible, the army wanted the power to pursue the rebels with a vigorous campaign centralized under one command, ideally that of a military man, unrestricted by local authorities. Such ideal conditions seldom existed; either there was existing and competing local authority or serious limitation in the degree of force to be used or both. Largely, however, the military attitudes toward the rebels differed in no significant way from those of other parties involved in policy formulation.

In sum, within the process of devolution the basic British response to revolt, honed by experience, not always properly absorbed, remained largely the same. Firt came surprise, followed by shock, and the processes of defining the rebels as a minority of evil men using force to garner support from the basically loyal people. If the rebels were beyond compromise or had taken up arms openly, the army pursued an anti-insurgency campaign in sure and certain knowledge that their efforts in the field could succeed only if a political formula were found and supported for the long run by London. The means to fashion such a formula might, however, be limited by the very needs of the military, thereby protracting and complicating the problems of suppression. Seldom were economic factors decisive, even when in Malaya or India or the Gulf they were important. In large part the British managed to avoid open revolts and even then devised solutions other than absolute suppression or evacuation. Given the number of "natives" involved, the opportunity for misunderstanding, the international interference from various friends and enemies, and the nature of partisan politics, the dialogue of devolution seldom broke down.

With the evacuation of South Arabia in 1967 and the end of a British presence east of the Suez, the end of Empire appeared to have arrived. There were a flurry of ceremonial flag raisings on small islands and in tiny enclaves and a spurt in Commonwealth membership. Little was left under British sovereignty but rocks and reefs. There were marginal and distant responsibilities in Oman or Borneo, but with the end of Empire the problem of revolt seemed to belong to the past. Such did not turn out to be the case, for once more the Irish question, this time in a particularly violent form, appeared. And once more, whether or not Ulster was an integral part of the United Kingdom, the British response followed the imperial model.

13

On Revolt: An Irish Template

By 1968 there was no doubt that the end of Empire had come. Little remained but the odd rock and a small colonial residue the Labour government intended to encourage, ready or no, into independence. With the end of Empire one might also have expected an end to the long series of imperial revolts, leaving the British army free to concentrate on conventional war on the European continent. Yet within a year civil disturbances severe enough to require the army occurred, not on some distant imperial backwater but on the home islands, in the province of Northern Ireland. The army's peacekeeping mission—separating the Protestant majority from the Catholic minority—gradually shifted between 1969 and 1971 to an exercise in irregular war. Britain in 1971 once more faced a revolt, this time within the United Kingdom, directed by the Provisional Irish Republican Army, an organization that had not even existed two years before.

As always this revolt was unique, but events in Ulster, maneuvers out of London, and the essence of the lethal dialogue between rebel and ruler were not unlike previous imperial experience. The problems facing the IRA, neither surmounted nor solved, were as complex and special as those facing any rebel, the difficulties of fashioning a relevant and effective strategy if anything greater, and the ultimate level of violence if anything higher. Most important, the rebel experience in Northern Ireland by 1971, although peculiarly Irish, also reflected the experience of earlier rebels against the Crown. The Irish template might not fit everywhere exactly, but even a revolt within the United Kingdom rather than on the edge of Empire was not alien to distant observers, old rebels, experienced journalists, or military officers who saw, if uncertainly, the analogy.

Although in London staunch Tories were wont from the comfort of their clubs to insist that Northern Ireland was as British as Kent, and as dear, this was not true. In fact, few in Britain really knew very much about the province, its people, or its problems. It was a strange sort of place stitched together during the Irish Troubles, inhabited by dour and difficult people involved in old and irrelevant quarrels. There was good fishing, scenery, run-down industry, high unemployment, and primitive politics. In 1921

Lloyd George and his advisers managed to separate six of the nine counties of historic Ulster from the rest of Ireland and establish the Province of Northern Ireland with a regional government at the huge marble hall at Stormont outside Belfast. Ulster thus was maintained as an integral part of Britain, while the remaining twenty-six Irish counties became the Irish Free State, drifted out of the Commonwealth, and in 1948 evolved into the Irish Republic. In Dublin the Irish leaders with varying degrees of intensity claimed all thirty-two counties. In the north the loyal Unionists, Protestant almost to a man, did not want all of Ulster, which would be difficult to control, but only the six counties in the northeast where a two-to-one majority over the Catholics would guarantee "their way of life" protected by the assembly at Stormont.

Suspecting Catholic disloyalty and fearing the ambitions of the Papist Irish Free State to the south, the majority maintained the symbols of their loyalty to Britain and flaunted their domination every year in a series of provocative parades and demonstrations usually led by the massed militants of the Orange Masonic lodges. The Catholic minority responded in kind where possible, organizing commemorations in honor of Republican patriots and martyrs. From time to time various Catholic-Nationalist politicians attempted to work within the Stormont system, but to little avail. Injustice became institutionalized in gerrymandered election districts, in housing allotments, in weighted ballots, in council employment. Privately, the two communities led lives of self-imposed isolation. The two tribes were distinguished by religious labels. Only rarely could a common interest, such as mutual poverty or community loyalty, breach the wall of suspicion and distrust. Once the minority opted for civil disobedience, order decayed to IRA advantage. The Provos rushed toward rebellion.

Between July 1970 and January 1971 Provo strength in Belfast alone had grown from a few hundred, often self-selected volunteers to a thousand. There were arms, often ill-matched and insufficient, explosives, often primitive and unstable, and vast enthusiasm, but not yet a direction other than area defense. Belfast's religious segregation meant that Catholic areas were safe ground, organized by local men and protected by their neighbors, who were in turn protected by the local IRA company. The city was divided into three battalion areas and commanded by a brigade staff, directed in general terms by the seven-man Army Council and the GHQ Staff in Dublin. There was a large unit in Derry and smaller groups scattered about the province, but the key was Belfast. There, until January 1971, the British army was still tolerated, though not welcomed as it had been a year before, and some Provo units even cooperated informally in keeping the peace. By that time, however, there had been a largely unnoticed change in Northern

Ireland; the Provo potential, husbanded by the leadership, was about to be revealed.

The British army that had "saved" the Catholics in August 1969 had gradually and not unexpectedly been alienated from the minority, a minority with different symbols, one which suspected or opposed "legitimate" local authority and never was convinced that Ulster was British. The activities of the British army were a prime cause for the shift. With a generation of experience in peacekeeping and low-level violence, the British army saw, and was allowed to see, its mission as the imposition of order. The doctrine was available and, with Aden only a couple of years in the past, so, for many, was the experience. This Irish mission, in spite of some institutional and political restrictions, was pursued with a vigor that seemed disproportionate to those most often gassed or beaten, the minority Catholics. The British army was perceived as biased, acting for Stormont, rushing in CS gas and Saracen armored cars to beat down a few lads tossing rocks at an Orange parade. The security forces insisted that they were merely getting on top of the situation, preventing worse trouble.

The British commanders in Belfast knew that although it might be possible to get on top of trouble for a while, without parallel political maneuvers the trouble would get worse. And it did. Yet in London this all but predictable decay of the new military order was ignored. Provo operations reached such a grave point by midsummer 1971 that the British cabinet had acceded to the wishes of the Stormont government and introduced internment. Open urban guerrilla war erupted and was supported by the outraged minority. The bombing and sniping escalated. There was rumor and then evidence of British torture and beatings. Large areas of Belfast and Derry became IRA no-go zones, beyond the reach of security forces. On a single day in December, the Provos mounted over thirty bombing operations throughout the province. The Provos had their *real* campaign at last, thanks to the efficiency of the British army, delay in London, and their own historic reaction to opportunity.

In an effort to maintain the pressure on Britain, both the civil rights people and the Republicans staged a series of demonstrations. The result was violent confrontation. Then in Derry on January 30, came Bloody Sunday, in Catholic eyes a massacre. The British Embassy in Dublin was burned by a mob. The Irish government, no friend of the IRA, was gravely embarrassed. In London at last came realization that "something must be done" in response to Catholic grievances rather than in opposition to the IRA. Meanwhile, Protestant militancy was rising. Paramilitary groups appeared, bigotry under a suave exterior disappeared, and raw hatred could be heard from Protestant platforms. In March the British finally terminated their long deliberation and announced the promulgation of the Stormont assembly. There would be direct rule from Britain. A year before the ground would have been swept out from under the Provos, but in March 1972 the volunteers were in no mood to quit. The British were on the run. Stormont was gone. The Protestants lacked the will and capacity to launch a fatal, sectarian civil war. There had been a brief truce in mid-March and now after the end of Stormont the Provos were willing to talk, but about an all-Ireland solution not a patched-up assembly. The bombs continued.

By mid-1972 Belfast and Derry were cities under siege. Large areas were demolished by bombs; British roadblocks faced those of the IRA; there was armor in the streets and constant sniping. The car bomb was introduced in March and more shops and offices were turned into rubble. Constant ambushes in the country and a border war drew British forces away from the urban areas. There was no peace with or without justice, and more observers began to feel that the Provos just might bomb their way to a place at some ultimate bargaining table. And in fact they did. In July 1972 the new British Cabinet Minister in charge of Ireland finally met secretly in London with leading members of the Provos. As a first step a truce was negotiated. The distance between the Provos—release all internees and prisoners, amnesty for all, British withdrawal from Ulster, and an Irish solution—and the British was vast. After all, Northern Ireland was an integral part of the United Kingdom whose inhabitants had by large majorities repeatedly declared their loyalty to the Crown and whose future was protected by parliamentary legislation. Still the impossible had happened and the Provos were in London to talk to the Cabinet. For rebels, most of whom had been retired, some for decades, or who were not involved in politics two years before, they had come a long way.

They were, it turned out, still a long way from the end of the road. The truce collapsed. The London talks were revealed by the Provos. The British Cabinet, outraged, decided to shift tactics once again. That a truce would lead to a formal accommodation had been a dubious prospect at best, but worth attempting. The British in Operation Motorman moved troops into the no-go zones undefended by the Provos. There were more bomb blasts in Belfast. More voices called for a pause, including even those of the Official IRA. The Provos paid no attention and settled down to a campaign of attrition. After the brief emotion of the Derry deaths receded in the south, the Dublin government took increasingly hostile steps to limit IRA activities: arrests, new security legislation, internment, and harassment. Repression (north and south), the British determination to stick it out, the criticism of all types of Irish political opinion, including the Official Republican Movement, the decline of international interest, the erosion of support by the exhausted minority, and the risks of renewed sectarian violence in no way diminished the determination of the Army Council to pursue the revolt.

Between the first great burst of sectarian violence in August 1969 and the campaign of attrition in 1973, the British response to Irish events, despite the special nature of Ulster, followed a pattern remarkably similar to those of the previous generation of imperial dissolution. It may be possible to say, and a good many Irishmen have done so, that this is so for an obvious reason: Britain's relation to Ireland has always been that of a colonial power. Although this might be a simplistic analysis of eight hundred years of very complicated history, a pattern emerges nevertheless. First, the British were surprised at the sectarian violence of August 1969, surprised at the rapid decay of the situation in 1971, surprised at the depth of hatred and the repeated recourse to violence, and perhaps it should be pointed out horrified as well. The initial tendency was to blame the new troubles on both Green and Orange bigots, but increasingly British animosity focused on the IRA. Indignation replaced horror at the tiny Republican minority's violent operations against the British army performing legitimate peace-keeping duties for the benefit of all. Clearly the IRA maintained support by intimidation, since most Catholics surely wanted only decent reforms and peace. The IRA, then, was illegitimate, outlawed in the north and south, composed of dreadful bombers who killed innocent civilians in an effort to force the Loyalist majority into an alien state against their interests, in opposition to the promises of the London government, to the inclinations of the Dublin government, and perhaps even to the wishes of the Catholic minority, who were the beneficiaries of all sorts of British welfare programs.

These Irish Republican terrorists, unlike the Chinese Communists in Malaya or the Mau Mau murderers in Kenya, were not all that alien to the British, but the aspirations of a secret army so disreputable as to be disowned even by the Irish Republican government in Dublin, not to mention most respectable opinion elsewhere, were alien enough. Thus, by 1971 British attitudes differed little from what they had been elsewhere in the Empire: surprise, shock, outraged indignation, a public determination not to deal with a small, illegitimate gang of violent men who used terror to garner support for a mistaken and flawed cause. In February 1971, when security forces slipped from peacekeeping into anti-insurgency, the typical two-pronged British attack on the problem began: military and security operations in the service of political initiatives that sought to erode rebel support by creating parallel options. Even the fact that the political option had been so haltingly deployed was not novel and much ground had already been covered before March 1972 by committees and investigations and consultations, as well as pressure on Stormont to do something more for the minority. The promulgation of Stormont was seen in part as a means to open up the road to a regional solution by devolution that would wean the minority from an all-Ireland solution. The Provo-Cabinet meeting in London probably resulted in large part from British hopes that a truce would work to British advantage by reducing the role of the gunmen and giving the minority a taste for the quiet life. Whatever the ulterior motive, it revealed once more British flexibility. London had officially, if secretly, talked to the terrorists, just as they had talked to nearly everyone. In the year since internment, Britain had kept on throwing out lines and floating balloons.

The Ulster Emergency is peculiar in that no longer are important British security interests involved. (There never were serious economic considerations since the province absorbs far more funds than it returns.) However, it concerns the future of a part of the United Kingdom inhabited by those who, despite their professions of loyalty, are cherished by few in Britain. In 1921 Britain managed to cope with far more unusual and complicated Irish challenges; now in 1976 London appears set on enduring the difficulties in the name of moral responsibility—to evacuate would insure sectarian civil war. Since the Conservatives, and now Labour, refuse to withdraw and have not found a formula to defuse the IRA, the Emergency may drag on for some time. All that an uneasy unilateral truce has accomplished is a decline in military casualties and a rise in sectarian murder.

The Irish rebels have remarkable similarities with their immediate imperial predecessors. That hard core of dedicated and zealous men who came into the streets of Belfast in 1969 to defend their people represented a movement, an attitude, a response fashioned by a heritage and an experience stretching back almost into the Celtic twilight. Their cause, a united Ireland, free and Gaelic, without religious distinction, had regularly attracted the idealistic and dedicated, often from a background neither Catholic nor Celtic. For two centuries the means had been the same: the use of physical force to break the British connection. Coupled with their long Republican heritage, the men in Belfast had lived their lives humiliated and oppressed in what should have been their own country by the injustice of the Stormont system.

As often was the case, the Irish Republican cause in Ulster was flawed; no matter how the province of Northern Ireland had been created, or why, it was inhabited by a million Protestants who abhorred the idea of a united Ireland. For them there were two Irelands. Their wishes had been respected in the legislation of the British Parliament, in the gradual and graceless acquisition to this fact by the Dublin government, and even by long toleration of individuals and institutions of the minority. The enlightened in the majority accepted that discrimination and oppression might have to go, but would accept neither need nor legitimacy in any all-Ireland solution. Irish Republicans contended that the Protestant minority had no right to stand in the path of a nation; that the "majority" had been manipulated for British interests and that once the connection was broken it would be absorbed to great advantage in a new Ireland; and that in any case there could be no justice for the Ulster Catholics outside a united Ireland.

Thus, in 1969 a small group of zealots had a cause, flawed or not, a remedy for the existing intolerable troubles, and a heritage of revolt. During the autumn and winter of 1969–70, the Provisionals created an alternative IRA and absorbed some units, north and south, or built up new ones. They did not alter the old form. Because of the habits of the past and the limited number of arms, the Provos remained a conspiracy of rebels tied into local neighborhoods, a structure guaranteeing an urban guerrilla strategy. No one really considered novel structures; the old structures would do; they were comfortable and reflected the reality of the situation in the North. Unlike other rebels, once the organization was set and to a degree armed, there was no sense that time was running out, that someone must strike soon, nor any feeling that victory must be grasped immediately. Delay was for specific purposes since all were confident that sooner or later a revolt would occur. Between 1969 and 1971, the Provos concentrated on transforming themselves from Catholic defenders to rebels against the Crown, without losing the support of the people. This point was reached by February 1971, when sufficient arms had been acquired. Internment in August simply made the shift more obvious.

The IRA did not create long-range scenarios. Its prime concern was to manipulate conditions so the revolt could begin. When the point was reached, the Army Council assumed that escalating operations in Northern Ireland would make the province ungovernable, destroy the Stormont regime, and coerce the British into withdrawing. Few recognized that because of a long heritage of attitudes and previous experience, tactical options would be limited unless seriously reappraised. Whole categories of tactics or techniques fell outside intended Provo practice: assassination, operations in either Britain or Southern Ireland, spectacular "stunts," or calculated casualties in large operations in the North. The Official IRA was more flexible, but it fell along the wayside, abandoning most military activities for political ones. Also, Provo tactics, although they created great sound and fury, were not carefully orchestrated for effect or cunningly directed at a target beyond the victim. The Ulster campaign did not become an intolerable burden to Britain in funds, pride, or lives, although normal life collapsed under the detonating bombs. Therefore, as time passed Provo hopes shifted from coercing the British into leaving to the prolonged effect of violent attrition. There was *some* hope that leverage might work, perhaps within the Labour Party, but centuries of exposure to British hypocrisy had convinced the Irish that London would rule without shame. And the official reports and explanations concerning outrages in Ireland—whether torture or Bloody Sunday or internment—underlined the lessons of the past. Unlike Palestine, Ireland was not a glass house, the Provos had no prominent friends, and the British public would support their army's exercises against the Irish terrorists most of the time. The only hope was that the British would tire of defending "a bloody awful place" and withdraw under some face-saving formula. Accordingly, the same tactics, improved or elaborated, were continued: commercial sabotage by means of bombs, sniping, mass confrontations, and ambushes in the countryside. There was some improvement in techniques and more sophisticated weapons were introduced, but, with one or two exceptions, no novel tactical innovations were attempted.

As always, the armed struggle dominated the revolt and absorbed the interest and talent of the most committed; also, as always, it managed to send out but one message unit. Provo efforts to devise a political face with a political party, Sinn Féin, and support of a nine-county Ulster assembly, were largely ignored. In spite of unilateral truces, massed demonstrations, and the rent and rate strikes, it appeared obvious that if conventional politics prevailed the Provos would be a small minority. Not unlike the dilemma that faced Begin in Palestine, they were in a position of bombing their political opponents into positions of power once the campaign ended and the ballot returned. The Army Council, reluctant to recognize this fact, hoped that once the British connection was broken the political scene, north and south, would be transformed. Thus, the Irish rebels against the Crown concentrated on military operation in the North, determined to wait it out and convinced that this time the connection would be broken and Ireland free at last.

If the British in Ireland followed the script without much editing and the Provos nearly so, the nature of their lethal dialogue hews even more closely to previous experience. No matter how complex and sophisticated the overt strategy of revolt may be, the basic essential for the rebels is to send a single, violent message unit, loud, persistent, adamant, and, if possible, only interrupted to rebel advantage. This effort in communication ordinarily absorbs almost all the movement's available talent and energies. And it does in Ireland. Subsidiary activities, civic disobedience or strikes or demonstrations, all those aspects of the strategies of agitation and confrontation, would be inappropriate and futile unless orchestrated with the armed struggle. In addition, much "political" activity is aimed at supporting the military: money, men, weapons, communications, intelligence, and propaganda maneuvered by the men behind the guns. Much legitimate agitation—demonstrations of mass support, riotous meetings, boycotts, displays, and gestures—is a means to increase the din of the armed struggle and erode the assets of the opponent.

The key for the rebel is armed violence. Once that is controlled as in Malaya or Kenya or Egypt by security operations, all is lost. A deaf British ear can be turned from the fainter and fainter message unit of violence. The rebel may be defeated by a combination of factors beyond the scope of his message unit, as was Grivas, or succeed because of decisions equally beyond his capacity to alter, as was the case in Aden. But as long as the message can be sent at volume, he has not lost. Consequently, a movement must be so shaped and so directed that the message unit can be sent even under severe pressure. After that, other messages taking other forms—a unilateral truce, a United Nations resolution, a petition to the Commons, or the intervention of friends—may be devised, but the overwhelmingly important question remains how to persist and perhaps to escalate the most effective means of communication.

There were not in Ireland or elsewhere a great many strategic options considered nor detailed expectations. Armed revolt is a crude and costly means of communication, and rebel analysis tends to reflect this. The strategy of most of the movements against the British can be set out in slogans: (1) Begin before it is too late, because we must; (2) Keep up the pressure, without risking too many of our people; (3) Because of the winds of history and the righteousness of the cause in time, willingly or not, the British, being British, will concede. Whether in Belfast or Aden, the rebel arrives at the sticking point with all but one of the big questions answered: how to devise tactics that will amplify the single message unit.

Rebels concentrate on techniques and tactics, not strategic scenarios: which operations are possible; which will be effective in humiliating or damaging the British, especially (often solely) their security forces? And, as in Ireland, the possible has already been determined by the limitations of ideology, by the attitudes and values of the rebel and his people, by the structure of the organization, by the limitations of the campaign site, and by the assumed response of the British. No matter what the conditions or the situation at the moment the struggle begins, usually only a few tactical options remain to open the lethal dialogue.

Once under way, a rebel movement can rarely draw back; even a truce carries great dangers permitting decay of caution, guaranteeing exposure of the hidden, and encouraging a decline in militant support. In a real sense the rebel is doomed to his original either/or proposition. His only really effective means is violence; the protest and agitation often engendered by the armed struggle would fade away in normal negotiations—or so the rebel fears. Except in the realm of violence the British opponent, legitimate, replete with talent and funds, and practiced in diplomacy, has all the assets. This was a major factor in engendering the revolt in the first place; the British would not engage in a decent dialogue with alien spokesmen. All that remained was armed struggle or bitter resignation. In Ireland, more than anyplace, a heritage reflecting this analysis had been handed down through the generations. For Wolfe Tone, as for every Irish Republican since, the only effective means of freeing the country has been physical force. Others may place their hope in conciliation or confrontation, in agitation in the streets or election to parliament, boycott or general strike, but not the zealous and adamant Irish rebel. He knows from his reading of the past centuries that regarding Irish matters Britain listens to but one message, physical force. And few of his distant peers in Aden or Malaya or Cairo would disagree. If, then, the Irish template is placed over the entire recent British imperial experience, the fit is more than adequate. The British response to the revolt in Northern Ireland coincided to a remarkable degree with those of the generation of imperial dissolution.

The British had experienced all sorts of problems in Ulster. As noted, one of their difficulties was orchestrating an effective response to conflict. The army complicated matters by reacting to violent agitation as if protest were the same as rebellion, thus assuring that this would be the case. The government of the moment, any moment, complicated tomorrow's policy by avoiding today's decisions—delay between 1969 and 1971 proved deadly, and, ultimately, time lost could not be made good or made to seem good. No one in London ever knew quite what to make of the Unionist and never quite recognized a community of interest with Dublin, no matter the government of the moment, until too late. And despite all the political initiatives, the social and economic programs, the reforms and renewed starts, the elections and referendums, the discussions, seminars, private conferences, and public promises, despite even the royal visits and rumors of torture, despite corrupting the judicial system and unleashing the police, despite everything, the problem, except immediately after an atrocity or briefly at the end of a busy agenda, remains a marginal matter in London. Ireland, still a mix of Cornwall and the Congo, charm and black violence, is a far away place, little understood, seldom visited, rarely a crucial matter in Parliament or Westminster—a bloody awful place. And the British are hardly singular in this respect, in Dublin too, their are all sorts of problems without solutions; in fact the problem of Ulster is that there is no solution.

14

Democracy and Armed Conspiracy, 1922–77

It is not those who can inflict the most
but those that can suffer the most who
will conquer . . .
—Terence MacSwiney

In Dublin the government, overtly or not, has since 1923 been forced to cope with the residue of the civil war, the legacy of thwarted dreams, the nation not risen but receded, the persistent malignant node of pure Republicans. At the best of times, erosion of enthusiasm, aging, private ambitions, the hard edges of reality grating against the ideal, the futility of action may allow a time of calm—the IRA quiescent, the gun in storage, the era aclamor with other options, other ambitions, other rewards. The British at worse can oppose the gun with a greater gun, the dream with imperial reality, and can act without question, without guilt, in London's interest for London's purpose, and perhaps in the interests of the militant, unpleasant Loyalists as well. The power center at Westminster can deal from strength with, impose order on, pass with faint protest compelling legislation against, imprison, exile, execute, and best of all ignore the Irish rebels. The Dublin government can so do only with some qualms, regular second thoughts, and considerable political danger. For that pretentious and violent Irish rebel, equally revolting from Leinster House as Westminster, speaks with patriot tongue in sacred words, claims the same ancestors, engenders in the countryside echos and emotions, if not presently relevant, still real.

Dublin must deal with a mutual history as well as present muddle, deny in quiet what cannot be jettisoned in public, and hang the patriot boy. It was not easy for the Dublin government to honor the patriot Roger Casement for encouraging Irish–German trade, as it were, and on the same day arrest his descendents who were smuggling arms into Kerry from afar. It was easy to read the old Easter speeches, visit Tone's grave, love the dead

213

rebel and at the same time imprison the lad who lives the testament and dies for Ireland. But times do change, and dreams do fade. Much of the island is a nation once again, and Fenians are very long dead. Notwithstanding Europe and the green pound, VAT, divorce and abortion, ring roads and ticky-tack glass boxes in Dublin, the North matters; the new Troubles, a tragedy in endless acts, matters; the old speeches, the dream, the dreadful never-dead past matters. And Dublin, responsible, adult, moderate, and decent, must cope, especially with the alien North. Ulster for the rest of the island, the free Irish and the partly free Irish is still an alien place, dour, dark, narrow, grey stone edges; it is a place filled with not only Protestants, fanatical preachers, arrogant landlords, ignorant gunmen with Union Jack boutonnieres, and ship workers with different songs, psalms, and bias but also a province filled with Catholics who are lost, hard, radical, unforgiving, pious, equally unpleasant, often betrayed, and impossible to forget. On a soft, amber day in dirty Dublin, the Falls and the felons are forever away, and no plow boy would rush to the low green hills of Armagh or Down even to play the patriot game.

Few national governments, perhaps no other, have for so long been required to respond to rebels within the body politic who, more than the state, possess the symbols of the nation and encorporate the dream of a people. Ruthless, brutal, inept, arrogant, narrow, often bitter, dubious friends, awesome enemies, generation after generation, the IRA gunmen have cast a cold shadow across the warm pleasantries of Dublin politics, over the smaller triumphs and tragedies of parliamentary politics. Many states have overt rebels and cope—a lost generation, a lost cause, the adamant in prison, the fanatics across the seas in exile. Many states have institutionalized tyranny, oppressing those who by race or inclination would rise against the center, but few democratic states have to cope with resistance beyond the generation of convulsion. A few states do have persistant problems, but for democracies, an unresolved ethnic problem may be accommodated (there is federalism or absorption or regional reward), and few rebels manage to recruit decade after decade—times change, issues shift, priorities are transformed, and unnegotiable demands become irrelevant. Thus within a state, the Fascists win or lose, the Brigate Rosses come and go, the young pretenders are across the water, and the legions of the Confederacy are gone with the wind, subjects for novels. In Ireland the IRA persists; the Legion of the rear guard cannot be relegated to fiction, polished into old legend, and dipped in amber. A real government must cope with both real rebels and real myths, ill winds for the conventional; those who must balance law and order, liberty and security, must cope with the realities of governing against the power of myth.

All nations are special, their experience difficult to transfer. Ireland often seems more special than most. Despite a heritage of violence and a tradition of rebellion, there has not been for nearly two centuries any real debate on the ideal physiology of government (parliamentary democracy), only debate on the forms of the state (British province, Home Rule, the Republic) and the bounds, thus, of the nation. Since the establishment of the Irish Free State in December 1922, no serious political organization has considered an alternative to democracy. The Irish struggle of national liberation, the first of the twentieth century and archetype for all others, has not only led to a democracy but also to a democracy accepted by nearly all—the fruit of a long tradition, a heritage or compromise and accommodation as well as violence and rebellion.

Yet since 1922 Irish governments have been troubled by the presence of unreconciled Irish Republicans, organized overtly and legally as the Sinn Féin Party and covertly as the Irish Republican Army. And since 1922 Dublin governments, manipulating various strategies of accommodation and repression, have sought to achieve as much of the ideal Republican as practical while simultaneously opposing the pretensions of the IRA. Ultimately, the primary obstacle proved to be the existence of the Province of Northern Ireland, as an integral part of the United Kingdom. Thus, Dublin managed in the twenty-six counties to remove the symbols and trappings of the British connection, to cut the Commonwealth ties, but not to end partition. And so with this last grievance, coupled with a general concern for the fate of the Northern Catholic minority, the IRA has maintained both a mission and a means—physical force—that Dublin denied itself.

A great deal that goes on in Northern Ireland, then, has a tremendous impact on Southern events, but can only marginally be shaped by Dublin. After the establishment of the Irish Free State in 1922, there still remained, decade after decade, the dream of the ideal Republic that in public at least all Southern politicians revered. Most of the Irish recognized it was a dream but always some were willing to die for it. An IRA volunteer sought the Republic, denied the validity of the puppet regimes at Leinster House in Dublin and Stormont in Belfast, and sought to break the British connection.

Background

About the only general agreement concerning the present Irish Troubles is that the violence has long roots, at least back to the seventeenth-century planting of large numbers of English and Scottish Protestants in Ulster, sponsored by the British Crown. Their descendants form the loyal base of the Province and the British connection. For many Irishmen the British connection is the source of all Irish ills and must be broken by the only effective means—physical force. These, the "men of violence," heirs to a long revolutionary tradition, and members of the IRA, dedicated to the establishment of a thirty-two-county Republic first declared by the leaders of the Easter Rising. The 1916 Rising failed, but the separatists after 1918 waged the archetypal national liberation struggle. In 1921 Britain, exhausted by the war and frustrated after centuries of the Irish Question, unable to win by acceptable means and unwilling to resort to terror, sought a negotiated settlement. In effect the IRA, unable to win, had refused to lose, thus bombing the British to the bargaining table. What evolved was an Anglo-Irish agreement, accepted by the Irish Dáil on 4 January 1922. And from that agreement and what it implied flowed all the subsequent challenges to the Irish state. Its advocates claimed that it gave Ireland the right to be free, its opponents that it betrayed the Republic. According to the dedicated Republican leader Eamon De Valera, the people had no right to do wrong—a nation could not be denied by sixty-four votes to fifty-seven in the Dáil.

The Free State Years

The Anglo-Irish Articles of Agreement tied the new Irish Free State to Britain with a governor-general and an Oath to the Crown for Dáil deputies. The articles also delineated certain British-held military bases and various schedules of payments for land annuities, and incorporated a previous act of Parliament, the 1921 Government of Ireland Act that had established a separate Northern Ireland government in May 1921. But the big issue was the lost Republic, and in its name the IRA fought a brief and bloody civil war with the new Free State Army and lost. The IRA then went underground.

On 24 May 1923, Eamon De Valera sent the volunteers still in the field a final communiqué accepting that the Republic could not be defended by arms and other means had to be sought. The most apparent means appeared to be the Republican Sinn Féin Party that under De Valera's direction contested seats with the government dominated by the Cumann na nGaedheal. They did so, however, on an abstentionist platform—refusing to take seats in the "puppet" Dáil at Leinster House. The IRA did not disappear but reorganized for another round. In order to counter this potential threat to the Free State, the Dáil in August 1923 passed a Public Safety Act, an extension of existing emergency powers that permitted the continuation of internment.

This was merely the first step in the confrontation of the Cumann na nGaedgheal government with the Republicans. After some initial Sinn Féin successes, it became apparent to the pragmatic that absentionism denied the electorate effective representation and would assure an erosion of electoral strength. Sinn Féin split, and De Valera took the pragmatists out to form the new Republican Party of Fianna Fáil on 12 April 1926. Still refusing to take the Oath, Fianna Fáil ran a strong race in the June 1927 general elections, gaining forty-four seats to Cumann na nGaedheal's forty-seven. De Valera—if he and his allies went into the Dáil—might even form a government and win by the ballot what the IRA had failed to do with the bullet. Yet De Valera would not swallow the Oath. And the President, William T. Cosgrove, would make no concessions: if Fianna Fáil wanted to stay out of the Dáil, then they, like Sinn Féin, would become irrelevant. On July 10, the Cumman na nGaedheal minister of justice, Kevin O'Higgins, was assassinated. In the extremely tense atmosphere that ensued, De Valera and Fianna Fáil appeared at the Dáil and signed their names while insisting that they had not taken an Oath. In any case Fianna Fáil as "a slightly constitutional party" was in the Dáil, where their deputies glowered in opposition. A new Public Safety Act was passed and, outside parliamentary politics, abstentionist Sinn Féin soon decayed to a faithful few. But the underground IRA still created a very real security problem for the Free State government. The Special Branch detectives, using the new powers, sought to crush the IRA with some success. Yet large segments of the public if unwilling to sacrifice for the Republic still sympathized with the aspirations of the IRA. In the nearly five years of the Cumann na nGaedheal government, the IRA remained largely a potential rather than a present threat to launch an armed revolt. The Republicans talked about a second round but really did not want one.

The potential threat of the IRA engendered further legislation—in May 1929 a Juries Protection Bill was introduced in the Dáil. For a variety of reasons—IRA coercion being one—juries had shown a reluctance to convict accused Republicans. It was not, however, until the impact of the world depression on an already depressed Ireland inspired radicals to organize that the Free State government felt it necessary to seek additional legislation. The IRA had in the meantime shot several active policemen, intimidated juries, and became deeply involved in various militant organizations dedicated to socialist revolution or communism or worse. Some in the Cumann na nGaedheal truly felt threatened, and some members, not unmindful of the approaching general elections, could see political capital in a "Red scare." The result was Article 2A (a Public Safety Bill) inserted in the Constitution in October 1931. This permitted outlawing subversive groups and parties, the arrest of radicals, sweeping searches, and the establishment of Military Tribunals to try the suspects.

The Cumann na nGaedheal government saw the problem of rebellion after the end of the civil war as one of legitimacy. Their opponents must be persuaded or forced to accept the reality of the Irish Free State. If they did not, they faced arrest and imprisonment. Thus, the greatest triumph of the Free State was the entry of the "slightly constitutional" Fianna Fáil Party into the Dáil and into the system. Although Cumann na nGaedheal in 1929–32 chose to see the IRA and the radicals as a threat sufficient to require emergency legislation, any real danger to the institutions of the state from unrepentant Republicans had eroded. The second greatest accomplishment was the transfer of the power to their Republican enemies after the election of 1932. This was hardly remarked on at the time and yet, given the bitterness of feeling and the possession of the assets of the state, Cumann na nGaedheal's smooth shift to the opposition benches remains admirable.

The Eire/Ireland of Fianna Fáil

During the autumn of 1931, the IRA did not react to the arrests by recourse to the gun, in large part because of the impending general elections in February 1932 that gave Fianna Fáil seventy-two seats to Cumann na nGaedheal's fifty-seven. The interned were released. The banned publications reappeared. Article 2A was a dead issue along with the "Red scare."

What followed was a carefully wrought De Valera strategy to steal the IRA assets, thereby ending the necessity for an alternative secret army within the state. The Special Branch of the police, an IRA *bête noire,* was reorganized into the S-Branch under Colonel Eamonn Broy and staffed with ex-IRA people. A volunteer militia was set up giving potential IRA volunteers a uniform and a bit of money. Compensation was given for civil war losses and pensions for the Republican wounded. A Military Service Pensions Bill was enacted. Old grievances were thus transformed into new loyalties to the government. The government permitted the IRA to harass the Irish neo-Fascists, so the Army Council thus had a "mission."

De Valera dismantled as much of the Treaty settlement as possible. The governor-general was ignored and ultimately replaced by an obscure Fianna Fáil politician. The land annuities were no longer paid. The Oath, of course, was discarded. When Edward VIII abdicated, De Valera swiftly removed the Crown from the constitution and in 1937 a new Irish constitution was introduced, creating Eire/Ireland and claiming domination over all thirty-two counties. If it was not the Republic, at least it was not the Free State.

It was increasingly clear to the IRA Army Council that De Valera was not going to opt for the real Republic and was not going to end partition. And it was apparent to the Fianna Fáil government that the core of the IRA could not be co-opted and would not be satisfied with concessions. In 1936 the IRA chief of staff was arrested under Article 2A, no longer a dead issue. The following month the IRA was declared an unlawful association. Thereafter, nothing went right for the IRA. There were damaging arrests in the North. In July the Spanish Civil War began and many Irish Republicans left to fight for the Spanish Republic. The movement remained split between the Left radicals and the Center military types. There was constant seepage into Fianna Fáil or retirement. In 1938 an Anglo-Irish Agreement returned control of the British military bases to the Dublin government—a tremendous victory for De Valera and, many thought, a harbinger of an agreement to end partition. Seemingly the IRA had become, like Sinn Féin, irrelevant.

In fact the IRA entered a period of new militancy, presenting unexpected and unwelcome dangers to the state. On 12 January 1939, the IRA Army Council sent the British an ultimatum to withdraw from Ireland and three days later, when there was no response, issued a Proclamation of War. The major arena of IRA activities during 1939 and 1940 was Britain. IRA active service units detonated a long series of sabotage bombs, usually small, seldom effective, and without any real strategic purpose. British prisons began to fill up with those involved in "terrorist outrages," and except for the odd vicious incident—the worst being an explosion in Coventry that killed five and injured sixty in August 1940—life went on as usual. The major public concern was the war in Europe that began in September 1939.

In Dublin, in December 1940, the IRA under the direction of Stephen Hayes raided an arsenal in Phoenix Park and cleared out most of the "other" Irish army's ammunition. But what concerned the De Valera government was not so much this raid but evidence that the IRA had close contacts with Germany—Britain's foe and therefore a potential Irish ally. De Valera was determined on neutrality, a posture that would at last indicate complete separation from the United Kingdom. Any IRA-German connection could easily prompt a British invasion. Thus, the IRA seemed to De Valera to be dangerous and violent, waging a bombing campaign in Britain, dragging in German agents, indulging in bank robberies and gunfights.

The government first set up Military Tribunals in 1939 to try IRA suspects. The government at that time found the existing emergency legislation insufficient. The Offenses Against the State Act that permitted the suspension of civil and personal liberties was enacted. Various loopholes were filled when it was amended in 1940. The act largely paralleled the Northern Ireland Special Powers Act of 1922, allowing, for example, the government to imprison a person without holding a trial or making a charge. In 1940 hundreds of known Republicans were interned at the Curragh Military Camp; others were tried and convicted of various offenses.

The Special Branch police concentrated on tracking down and arresting those—many old comrades—on the run. To complicate matters for the IRA, members of the Northern Command in Belfast came South, found the organization in disarray, arrested, tried, and condemned Chief of Staff Stephen Hayes. He managed to escape from his former colleagues by leaping out a window and running to the nearest police station. Further arrests followed. There were one or two more gunfights. With tight censorship, IRA activities attracted little notice. The men in prisons and internment camps were largely forgotten. In 1944 the last chief of staff, Charlie Kerins, was captured, tried for the murder of a policeman, convicted, and hanged in December. By 1945 the IRA had apparently been destroyed as much by its own splits and schisms and futile campaigns of violence as by the repression of the governments in Dublin, London, and Belfast.

At first Fianna Fáil did not necessarily see a conflict of interest between the IRA and the Fianna Fáil government. As fast as possible, the hateful Anglo-Irish agreement was to be dismantled and as realistically as possible the country moved towards the Republic. In the process, of course, De Valera quite consciously co-opted potential opponents by eliminating old grievances, rewarding old services, opening new doors. While Cumman na nGaedheal had felt there could not be any legitimacy in Republican pretensions, De Valera believed that there could no longer be any purpose in them. When the hard core of the IRA persisted, Fianna Fáil, beginning in 1936, used the same tools of repression as had the Free State. After 1939 when the IRA threat not only to neutrality but also to internal order became serious, Fianna Fáil opted for more stringent legislation, more rigorous repression, and at least an end to sympathy for the misguided— IRA leaders were hanged, imprisoned for extensive periods under primitive conditions, and allowed to die on hunger strikes. Undertaken during a period of strict wartime censorship and in the name of the popular neutrality, Fianna Fáil's policy shift did not result in a similar political shift. The party still sought an end to partition, thus condemning not the IRA but only the IRA's means.

The Northern Campaign

Soon after the end of World War II, two initiatives were undertaken in Ireland to secure the ultimate Republic. With the aid of nationalists in Northern Ireland, Fianna Fáil mounted an international antipartition campaign, employing any available forum and relying mainly on publicity. Another approach was the formation of the Clann na Poblachta Party by Seán MacBride, a former IRA chief of staff, and a group of militant Republicans and radical reformers. In an Ireland that was stagnant without economic prospects, after sixteen years of De Valera, there was a tide toward change. In the February 1948 general elections, the Clann won ten seats and came close in others. Then, to everyone's amazement, MacBride formed a Dáil alliance with Fine Gael, the descendant of the Free State Cumman na nGaedheal, that put an end to the Fianna Fáil reign. Despite the presence of the Clann in the cabinet, there was little that the government could do to act on partition. In an effort to get the "Republican" issue out of politics, Taoiseach John A. Costello simply declared Ireland a Republic and the Dáil in 1948 passed the Republic of Ireland Act. The British Parliament responded with the Government of Ireland Act that assured there would be no change in the status of the province of Northern Ireland without the consent of the population of the six countries. There the matter rested. Antipartition had fizzled out. The "Republic" had been declared. And in the general elections in 1951 Fianna Fáil came back into office and the momentum of the Clann disappeared.

In June 1954, old Fianna Fáil was again replaced by another interparty government. By then, for the first time in a decade, there was evidence that the IRA had been buried too swiftly. In the North there were two spectacular arms raids on British army barracks in Armagh and Omagh in 1954, and then in December 1956 the guerrilla campaign opened with a series of cross-border attacks and lasted until February 1962, a low-intensity affair. In the North the Stormont government had depended on the Royal Ulster Constabulary (RUC) and the mobilization of the B-Specials. Suspected IRA people had been interned or tried and sentenced to prison terms. In the South Fianna Fáil, back in office in 1957, had interned suspected IRA volunteers and, when the campaign seemed likely to drag on in 1961, reintroduced military tribunals and long sentences.

During the period 1956–62 the response of the Dublin government to the IRA had become almost tradition: arrests, internments, police harassment, censorship where possible, refusal to concede to hunger strikers, and a continuing condemnation of violence. While there was some evidence of sympathy for the IRA, by 1962 physical force seemed outmoded by events. There had not been any great support from the Northern minority. Perhaps the old Republican "issues" no longer had an appeal. Tensions had so far eased that the Unionist Premier Terence O'Neill and the new Fianna Fáil Taoiseach Seán Lemass could exchange visits. Gradualism, a community of economic interest, and the easing of old grievances, bridge building appeared to be the new direction. In 1968 a small but vocal civil-rights movement was created seeking Stormont reform, not revolution. Even the IRA had put the gun on the shelf and gone into radical politics.

In the postwar years the only difference in the response of the interparty and the Fianna Fáil governments to IRA provocation was that the latter proved firmer. Neither could make any substantive contribution on the issue—partition—but then neither really felt that the IRA campaign was a very great threat. One or two of the highly emotional demonstrations certainly worried Leinster House, but the old tools of internment, imprisonment, military tribunals, police raids, and the rest did not need reinforcement.

The Northern Troubles, 1968–1977

For the Irish Republic the escalating turmoil in the North after 1968 produced a series of unexpected traumas, rekindled old fires, and ultimately produced a dedication to new realities. The major problem for the Irish government at Leinster House was an inability to act legitimately on Northern events and an unwillingness to stand idly by, mute and futile. The civil disobedience campaign was greeted with complete enthusiasm by Dublin—"our people" in the North had found a means to remove the inequities of the Stormont State. As the shrewd had expected and a few intended, the campaign engendered a violent Protestant blacklash by militants who already suspected that the moderate O'Neill was going to sell them out to the "Papists." Dublin deplored the violence and urged reform on Stormont and London. London, with the Irish Question back after a lapse of fifty years, responded lethargically. The rising aspirations of the minority made it impossible for Stormont to keep pace with new reforms while damping Protestant anguish. The ultra-loyalists knew that "civil rights" was a code word for United Ireland and "civil disobedience" the harbinger of an IRA campaign. Ultimately in Derry, in August 1969, Stormont could no longer maintain order and the British army had to be moved in.

The response in the South was an anguished concern about the fate of the Northern minority, open to Protestant pogroms, "protected" by Protestant police and a British army that would hardly be congenial to minority concerns. There was little that could be done. It was difficult enough for a member of Fianna Fáil to welcome the presence of British troops in Derry and Belfast. It was quite impossible to send in Irish troops, even if there had been enough. Calls for United Nations action or contacts with Northern Irish political leaders hardly produced the stuff of drama.

What some members of the Fianna Fáil government undertoook was to underwrite a dissident segment of the IRA disenchanted with the Dublin Army Council's "political" approach and by their inability to aid the Northern minority in August. By the end of the year, the new Provisional IRA had evolved and until April 1970 operated in a tacit alliance with the Fianna Fáil ministers who donated money and endeavored to arrange arms shipments. Those in Fianna Fáil involved with the Provos were revealed as plotters, indicted, brought to trial in the autumn of 1970, and, as expected, acquitted. By then the Provos, with the Official IRA at their heels, were moving out of the role of Catholic defenders into that of urban guerrillas.

During 1970 in the North, there was a gradual slide into chaos. The security policies of the British Army eroded Catholic goodwill. Sectarian clashes continued. Moderate politicians disappeared. In April 1969, O'Neill had given way to his cousin Chichester-Clark, who had to balance the necessity for reforms urged by London with the need to placate the Unionist militants. The latter wanted the British Army to step in and crush the IRA. The IRA wanted them to try, thus solidifying their position as Catholic Defenders. Matters slipped out of hand. Desperate, the Stormont establishment urged internment. The London government that for so long had done little suddenly decided to authorize internment. The minority response to the internment "humiliation" was intense. There was a rent and tax strike. Most of the Catholic ghettos in Belfast and Derry became no-go zones. The province collapsed into open guerrilla war. More British troops were sent in and yet the violence escalated.

The two years following the arrival of the British Army in August 1969 had been most trying in Dublin. The apparent ministerial involvement with the Provos and the arms smuggling had been scandalous, but understandable. Some who were involved had no apologies. Many in the country condoned their motives if not their methods. In the South the government, thus, felt any moves against the IRA must be undertaken cautiously. The Special Branch did keep a close watch, but with two IRAs, hundreds of new volunteers, and all the unknown Northerners drifting back and forth, they were out of their depth. For many, the IRA rebels were the new heroes. Dublin was often jammed with international press and media people. Former Prime Minister Harold Wilson even came to Dublin to talk to the Provos, using a meeting with Irish cabinet ministers as a cover. No one abroad was interested in the real government of Leinster House. For Jack Lynch and the cabinet, the problem was to dampen the potentially explosive emotionalism that might lead to action—any action, no matter how self-destructive. All the news from the North made this difficult: The IRA campaign, the idiocy of internment, the revelation of British Army and RUC torture techniques, and then in January 1972, Bloody Sunday. Two nights later, while the police stood idly by, the Dublin mob burned down the British embassy.

For Fianna Fáil and subsequent governments, Bloody Sunday was the most dangerous moment. The mob was in the street. The IRA was immune. And the cabinet literally had no policy and no possibility of effecting Northern events. The IRA guerrilla campaign escalated. In March the British government promulgated the Provincial government. The Provos claimed that they had bombed down Stormont. For Dublin the hope was that this meant the time for violence had passed. This was paticularly true when on 7 July 1972 the Provos met in London with British ministers and agreed to a cease-fire. The officials had already unilaterally announced their own cease-fire. Although the Provo-British agreement collapsed two days later, Dublin insisted that the time for politics had arrived. Cautious moves began to be made to restrict the IRA freedom of action in the South. The army and police picked up those involved in cross-border attacks. Selected Republican leaders were arrested and questioned. All sensible people in London and Dublin and Ulster urged political initiatives, all-party talks, and accommodation.

The IRA kept on bombing. On Friday, July 21, 22 bombs exploded in Belfast killing 9 people and injuring about 130. There was general revulsion. In the wake of Bloody Friday, on July 31, the British moved into the Derry no-go zones. Although it was not apparent at the time, the Northern Troubles had entered a new period. First, the IRA could now only pursue a campaign of attrition; the struggle could not be maintained at the July level, but could not be wound down by the British. Second, it was reluctantly accepted that the new Protestant paramilitary organizations had undertaken a campaign of random assassination. The British strategy was to attempt to hold down the violence while fashioning various institutions, proposals, referendums, and initiatives that would permit conventional politics at the center. The Irish response was to encourage all sorts of efforts while hedging about the IRA activities.

Yet every maneuver to create a center for politicans in the North failed. Between March 1973 and May 1975, the North went to the polls seven times and remained polarized. The IRA wanted the British out and a united Ireland. The Protestant paramilitaries wanted no united Ireland, no power-sharing, and no compromise, so they continued to commit random murder. The moderate Catholic and Protestant politicans often found their communities alienated, their gunmen with a veto, and their friends in Dublin and London unable to help. Britain could keep the army in place to prevent open civil war, but it could not pacify the provinces or operate by any other means than direct rule from London. Dublin's only formal involvement had come after Anglo-Irish talks led to an agreement that foresaw some vague Council of Ireland—one of the reasons the militant Protestants refused to cooperate in power-sharing. With no Council of Ireland, Leinster House was left urging moderations in the North and trimming IRA wings in the South.

The end of Stormont and the increasing discussions by Britain of an Irish dimension to the Northern problem at least and at last gave Dublin some leverage. Spokesmen claimed that the IRA campaign was no longer needed, that it alienated decent Protestants and inspired the paramilitaries to sectarian murder. The continued IRA bombing and the rising toll of civilian casualties also had convinced many that the Dublin position had much to offer. Many insisted that the Provos should have quit while they were ahead. Various voices were raised in the cause of moderation. And Fianna Fáil decided to act, to take the risk of closing down the Provos. On 19 November 1972, Irish security forces arrested Seán MacStíofáin, chief of staff of the Provisionals, under section 30 of the Offenses Against the State Act. He went on a hunger and thirst srike. On November 25, he was sentenced to six months imprisonment. An IRA attempt to free him failed and he was moved to the Curragh Camp. On November 27, the government announced details of a new antiterrorist bill to be introduced in the Dáil. There were further arrests of Republicans. MacStíofáin ended his thirst strike. There were pro-IRA demonstrations, but the government pushed on. Then, during debate on the second stage of the Offenses Against the State (Amendment) Bill in the Dáil, bombs exploded in Dublin killing two people and injuring eighty-three. Fine Gael opposition collapsed, and the bill passed by a vote of seventy to twenty-three. In December the president of the Provisional Sinn Féin, Rory O'Brady, was arrested. Sinn Féin offices on Kevin Street were closed. IRA leaders from the North were arrested. The pattern had now been set; the Provos would not be tolerated. In Ireland the Curragh Camp began to fill up. On February 5, Taoiseach Jack Lynch dissolved the Dáil and went to the country—as a law and order candidate.

On February 28, the electorate transformed Lynch into the leader of the opposition. The Fine Gael-Labour Coalition now had seventy-three seats to Fianna Fáil's sixty-nine. As far as repressing the IRA was concerned, the coalition intended to follow Fianna Fáil's lead. Every effort was made to cooperate with British initiatives in the North. Dublin was frightened of a doomsday war in Northern Ireland as was London, and also as little interested in unity, as concerned with shoring up the Belfast center, and most of all as dedicated to ending the Troubles.

The posture over the next three years simply made Britain's impossible job easier but no more effective. All the elections, proposals, commissions, new groupings, and gatherings of old faces ended futilely. A power-sharing Assembly coalesced in January 1974, and four months later collapsed as a result of a Protestant general strike. In 1975 a new constitutional convention met, wrangled, and ended without a constitution. The Provos soldiered on. The Protestant paramilitaries continued the random murders.

The Troubles went on and on. There were no-warning bombs planted in British cities. There were book bombs and letter bombs. In the North there were car bombs, some driven by the Provos and some by the Protestant paramilitaries. There were bombs placed in Dublin streets and Irish hotels. And in August 1976, outside Dublin a massive bomb in a culvert detonated and killed the new British Ambassador Christopher Ewart-Biggs. The coalition government seized the opportunity to postulate an Irish emergency and push through further antiterrorist legislation that would increase sentences and narrow the opportunities for subversive publicity. Again civil liberties would be hedged about more narrowly than many thought proper. The most unexpected development was the decision of the Irish president, normally a figurehead, to send the bill before the Supreme Court. The court, albeit reluctantly, agreed to the act's constitutionality. A coalition minister sharply criticized the president's action. The president then resigned in protest, forcing a presidential election that the coalition refused to contest, anticipating defeat. All the maneuvering ended with emergency legislation that many felt was unnecessary and probably ineffective. The coalition's efforts over three years had been little different from those of previous challenged governments: arrests and sentences (on the evidence of a police superintendent's statement that the suspect had been a member of the IRA); harassment of known IRA members; increased cooperation with British and Northern security forces; increased responsiveness to all moderate initiatives; and condemnation of the men of violence and their pretensions. And at the end of the delicate waiting game, they kept faith in the realism of the Irish public and the eventual end of violence in the North. Without the carrot of unification, without even a desire to absorb the troublesome North, the coalition stressed the dangers of unification now, the potential horrors if the Provos continued their wicked ways, and the need for sensible compromises by men of good will.

When the Northern Troubles began in 1968, Dublin faced a problem. In public the state's ideals were the same as those of the IRA. In public and private there was universal concern about the safety of the Northern minority. In private there was a fear that the IRA might exploit that fear and the Dublin government's impotence to disrupt the democratic system. Thus, the IRA campaign in the North did not challenge the state as had the embittered IRA in 1923 or the IRA-German connection in 1940, nor could it be simply closed down by coercion as it had between 1957 and 1962. The IRA after 1969 had a mission that Dublin could not undertake—as Catholic Defender.

So far the Dublin solution has been to use every opportunity arising from shifts in Northern events—and consequently Southern opinion—to limit IRA activities. Even the ministerial involvement with the Provos in 1969–70 can be seen as an effort by some to co-opt a potentially dangerous organization. The major direction of both Fianna Fáil and, after 1973, the

coalition has been to make matters difficult for the IRA while choreograph-
ing a change in public attitudes: violence does not pay and is counterproductive; the IRA campaign has set back unification; it is impossible
to bomb the million Protestants in Ireland; the gunmen are wicked, cruel,
pretentious, and will assure that Northern violence bleeds into the South.
There has indeed been a change in Southern attitudes. Many in public
doubt the wisdom of a united Ireland. Although the defeat of the coalition
by Fianna Fáil in the June 1977 elections, in which their spokesman of the
North, Conor Cruise O'Brien, lost his seat, may give some pause. Still, few
see physical force as an effective or morally acceptable means. Thus, it is
not so much the stringent new emergency laws, continued police harassment, threats of censorship, or cooperation with the British government
that have changed in the government's response to provocation, but rather
the public political reasoning behind the necessity for such acts.

Review: The Nature of the Response

Any governmental reaction to a lethal challenge almost inevitably includes both "carrots" and "sticks." In the Irish case, for fifty years by far the
most important was the mix of carrots. By the 1960s, however, all the
carrots had been used but one, and that was owned by the British. The
major difficulty for Dublin is that this focus of discontent—Northern
Ireland—lies beyond the legitimate authority of the state. Except briefly,
when the British introduced the Council of Ireland as the Irish dimension,
formal Dublin involvement in Northern matters did not exist. More troublesome, until very recently Dublin could not persuade the British authorities in London of the communality of interests. London assumed,
when time could be spared for Irish matters, that Dublin on the subject of
unity meant what various officials had said, what the 1937 Constitution
claimed. Dublin thus had little leverage in London or Belfast. The Dublin
dilemma was not unique but was certainly an extreme example of the
difficulties of devising an effective strategy to contain those beyond the
reach of coercion or reward. Ultimately, a high degree of tactical cooperation with the British evolved and an often unstated acceptance of British
intensions and strategy. In time Dublin ran out of ideas, clung to the hope
that time and exhaustion would permit an effective Northern political
initiative, and concentrated on closing down the IRA in the twenty-six
counties, where effective tactical repression was possible.

The various Southern "sticks" of repression have been used to effect for
sixty years. The present basis for their use is the Offenses Against the State
Act of 1939, variously amended and elaborated by subsequent legislation.
In essence it all but puts members of the IRA beyond the protection of the

law; they can be arrested without warrant, imprisoned without charge or trial, and their homes, offices, organizations, and property become vulnerable to the security forces. On the word of a police superintendent alone they can be sentenced to prison. The latest legislation, passed by the National Coalition after the assassination of the British ambassador, among other features greatly extends the government's privileges of censorship. One of the primary reasons that such gross invasions of civil liberties have been tolerated by the general public is that as long as coercion is directed at the known Republicans, the restrictions are not seen as relevant to Irish society in general, not unfair for use against those dedicated to dismantling the state. Sympathy for the IRA may or may not exist, but few doubt that those interned or sentenced are guilty as charged, and the state is not unreasonable, for usually the state has not acted until IRA activities appear a real danger to cherished goals.

Once the IRA volunteer is imprisoned or interned, his life remains dedicated to the cause. Prison is an opportunity, not a penalty. Efforts by the authorities to prevent IRA people from having special treatment, to punish when possible, and to withhold privileges, educational benefits, or visits often tend to harden resistance, producing martyrs. It is, indeed, a policy of the state, quite unstated, to make life miserable everywhere for Republicans. Parents and employers are warned of the dangers of Sinn Féin membership. Suspects are questioned where and when the major amount of embarrassment will occur. Cars are stopped, tickets given, homes searched, members followed for little other purpose than to cause trouble. When arrests and imprisonments are the policy, often those most vulnerable, men with new jobs or sick wives or heavy mortgages, are lifted first. Once in prison and in the power of the state, the process becomes more intense. Irish prisons—cold, stone, Victorian monsters—are unpleasant at the best of times, with little heat, few recreational resources, limited exercise space, inedible food, and cursory medical attention. At times, in response to Republican provocation, prisoners have been allowed to remain naked—if they refused criminal prison garb—denied visits and letters, kept in solitary in cells without furnishings, denied medical attention, and denied Catholic communion. The authorities, when any public notice is taken, insist that the prisoners have brought on their own troubles or in some way provoke authority.

Those responsible for IRA prisoners—the prison wardens or army guards—rarely have any understanding of "political" prisoners and are permitted or encouraged to see *them* as beyond conventional bounds and dedicated to causing unnecessary trouble; therefore, they are fair game. Outside the prisons, this attitude has gradually been institutionalized in the Irish Special Branch, a force made up of plain-clothes detectives responsible for political subversion, often to the exclusion of all else. The regular unarmed police are nearly everywhere respected and seldom concerned with political matters. There has, however, been a noticeable erosion in their restraint with the escalation of Republican activity in the South. There have been accusations of brutal beatings, arrests on unfounded suspicion, coercive interrogation, and use of excessive force during the policing of various demonstrations. The Special Branch remains the cutting edge of the security forces. Yet the dialogue between IRA and Special Branch is a curious one, since Republican policy allows no armed action in the South—the shoot-outs in Dublin during the 1940s have never been repeated. This policy has prevented a cycle of vengeance and retaliation but has done little to moderate mutual antipathy.

Far more important than all the normal tactical police and legislative responses to the IRA have been the government's efforts to transform old Irish attitudes. Every effort is made to paint the IRA as a band of wicked murderers, as criminals who have nothing in common with the litany of old Irish patriots and martyrs. The IRA is illegitimate, brutal, without vision, unwittingly dedicated to destroying the very ideals it supposedly cherishes. And every effort is made to see that the IRA is denied any forum to respond. New legislation will deny Republican spokesmen the "right" to be questioned on Irish television, for example, or even to have their views quoted—a limited ploy, since the easily accessible British television networks have not accepted such a policy. Backed by the immensely powerful and immensely conservative Roman Catholic Church, by the men of property, by most newspaper editors, and by nearly all people of substance or reputation, the government's campaign has clearly had an effect. This is, in part—in large part—because of various IRA blunders. And it is in part because the prospect of a united Ireland containing not only a million embittered Protestants but also (far, far worse) a half-million radicalized and armed Catholics from a betrayed North is a frightening one. In this case the "stick" of reality has been used on the opponents of the IRA whose Northern campaign will endanger the existence of various Southern "carrots."

Summary: The Foundations of the Lethal Dialogue

The IRA Assets

A Traditional Legitimacy. The foundation that permits the operation of the Irish Republican movement has quite literally been centuries in the making and cannot readily be eroded by right reason or by the grating of a new reality. The Republicans have been strengthened by nearly two centuries of uncompromising efforts to break the British connection. They have claimed, and their claims have until recently seldom been denied by those seeking office, that the Republican revolutionary tradition has been largely responsible for what freedom Ireland has gained and that violence works—that all the democratic maneuvers, political agitation, and civil disobedience would have proved ineffective without recourse to physical force. This legacy of patriots has been accepted in Ireland as real history, not as myth or legend. Those who would deny the benefits accrued through an armed struggle have until recently been in a minority. Even today a great many of the Irish read their past as a long confrontation with British power and consequently accept the present IRA as, deserving or no, heirs to a heritage of struggle. Nearly all the effective symbols of the state and almost all the most gripping patriotic myths authorize this legitimacy.

When, at the funeral of a fallen volunteer, the Provos march slowly to the wail of pipes, impassive under black berets and hidden behind dark glasses, awaiting the final volley over the grave of another patriot and martyr, there is a moment of deep emotion that no rite in the Dublin state can equal. No one feels as deeply about an Irish army parade or the inauguration of a president. For over fifty years the elected politicans have in fact employed the Republican rhetoric. Those who did not largely kept their convictions out of sight of the electorate. So for almost the entire history of the state there was no dissent on the "national issue." The efforts of the major parties to defuse the Republican bomb in no way tampered with Republican ideals and in no sense created a parallel rhetoric. The strongest attraction of the Republican movement increasingly became the obvious hypocrisy of the legitimate institutions. Politicans who served in the "official" Republican party of Fianna Fáil were all too willing to jail and intern those who sought to turn oratory into action. Thus, a Republican commemoration is real—a real young man is dead; the flag on his coffin is not just a banner; the volley over his grave is not a sordid ritual but a reward and a promise. The state has been left without the rites of legitimacy. And emotive ritual dramas cannot be easily repossessed or new ones easily created.

The Old Attitudes. What the IRA ritual summons forth in public is an attitude toward existing institutions. For a great many of the Irish, all with long and exacting memories, there has seldom been an intimate connection between justice and law, or law and order. The agencies of order were often considered, justly, as imposed, the laws constructed to preserve others' privileges, and the Crown's justice no more than mean self-interest. Forbidden their religion, paupers in a green land, denied education, advancement, or common decency, few could see a communality of interest with the Ascendency landlords, or with the agencies of the Crown. Laws were to be evaded or changed, not obeyed. Concession, compromise, changing times, prosperity, or prospects did indeed erode this posture but, basically, an abiding suspicion remains. Injustice is no longer institutionalized as it was in Northern Ireland, but still and all, the IRA advocates the ideals long proclaimed, and to deny them—and with them, the dreams of the past—is difficult. "Political crime" truly exists in Ireland, and the IRA, whether engaged in train robbery or random bombing, can continue to feed on a considerable pool not so much of sympathy but rather of toleration. The informer, no matter how highly motivated by democratic ideals or by loyalty to the state, remains hateful. Thus Ireland, a really most law-abiding state, still is populated by those whose dedication to democracy, to the proposition that now law and justice are truly linked, cannot easily betray those whom Dublin calls "men of violence." This by no means indicates that all the Irish support the IRA or that the Irish ocean largely is friendly to the IRA fish, only that the habits of the past coupled with the situation in the North create an ambivalence. The public tolerates the presence of the IRA.

A New Role. It is in fact the Northern events that give the present IRA a legitimacy related neither to the old rituals nor the old attitudes. Once the civil rights movement had engendered a Protestant backlash, very few in the South trusted the policy of the British Army to defend—effectively, or in time, or perhaps at all—the Northern Catholics. The revelation of the arms trial indicated that the Republican Fianna Fáil had opted to stand back. The victory of the coalition brought to the fore those who at last, if haltingly, denied in public the historical aspirations of the Nationalists. There was no longer an inalienable right to unite, and increasingly there was no longer any interest in a unity that would cause chaos and undesired change in the North and South. That very few in the South would benefit by a united country and many might suffer, that without harsh sacrifices no Dublin government would be capable of acting on Northern events, all might be true. But the desertion of the Northern Catholic population, whether logical or inevitable, caused grave concern and some guilt. Thus, *at least* the IRA was there, doing something, holding a thin line. If the IRA were hounded and crushed, what then?

Thus, the IRA has three factors to exploit: possession of living historical rituals that grant the legitimacy of a long tradition, the reluctance of the population to betray those who advocate the old ideals of the people, and a position as Catholic defenders in the North. It would appear that certainly the first two, and perhaps the last, are wasting assets. Yet old ways and old dreams change but slowly. There is a charm about myths that the new realities of the democratic state cannot quickly or easily erode. Fifty years of political cant are not suddenly discarded. There are years of debts still to fall due. New rituals and myths cannot be fashioned at will, new attitudes summoned up by emergency legislation, and old responsibilities discarded in the name of practicality. Ireland has not always been a very practical country and still can be touched by the old dreams made manifest in the old ways.

The Government's Assets

Legitimacy. The response by the Dublin government in the broadest terms has been directed, often quite consciously, against IRA assets, to stress the real rather than the ideal. The prime effort has been to strike at the pretensions of the IRA while stressing the legitimacy of the democratic institutions of the state. It is the position taken by Kevin O'Higgins in 1923 that "we will not have two governments in this country, and we will not have two armies in this country." And as long as the IRA continued to advocate the bomb in the North, the Dublin government sought to deny them a platform in the South. Over and over again the government's spokesmen have insisted that there is no place for secret armies in a democratic state, that no political movement can represent a higher authority than the elected Dáil, and that finally, in effect, the IRA is betraying the state and hence the nation. The legitimacy of the democratic institutions is everywhere accepted—except by the purists in the Republican movement. It is a very strong card and regularly played. And the Republicans are left isolated with limited electoral support in the best of times and few converts to the proposition that the people have no right to do wrong—that is, abandon the dream of a united Ireland, abandon the North, abandon the old ways for new profits. The government's problem is that many do not see a contradiction in supporting democratic institutions and tolerating the IRA. While the legitimacy of the existing institutions is unquestioned, the presence of the IRA is also accepted—if less universally—although not its claims to represent the nation.

IRA Faults. The government has stressed not simply the pretensions of the IRA in contrast to the reality of the state but also the failings of the men of violence. The leaders are scorned as incompetent, narrow-minded, brutal gunmen. Occasionally there is some indication that a few volunteers might be misled idealists, but for the most part the repeated charges have been that most are callous murderers of the innocent. Dublin accuses the IRA of setting back any hope of unity through the long and vicious bombing campaign that has alienated the Protestants and caused immense Catholic suffering. Violence does not pay, and the little cruel men of the IRA have once again disgraced the nation. And there is little doubt that the war in the North is brutal and often degrading, that many accept the government's version of events, and that the long tale of horror has left few in the South who believe that the IRA is still embarked on an unstained crusade.

IRA counterpropaganda points out that all wars are brutal, but it has not convinced a great many. One horrid incident and the government's case is made again. And more so, since the war has oozed South. Dublin is in danger of violence because of the gunmen; that those gunmen are killers unworthy of Ireland is a theme with increasing believers.

New Pragmatism. Finally, and at last, the coalition government discarded at some cost the patriotic rhetoric of the past. Ministers have indicated that now a united Ireland would be an error. This does not mean that the Irish government has ended advice to Northern Catholic politicians; or given up the concept of an "Irish dimension" to the Northern problem; or even foresworn some ultimate union. Rather, for the forseeable future, the coalition contemplated the continuation of partition, urging only sharing of power, reforms within Ulster, and an end to violence. A union achieved by violence would be a disaster. Violence is and always has been unnecessary. Some insist that Irish independence would have come through concession, that the Easter Rebellion of 1916 was unnecessary, and the Tan War unneeded. This, so far, has not converted generations raised on the glory days, or Fianna Fáil (swept into office in June 1977), to similar disavowals; but the recourse to pragmatic analysis has quietly convinced many that unification would cost a price not worth paying. Clearly, partition has advantages for the Roman Catholic Church—people's protector in the North and government confidant in the South. Clearly, too, no Southern political party could expect to gain much nor would the existing governmental institutions benefit. Thus, the coalition government's effort to stress the real world over the mythical was a pragmatism desperately trying to erode the old loyalties before too late.

In a sense, then, the government, especially since 1972, stressed the new realities. They had reason to believe that *their* assets were accumulating, not wasting away, and that, as time passed, the old symbols and rituals would become barren, the old loyalties erode, and the new gifts within the power of the state attract. The government's defeat, however, may slow this trend, although it is unlikely that Fianna Fáil's response to the IRA will differ greatly—the same familiar sticks are ready at hand. Any vote today would go against the aspirations of the IRA; overt sympathy for the Northern campaign is slight. The democratic institutions engender deep loyalty; the incompetence and arrogance of the IRA (in North and South) are accepted, and the dangers of unification are now realized. Yet no one in power rests easy, least of all the new Fianna Fáil government of Jack Lynch—supposedly the *real* Republicans.

Ireland is an effective democratic state with a nationality problem beyond resolution. Britain must "solve" the Ulster problem, not Ireland, and solve it in such a manner that the IRA becomes irrelevant and physical force no longer legitimate in the eyes of the militants. Unlike the aspirations of the South Moluccans, the goal of the IRA—to break the British connection—is feasible. Unlike the ideological goals of the Baader-Meinhof Group or the Brigate Rosse, the forms of the future sought by the IRA are feasible. A Republic of thirty-two counties may not be likely or around the corner, but it is a reasonable aspiration that has for six decades attracted the purists and for six decades been the proclaimed goal of the state. The contradictions between the ideal and reality have left a space for an armed conspiracy acting in the name of the nation.

It is clear that one of the major, often unstated, responsibilities of various Irish governments was the co-optation of nonconstitutional dissent—the legitimization of the state by real movement toward the ideal. When the process no longer worked, Dublin was in trouble and had to choose between the ideal and reality, adventure and honesty. The strength of the IRA eroded because most people took half a loaf and settled for the easy life.

Second, the pattern of repression must be shaped to appear legitimate. For example, in Ireland emergency legislation, whatever the motives behind it, is a scandalous assault on all civil liberties. Yet with rare exception such legislation has been used solely against Republicans and with relative restraint—when the IRA grows too arrogant. Hence, much of the public understands and accepts the rituals or internment or imprisonment. Since Ireland is so conservative, there is almost no real radical Left; the only dissent is the Republican movement. No one else is penalized. After all, in a little country everyone knows just who belongs to the IRA and what they can legitimately do. Consequently, in Ireland, except for the radicals and libertarians (few on the ground), the emergency legislation is seen as legitimate, perhaps an exercise for narrow political purpose, but not a danger to a free society. And it must be remembered that in Ireland a variety of institutions narrowly define just how free such a society may be. In sum, it would appear then that, when possible, accommodation pays and that, when necessary, the mix of repressive techniques must be regarded by the people as a legitimate exercise of authority.

So at the very end, over six decades, the Irish strategy of carrots and sticks—co-optation, coercion, faith, hope, and the aid of the bishops—has protected the democratic government if not eliminated the idealists. There would be less trouble if those in power were more willing to talk about new realities rather than the old myths, but that is asking more than most politicans—Irish or otherwise—can willingly offer. For democratic governments elsewhere, the Irish experience with sixty years of armed subversion appears not to be readily transferable, except in demonstrating that carrots are effective, may cost less, and certainly taste better than the bitter dregs of police vengeance, unnecessary emergency legislation, and prison brutality. Apparently effective and swift accommodation and cunning co-option have a great part to play—certainly as great a part as coercion and repression, where less is most often more.

15

Terrorism: Nets and Oceans

Strangely enough, governments generally do not welcome being told in moments of crisis to do nothing, that less is more, that benign neglect will pay best benefits in time. Most governments are staffed by activists, doers not thinkers, determined to enact legislation, and determined to act. They want most of all to be seen as the cause not the response. There are only a few for the easy life. And, too, few truly want to be responsible for disaster, embark on risky adventures, sail in harm's way, and lead the charge. Nothing then satisfies as advice to act within restraint, lead without risk, and adventure with assured results. Such advice, simple and compelling, must rest on accurate analysis of the present, a display of assets, a portrait of the threat in all ramifications, and the presentation of a sure solution, quick, cost-effective and resonant with virtue that will reflect well on its sponsor. Such advice is rare indeed. In Ireland in matters of security related to the Republican problem, all the involved recognize all too clearly the problem, the risks, the potential pitfalls of coercion, and most of all the dangers of a public position. A few like Conor Cruise O'Brien, late of the Dáil Labour Party, rather enjoyed riding point on Northern matters, slashing Republican pretensions, skewering the IRA balloon, daring the stolid and the simple to protest with yesterday's clichés the dreary, dead dreams of bogmen. O'Brien is no longer in politics, a point taken out in the bogs, but the job of coping with the IRA has in many ways become simple—and in a few ways more complex.

Mostly, the position of 1977 has simply hardened with an advantage for Dublin in the decade of practice, since the IRA response to repression has been resistance without accommodation. Then, too, the Provos have moved some operations into the Republic—alarming many—and have garnered the opprobrium as a result of brutal actions, killing of innocent people, cruel murders, and policy of theft. Their crimes represented assets for the Dublin government: the botched and unauthorized murder of a Protestant senator, a kidnapping attempt, a penalty murder in a Dublin pub, a bank raid (one of dozens) and the assassination of Lord Mounbatten with the ensuing death of an old woman and an Irish boy. Not a pretty list,

236

even if the result of military necessity. Not the stuff of the deathless dream nor the patriot game, but the world of revolution, irregular war, terror and extortion for the cause. Certainly a traditional arms smuggler figured in the list, but from a failed attempt; there have been too many public examples of covert atrocity, too many failures, too many bank raids, too many innocent deaths, and too many no-warning bombs. True enough, the IRA's greatest asset—official hypocrisy—has shown little sign of erosion, and the old myths have a longer staying power than most politicans and many observers would have assumed. And, in addition, the IRA has unearthed unexpected—and for Dublin unwanted—assets in growing electoral support in the North and before that in the impact of the hunger strikers, hardly the tactic of psychopathic, mad-dog killers. So, little has changed. Dublin may have overreacted, especially in barring Republican spokesmen from the media, but there was ample provocation and fine tuning repression in a democratic society is no easy task (especially for men who would really like to come down with the boot if they could). Still there is no easy, simple advice to offer a Dublin government except to observe moderation in all things, have patience and prudence, and eschew the patriot game where Republican dragons regularly spring from careless seeds of oratory.

America's government, much larger, more various, and rich in assets and problems, is little different in matters of advice. Those responsible to the electorate want sure things, simple explanations, viable solutions, and a quick, cost-effective fix, swiftly deployed, and swiftly effective. Congressmen—or for that matter most people besides academics—do not want complex dissertations, exceptions, quibbles, and distant historical examples. What is wrong? What can be done? What will happen? A sleek proposal underlined in red, printed on one side, in a few paragraphs, effective and politically desirable, that is what is needed—not that it is anticipated. Members of Congress, whatever else, are realists. Journalists and television reporters may want the spectacular and the novel, perhaps even the significant, but the responsible want something that works to everyone's advantage. Thus, on Irish matters the U.S. State Department, when interested— which is rarely—mainly focuses on extradition or presidential visits; the Ulster Troubles is one of the few problems that rarely troubles Washington. If—even more rarely—the Irish Troubles can lead to general consideration, Washington is apt to be interested in answers to the wrong questions: Who conspires? Who are the Communists? What about the arms? How will it all end and to whose advantage?

The American questions of policy and priority are at least easier to answer or approach since they are so far from Ireland. The answers are not always welcome. The concerned prefer to believe in a conspiracy, a vast international terrorist net, a web woven by the KGB and manned by surrogate spiders. Washington cherishes the Communist conspiracy, the great Satan to be found everywhere, that necessitates all sorts of expense and commitment. And it is most depressing for Americans to learn that the arms of the IRA generally read "Made-in-America"; the few other arms have been scrounged up at great cost, with no visible evidence of spiders anxious to provide Provos with missiles or diabolical devices. So Ireland is a bit of a disappointment; there is no conspiracy, no Communists, especially Celtic, no alien arms, and even worse, no prospect of a surprise-free future to American advantage. In fact Ireland remains of no interest to any but the Irish-Americans, a scattering of responsive politicans, mostly with Irish names, and a few analysts who seek to draw general answers from very specific Celtic experience: trends in terror. For if Ireland is not trendy, terror is, and therefore Ireland may find a small place in a State Department conference on terrorist conspiracies or a congresssional hearing (Subcommittee on Civil and Constitutional Rights of the Committee on the Judiciary) on the irrelevance of such conspiracies. Even a decade apart the conclusions presented to the State Department Conference on Nets and Oceans remain the same as those arising from Terror International for the House testimony.

Terrorism, always trendy, has lately engendered considerable interest because of suspected or discovered linkages not only between patron states but also between various revolutionary organizations. Authors and analysts of generally conservative posture have found conspiratorial nets implying at minimum that many strands lead to Moscow or the capitals of Moscow's friends. There are voices of caution, and even the most devout advocates of a KGB terrorist conspiracy admit that the origin of every massacre cannot be traced to Moscow or Havana or Tripoli; matters are much more complex. Still, the fashion of the moment is to stress the nets, the links, the contacts, and the conspiracies.

The analytical problem, putting aside the need to define terrorism, is that matters *are* very complex and not especially amenable to conventional approaches. The use of the word *net* implies actual lines or threads from a specific point to a specific point, routes and passsages that have visible patterns and some permanence. Unfortunately for the orderly mind, the real, clandestine, revolutionary world is more like an ocean with varied currents, differing temperatures that fade away, dark holes, eddies, and froth. And in this ocean, from time to time, swim an enormous variety of terrorist fish often changing form, especially when netted by the eager analyst.

There are presently an enormous variety of these revolutionary fish. Each has special assets, exists in special conditions, and seeks particular ends. Some, like the IRA, have a long, long organizational history. Others appear for a single Italian operation and disappear forever. Some have acquired considerable legitimacy, like the PLO, and are represented at international meetings. Some represent no one but their new members, like the team that kidnapped the OPEC oil ministers. At times one or two men is the total membership. Some like the Wales Free Army are unknown but to specialists. Some control tens of thousands of members. Some cannot even control their own members. Most claim constituencies—the Puerto Rican people or all Croatians—that deny them. Many have bleak prospects or none. Others are serious factors in regional politics. Some are secure in sanctuary states or control liberated zones. Some operate with overt political wings and clandestine operational groups. In general, to lump together the Armenians and South Moluccans, the Brigate Rosse and the PLO, the IRA and Carlos the Jackel is not very rewarding; however, there are some aspects of revolutionary contact within this ocean that might warrant examination.

Organizations

With some rare exceptions most revolutionary organizations aspire to power even if built on the ruins of the nation; they are in a sense counter-states, and the nearer to power, the more state-like. In the most promising cases, the organization is in place in the nation to be liberated and operates as an alternative government. At times a government-in-exile is proclaimed and again dons the attributes of sovereignty. Most groups, however, have to settle for being recognized as "national liberation movements" by their friends and patrons. They may have exile headquarters, receive official or unofficial legates, seek various kinds of formal recognition, and arrange political and military alliances with other movements. All of these, of course, maintain operational units—guerrilla armies or columns in the hills. Those groups, when more hardly pressed (like ETA or the IRA) try to maintain an overt political presence and persuade potential patrons and bountiful movements that they are legitimate. The most clandestine movements, Brigate Rosse or Prima Linea in Italy or the remains of the RAF in Germany, are reduced to a fully clandestine life with only covert contacts with their friends. With very rare exception, all such organizations, for a variety of reasons, seek to touch similar groups and tend to do so in similar ways.

The Ocean

Automatic Response

In Italy one of the more curious revolutionary innovations has been *autonomia*, which purports to structure spontaneous response to state provocation. This means that given the appropriate oppressive stimulus the enlightened sections of the masses would act without instruction. (Alas for the *autonomia* theorists in Italy, there turned out to be a highly organized, conspiratorial core to the movement.) What this means in most parochial terms is that under provocation in Belfast no one need contact "the masses"; rather, little old ladies will rush to the street automatically, autonomously, banging their bin lids. Under certain circumstances, the equivalent demonstration may take place all over Western Europe without prior planning or preparation, although by some means or another, years of intense education may have occurred. When IRA hunger striker Bobby Sands died, stones in Europe were thrown by those who could not find Ireland on a map. The terrorist ocean suddenly ran warm without the turn of a tap.

Sympathetic Response

Over much of Europe, there were also friendly hands on various taps who intended to turn on displays and demonstrations the moment Sands died. A great many of these responses were far beyond the control of the Irish Republican Movement, although their wandering emissaries over the years had made many appropriate friends. Essentially these responses were unauthorized, yet welcomed. Usually these sympathetic responses are rituals of protest, escalating at most to smashed windows and burnt cars. From time to time, however, the line of agitation is passed and bombs are detonated or shots fired. Usually with the IRA or others, there is a reluctance to become involved in operational matters without control: stones and banners yes, bombs and bullets no.

Structured Response

Here cooperation is planned by delegated agents of two or more existing organizations. Again, more often than not, the cooperation concerns agitation and demonstration; there can never be enough revolutionary display in support of the starving prisoners or the slaughtered peasants. The maximum number of forums for violent protest are desirable. In other cases this overt response—support for our Palestinians friends or the freedom fighters in Southern Africa—may involve various covert agreements. Most such "structured" arrangements are not very structured, but simply personal contacts, extended discussions, or an exchange of ideas and problems. There may be public meetings—guerrilla summits or terrorist conventions—where the like-minded circulate and exchange telephone numbers. These contacts may lead to more serious arrangements than panel discussions.

Issue Coalition

From time to time covert organizations agree, seldom in writing, to intimate cooperation on certain matters short of operational actions. In the course of the anti-imperial struggle in Africa, various liberation movements formed coalitions, met with some regularity, and stressed publicly the appropriate ideological positions. These issue coalitions most resemble treaty organizations for defense in times of peace. The major exchange remains simply words of comfort intelligence, and past experience, but all on a formal basis. In Palestinian matters, the PLO as an umbrella functions in this sort of role, although proporting to be the outward symbol of an action coalition.

Action Coalition

A time may come when words prove insufficient and operational matters are a matter of cooperation. Those with secure sanctuary, like the Palestinians, may offer training not easy to acquire in the clandestine world of the Provos' Ireland. Those with excess weapons may trade in kind or out of kindness. Those groups with too much money—and some exist—may bankroll the poor. Passports and papers can be arranged, holidays on the Black Sea or Lake Michigan assured, Skorpion submachine guns and night-sight binoculars distributed. This is essentially the romantic world of the clandestine terrorist. It is small, shifting, difficult to penetrate, and rarely operationally significant. Such coalitions between ETA and the IRA, or the IRA and the Palestinians, are as much a matter of ease and convenience, visible comfort in a hard world, as an operational necessity. At the most they may lead to joint operations, such as the ANC-ZAPU foray into Rhodesia a decade ago, but for the most part each revolutionary group prefers to tend its violent garden alone.

Coalescence

In special cases it is possible that a movement may be created or absorbed by another. This is usually the case in an area where a variety of competitors become a "front," but at times a patron-state manipulates the group as an extension of policy. Presently there exist a small pool of transnational terrorists, ideological mercenaries who can be hired with a slogan and a promise of sanctuary. They—the individuals—have spun off the wilder fringes of the Japanese Red Army or the German RAF and can be employed to kidnap the OPEC ministers, hijack a Lufthansa plane, or shoot a symbolic target. These captive organizations, as organizations, rarely have contact with any but patrons, for they exist but for a single violent display. A few groups, like Che Guevara's in Bolivia, are international columns but in action beyond patrons and beyond contact.

The Provos

A specific example of how these various contacts may work in practice can be found in the experience of the Provisional IRA, a group that began as hopelessly parochial and to a considerable extent has so remained. The Provos had no need for alien volunteers. They had too many volunteers as it was. They had little need for money, for at the beginning of the decade funds poured in from the Irish diaspora, and when these began to ebb bank robberies supplied both funds and action for the bored. For arms there was a steady and reliable stream from America. The Army Council and the Executive of the overt Sinn Féin political movement did not feel especially isolated; they had sufficient problems in Dublin briefing the foreign press and taking the gullible on television tours of the camps and training grounds. The first ventures into the arms trade in Europe had been a disaster brought on by innocence. The suppliers were selling arms to the IRA and information to the security forces—if, in deed, they were not fronts for British intelligence.

In any case, the IRA regrouped and undertook a halting series of policies to swim in the terror ocean for advantage. The most publicized outcome was an arrangement with Libya that produced a shipment of arms, a shipment monitored by various intelligence services and seized by the Irish Republic on arrival. Other contacts were made through mutual friends at cities in Europe that produced smaller arms shipments—and larger failed shipments—and visits to Palestinian camps, especially in Lebanon. Training there in any military sense was marginal—the IRA has used their RPG-7 rockets properly only a few times. But increasingly the main thrust of Provo activities in the terrorist ocean was to encourage overt political support. Sinn Féin established a foreign department, and various members of the Executive criss-crossed Europe making new friends just as they had visited America encouraging old ones. Mostly they concentrated on European national liberation movements, avoiding the mysteries of the radical ideological groups. They knew no one in Brigate Rosse and did not wish to. Thus when needed, on Sands' death, these friends could orchestrate protest, could from time to time be of marginal, operational aid and comfort, but this is another and minor matter.

The purpose of such contacts is much the same for all: the erosion of isolation, the comfort from association with those of the same vocation, the creation of agitational support, and the exchange of ideas and experience. At times there can be logistical aid and comfort, sanctuary may be offered, training given, and funds and money made available. But common operational action is very, very rare and real action alliance novel. In any case, the terrorist ocean shifts and flows constantly; friends come and go as do the warm places and useful currents. Old nets collapse and are blown away, not to be replaced. Telephone numbers and ideological postures change. New people come into the center of the circle, old ones grow tired. No one from the IRA now remembers how to run the old Middle Eastern routes. The new currents do not seem helpful this year, but next year there may be a neap tide. For the IRA, for most, there is no conspiracy but a community of interests, a shared vocation, a ragged collection of telephone numbers, a few friends without names, and if need be a sense of which current to swim with and which against. It is a murky, shifting world of intuition, emotive response, dissolving arrangements, uncertainty, tacit understanding; a vague, fluid, violent world, uncertain, and, in the heel of the hunt, not especially amenable to academic, analytical investigation, not easily revealed with numbers, charts, and graphs. The terrorist ocean contains very troubled waters, and the fishing is complex.

16

Terror International: The Nature of the Threat

For over a decade we have apparently lived in a time of terror—aerial hijackings, car bombs, assassinations, the slaughter of innocents, hostages, and urban guerrillas—the politics of atrocity. The contemporary, postindustrial Western world seems particularly vulnerable to bloody spectacles, as our complex technology is attacked or warped to the uses of the gunmen: diplomats may be held in a basement along the banks of the Nile at Khartoum and the terrorists demands arrive on our evening television news, not weeks later by forked stick. And there are ample prophets of doom who correctly predict that matters may grow worse. The fanatics may poison the water or spread plague or build their own nuclear devices. Many see us about to be swamped in a terrorist ocean. The contemporary revolutionary ocean is murky, filled with unexpected currents, dark with varying temperatures, and ateem with fish both elegant and awful. It is not our world nor is it likely to flood us out. It is a strange, alien ocean world.

There are many conspiracies and many contacts. All those rebels involved want an erosion of the isolation of the revolutionary vocation, the comfort of association with their fellow rebels, the agitational support of friends, and the exchange of ideas and experience. At times real governments, especially Marxist-Leninist regimes, may offer logistical aid and comfort; sanctuary may be given, training and funds and money made available, schooling or passports promised, or resolutions discussed at the United Nations. There are some proxies owned and operated by masters in Tripoli or Moscow or even Washington. There are those up to dirty tricks and black agents of distant powers and thrones. The IRA has for the moment left the Middle East. The Eritreans have different patrons, their enemies different allies. The Kurds still have no friends and the rebels in Mozambique no program. For the IRA or the Eritreans, for most, there is no conspiracy but a community of interests, a shared vocation, a few friends without names, and if need be a sense of which current to swim against. The fanatics out of Persia will find a warm spot perhaps, filled with

244

exotic creatures, and perhaps even kept warm for a time with heat funded by Moscow, perhaps not.

Washington is concerned with what seems to many a grave, great unexpected wave of "terrorism" sweeping about the foundations of the Western world. The Ulster Troubles are innocently lumped in with Brigate Rosse, Philippino rebels, the bush wars of the Horn of Africa, and the guerrillas of Latin America—unconventional all. There were of course certain similarities in all these low-intensity campaigns, just as there are in all conventional wars. But unlike real war, in unconventional war the conflict is only a small part of the contest, a violent part; the contest is always largely special, moored with long historical roots and focused on particular, obdurant disputes. No matter, after the gun enters politics the concerned want general explanations; this was especially true when gunmen arose seemingly from nowhere, killers without roots, rebels without causes, in the midst of postindustrial Europe. Imported killers from distant parts of the world who slaughtered the innocent were explicable, but for many the gun in Europe was not only novel but irrational.

The Gun in Europe

For a generation there was a general assumption that postindustrial Europe was immune to the more violent fashions in political extremism. One Budapest appeared enough to demonstrate the stability of the authoritarian East, and one Paris spring to show the irrelevance of the barricades in the West. If there was to be illicit change, it would come in the more traditional form of a formal and bloodless military coup, as has been the case in Greece and Portugal—and even then democracy appeared the ultimate winner. If terrorists did appear in Europe at the Rome airport or at the Olympics, they were driven by distant motives, bringing with them the violence of the periphery. If Algerians were fished from the Seine, they were, after all, Algerians. Thus when Northern Ireland slowly collapsed into chaos after 1970, the violence seemed incomprehensible to most observers, the child of Celtic malice, a religious war in the twentieth century. The fact is that in recent years Europe has become a battlefield for all sorts and conditions of secret armies engaged in liberating unsuspected or unwilling nations from previously unnoticed oppressors. Much of Western Europe has become a free-fire zone for this new and violent generation of guerrillas.

In recent weeks, two Turkish ambassadors have been assassinated in Vienna and Paris, a Dutch businessman kidnapped in Ireland, Spanish police shot down in the streets of Madrid, a car bombed in London, another kidnapping in Italy, more bombs in Portugal, and a massive, world-wide display of indignation at the execution of Spanish revolutionaries. A quick flutter through last year's newspapers reveals that this is by no means a special or particularly violent period. Even to the optimistic, there appears to be more trouble in store for Portugal, for Spain, even for Italy, and there are always the Irish. The pessimists foresee an era of revolt and reaction that may seriously strain European stability. In a large degree it has been that very stability, the economic miracle, the free movement of working populations, the easing of old tensions, the consumer revolution, all the supposedly good things of the new European life that have been responsible for the rising resort to violence by the few. Many Nationalists see this next generation as crucial; independence must be achieved before all Europe slips into a homogenized Coke-culture. Now is the time for a united Ireland, a Welsh republic, a free Brittany or Corsica or Catalonia before the language is lost, before the iron laws of the Common Market drain off the people to the Saar and replace them with German tourists, before the European edges become parklands. Then there are those on the Left who see an apparently indestructible postimperial system of oppression, a system that buys the workers' loyalty with color television sets—the opiate of the people—a system so complacent, so coercive, that only terror can engender change. And finally on the Right are men who abhor the drift to secularism or the acceptance of the Communists as respectable or the drift to Americanization. They speak for the old values, the old ways. They speak with the bomb.

Europe is currently most vulnerable to the bomber. An Italian anarchist can drift through the restaurant underground of London without attracting notice. Greeks in Volkswagens are everywhere to be found. The Irish are in Liverpool, the Basques in Paris, and the components of infernal devices easy to purchase. And there are so many soft and symbolic targets: the giant national airlines, the embassies, the computers, the prime ministers, and the refineries. When driven and dedicated men are determined to act no matter what the risk, the forces of order are sorely pressed. In Germany the spectacular operations choreographed by the Baader-Meinhof group forced the security forces into an intense, extremely expensive antiterrorist campaign. Even the present trial of some of the members is being held in a huge, high security structure built solely for the event. A very few can produce the most disproportionate results; a single dramatic operation can be magnified by television; one person can change history.

What is crucially important is that Europe can rumble along under such a threat. The various bombing campaigns of World War II by the Allies and the Axis powers dumped far more tonnage on the vulnerable than any terrorist is likely to do. Life then was more uncomfortable, more dangerous, but until near the end everyone coped. Despite all their bombs, the

Provisional IRA has not been able to force the British to evacuate Northern Ireland—yet. No one can really take seriously a grasp for power by the
Red Brigades in Italy or the new breed of German revolutionary. What is
far more likely and far from a pleasing prospect is that the gunmen may
unwittingly either unleash the forces of reaction or precipitate a civil war.
And some of the more radically inclined revolutionaries feel that either
eventuality will ultimately reward them.

In the past few years in Italy there has been a revival of revolutionary
fascism. As early as 1948 a Black Legion of the unrepentant was formed in
Northern Italy. Broken up by the authorities in 1951, it appeared in 1954 as
the New Order. In April 1974, the name changed to the Political Movement
of New Order and from that to the Black Order. All this elaborate verbiage
may cover as few as 300 militants, but there are similar militant groups,
mostly north of Rome, some linked by loose ties, but all dedicated to
violence. This new Fascist underground in Italy assumes that if they can
create a rising level of chaos at the same time the Italian Communist party
creeps closer to power, there will be another march on Rome.

There are those in Ireland who can envisage a doomsday situation in the
North—civil war without a British referee—that will create a situation in
Dublin to the advantage of *real* Irish Republicans.

The Provisional IRA has waged a classic insurgent campaign against the
British army. With several thousand members, especially effective in the
Catholic ghettos of Belfast and Derry and certain rural areas, with arms
and money seeping in from abroad, with friends to the south in the Irish
republic, the Provos under the hardliner Seamus Twomey all but hold a
veto in regard to British policy options in Ulster. Their Republican rivals,
the Offical IRA, somewhat smaller, more radical under Cathal Goulding
and Seán Garland, is no whit less violent and perhaps more talented. The
latest Republican splinter, the Irish Republican Socialist party of Seamus
Costello, broke away from the Officials as too tame. All of these groups plus
independents and individuals, the hard men of Irish politics, agree at least
on one principle: Ireland was divided by force and will be united by force,
and some are not beyond detonating bombs in Birmingham to underline
their logic.

Not all the revolutionaries have such luminous dreams of a terrible
beauty born out of blood bath, but then a few shots in the right place might
just do the trick.

And there are throughout Europe these small groups—a hundred ill-
organized Corsicans or a dozen Cypriot Greeks—quite willing to shoot.
Some, in fact, have been shooting for years without, until recently, attracting any great interest. The Basque liberation front of ETA, split not unlike
the IRA into a political and military wing, has for a decade been involved

in a separatist campaign. They have a few hundred activists, often in exile, but tens of thousands of sympathizers. At times Spanish repression has reduced the militants to a handful, pursued even into their French sanctuaries by police gunmen. But they have succeeded in assassinating Prime Minister Admiral Luis Carrero Blanco in the process. Now under extreme pressure, after the executions and waves of arrests, ETA gunmen can shoot down police on the streets of Madrid.

There is at the moment no place so vulnerable to the inappropriate shot as Spain. A long forty years have passed since the civil war. The immunization has been wearing off, for a new generation appears willing to take risks without their fathers' experience of the costs involved, even if by miscalculation. No matter that all the more formal underground parties insist they want nothing more than democracy, toleration, civil liberties and a peaceful transition to the post-Franco era. There are those, well-armed and in power, who believe that democracy is a code word for decadence, that civil liberties open the door to paganism, and that toleration would destroy the state. How, indeed, can Spain tolerate a Basque republic? And for the Basque guerrillas, why should they assume any Spanish government would acquiesce in secession, or any French government? Even a wise and talented government in Madrid would have great difficulty in creating a federal Spain. And it has been a very long time since a wise and talented government met in Madrid. The pent-up frustations of four decades, the nationality problem aside, will be difficult to control; the demand for vengeance is real, the fears of the powerful and contented extreme. With gunmen on the street the prospects for an era of good feeling appear bleak. Only oppression has been able to maintain order in modern Spain and a continuation of the old system no longer seems a possible option; a police state can run short of policemen. Moderation, compromise, and accommodation may indeed be about to have their day. The sensible will recognize the risks, ignore the bombers and the old quarrels and move on. Yet restraint and sweet reason have always had few takers in Spain.

If elsewhere in Europe the prospects do not seem quite so bleak, only in Scandinavia does there appear real stability. The Irish troubles go on and on; no one can see how things can get better, and everyone knows they could get worse. There have been bombs in Scotland and Wales. The Bretons and Corsicans could, again, choose violence. All the Italian political parties are concerned with the men at the fringe. There are Croatian guerrillas, German anarchists, Portuguese Maoists, all waiting in the wings. There are language problems in Belgium and Switzerland, cultural separatists in France, irredentists in northern Italy, and always the transients: Palestinain fedayeen, EOKA-B Cypriots, the Japanese Red Army. And Europe makes a splendid stage to play out their ambitions with violent deeds. One hopes those in power recognize that the revolutionary threat is not lethal but tolerable. Few want a march on Rome or a Spanish Civil War, but without care neither is impossible. The gunman knows that, and so he has written in a role for his opponent.

Too often the role seems likely to be attractive to the threatened. Car bombs and dead policemen produce indignation and a demand for action, an end to terrorism. Outraged indignation should fit uncomfortably on those who gave us the holocaust or the fire bombing of Hamburg or a century of large scale brutality, but it does not. More to the point, such indignation is partisan. The wave of protest over the Spanish executions indicates that some gunmen are more acceptable than others, especially if they have an odious enemy in a distant country. Thus, some may approve of the Red Brigades, but not the Black; Irish unity, but not Spanish; cultural independence, but only for foreigners. One man's terrorist is another man's patriot. From the seat of power in Rome or London or Madrid the gunmen are wicked, evil men who must be destroyed by any means, by all means, And therein lies the danger. Without a sense of proportion, the effort to get terror by the throat, end murder from the ditch, may do more damage to order than to the gunmen.

In Irish matters it was possible as time passed and novelty faded to report from time to time to a more general public with word from Ulster. Mostly in the mid-1970s the word seemed to be the same: Ulster was now familiar in an unconventional world. Increasingly, to be thought newsworthy, hard and hot, an event had to be spectacular; there were few extended stories and few stories that delved beyond electoral results or atrocities. Violence, Irish violence, had become institutionalized at a tolerable level. The odd crisis could be exploited or ignored, for if doomsday did not recede neither did it loom as large. For the most part, matters moved along, the body count rose, the IRA operations continued, the police took advantage and at times the concerned were concerned. By 1976 the Ulster Troubles remained dangerous but somehow dormant; Ireland was a comfortable if uneasy hostage to random, irradicable violence. Once thought pandemic, sufficient antibodies had arisen to maintain surface order much of the time, except in a few pestulent centers, but the country continued to suffer from a low-grade fever. And always the fever of hostage Ireland threatened to peak and overwhelm the antibodies, and the proposed treatments meant even more deaths and more threats.

17

Hostage Ireland, 1976, 1982

For the most part, summer 1976 in Ireland has been a season of mists and soft skies, the green countryside dotted with tinkers and ruins. The tourist board stresses fishing and golf and unspoiled beaches. And for much of the island and most of the tourists this will be the case: a quiet time of easy ways, a land of pleasant people and uncertain weather where time runs a little slower. For others, especially those in Ulster, Ireland is a cruel and bloody arena. No tinkers or ruined castles but gunmen and bombed pubs. Like the inevitable rain, murder has become accepted, certain, unavoidable. So far in 1976, the deaths from explosions and shootings average one a day and are running ahead of deaths on the road, which is always a vital indication of serious political turmoil. And, more to the point, most observers foresee an escalation. In the words of a spokesman of the Provisional IRA, it will likely be a long hot summer.

For the Provisionals the time has apparently arrived to give up the pretext that they are observing a unilateral ceasefire and return to the gun. The primary reason is that the British authorities, having tried practically every form of political initiative except a royal visit, appear determined to ease out the British army and allow an increasing proportion of the slack to be taken up by the police UDR, a militia force. Although many loyalists see this as a harbinger of an ultimate British withdrawal, the IRA does not. But they regard it as a maneuver to ensure a sectarian war that will require a continuing British presence. Although the UDR was established six years ago as a community force, there are now probably no more than 200 serving Catholics out of a total of nearly 8000 volunteers. There has been, moreover, evidence that some members of the UDR are also members of Protestant paramilitary groups like the Ulster Volunteer Force—ill-organized vigilantes dedicated to random assassination and no-warning bombs in Catholic pubs. The RUC, too, is largely Protestant. Neither force is particularly well trained to fight a real insurgency campaign. The RUC at 9280 full- and part-time police is 26 percent below strength and the UDR has only 1550 full-time members. There have been suggestions, of course, by loyalists to beef up *their* security forces and by Conservative politicians in London to create a new and more effective Ulster security force. The Provisionals' Army Council decided to challenge what they saw as a British attempt to manipulate the Ulster situation. The IRA thus declared an open season on the RUC.

On Saturday, May 14, a small IRA armed service unit crossed the border from the Republic of Ireland at Belcoo in County Fermanagh and ambushed a two-man UDR patrol. Before they withdrew, without causing any casualties, they planted a land mine at the point of the ambush, aware of British security and search procedures. The susbsequent RUC patrol detonated the land mine and an RUC constable and two reserve constables were killed instantly. Another RUC constable was shot and killed in an ambush near Warrenpoint. It was the start of a spate of weekend violence that cost eleven lives. It is now almost inevitable that an effective IRA attack on the security forces engenders violent retaliation by the Loyalist paramilitaries. Although IRA policy is to oppose counter-retaliation, especially random retaliation, the army council often has only tenuous control over the volunteers in the field. The result has been a cycle of tit-for-tat killing. The green and pleasant Irish countryside, the beautiful hills, twisting lanes and tidy fields have become a deadly battlefield. War has come to the Irish countryside, a vicious, anonymous and cruel war that shows no signs of abating.

Larger sectors of the southern part of Ulster are all but controlled by the IRA. To talk of the Republic of South Armagh is not simply a quip. RUC patrols drive at 60 miles an hour with orders not to stop. British army forces appear in force or not at all. The danger of snipers is so great that helicopters remove the garbage from British military posts. In many of these Nationalist areas, the IRA is conducting an almost classical rural guerrilla campaign. The introduction of the elite British Special Air Services (SAS) counterinsurgency troops has resulted in a series of incidents where hot pursuit led the British into the Irish Republic. It is not the IRA-British confrontation or even the IRA attacks on the police that have appalled the distant and the immediately threatened, but the growing toll of innocent civilians, innocent of all but their faith. Stretching across southern Ulster is the Murder Triangle where Protestant paramilitary gunmen have murdered the isolated and vulnerable and the Catholics have replied in kind. Several tiny towns have been bombed repeatedly, men have been shot down before their families, car bombs have gone off in village squares, shops, restaurants and offices have been hit. In August 1975, a minibus carrying the Miami Showband was stopped, the members taken off, lined up and machine-gunned to death. An unknown group soon thereafter stopped a worker bus, let the one Catholic aboard go, and machine-gunned Protestants who had been lined up by the ditch. In the mixed areas everyone is vulnerable. And the killings go on—one a day, and the bombs go on—four a day. And no one can see an end to a violence that is rapidly becoming institutionalized or any hope for a population that is divided, brutalized, and beyond compromise.

The war in the countryside and in the ghettos of Belfast and Derry is only one aspect of the Irish Troubles. The Provisional IRA struggling in Ulster during a campaign of attrition took the war to England or, in some cases, Irishmen fought it there for them. The British bombing campaign—the IRA second front—has not been especially effective. No-warning bombs in British pubs have horrified and alienated public opinion. A great many operations simply failed through incompetence, and most of those involved were arrested, tried, convicted and imprisoned. What has happened is that the Irish Troubles, so long only on the evening news, have come to Birmingham and London. And understandably the public wants *something* to be done. Much the same problem has arisen in southern Ireland, where from time to time Ulster Loyalists have detonated no-warning bombs. The Dublin government has tended to see the culprit as not so much the Northern Protestants but as the IRA, whose operations provoked the bombs. In Dublin the politicians threatened by the ancient loyalties of some of the Irish population, by the dreadful prospect of a real sectarian war in the North, and by the activities of various subversives, too, have felt that *something* must be done.

If the brutal murders in the country lanes of Armagh have no real lesson to teach elsewhere, the response of two democratic countries to revolutionary violence may have. In both Britain and Ireland, public opinion, as far as such things can be gauged, responded to provocation and massacre with outraged indignation. In London there was a demand for the return of the death penalty by many Conservatives—even though only the IRA would benefit by the creation of patriots on the gallows tree and even the police had no interest in such a maneuver. What did evolve after a particularly grisly pub bombing at the end of 1974 was new, antiterrorist legislation that gave the police new powers that from a distance hardly seemed necessary. During the violence in mid-May, the RUC held eighteen suspects under the Prevention of Terrorism Act, but holding suspects for seven days without filing charges was hardly going to prevent future terror. In both Northern Ireland and the Republic, formidable emergency legislation had long existed. In Dublin, however, the Minister of Justice Patrick Cooney and his cabinet colleagues insisted on a further Criminal Law Jurisdiction Act that many saw as unnecessary and that would likely remain a permanent weapon in the hands of an authoritarian government long after the present troubles had ended. Cooney insisted that unusual times and a demonstrable subversive challenge demanded the State adopt a policy "as tough as their opponents." Thus, the Provisional Republicans' Easter commemoration parade was banned, took place anyway, and has led to summons for practically the entire leadership of the legal political Sinn Féin party.

Cooney notes that "the Government's first duty when faced with violent attacks on its institutions is to strengthen its laws. As a consequence there may have to be a derogation from laws protecting the freedom of the individual." Americans are all too aware that some politicians have difficulty in distinguishing between attacks on institutions and attacks on party or even personal aspirations. In the Irish case Cooney's insistence that such laws should be temporary and subject to review, while splendid in theory, suffers from the government's refusal to accept just such an amendment. More distressing, the campaign for law and order has seemingly encouraged members of the Irish police to adopt most dubious practices—persons suspected of a major and political train robbery insist that they were brutally beaten and presented with detailed confessions to sign. If they're telling the truth and if this is the sort of thing that was meant by being as "tough as their opponents," it is an ill omen for Irish democracy, not to mention Irish stability.

In fact most of the omens are ominous and most of the comfort that can be given is cold. The Provisional IRA, according to a member of the Army Council, is content that the anti-RUC campaign is paying dividends, that the police do not want to be in the front lines; furthermore, internal pressures within the organization are building up. Many IRA men want an escalated campaign, want more bombs in Britain. Some close to the border in the Republic of South Armagh see little reason to tolerate arrests and internments in the South while shooting the RUC in the North. The Protestant paramilitaries in turn have promised a campaign of retaliation, and there is no reason for them to deny themselves soft targets in the South. After regularly releasing British soldiers found in the South, the Irish recently jailed eight SAS men for a border incursion. For the Loyalist, that's sufficient evidence that Cooney's law and order campaign is a façade. And in London there is fear that bombs in Birmingham or Liverpool will produce a violent backlash against the resident Irish population and begin a chain reaction that could cause untold damage to British society. Yet London has run out of political initiatives. Each elaborate and lovingly constructed proposal has collapsed in Ulster. There seems no center in Northern Ireland. Those who attempt to find the middle of the road have been run down and destroyed. The future is still held ransom by gunmen and bombers. Guns and bombs can kill only so many, but in the process they threaten to destroy two open societies. In Ireland, laws, however Draconian, cannot create order as long as there are those who see existing order as institutionalized injustice. Those concerned not especially with

Irish matters but rather with liberty and justice might consider that perhaps in the face of provocation less is more and freedom more precarious than retaliation.

By 1982, well into the next decade, the Troubles had truly become an Ulster norm. At times it seemed as if there had never been peace for those who lived in the danger zones, and for some there never had been, children in the civil-rights days, volunteers and prisoners on maturity, felons in retirement. What had once been threatening talk of a twenty-year war, increasingly appears rampant optimism. The problem was that there was no solution, accommodation was reached, if rarely, solely due to exhaustion and spent recources. Politically on the ground, the game could still have only winners and losers, compromise was a promise by those denied a role, agreement was treason to ideals and to those sacrificed, concord was a cruel hoax. Socially, if possible, Ireland appeared an expanding universe, each group rapidly moving away from all others at increasing speed—no class solidarity, no mixing, no understanding of the other tribe, division of North and South, rich and poor, Loyalist and Nationalist, the center gone and the genial driven away. Militarily, with the accepted, unwritten givens, the British could not win nor the IRA lose, and no one could balance an unleashed Loyalist militia on the scales of deadlock. The decent institutions were warped by crude usage, the courts corrupted in the North, free speech limited in the South, the police too often grown brutal throughout the island. Yet on the island much remained the same, green hills, regular elections, regular rain, sport followed and churches attended, inflation up and too many unemployed, new houses spreading out over the country, and the same quarrels about the parish pump. For most, the long war would be fought out on battlefields distant in perception if not in miles. The white-hot causes, the dying and the sacrifices, the extortion and the betrayals, the erosion of rights, the denial of justice, the hypocrisy and the lies would be the concern of others, mostly. For the most part, life went on, papers were printed and positions secured. It was to be a quiet, long war, grinding, painful, the cost in freedom and justice long delayed, the cost in dead and maimed uneven but endless. A war without battles but always with victims. The innocent were often more at risk than the dedicated. A small war ever on the rim of chaos so that the Ulster Troubles could not really be forgotten by anyone, so that nothing was forgiven and no foundation for accommodation crafted. It was a war that could not escalate with the assets open to the players. Yet the conflict had made parts of Ireland, some Irishmen, many institutions bloody awful. Still the Troubles were and are still only part of the main, not the whole island, not the whole story. As prologue, the war had swallowed the future. The next generation gave every indication of repeating the past, if in novel and bloody ways, hostage to a history seized on irreconcilable grievance. The IRA gunmen, lay pilgrims on a corrupted crusade, moved into the next decade as dedicated, certain, and obdurant as ever, determined to suffer, if need be, when necessary and, if possible, inflict pain on their foes who would maintain the hateful British connection.

Into the Next Decade with the IRA: A Long War

The last year or so has been the worst of times and the best of times for the Provisional IRA. While the leadership has struggled with an eroding military capacity, there have been spectacular bombs and even more spectacular political triumphs as a result of the hunger strikes and the electoral process North and South. In fact the long, dramatic trauma of the hunger strikes with Bobby Sands' death, followed by those of nine other Republican prisoners, coupled with the returns in Fermanagh-South Tyrone in the North and in nine constituencies in the Irish Republic during the June 1981 general elections, absorbed most media attention. Much the same was true the following year when the 1981 gains in the Republic were largely eroded in one more general election, but were recouped in the vote for seats when the new Northern Ireland Assembly showed an unexpected 10.1 percent for the IRA's political arm, Sinn Féin. Of course, the same old murder and maiming continued, 112 people were killed in 1981, not an especially violent year, and the same rate for 1982. The fact was that the IRA did not do badly in attacks on security forces, particularly locals, in the occasional assassination, and in the summer bomb explosions in London that killed ten soldiers and wounded fifty people. What was not as immediately clear was that the IRA leadership had during much of 1982 serious problems in maintaining the momentum of a long war of attrition.

Some of the IRA's difficulties are long standing and largely beyond solution. The persistant problems do have an obverse side, but one that provides usually only secondary benefits. The IRA's constituency in the North (friendly or tolerant Nationalists) is very small, but economic and social conditions, not to mention historical grievances, have assured a ready supply of volunteers (better in the IRA than on the dole). The IRA is also isolated geographically and to a lesser degree politically, and Britain has fewer enemies these days who might be Irish allies. But the Irish diaspora, particularly in the United States, fuels the organization, and foreign contacts, particularly during crisis moments like the hunger strike, supply distant if real enthusiasm. Then, too, after ten years of violence with no end in sight simple exhaustion even among the faithful is a debilitating factor, *but* not a crucial one since militant Irish Republicans, despite moments of optimism, always have been involved in the long haul, one aborted campaign after another, one failed generation after another. No matter the opposition of the proper people or the priests, those of no property will soldier on in the cause of the ultimate Republic. Actually, the fact that the IRA is almost entirely composed of volunteers of no property is an unexpected and often denied obstacle. The IRA is what the fashionable Western intellectuals have always wanted—a purely working-class liberation movement. There is the odd teacher, publican, or solicitor, but the IRA is unrepresentative of Irish society as a whole—no bankers or scientists, but only the volunteers from the unemployed, many whose only careers have been with the IRA. However ideologically attractive this conglomerate of friends and neighbors may be, the resulting organization has had to make do with a paucity of the types of talent necessary to fight a revolutionary war in an advanced industrial nation.

Two present cases indicate the problems posed for the IRA: arms and money. The IRA has not been able to acquire the arms desired, although to an alien eye they have at present the arms they need. For ten years there has been one disastrous "smuggling" failure after another. There has been a reliance on romantic arms drops from boats or shipments smuggled on planes. There is still a reluctance to spend money on paper, or to employ the traditional means of all illicit arms dealers. Most of their forays into the Middle East have been aborted due to the most primitive security measures, not to mention Israeli distaste for any friends of the PLO or Kaddafi. They have been sold out in Europe and found out in the United States. Bartenders and telephone repairmen, however dedicated, seldom possess the skills to acquire and ship missles or machine guns or sometimes even legal deer rifles. Most of the IRA armament from the United States has come into Ireland in "conventional" covert shipments independent of the organization. These stocks plus what the IRA has acquired, however, have proven sufficient when coupled with continuing experimentation with explosives. The IRA may not fight a high-tech war, but they can fashion mortars and rockets, bombs that can be set off years later, home-made napalm, and all sorts of diabolical devices.

Much the same problems arise in money matters; diaspora funds still arrive in cash in brown paper bags, while in hard times bank robberies make up the difference. Yet the IRA has in the North, especially in Belfast, set up a whole black market of taxis and pubs and co-ops, plus contributions, that keep the movement solvent. The main point is that the IRA with more talent might do far better, but even without the talent they have done well enough.

During 1982 the IRA appeared to maintain the momentum in what in 1977 the Army Council decided would be a long war of attrition. There were to be no more years of victory or large, soft "military" units but rather a dedication to persistence and a cell structure. Yet several continuing problems hampered military action. In 1976–77, the British army interrogation center at Castlereagh had secured 2500 convictions for terrorist actions as a result of induced confessions. The IRA cell structure after 1978 had put a stop to the leakage, but in 1981–82 the British made use of a few nicely placed informers ("supergrasses") whose relevations had a devastating effect. In Belfast, the IRA's ally the INLA, a violent splinter from the old Official IRA, was particularly badly hit. Then in the summer of 1982, the IRA lost practically all of the Derry unit, long in place, too long it would appear. The IRA did respond. The pregnant wife of an informer about to appear in court disappeared only to return from "visiting friends" after her husband forgot his proposed revelations. Largely, however, the damage was done. All the arrested could be replaced. Some have been. Operations continue in Belfast and Derry. Yet the impact of informers, the most deadly disease that can affect a covert revolutionary group, has been very serious indeed. Even if the Derry man was only a "friend and neighbor," the loss of trust was still real. Even if the British were trading freedom from criminal prosecution—for real not political crimes—the betrayal was real. Yet, and again, the IRA has lived through other eras of informers, real and imagined.

The present leadership has another serious problem, not fully recognized, that of their own image within the IRA. The existing Army Council and all IRA policies are dominated by men from the North, especially but not entirely Belfast, who came into the movement in 1969–71. Perhaps congenial and reflective in conversation, they are hard men possessed of deep and narrow ideas, radical in spirit, intolerant of compromise, often uncertain in "political" matters, but absolutely determined. Their political radicalism tends to alienate the more traditional Republicans in the South and the United States, but it is the norm in Northern Ireland. Their provincial parochialism is increasingly a problem. Presently the significant figures in the IRA seldom come to Dublin and have probably never been in much of the Republic beyond the border. They, the Northerners, are, or course, the ones doing the killing and dying, but there is growing unrest that the Republican Movement is narrowing. The leaders of the last generation now in Sinn Féin like its president, President Rory Brady, and Vice-President Dave O'Connell are presently isolated from most decisions and are rumored on the way out. If Sinn Féin is to become only an adjunct to the Northern-directed IRA, the movement may well lose more than is gained. The leadership of the IRA already suffers from the drains of simultaneously directing the military campaign and the various political initiatives. Thus when more talent is need, this most parochial of national movements has moved along the road to being a provincial rump, thus further limiting the shallow pool of skills. And again this, too, has happened in the past and the IRA persists—practically everything bad or good has happened to the movement in the past. And in some cases the leadership has parsed previous errors to advantage.

With all the problems, what now and what next? What are the IRA prospects and intentions? What of the next decade of the long war? What is the IRA really like? The conventional and analytical always want to know the wrong things about revolutionary organizations: the number of active members, the size of the war chest, the kinds of arms, the agents abroad, the weight of stored explosives, perhaps international contacts or future strategic priorities. Mostly they want hard numbers and firm data. The IRA cares, and properly, only marginally about such matters. There are *never* the weapons wanted, but there are always enough. Too many weapons, as the PLO discovered, may not mean victory but rather defeat on the wrong battlefield. There are usually too many volunteers, not too few. There is a guerrilla overload already, too many who want to serve and no place to use them, no money to keep them, and no arms for them to use effectively. However, numbers do not matter, but the capacity to perform the needed operation does. A very few men can kill Lord Mountbatten or scatter horses and corpses across Rotten Row in London. Money is almost always a problem—except when there is too much, as the RAF found in Germany when spending began absorbing more time than the cause. More elegant arms are always useful but not necessary—a match or a chain saw may do. The IRA would, indeed, like missiles and machine guns, but can manage without. There are no agents abroad, but old friends here and there. Explosives can be made when needed, but found when stored too long. International contacts long lost could be renewed if needed. And most revolutionary organizations have enough trouble with present priorities, present personnel, and present problems so that they can give little time to the morrow. It is not the numbers that count for the IRA and the others but the will to persist in view of the assets, political and material, to hand.

The IRA can struggle on for the next decade, making do, hitting the headlines with a spectacular operation from time to time, and exploiting their opponents' blunders. They can suffer what the British can inflict and persist. And they will. The British have what they always wanted—a tolerable level of violence—but just barely. And there is no hope for better short of recourse to state terror. And the IRA has probably bottomed out; things could get worse, but not much. There is nothing in sight that could destroy the organization, and things might get a great deal better. There could be new and talented men on the scene or an unexpected friend abroad, a shift in the Irish political tides, or idiocy in London. The IRA is not going to fade away. There are too many real grievances. This time there have been too many deaths, their own and others, to shut the campaign down. The dream persists. The volunteers still come. The North faces even harder times. Every British attempt at agreement or accommodation has failed, often to IRA advantage. For Irish Republicans the obvious step is to sever the connection with England, and they believe eventually the English must accept this as well. Then the Loyalists can either make their peace with reality, become as Irish as they ought to be, or leave. Then the Thirty-Two County Republic will be a reality and Ireland a nation once again.

If there is any reality to such a scenario, London has showed remarkably little understanding of this direction of Irish history. Not that London has *ever* been very understanding about the revolting Irish. More is known in most London clubs about obscure African tribes or the habits of the bedouin than the Irish, much less the IRA. No matter, it would appear from the rhetoric of Margaret Thatcher and the example of the Falkland Islands that the British intend not to desert their own or to compromise with violent men. Still, there was similar rhetoric and similar examples of sacrifice during the end of the Empire, and the British did finally withdraw. The martyred mayor of Cork Terence MacSwiney said before his death on a hunger strike, "It is not those who can inflict the most, but those that can suffer the most who will conquer." And this IRA, for this decade, is prepared to suffer, and when possible to inflict what they can. They believe that sooner or later Ireland will be free—in their time or others. And so the Irish tragedy in endless acts shows no sign of closing for lack of demand. The IRA refuses to allow the British to set the bounds to a nation that London denies exists. For both, still, the conflict is a zero-sum game, and both seem determined to play on.

And there can be no terse final sentence on the Ulster Troubles, the long war, the IRA, and the gun in Irish politics. There is no last chapter to the Troubles, no conclusion, and for the Republicans no surprise that the past is prologue; crusades may offer salvation to the pilgrims but cannot promise Jerusalem at the bottom line. For the alien dedicated to efficiency, the arts of the possible, even the sacrifice of a pawn during an end gambit, the game must be worth the prize. In sports, participation may be all, not winning or losing but playing the game. In war and politics the costs at the entry gate and the price on the field are higher, rich in blood and ruined lives. Spectators are at risk in the real world, and the innocent cannot be replaced on the board. A long war should be waged to effect, for victory, not entered or maintained as witness to virtue, as a necessary foundation for future battle, or as a symbol of justice denied or a nation unredeemed. Not all long wars are so waged, nor are the Celts in general or the IRA in particular unique in persisting.

Unconventional wars are unconventional in various ways; all great conventional battles, clashes of main battle tanks in the sands of Sinai or the crash of the Imperial Guard against a thin red line in Belgium, are the same; each irregular war is special in its own way, unconventional, unique, particular. And so the Ulster Troubles are more special, the motives of all mixed, the symbolic totems often more important than the tribe. The old realities of irregular war are everywhere to be found, and so, too, are the old myths. It often seems nothing is new but a handful of elegant weapons and the concern of distant academics with strange tools of analysis. Every violent novelty proves to have an ancestry, every outrageous perfidy a lineage. The same heroes and villains, martyrs and patriots, all the old actors return for their usual roles without a need to read the script. Not true, of course. A prologue does not of necessity determine the plot, and even Irish history cannot predict the future. Continuity does not deny change nor the pressure of the past assure a surprise-free future. The long war is not forever, nor the Troubles indeterminable. At the moment, however, the problem remains that there is no solution—to hand. Tomorrow is another day. Certainly in the turmoil of the Troubles, the fury and anguish, the novel disasters and spectacular atrocities, the public pain, the long butcher's bill, it is crucial to note that the gun plays but one, often small, often irrelevant, role in Irish politics. The Troubles do not trouble all and are, if not aberration, at least not dominant on much of the island. And that hallowed, often warped, past of reality and myth has been prologue to agreement, accommodation, democracy, and justice, as well as to this long war and these troubles. The Irish trumpet calls have not all been martial, sounded only over patriot graves.

PART IV
The Ulster Troubles: New Surveys, New Problems, and Analytical Perspectives

> What experience and history teaches is
> this—that people and governments never
> have learned anything from history, or
> acted on principles deduced from it.
> —Georg Wilhelm Hegel

Analysts and academics are no more immune to the allure of the novel and spectacular than the media. And the simple fashions of the times shift unexpectedly: one year Oriental religion attracts only a few and the next year long lines of eager students wind across the campus, women's studies, neo-Marxists, structuralists, annalist historians, and psycho-biographers appear suddenly, ice floes endangering the warm waters of the traditional university's streams. Thus, in the last generation the foci of concern, often poles of chaos, attract the trained and potential specialists abuzz with theory and eager to practice. Some events are distant, alien, devoid of convenient data, wars fought in strange tongues or within forbidden zones, seemingly without consequence or perhaps with readily identifiable symbols and sides. No one cares much of slaughter along the upper Nile or can get into northern Burma or has the proper background to pursue the Ayatollahs in power. On the other hand, the hand of Satan can readily be found in Nicaragua or the KGB conspiracy against the world, thus filling previously barren library shelves. For the most part, trendy topics have a brief half-life; the wars in Mozambique may continue, but the age of academic heroes and media villains has passed and who but the regulars care for Argentina without gunmen and Fascists? Mostly, the hot lava flows of analysis, special pleading, innocent memoirs, potted history, and tracts for one time do no real harm; later the institutes and libraries will amass the residue and less fashionable scholars will order the old ashes. Thus, it is hardly surprising that the sudden, unexpected advent of the Irish Troubles set off not only a paper chase but also a cottage industry of analysis, explanation, and advocacy. Ireland as crisis-site had much to offer.

261

At the very beginning, Ireland was, mostly, an advanced country where accurate and plentiful statistics were available, where the press was various, largely accurate, and in touch with the real world, and where a long and agreed history written out by specialists awaited the concerned. The language of the world, English, was spoken usually by articulate and educated spokesmen. There were real governments and real institutions, not aspirations clothed in rhetoric and authorized only by treaty. Ireland was in every way a modern and comfortable country moving apace into the postindustrial world, an arena in theory familiar to many; there were no dragons, no cannibals, no miasma of revolutionary politics rising from swamps, and no desert ghettos filled with strange dialects. The hotels worked. The universities produced scholars. There was real law and order outside the riot zones and havens near to hand. Also, of course, in the beginning there were highly recognizable symbols and sides. Everyone, journalists, scholars, transient observers, knew about civil rights and police brutality, had seen films featuring the IRA gunmen, and was soon familiar with Orange and Green history, the bar at the Europa, the door on Kevin Street, and the briefing by the responsible. All this in English in a world only slightly different from the familiar. Not only the Irish Troubles but terror in general had become matters of pressing concern, and unlike more transient disasters—industrial pollution, nuclear accidents, coups, plagues, famines, and small wars—Ireland remained a concern, if not always so pressing, and hence an open-ended analytical event with all that it implies for the observers from afar.

18

Terrorism International: Academic Branch

Terrorism has become trendy, not only as a revolutionary means and a threat to order but also as a new and promising field for academic "specialists" who have rushed into a virgin field to sow hurriedly assembled words of wisdom. Every two years, meetings take place in various Italian sites under the auspices of the International School on Disarmament and Research on Conflicts, ISODARCO.

Directed by a Roman physics professor Carlo Schaerf, ISODARCO has become an institution attended by Soviet generals, Asian diplomats, American arms control experts, Third World students and other oddbods. This year, edging away from disarmament and the wonders of the cruise missile and multi-targeted MIRVS, ISODARCO focused in part on "Substate Violence" and the Irish Troubles were allocated a full day of discussion.

There was quite a splendid overview of the Ulster situation, stressing economic verities and political postures by Frank Wright of Queens, an Englishman who has spent eight years in the midst of his subject. Perhaps one of Wright's most intriguing suggestions in a lecture studded with as many goodies as a Christmas cake was the proposition that the form of the labour requirements of Ulster industry had as much to do with subsequent Loyalist attitudes and values as the supposed Protestant ethic. Given the level of ignorance of those responsible for Ulster—or those who seek to be—nothing would be more profitable than an exposure to Frank Wright's exercise—and his suggestion that economically at least the good times are past.

Then there was my trot through the Provisional IRA—who was who and from whence they did come. Most academics have never met a "terrorist" and find the real-people-approach somewhat disconcerting, being quite content with red steel doors between them and their subject matter. Next, a "holistic analysis of the Northern Ireland conflict with a time series analysis" by Steve Wright of the Richardson Institute, Lancaster University, that despite the arcane methodology came to the quite sensible conclusion that the British Army's effort to solve the problem with technological fixes (cures, i.e., CS gas) only aggravated the problem—not that the innocent could dig this out of the charts and graphs without help. Then, after a pause for pasta, there was more discussion: what will happen next (nothing good), and some indications of British intentions (nothing much); now operating on a Scarlett O'Hara policy from Gone With The Wind—"I'll think about that tomorrow"—And off to wine, ice cold, served at a garden cafe at 40p a bottle.

And what did the Iraqis and physicists and denizens of social science make of the Troubled North? In time the rapporteur told us that our conclusions had been that the Irish Troubles were incredibly parochial, embedded in long historical processes and not amenable to comparisons to other substate violence. Which seems fair enough if not very hopeful, still better than the German morning where it was claimed personality explained all or the Italian afternoon when it was denied that personality played a significant part.

An unbombed with whole knees, the red doors closed behind the assembled; some were off to another display in Bulgaria on nuclear matters, others to the beach, many to reassemble in Berlin in November for the next meeting of the academic branch of Terror International, where surely once again out of the Celtic mists will charge the shadow of the IRA gunman, a feature player, parochial or no; and a ticket on the terrorist tour.

In general, before the Troubles made Ireland trendy in 1969, there were serious problems in contemplating recent history and politics. While not as bad as the Sudan or Chad, Ireland had not been especially well served by contemporary historians; the American invention of political scientist replete with quantitative tools had not as yet taken hold. Many small countries—Norway and Bulgaria—have similar problems: there are only so many indigenous scholars who drift to subjects of personal concern and only so many events that might attract the alien. Thus, the 1916-22 period was well covered by all sorts and conditions, but because of native reticence to examine the immediate past (a scene of bitter schism) and because of the lack of novel and spectacular events (nation building and constitution writing did interest a few) to attract the distance, history petered out. Until Tim Pat Coogan produced *Ireland Since the Rising* in 1966 there had been no attempt at either the plain tale of events or a survey of Irish conditions beyond the publishing industries' annual pop-sociology volumn entitled *The Irish*. It was difficult to find the results of elections, the tale of parties, or the battle of budgets in print, much less a history of a secret army. Basically, Ireland did not want to replow salted fields. The books stopped in 1921, and the classes went no farther; for a nation seized on history there were nearly fifty years of blank pages, rumors, yellowed newspapers, tribal tales, and no sign of serious investigation. No place was this more evident than in the concern with the sources for any future history when, as it must, such a project had advocates. Ireland was not *really* an everyday country with an immediate past fashioned by professionals in consensus. Ireland has not an agreed upon past, but an almost conscious policy of authorized ignorance to evade unpleasant contention. Many felt Ireland could not be a nation once again if the immediate past was up to plunder—better to stop time in 1922 and fret about a penny on the milk, throw away the documents, and sing the past in pubs. To the alien eye, Ireland only appeared normal briefly before the mists drifted across the roads, before charm became a cloak, and the common language a bar.

19

Contemporary Irish Archival Resources

The scholarly study of contemporary Ireland has remained largely an arcane pursuit of the very few. Despite extensive policy-oriented research on contemporary Irish affairs, particularly economic policy, public administration, and governmental planning, serious primary research into recent history has barely been initiated. Ireland lacks not only a standard, not to mention definitive, survey of the past fifty years but also any substantial body of specialized studies. Even secondary works on contemporary Ireland are relatively rare. Thus, for Irish history there is nothing faintly resembling the studies available to a student of public administration or state planning. Other than the restraints of academic fashion and the fear of controversy, one of the most awesome obstacles has been and is the paucity of readily available documentation. This has meant that much of the understanding of modern Irish history has been based not on the written word but rather on personal recollection, secondary sources, and more than likely dearly held illusions. In order to act on the future, Irishmen should have some command of their recent past and such a command depends largely on extensive, disinterested investigation by reputable scholars. To date, both Irish and foreign scholars have been severely handicapped by inadequate access to the basic, primary material—the papers out of which history is made.

In modern Ireland access to written documentation is limited—in some cases barely existent. Private papers for the 1916–23 period have often been retained, too often in unknown private hands, but also few records were made and fewer kept. Men intimately involved in the period like Frank Aiken, Séan Lemass, Gerald Boland, and James Ryan replied also uniformly that they really had no "papers" for that period and by implication for any period.[1] With rare exceptions, President De Valera being a welcome one, the Irish politician in the South at least apparently has found the concept of private papers to be alien. Although a very considerable number of what might be called the 1916-papers have found their way into the National Library,[2] holdings after that date fall off rapidly. Some collections, like Ernie O'Malley's, remain unexploited, some, like Michael Collins', until recently "hidden,"[3] and many others have disappeared. But it is to be hoped that at least those of former members of government remain in part somewhere in the closed archives.[4] One highly commendable step was the government sponsorship of an extensive series of interviews with the 1916 participants, who often carried the story further than 1916. But these "papers" held by the Bureau of Military History are closed for fifty years and will do even the next generation little good.[5]

The prospect for new and extensive collections of private papers appearing is not hopeful. And access to government archives is not a much better prospect. The policy of the British government, followed generally by the government of Northern Ireland, concerning archives is long-standing and well known. Essentially, most enlightened countries tend to recognize the ultimate value of their archives and most Western countries allow access after sufficient time to chosen individuals, then to accredited scholars, and finally to the public. The time span varies from country to country and according to the nature of the documents. For example, in the United States the Foreign Relations series based on diplomatic correspondence is published in theory twenty years after the event, and limited access is granted before this. Although Great Britain adhered in theory to a more rigid thirty-year rule, much is published well before then; for example, the Cabinet papers come under a thirty-year rule—the background to the Anglo-Irish Agreements of April 1938 being a recent goodie. Sometimes there are unexpected revelations (e.g., the rapid exploitation of the German archives captured in 1945) and at other times an unexpected hard line (e.g., the British closure of the 1916 courtmartial records for one hundred years). But at least, there is usually a recognized policy; in the case of the Republic of Ireland, there is a prevalent uncertainty.

In an endeavor to discover not only the existing rules and regulations on archival material but the attitude of those involved in Dublin and Belfast, a set questionnaire was sent to every government department North and South (except by an oversight to the Department of Labour in Dublin, an inexcusable example of scholarly fallibility) requesting the regulations on access, among some other questions. The result was mixed. Clearly the government of Northern Ireland had a standard policy and had anticipated such a query. All of my questionnaires were forwarded promptly to the Public Record Office, which replied at length as to the specific policy regarding archives as well as forwarding other detailed information.[6] Two Ministries, Education and Agriculture, also answered directly, supplying additional suggestions in the light of my interests.

The result from Dublin, however, left something to be desired. Apparently there has never been a considered policy for the government holdings after 1921 except to assume that no one would want to, or should be allowed to, root through old papers. The most detailed official information was eventually, six months after the original request, supplied by the Taoiseach's Office, but only in reference to the holdings of the State Paper Office and the Department of the Taoiseach. By and large, the other departments simply did not answer—at all—or felt that my question was irrelevant: e.g., "this Department is not concerned in matters of this kind and is not, therefore, in a position to supply any of the information you require."[7]

There was, fortunately, one exception: the reply from Mr. J. A. Scannell, secretary of the Department of Post and Telegraphs, who was quite aware of the eventual value of his records, the need for preservation, and the reason for my query. Both Breandán Mac Giolla Choille at the State Paper Office and Margaret C. Griffith at the Public Record Office answered in detail as to their holdings and policies, but they are not responsible for the mass of government papers after 1921. That there is no official access policy for later material—or interest in one—is hardly crucial since total denial is an effective policy and hardly a novel one. In time, under repeated requests, an Irish government will decide on a formal policy; however, unless the government and the civil service are made aware of the value of their archives to future scholars and the present need of preservation, much that is irreplaceable may be destroyed. While considerable reliance can be placed on the traditional bureaucratic reluctance to discard paper, the lack of official policy can only be worrisome.

The departments of the Irish government were hardly alone in responding with some uncertainty as to the nature of archival policy. With two exceptions—Aer Lingus and Bord na Mona—the selection of state-sponsored bodies contacted simply never answered what was admittedly a form letter. As to the two responding bodies, the assumption seemed to be that as long as staff were not involved and the request was legitimate, due consideration would be given, but "no one, however, has shown interest in access to these, and consequently no policy has been formulated regarding access to them"[8]. Answers to form letter or no, this generally proved to be the attitude of nearly all individuals or institutions contacted.

Commercial and financial institutions generally showed, as might be expected, a reluctance to consider any access to business records: as Harland and Wolff pointed out, "as a commercial undertaking we do not normally allow access to our archives."[9] The Bank of Ireland did forward the substantial *History of the Bank of Ireland 1783–46*, and Arthur Guinness supplied information concerning industrial archaeology. But few concerns seemed aware of academic interest in business and financial history. The danger here, even more than with governmental archives, is that records will be discarded. The Irish Economic History Group, established in 1967, is intent on the preservation of significant collections of these business records. In 1967–68 a survey of business records in Dundalk and Drogheda was undertaken and submitted to the Irish Manuscripts Commission. An overriding impression gained for the report is that most businessmen were, until contacted, unaware of the value of their old records but were more than willing to cooperate. There is no reason to doubt that a similar situation exists in most of Ireland where solicitors' offices, small family concerns, and private individuals possess copious records and letters that may provide valuable historical materials for this generation or later ones. General knowledge of historical significance is probably at the moment more important than funds to collect and catalog vast amounts of paper.

In theory some of the most useful archives in Ireland must be those held by the Churches, but in practice it is most unlikely any will be available to historians in the foreseeable future. Rev. Seán Corkery of the Library, Maynooth, reported that the only archival material potentially available would be Diocesan archives and access through the Bishop or Archbishop is not easily obtained. Less specific replies from Dublin, Armagh, and Belfast might perhaps be supposed to indicate an ecumenical agreement to read my questionnaire, not as a request to gain access to archives closed even to the faithful, but only as a vague query for information on church history!

Similar requests to more worldly institutions, in particular political parties, engendered more interest. In time nearly all parties contacted, North and South, replied with varying degrees of enthusiasm. Whether a keen awareness of public relations was the basis or not, the result was heartening: "full co-operation assured,"[10] and "we would co-operate fully with such an investigator."[11] In Dublin the Labour Party reported a "couple of ardent historian members cataloguing our records."[12] In a specific case, for over three years Sinn Féin gave me the most commendable cooperation, and others have had similar experiences with various Irish political parties.

The trade unions, too, replied hopefully, although the late James Larkin, general secretary of the Workers' Union of Ireland, felt that they had no materials that would be interest. As usual some queries to farmers' or women's organizations disappeared into limbo, but it should be pointed out that most organizations are not oriented to answer strange form queries in an area not of immediate interest. Experience has shown that with rare exceptions Irish institutions like Irish individuals, when approached personally, are most receptive.

The general result is that outside of government archives, where different ground rules operate in any case, a willingness to aid scholarly research could be found in most of the areas of potential interest, such as business houses, labor unions, political parties, and even state-sponsored bodies, though not unfortunately in the churches. Thus, the situation is hardly as bleak as might first appear. In other countries the lack of access to official governmental papers and files has not prevented historians from making do. In Ireland a great deal of material is available, even if it is not *readily* available. All that remains is to tempt the scholars into activity.

The Impact of Turmoil: 1972

By 1972 it appeared as if everyone literate had been tempted into Irish matters, not just reluctant scholars. The lava had begun to flow and the slag thrown up could soon be examined. As an example of the confluence of literacy and political crisis, ambition, skill, the demands of the market, public anguish, private certainty or despair, and greed for place, the new Irish Troubles had few equals; the very response to Irish violence itself was a case study once removed from the real world of riots, protests, ambushes, and arson, but still just as real. The anticipated trend tracers, as expected, coupled with the tractarians could be found—and for years and years would continue to be found. In that respect, except for the length of concern, Ulster was little different from other spectacular eruptions: Cuba or Chile, Indochina, Algeria, or Israel. The ease of access, comfort of investigation, congenital language, advanced and available data, and extended analytical roots continued to attract a spectrum of talents. The violence, the novel and spectacular, drew the media and the trendy. And the participants proved literate, often relevant, and continually productive. The great lava flow of publication—as well as television documentaries, transient news programs, poems and plays and paintings, novels, legends, and ballads—did not burn up the good in the river of awful: no Gresham's law. And much would be good and quite a bit interesting, with no end in sight. Thus, it was possible to include most of the available material in the early surveys, where presently the sum total to date would be, as bibliographic reference alone, a substantial book. And there was, as well, material not so readily available, often found later or rumored sighted in distant parts: the journalists reported back in various tongues—Italian, Spanish, Japanese— in works of local interest and short shelf-life; the scholars crafted papers and articles beyond the computers' reach; the idealogues wrote for party in private papers; and very small presses printed very special pleadings.

And there was no sign of an ebbing tide. A new generation of historians were at work on the Irish past, not unmindful of the present; they deployed the tools of the analysts, noted the new Marxists, and focused on many odd but significant corners. The steady state of Ulster violence continued to intrigue the more contemporary, replete with social science models, quantifiable questionnaires, and psychological concerns. There was more of the same, biographies and memoirs and surveys and summaries with uncertain final chapters.

Notes

1. Correspondence, various dates. As an aside, the very first two answers I received were from what are reputed to be the most efficient institutions in Ireland: Guinness and Seán Lemass.
2. A reasonable estimate of the holdings of the National Library for the 1916 period would be 80 per cent. The great gap will be the papers of President De Valera, which will go to the Franciscan Library, Killiney.
3. Nothing reveals more clearly the obstacles still present for the contemporary historian in Ireland than Mr. Peter V. Collins' letter in the *Irish Times* (18 February 1969), which reads in part:

   > Many papers, both Collins' personal papers and those of other people concerning Collins and his work, have been in my possession for some years, having been passed on to me by a now deceased member of the family. Of these, many are commonly believed to have been destroyed . . . When the time comes to pass on these papers, they should be given only to the individual who in my opinion, is most worthy of the name Collins and who bears the name and memory of his great ancestor proudly.

   This attitude is neither novel nor limited to Ireland and is quite understandable even to historians.
4. There is very little understanding of the difference between public and private papers.
5. It is possible to hunt up the living contributors and request permission to read their personal copy, but for almost all purposes the records are closed. In an otherwise admirable project, the only quibble is that at the time of the interviews the results were not correlated with each other, thus missing an opportunity to clear up what may now remain controversial points.
6. "I would also draw your attention to an article on the office in *Archives,* The Journal of the British Records Association, Volume 6, No. 30, published Michaelmas 1963, page 108. In addition you might find of some interest an article of mine in the *Journal of the Society of the Archives,* Volume 2, page 361. I would also draw your attention to our Annual Reports published since 1924; the last one published in 1966 covers the period 1954–1959 and one to be published this month covers the period 1960–1965," K. Darwin, *Letter* 3 April 1968.
7. J. A. Butler, Department of Agriculture and Fisheries, *Letter,* 18 April 1968.
8. David Hayes, Aer Lingus, *Letter,* 11 April 1968.
9. Alan Hedgley, Harland and Wolff, *Letter,* 2 April 1968.
10. E. McAteer, Nationalist Party, *Letter,* 2 July 1968.
11. Brendan Halligan, Labour Party, *Letter,* 17 April 1968.
12. See footnote 11 above.

20

The Chroniclers of Violence in Northern Ireland: The First Wave, 1972

Perhaps the only undeniable blessing to evolve from the recent troubles in Northern Ireland has been miniboom in the publishing industry. Seldom have so many, written so quickly, on a subject understood by so few—and turning, one assumes, a decent profit for their effort. Traditionally, contemporary modern Ireland has attracted the occasional coffee-table volume or the nearly annual *The Irish,* potted "sociology." Until quite recently, few scholars have ventured into contemporary affairs—those events after the revolutionary years of 1916–21—and almost none of the tools of social science have been put to use on Irish society. Thus, the latest commentators found a truly virgin field, bereft of valid experts, congenial to anecdote, fashionably violent, amusingly Irish and if not fit for the coffee table certainly attractive in the marketplace. The result has been a twofold outpouring: first of those who would chronicle in print what had been for the British audience nightly fare on the television, and second of those more committed or more daring who would interpret, analyze, explain and predict. The former, however ill-prepared, sought to write history, however superficially, while the latter sought to make it by rearranging the past to buttress their vision of the future. Neither the observers nor the participants have in print as yet produced a single definitive work nor in fact a very satisfactory plain tale of events—much less a revelation into the nature of the conflict in Northern Ireland. The attempts of this first wave to date, however, offer some insights into the Northern Ireland problem, into the nature of Irish and British scholarship and, perhaps, into the future that awaits the most distressful six-counties.

To begin at the very beginning, no one who has yet taken pen to hand on matters concerning Northern Ireland has failed to indicate that the violence was not born yesterday. The bombing in Belfast and the sniping in Derry are almost without exception seen as the products of forces, institutions, currents of thought, social structures, and habits of mind that have long, long history. Those who stress the relevance of the Celtic past to

272

recruitment in the Royal Ulster Constabulary are often hard put to say at which point the descent into first sectarian violence and later guerrilla war truly began, but no one doubts that the present has not so much been molded as warped by the past. Even those journalists who arrived in Belfast with minds like blank slates soon found that *their* book must begin back there in the grim Celtic mists of old grievances, old war, and old hatreds. And, like the Irish, soon they too were fingering the rosary beads of the past to explain what to the common viewer of BBC seemed almost inexplicable—a "religious" war in the mid-twentieth century in Great Britain. Even the most quantitative social scientist accepts that the current crisis has contributing factors—the most striking fact about the works on the Irish Troubles is the universal acceptance of the heritage of history. Liam de Paor in his sound, historically based *Divided Ulster* (New York: Penguin Books, 1970) is one with Professor Richard Rose of Strathclyde in his analytical survey-based *Governing Without Consensus: An Irish Perspective* (Boston: Beacon Press, 1971). History seemingly in the case of Northern Ireland is destiny. Just exactly what history is and means then becomes the very stuff of the conflict.

Most of the material—stuff—included in the first wave of works on Northern Ireland has been snatched from secondary works, often of doubtful merit, and arranged often with a fair mind if a heavy hand. With one or two exceptions no one has done any original research on the roots of the problem or sought analysis beyond the conventional, historical narrative of battles and bombs. Typical are two solid, fair, balanced works by prominent journalists, Max Hastings of the *Evening Standard, Barricades in Belfast* (New York: Taninger, 1970) and Martin Wallace of Radio Telefis Eirean, *Drums and Guns: Revolution in Ulster* (London: Geoffrey Chapman, 1970). Hastings came to Ireland unprepared and, like his English readers, was appalled and totally bewildered. One suspects he is still appalled. Wallace, on the other hand, as former deputy editor of the *Belfast Telegraph,* began his task no less appalled but somewhat less bewildered. Both, however, begin in the seventeenth century to explain the twentieth, both recognize a bigot whatever his color, both tend to find against not only the Protestant powers and dominations but against the concept of Northern Ireland. Wallace, the more subtle, hopes for some sort of agreement between the three governments involved: "Ireland will not be united without the consent of a majority of people in Northern Ireland." Hastings foresees—without details—"that distant but inevitable day" when "Ulster and the Irish Republic are reunited as logic dictates." And this largely has been the analysis of the Irish press, even of British liberal opinion, and of the common wisdom. It is also essentially the "Decent Dublin Case."

Those less decent, that is, more militant, are usually lumped with the problem not the solution. The "extreme" Protestant Unionist case has usually been made so badly and so bluntly that no one has paid any attention to it. The bland, slick apologies of official Unionism are thought a cover-up of jobbery and polite bigotry. The pure Republicans who blame the British Empire for everything and insist the only recourse is force (guerrilla war) are pigeon-holed as terrorist-radicals and ignored. And the Marxist-Leninist analyses of the young people of the Peoples Democracy or the political Left are rejected as the blathering of the immature and misguided. Yet each analysis offers more than a recital of the past and a "hope" for the future—a past seen largely from an Irish perspective and a future that would be anathema, apparently, to any but the already committed.

When Avro Manhattan produces *Religious Terror in Ireland* (London: Paravision Publications, 1969) on a level little different than the skilled rabble-rousing of Dr. Ian Paisley, he answers to a need, elaborates a view of man and history, and if he offends good taste and good sense, he most assuredly indicates a world view that in part is responsible for the violence but guarantees the past as prologue. As long as the Paisleyites—and Paisley is not necessarily one—*believe* their vision of history, act out their fantasies and fears in the street, then the people of the North are doomed to repeat themselves. And Andrew Boyd in the *Holy War in Belfast* (Tralee: Anvil, 1969) outlines episodically the chronicle of sectarian violence of nineteenth-century Belfast—long before the pressures of partition and the establishment of the Republic.

The Unionist view repeatedly expressed in public speeches and Stormont debates, published in a variety of pamphlets, read only by the faithful, has also surfaced in Patrick Riddell's *Fire Over Ulster* (London: Hamish Hamilton, 1970). Almost for the first time the "decent" Unionist vision is delineated, if not without passion at least with care and detail. It does not matter that the vision is faulty, based often on error, exaggeration, and willful ignorance, but that the view from the top of Stormont, from the proper suburbs and from the big offices has been shaped into something more than platitudes or lies or evasions. Nothing more reveals the awesome gap in the vision of the Stormont establishment and that of Dublin than the meaning of "1916." For the Unionists of the North this was the date of the Somme—July not April— and the "Slaughter of the Brave." The Rising to the south was only additional evidence that the Nationalists were traitors. The feeling, however self-righteous, that Northern Ireland is a small, beleaguered state, seldom understood, almost never appreciated, particularly in London, attempting to create a decent life for a decent people in trying and most difficult circumstances, may not and surely is not going to sway the skeptical, but it is most important to accept that it is real. The decent Orangeman is not a bigot—in his view—he simply neither likes nor trusts Catholics, and Riddell explains why. Riddell's work then is quite important for it details a different Irish history and brings the story down from the Banks of the Boyne—the world of pageants, symbols and Paisley—to the raw material of the past fifty years. As long as one segment of Northern Ireland immediately thinks of the Somme and all that it means when 1916 is mentioned, then bridge building is not a matter of social engineering alone.

The Republicans, not readily visible in print but present in the crisis, also have a vision of the future when the common name of Irishmen unites Catholic and Protestant, now divided in an Ireland partitioned for British imperial gain. If their visions hold more charm for many than the fantasy of Paisley, their cherished means—physical force—offers little expectation that Ireland will be united peacefully. As Cathal Goulding, Chief of Staff of the IRA, has pointed out, Ireland was divided by British violence and there is no evidence—for most Republicans—that the island can be united without further violence. And increasingly the two IRAs have devoted their energies to furthering that violence.

The civil-rights movement, as yet, lacks an adequate historian; the time and talent of the participants has been largely absorbed elsewhere. Much that is written is polemic, often arcane, and seldom convincing. The contemporary "language" of radical politics is the new Brutalism, appalling, and difficult to digest. The one inside job on the movement, Bernadette Devlin's *The Price of My Soul* (New York: Vintage, 1969) is, fortunately, more about the girl than the movement. Much of the polemic material does not seem real—a Thirty-Two County Workers' and Farmers' Republic—nor do the issues, largely tactical differences within the movement, seem important. What is clear is that *their* Ireland happens to be similar to that of Riddell only in geographical location.

What neither the chronicles, with their brief histories and gentle aspirations, nor the committed, with their tunnel vision and polemics, offer the reader is depth of analysis or an effective program of conciliation. Of all the committed books on the new troubles, the most promising on the record should have been *The Sins of Our Fathers: Roots of Conflict in Northern Ireland* (Dublin: Gill and Macmillan, 1970) by Owen Dudley Edwards. The title implies a serious academic study that the reputation of the author, a young, established historian of recorded insight and strong views, should have made possible. Yet *The Sins of Our Fathers* is not an historical analysis, not adequately academic for scholarly taste but too serious to pass as polemic, not quite an extended essay, part memoir larded with historical example, part inchoate study of the Irish working class and part special pleading for one man's view. About all that can be said for certain is that in the broader sense the work is definitely nonfiction, no small accomplishment in writing on Ireland. First, as seems to be incumbent on all authors on Irish matters, Edwards feels called upon to assert his views on not only God but on the Mass and Redemption so as to make his bias clear, one assumes, to the common reader. Few other common readers but the Irish insist on a catalog of an author's theological and political attitudes before turning to the body of the work. Thus from the very first, *The Sins of Our Fathers,* despite the occasional patina of historical objectivity and scholastic underpinning, is part of the Northern Ireland problem not the solution or resolution as the case may be.

Edwards who clearly feels very strongly and very deeply about the "conflict" would not take it amiss, it is assumed, to be labeled as engaged, a man committed, a political man even though the ideals of his profession indicate that the way of the disinterested, the objective, leads most swiftly to the truth or that part of the truth open to historical investigation. Yet he makes it clear that he does not talk to those in Northern Ireland with whom he disagrees. Thus, despite some most interesting and germane chapters, particularly on "The Breaking of the Irish Working Class"—certainly the embryo of a brilliant and badly needed book—Edwards has written one of Ireland's longest, most brilliant, most irritating, political pamphlets. The tone shifts—as does the subject matter—between that which might be appropriate on a television panel show and that of a seminar of graduate students at the University of Edinburgh. And all through the ups and downs and digressions, Edwards whips about with his sentences like chain saws demolishing pomp and pretense, scattering the wayside with dissected reputations, larding scathing comment with historical examples of folly.

And from it all, the major impression is that even Edwards cannot really make it *simple,* that he is too good a historian to find the easy devil in class or conservatism or original sin: the roots of conflict are complex, manifold, sunk far into a many-splendored past and have scarcely begun to be traced by the botanists of history. Edwards has not so much made a start as indicated the lay of the land. For generations, Irishmen have been building ideological castles on historical foundations that on even the slightest inspection have proven to be bogs of illusion and quicksands of myth. One simple suggestion—thesis—that Edwards proposes is that Joe Devlin and his Green Horde had as much to do with Orange prejudice as did the cynical maneuvers of the establishment. The view from Dublin has always been that only the Orange gain by the border, only the Unionists profit by partition, only the British or the Protestants or "Them" receive returns on the "theft" of the six-counties. Devlin, however, made a career of division, a virtue of prejudice, and Ireland abounds in Devlins, Green, Orange, Red and Lily White, in collars and caps, and few of them would look with favor on too many Owen Dudley Edwards laying about him with the printed word, too clever by half, shrewd, opinionated, and dangerous for those who like the easy life.

Some of the recent contributions, official, authorized and academic are as predictable as rain in Donegal. One of the most delightful of all, for those with arcane tastes, is *Disturbances in Northern Ireland* (Belfast: H.M.S.O., September, 1969), the Cameron report, that is an archtype British White Paper, fair-minded, just, thorough, so loaded with "balance" as to positively creak under the strain and so far from the reality of the "disturbances" that the bombs and arson and riots in the streets are tidied up, ordered into subsections, and lost in the mysterious language of civil servants—fair-minded, just, precise, and irrelevant. *Disturbances* (Cmd. 532) is a glittering example of British bureaucracy at its very best, so tidy, so well-meaning, so intent on doing the right thing that no one really notices the peculiar tunnel vision, nor the unspoken commitment to the elimination of waves, nay ripples. Between the black of sin and the white of purity, formal British investigations opt for a way station equidistant from the two poles, the good grey area of officialdom, moderately sinful, moderately pure, decent failure, and nothing could be more appropriate for Northern Ireland given the British record.

A similar distortion of the unpleasant reality by the application of blinders and the exercise of good taste is Terence O'Neill's *Ulster at the Crossroads* (London: Faber and Faber, 1969), a carefully edited and arranged selection of the former Prime Minister's speeches. Despite the O'Neillolatry in the editorial commentary, the speeches like the man are urbane, balanced, well-meaning, decent, very much liberated British Tory, but basically conservative—and reflect a Northern Ireland-that-never-was.[1] All the bridge building, all the hopes for economic progress, regionalism, improved community relations, social progress and cultural revival, all the surface of O'Neill's well-publicized and well-received administration proved insufficient to hide the real Northern Ireland. By the time Ulster—or six counties of it—reached the Crossroads, all roads led downhill from Stormont. When O'Neill asks, "Is this *really* the kind of Ulster that you want?" he as much as anyone is responsible for the "present state of the country," and given all it could have been far worse. His collected speeches reveal nothing so much as the distance between the Northern Ireland of O'Neill's public declaration and the real country in the back streets of Belfast and the bogside of Derry.

Since the academic community usually takes somewhat longer to get up steam, the early returns are first found in scholarly periodicals and privately circulated drafts. A "typical" academic analysis by Anders Boserup, "The Policies of Protracted Conflict" in *Trans-action* (vol. 7, no. 5, March,

1970) brings to bear a set of presumptions and approaches, proven useful elsewhere, on Northern Ireland.

> In the case of Ulster, the key factors of the conflict that shape the social system are, I believe, the inherent weakness of her postcolonial institutions and ruling class, and the consequent need for privileges, sectarianism and discrimination to uphold the political system.

This like much of the well-written and often searching article is the swift substitution of description for analysis, largely because the basics for academic analysis do not yet exist in Northern Ireland, and the categories found useful elsewhere usually proved inadequate, if for no other reason than "admittedly insufficient evidence." The lack of a few facts has, however, never stopped the academicians any more than the existence of a few unpleasant ones has deterred the politician or the civil servant.

The first book-length approach based on conflict theory is that of R.S.P. Elliott and John Hickie, *Ulster: a Case Study in Conflict Theory* (London: Longman, 1971), which with the exception of the material gleaned from the interviews of fifty Northern Irish politicians (spring 1969), is more about theory than Irish conflict. Advocates of nonviolence who hurried to the Irish scene either published too soon in the first flush of the civil-rights movement or have withdrawn in horror from the rising level of violence that fails to fit earlier concepts. In effect, the theoretical foundations for instant academic analysis have increasingly proven irrelevant as the Irish troubles spin through one "level" after another.

And if there is one popular work so far that will last, so too is there one academic work—the exception that proves the rule. In part, Richard Rose's *Governing Without Consensus* is not an exception in that it was begun in the mid-1960s before a visible Irish problem existed and was as much concerned with British politics in particular and the question of legitimacy in general as with Irish matters. The basis of the book was an extended questionnaire that alone is one of the more, probably the most, fruitful academic ventures into contemporary Irish politics. Questions of British politics and legitimacy aside, on Irish matters Rose has revealed with hard data a great deal that was suspected, and much that was not, about Northern Irish political attitudes. It is a major step away from the myths of the past, and may it be followed by further rigorous academic investigation such as those soon to be published by Cornelius O'Leary of Queen's University, Belfast, and Ian Budge of Essex (a community power survey), and Robert Baxter of Queen's (a constituency survey in East Belfast). James L. Russell of the University of Strathclyde has finished (1970) the field work for a political socialization study as well. Rose, however, was first in and first out, and for anyone concerned with Irish matters he came out with a truly important pioneer work.

Of all the bits of evidence left on the Irish tidal flats the most surprising is undoubtedly Bernadette Devlin's *The Price of My Soul*. For anyone familiar from afar with her meteoric "rise" in Irish politics, the work of many hands, and the content of her various public statements, *The Price of My Soul* was either going to be a callow political manifesto or a sentimental harangue. It proved to be neither. Bernadette Devlin may not be a profound political thinker or even the Saint Joan of Northern Ireland, but she is shrewd, realistic despite her "radicalization"; she writes well if not beautifully and has in her pages told us a great deal more about Northern Ireland than most of the more formal attempts by the professionals. While *The Price of My Soul* was sure to go into paperback—and has in various countries—on the scandal and esteem of the moment, it is also the only publication that so far seems likely to be popular a decade hence when the sound and fury of this generation's troubles have been forgotten.

In the heel of the hunt, perhaps, it does not really matter if anyone of competence writes on or anyone of influence reads about Irish troubles. The Irish are supposed to be historically minded, nurturing past grievances and former triumphs, versed in their past, custodians of a rare history. Yet no one in or out of Ireland can agree on the meaning of this history, often in actuality not so much a thing of rags and patches but a picture of blinding white and darkest black, not history in the grand sense but the stuff of the patriot game. No nation has used "history" for good or ill more often than the Irish, for often it was their only asset, a comfort in troubled times. There is little reason to think that a new, even non-Celtic generation attracted to the old past no matter how skillful their tools (and social science is hardly an Irish *forte* as yet),[2] how pure their hearts, and honest their intentions could do much more than create new bricks to build the same old mansions of bigotry unless their readers have a sudden change of heart.

For those who feel an urgency that cannot be satisfied by hopes for a sudden revelation or quiet hope for eventual change, there remains hope that man can do something—but exactly what is illusive. The aspirations of the Devlins and Farrells for a Workers' Republic, the Irish Republicans for the expulsion of the British and a return to a state of innocence, the Irish Orangemen for the triumph of "Protestantism" and the confusion of Rome, the hopes of the Unionist establishment for a moment of peace, the ambitions of the Dublin establishment for a bit of the action, and, most of all, the longing of many for a bit of quiet are not going to be reconciled by the formulas offered heretofore by the authorities or by the analysts. Perhaps as the social scientists complete with polls, systems analysis, theorems of conflict resolution, and the weightier tools of social engineering continue to report in, there will be a direction more earthly than prayer, more immediately relevant than history, and more *useful*. And maybe not. The involvement of American social scientists in such crucial crisis areas as urban renewal, welfare, racial relations, and more recently Southeast Asia has not exactly been an unmixed blessing. Still it is difficult to see in Northern Ireland with madmen shouting through the streets and secret armies in the basements, with the most painful evidence of greed for power, corruption of purpose and decay of virtue in the mighty as well as the meek, how things can get too much worse.

In any case, the first flood of publications, largely the product of journalists, instant analysis, and official—not authoritative—investigation has if nothing more revealed "the problem" to a wider if still not very interested audience. And yet when all is read and done, there are not only no answers but no explanations. All agree that the Troubles have historical roots, but one man's history is another's myth. Even the alien from afar becomes involved; his perceptions adjusted to the Celtic mists and Orange passions. Even his book becomes part of the problem. For some the Troubles are the result of the Devil, Roman or Protestant, class conflict or imperial predilections. Some do find the simple explanation in the hidden hand of Roman power or the machinations of Perfidious Albion. Some see Northern Ireland as a typical postcolonial situation and others as a unique combination of the most diverse and peculiar historical trends. No one can convince the other and while all have aspirations none really offer solutions.

Perhaps serious academic investigation can reveal the basic common ground available in Northern Ireland on which those long forgotton bridges might be built. Perhaps such investigation might reveal no such ground, not all human problems have human solutions and not all problems are amenable to compromise or even conciliation. When children prattle different nursery rhymes, play different games, curse with different words, live from the moment of birth in an alien world to that of the child across the lane—and when full grown gain certain benefit from the difference—then books probably can do little at the moment for Ireland. But books at least, unlike bombs, are not a clear and present danger. And, who knows, each may come a bit closer to the truth and, despite all, the search for truth still seems an important activity, even in Northern Ireland.[3]

Notes

1. It should, one supposes, be pointed out that despite how fair-minded and decent Lord O'Neill was, he was very much one of his own, no island of enlightenment

but part of the main. Consider: "Protestant girl required for housework. Apply to the Hon. Mrs. Terence O'Neill, Glebe House, Ahoghill, Co. Antrim." *Belfast Telegraph*, November 1959.

2. For example, not until the mid-1960s did any academicians undertake survey research in Northern Ireland and the first commercial undertaking was commissioned by the *Belfast Telegraph* in 1966. See Richard Rose, "Ulster Politics, A Select Bibliography of the Troubles," forthcoming in 1972 in *Political Studies*.

3. The works mentioned in the text by no means exhaust the recent literature on Northern Ireland. The Dublin arms smuggling scandal has engendered several not very informative works: Seamus Brady, *Arms and the Men* (Dublin: Brady, 1971); T. MacIntyre, *To the Bridewell Gate* (London: Faber & Faber, 1971); James Kelly, *Orders for the Captain?* (Dublin: Kelly, 1971). On the other hand, several solid works on far broader subjects have relevance to the recent troubles: D.R. O'Connor Lysaght's *The Republic of Ireland* (Cork: Mercier, 1971), Harry Calvert's *Constitutional Law in Northern Ireland* (Belfast: Stevens and Sons and Northern Ireland Legal Quarterly, 1968) and Martin Wallace's new book on the Northern Ireland government since 1921. With rare exceptions, most elite newspapers felt it necessary to give at some point extended coverage to Northern Ireland (*New York Times Magazine* or Mary Holland's pieces in the Sunday *Observer*) and many periodicals accepted pieces on Ireland. *The Sunday Times* (London) Insight Team's Investigation will be published in 1972 by Andre Deutsch. One of the most astute and thoughtful of the journalists has been Michael McInerney of the *Irish Times*, whose analysis deserves more permanent form. The pamphlet literature, as might be expected, is massive stretching from the wilder shores of Unionism (Rev. Ian Paisley, D.D. *Northern Ireland, What is the Real Situation?* [Bob Jones University Press, 1969]) on through Unionist apologies or explanations (for example, the most curious *Commentary by the Government of Northern Ireland to Accompany the Cameron Report* Cmd. 534, Belfast, 1969) to Desmond Greaves' *Northern Ireland: Civil Rights and Political Wrongs*, published by the English Communist Party (London, 1969)—and see his forthcoming *The Irish Question, 1971* (London: Lawrence and Wishart). Of the massive lot, two stand out—neither readily available to an American audience. *The Orange and Green, A Quaker Study of Community Relations in Northern Ireland* published by the Northern Friends' Peace Board (Brigflatts, Sedbergy, Yorkshire, England, 1969) is the best short account of the problem comparable in tone and approach to the exceedingly valuable *The Northern Ireland Problem* (London: Oxford University Press, 1962) of Dennis P. Barrit and Charles F. Carter. The other is Mike Farrell's *Struggle in the North* (Belfast, People's Democracy, 84 Albert Street), detailing not only the strategy of the civil-rights movement but also the maneuvers of the Dublin politicians in the troubled waters of the six counties. See, also, Bowes Egon and Vincent McCormack, *Burntollet* (London: L.R.S. Publisher, 1969).

21

The Chroniclers of Violence in Northern Ireland Revisited, 1974

As the years pass, the Northern Ireland Troubles appear to have become institutionalized at an intolerable but apparently irreducible level of violence. There appears no light at the end of the tunnel and no firm evidence that the center can hold. The bridges between a divided society have long been reduced to rubble. The Provisional IRA appears capable, even eager, to continue a campaign of guerrilla attrition damned as self-defeating, immoral, and bloody-minded by all concerned including the Official IRA. In return, Protestant gunmen have opened the season on Catholics, all guilty of treason in some form, all enemies of British Ulster. And the British Army remains a tempting target even at times to the Protestant militants.

Politics beyond the gun remain polarized. The Unionist voters massively repudiated the concept of the Council of Ireland in the February 1974 general elections. Polls indicate they yearn not for power-sharing but for a return of Stormont or integration into Britain, both nonstarters. Huddling in the middle of the road are Brian Faulkner, heretofore considered a bigot only slightly more decent than Paisley, and Gerry Fitt, formerly of Republican Labour, tricolors and all, now beneath the green umbrella of the Social Democratic Labour Party. They are scorned by the pure in heart and militant in deed. So the bombs and executions continue. The association of the Dublin government with Britain at the Sunnydale conference, the coalescing of sentiment North and South against the mindless violence, the weariness of all, the new forms and formulas, the pleas of the righteous or reasonable have not brought peace, even at any price, with or without justice, with or without honor. And from this dreadful confrontation no one seems to have gained, no one has been purged of violence or has been permitted to fashion new and revolutionary changes. Only, one would assume, those who publish for profit or promotion have derived any real benefit from the Troubles—or just perhaps there are those who can plot the road from the past into the present turmoil or mine relevant lessons from the chaos.

The very first impression of the common reader would be that a Gresham's Law of Publication remains operative, if not driving out decent work at least burying it. Despite a veritable torrent of the printed word, instant history, special pleading, pamphlets and biographies created on demand, honest essays and academic adventures, there is not really a plain tale of Ulster events, and most assuredly not a generally accepted explanation. There is, however, a detailed chronology in Richard Deutsch and Vivien Magowen's *Northern Ireland, 1968-1973, A Chronology of Events, 1968-1971,* vol. I (Belfast: Blackstaff Press, 1973) so that if it is not possible to tell why, at least it will soon be possible to tell when. There has been a somewhat similar attempt to produce a simple chronicle with Richard W. Mansbach's *Northern Ireland: Half a Century of Partition* (New York: Facts on File, 1973). Something more than this is wanted, of course, and may even be possible. There seems to be relatively little of significance on Ulster matters still hidden, for revelations, leaks, trials, spite, and the quick "historical" polemic to rationalize the present have left few important secrets. Except for the names of the guilty, the acrimonious events within the Republican Movement, the details of the inner world of Protestant extremists, and the odd caper, most or much is known. The difficulty in surveying the Troubles has been that the plain tale of events keeps rushing beyond the proposed final chapter, confounding prognosis, producing instant obsolescence. If the first problem was to find the beginning of the Ulster Troubles—Strongbow, Wolfe Tone, Easter 1916—the second has been to fashion an end, if not in reality at least on the page.

If we are not to wait until the final act or at least an exhausted pause, it is necessary to be quickly in and quickly out. An excellent example of the problems and prospects of such an exercise can be found in Henry Kelly's *How Stormont Fell* (Dublin: Gill and Macmillan, 1972) that covers the period of Faulkner's Premiership, March 1971 to March 1972. Kelly, Northern Editor of the *Irish Times,* long a perceptive and knowledgeable if not completely disinterested observer of the Northern scene, has done a sound and balanced study, good journalism in the best sense of the word. And the book had an obvious beginning and end, came out in a rush while the iron was hot, and a ready-made Irish audience existed. The considerably more trendy *Ulster* by the Insight Team of the *Sunday Observer* (Harmondsworth, Middlesex: Penguin, 1972) was a similar exercise. The Insight Team tracked down a considerable amount of novel information, often shrewdly leaked by the self-interested, including the Official IRA. The result is more important than the usual instant history, but like Kelly's work will gradually be left on the farther shore as Ulster tides move on.

The most recent and reputable journalistic endeavor is a most detailed and depressing account of the rising wave of arbitrary murders that began in 1972. Two young journalists on the *Belfast Telegraph,* Martin Dillon and Denis Lehane, expanded earlier unprinted articles into *Political Murder in Northern Ireland* (Baltimore: Penguin Books, 1974) largely dealing with events since 1972, but with a flashback or two to the 1966 UVF shootings and the background of the Troubles. Their major and not at this date particularly startling conclusion is that Protestant groups have been responsible for the majority of assassinations. These murders have been, if random in selection, by no means motiveless. Until the public announcements claiming responsibility by the UVF or the Ulster Freedom Fighters or the Red Hand Commandos and the evidence that began to appear in court hearings, the authors' conclusion would have had few takers outside the Catholic community. But after two years, the evidence is overwhelming that Protestant assassination squads are killing victims largely chosen at random for a political purpose: to intimidate the Catholic community. That these are by no means the only killings is made clear in chapters on the IRA executions and the activities of the British Army. In the latter case, the Catholic charge of military murder is felt to be largely unproved. As for the IRA, particularly the Belfast Provisionals, clearly no favorite of either author, not all their killings could be explained as the authorized execution of informers or the murder of police and security men. In some cases they were simple, sectarian murders. Although the book has been harshly criticized for errors of detail (the danger of speedy publication), there can be no hiding the main thesis: the Protestant militants have for two years resorted to political murder in an increasingly brutalized Ulster society.

In sum the three entries by the journalists fill an immediate need. They set down for the record what can be discovered; they are sound examples of the craft. While lasting value may be in doubt, this is not a concern of most journalists who seek to reveal, expose, present rather than explain or interpret—although in Irish matters few so deny themselves. In fact, in recent years there has been a considerable corpus of "history," analysis, or revelation not by journalists but by those involved or about those involved, so that we have to hand Conor Cruise O'Brien's "Ireland" or Andrew Boyd's "Brian Faulkner."

Not all of this literature is narrow, special pleading; for example, a most useful work for the serious-minded who are still innocent of Irish matters would be Garret FitzGerald's *Towards a New Ireland* (London: Charles Knight & Co., 1972). A practicing Irish politician, FitzGerald at the time was Fine Gael shadow minister of finance and is presently foreign minister in the Coalition Cabinet. For such a man to write a sane, sensible, authoritative book on the most pressing issues of the day with neither hedging nor cant is startling. Positively astounding is the fact that he is quite willing to write what most politicians prefer to whisper and then only after elections. The work is sound and authoritative, fair if quite clearly the view from Dublin and the left of Fine Gael. FitzGerald addresses in detail those questions concerning the future of Ireland, especially a united Ireland, most politicians and a good many important observers have discussed in slogans. The nature of Irish economic differences or the detailed and delicate problems of federalism or the Common Market in relation to partition or unity have rarely been approached. In the end, of course, FitzGerald has many suggestions, offers many potential options, proposes many scenarios and formulas, but like all the others has no answer to the men of violence. And perhaps despite his own background, his urbanity and learning—or perhaps just because of those qualities—the feeling lurks that he does not understand or weigh sufficiently heavily the bombers and the bigots, both uninterested in charts and graphs, projections and electoral reform, but only in getting their own back or yielding not an inch. FitzGerald is for the sane, the sensible, for those who reason closely and assume that accommodation and a new Ireland fashioned on the present ruin are possible. As yet there is limited evidence that anyone is moving towards this new Ireland.

A similar sensible approach appeared in *The Ulster Debate* (London: Bodley Head, 1972) where the results of a study group under the auspices of Brian Crozier's Institute for the Study of Conflict were published.[1] Meeting soon after the promulgation of Stormont, several members—Professors J. C. Beckett and F. S. Lyons, Lord Chalfont, Garret FitzGerald, and Robert Moss—presented formal papers. There was as well an earlier paper (included as an appendix) by Frederick Catherwood suggesting the necessity for a two-thirds or three-quarters majority to pass legislation in Stormont. This was perhaps the most novel suggestion. All the other papers, often sound and sensible, were predictable. Beckett notes the characteristics, political, economic, and social, of Northern Ireland that will persist no matter what ultimate formula of accommodation might be found. Lyons suggests "The Alternatives Open to Government" at a moment when the sands of time seem to be running out. Chalfont gives the orthodox British version of events on the military front: light at the end of the tunnel, need for a political solution, but, of course, after the reestablishment of the rule of law by the military that in turn appears impossible without the political initiative. Neither the introduction of direct rule or power-sharing has yet broken Chalfont's cycle.

FitzGerald puts the Troubles in a European context, an intriguing exercise but again somehow divorced from the bombs in Belfast and Derry. Finally, Moss sums up the common wisdom of the participants. Two years later in a sense the exercise appears hopelessly dated: Stormont is gone, the Assembly a reality, the Provos bomb away, and the Protestants are into assassination. Yet *The Ulster Debate* outlines the problem (and it is the same problem), scans the possibilities, and largely the same possibilities still exist. The participants, Catherwood's formula aside, suggested nothing new but did add a sense of perspective, often sorely lacking, and placed their hope in men of good will and the eventual erosion of extremism. Two years later those seeking an end to the violence have largely the same fears and the same hopes and have seen some progress and continued violence. The elusive majority of men of good will appears as far off as ever.

When one of those men of good will, James Callaghan, arrived at the British Home Office in December 1967, Northern Ireland, then a cloud smaller than a man's hand, was administratively squirreled away in the General Department along with British summertime, London taxicabs, and the protection of animals and birds. When he departed after the General Elections of June 1970, Northern Ireland was on the front pages of the daily papers and in the forefront of his mind. His *A House Divided* (London: Collins, 1973) is a straightforward chronicle of Irish events seen from Labour London without startling revelations, scathing comment, or intimate asides, whose absence may indicate that Callaghan recognized that power had not drifted into Tory hands in perpetuity. Callaghan in Irish matters was neither as skillful nor as lucky as William Whitelaw, one of the very rare British politicians to accrue credit during an Irish involvement, but since the major violence occurred after his departure, and Labour's Irish initiatives have remained the foundation of British policy, he has not been ruined or revealed a fool. In fact what emerges, and is intended to emerge, from the work is a picture of a sound man applying a sound political solution that should or would have worked out, the intractable nature of Northern Irishmen aside. Somehow to Callaghan an accommodation was possible, will be possible, if Labour is allowed to push on through the thicket of difficulties so disastrously ignored during Reginald Maudling's tenure at the Home Office. He believes the decay in 1971 and 1972 would have been checked by Labour. To politicians out of power all things in retrospect appear possible. Yet despite his good will, undeniable talents as a negotiator, innate reasonableness, even accepting Labour's willingness to contemplate serious changes in the North, Tory lethargy cannot bear all the blame. There was a lack of urgency in London after August 1969, a difficulty in grasping the problems of operating through Stormont, and a grievous misreading of the potential for violence by those in Ulster who cared little for the delicate formulas and carefully wrought institutions of compromise that Callaghan sought to fashion. Maybe with more time Callaghan could have avoided the worst, maybe not.

If Callaghan has written the Labour version of the big events, an eagerly awaited entry was the revelation of life among the Provo bombers—the underside of the Troubles. A reasonable assumption was that Maria McGuire's *To Take Arms, My Year with the IRA Provisionals* (New York: Viking Press, 1973) would be a bomb-and-tell diary of a woman scorned, rationalized as an act of political courage, a swift capitalization on a romantic interlude. This did not exactly prove to be the case. Ms. McGuire turned out to have very little to tell about the Provos that had not long been common knowledge to the interested, but she did reveal a great deal about herself. Within the rather dowdy ranks of the Provos, she had for a year been an exotic, with her pop clothes, elaborate makeup, foreign travel, and advanced ideas, the latter used largely by the president of Sinn Féin, Rory Brady, who employed her as a personal secretary and as a symbol of the new magnetism of the ideas of Kevin Street. Her recruitment for the one great adventure, the arms purchase trip to Europe with Dave O'Connell, indicates the paucity of certain talents then available to the Provos, since with rare exceptions the *real* Republicans neither trusted nor accepted her. During this time she may have felt to be at the center of events, but this was hardly the case, for the complex inner world of the Provos, with their Byzantine politics, shifting alignments and alliances, grudges and doubts, remains largely unrevealed and to some degree uninteresting. In any case, Ms. McGuire arrived at Kevin Street innocent of politics, violent or conventional, and departed the same way. It is very much a trendy book, not unsurprisingly the creature of the London *Sunday Observer,* and yet the mix of mild gossip, first impressions, and personal truth indicates an apparently innate Irish talent to turn lead into literary gold, not too much bullion in this case, but sufficient to have resulted in an intriguing book that reveals, not very attractively, a woman if not a movement.

A similar unanticipated revelation and one of the more curious byproducts of the Troubles is Kevin Boland's *We Won't Stand (Idly) By* (Dublin: Kelly Kane, 1972), which takes to task the author's old Fianna Fáil colleagues for deserting the Republican cause. While there are some interesting bits and pieces, including the fact that the famous arms importation of May 1970 was not illegal, the overwhelming response to Boland's present posture as an advocate of the old-style Republicanism, à la legion of the rear guard and De Valera of yesteryear, is disbelief. How could a practicing Dublin politician, son of Gerald Boland who hanged IRA men as minister of justice and boasted of the fact, who had personally lived through Fianna Fáil's reaction to the Northern IRA campaign of 1956–62, be so naive? Of course, it also took the British some time to understand that nearly every Southern institution, and most assuredly Fianna Fáil, viewed unification with horror and the prospect of sacrifice in the cause of Northern Catholics with distaste bordering on nausea. Somehow Boland has missed this, missed the real implications of the Lemass-O'Neill meetings, as did the

Northern Orangemen who doubted their own. He overlooked the hypocrisy of Fianna Fáil's position on the national issue and the plain evidence of the past. And during the arms trial when all became clear, he took pen to paper as a patriot unexpectedly wronged, a Republican suddenly betrayed: curiouser and curiouser.

No one would dare to accuse Conor Cruise O'Brien of naiveté, for he has always been too clever by half with the capacity to wound with a word or pull out the one brick that brings down an entire castle of pretension in an untidy and humiliating heap. For anyone who knows the least bit about the Ulster Troubles, his *States of Ireland* (New York: Pantheon Books, 1972) will be a splendid experience guaranteeing outraged indignation, resigned disappointment, or wild enthusiasm depending on how the orthodox-version-according-to-Conor meshes with one's personal predilections. For all varieties of Republicans he has become a figure combining the vices of Attila the Hun, Judas, and Brutus. And well he might, for he has little time for Republican pretensions or their more simple-minded scenarios for a united Ireland. These he sees as bad history, bad politics, dangerous, and even if possible a dreadful prospect given his own vision of the black and bleak soul of the Northern Protestant. And he had as little time as well for sentimental Southern Nationalists, for a good many recognizable political figures, spokesmen and pundits, and for the innocent and ignorant in general. Thus, for those who know nothing of Ireland, this elegant and cleverly constructed work, part family history, part memoir, part political narrative, all written with grace and wit, might surely become *the* explanation rather than as is actually the case at best an approach to the problem, and, at least as likely, a part of the problem. The author has over the course of his recent political career suffered a great many slings and arrows, a barrage intensified after the publication of *States of Ireland,* producing an inclination to view matters either/or, painting alternatives to his own vision in darkest hue. Thus, his two scenarios, the benign and the malignant models, contrast in stark terms a best-of-all possible worlds that, given the unwieldy forces at play, are devotedly sought by the Coalition Government, with a malignant future collapse into chaos and a Colonels' Republic. He has made too good a case to be taken quite seriously, although it might well be argued that the only means to attract the attention of Southern Irishmen, largely for whom the book was intended, from a bemused fascination with Celtic myths and the charms of Cathleen ni Houlihan was to strike repeatedly with the hammer of exaggerated reality. In any case, *States of Ireland* is a delight, with something for everyone even if it is not what they wanted to read.

While *States of Ireland* is very much of the moment, Terence O'Neill's *Autobiography* (London: Rupert Hart-Davis, 1972) is a strange script somehow out of touch with a real world, the tale of a life lived a generation out of date. Brought up in an elegant Anglican world on the margin of great events, O'Neill, decent but without driving ambition, fair-minded but without particular originality or critical sense, drifted into Ulster politics familiar only with his own kind. As Stormont prime minister he took innocent pleasure in his trips, his introduction to the truly famous, and his television interviews. He is proud of his efforts to improve both the image and economy of Ulster. In serious matters he remains pleased with his overtures to the Catholic community and his contacts with Southern politicians, still unaware that these few tardy gestures largely without content coupled with the limited and grudging reforms granted by his party could not, even if they should have, undo a century of bigotry and a half century of institutionalized injustice.

O'Neill was not a man for all seasons but a man for one. He proved an excellent and decent leader in tranquil times but no match for rough men and harsh currents. And at the end, the impression is that O'Neill does not think it fair that good intentions proved insufficient. Somehow it was the Catholics insisting on celebrating the Easter Rising in 1966 that sparked the rise of Protestant militancy. Or it was the unnecessary People's Democracy march to Burntollet Bridge in 1969 that opened the doors to chaos. Or it was the failure of Catholics to vote for his candidates and so transform the Unionist Party. There is from time to time a flash of bitterness at his treatment by old political friends or on the careers built on turmoil. Bernadette Devlin was blown "from obscurity . . . into fame and Westminster. The struggles across the Bann ensured a flat in Belgravia, a sports car and several visits to America." But mainly the impression is a twilight resignation at recent horror, vague hope for a better future, and a failure to understand that during his stewardship the Province required more than a generous gesture. His is the story of the limitations of a decent man. The prospects were radical surgery or yielding not an inch, and O'Neill could not credit the need for the first or the power of the latter.

An intriguing entry in the instant-biography category is Rosita Sweetman's *On Our Knees, Ireland 1972* (London: Pan, 1972), which in part avoids the inevitable problems of posture and prejudice by letting two dozen subjects speak for themselves. These range from the Rt. Hon. Desmond Guinness of the Georgian Society to a clutch of IRA leaders of various persuasions, new priests, and simple folk. There is no doubt where the author's heart lies—worn on her left sleeve—for she, too, does not suffer fools or the famous gladly, opts passionately for radical change in Irish society, and wields an acid pen. If *On Our Knees* had not contained the interviews, it would have been no more than another passionate editorial on contemporary matters by a radical journalist, fascination or fatuous depending on the reader's predilections. With the interviews the work becomes of some permanent value and retains, of course, considerable immediate interest. In this case good journalism triumphed over commitment, if only just.

This does not prove to be the case with Andrew Boyd's *Brian Faulkner and the Crisis of Ulster Unionism* (Tralee: Anvil Books, 1972), for the author opens with an "Introduction" beginning in part: "I take no pleasure in presenting this book to the public because it is the profile of a person who . . . could hardly be regarded as fit to be a Prime Minister, even of so miserable a place as Northern Ireland. If Brian Faulkner has been called a bigot it is because he has revealed himself as such." The book is, then, a passionate attack on Faulkner, his career to 1972, and his allies and associates. Boyd has in the case of his subject's more unsavory moments done little more than quote from old speeches to great effect. There is no attempt to treat Faulkner the man or even the politician, or to fashion a conventional biography. Rather, there is a chronicle of bigotry that gradually fades into a chronicle of Northern events, where the more unpleasant developments are blamed on Faulkner. Since Boyd completed his book in May 1972, Faulkner has shed his old Orange skin. The former outraged indignation with Faulkner in official Dublin circles has evaporated with the need for Northern Catholics to share power with someone—anyone. For many the perception of Ulster events has been transmitted, for are not the SDLP, Gerry Fitt, John Hume, and the rest sharing power if not the responsibility for internment? Such power must have a price. One suspects, however, that Boyd would still contend that once a bigot always a bigot. Even to the distant and disinterested, if not to Faulkner's new colleagues of the SDLP, Boyd has amply demonstrated a sectarian man, but in his distaste he has missed the flexibility of the politician with long-evident ambitions, and thus in the end has told us little about the *real* Faulkner, if there is one.

An even more difficult subject for fair treatment must surely be the Rev. Ian Paisley, for outside of certain evangelical circles on the far edge of Protestantism and hard-core Orange militants, some of whom are no longer so faithful, it would in truth be difficult to recruit a sympathetic biographer. Patrick Marrinan, as his title indicates, *Paisley, Man of Wrath* (Tralee: Anvil, 1973), does not try. All the old spectaculars, marches, and murders are recounted, the crude and cruel speeches, the crusades and confrontations. These remain vicious but have somehow faded, bleached out by the greater violence of recent years that Paisley neither unleashed nor could adequately exploit, although he most assuredly bears a part of the responsibility for encouraging it. Again, as with Boyd's book, it is difficult to grasp the essential nature of the man: in the heel of the hunt, to the author and the reader Paisley and his ideas, though part of a long and distressing tradition, still remain very alien. Do people truly believe these things in this day and age and, since obviously many do, what *sort* of people are they? Clearly, too, Paisley is not *simply* a crude and illiterate bigot, an evil man and a bad Christian. His career, despite peaks and valleys, has shown vast raw talent, an acute grasp of the location of the jugular, real skill as a demagogue, and a remarkable tactical flexibility. In the United States, in time, it became clear that Senator Joseph McCarthy cared neither about communism nor his victims but about power. But this is not so clear with Paisley. He apparently does care for more than the first chance; he does believe and can even, while his lumpen followers cannot, envision a future that he fervently opposes: a united Ireland. He can call for total unification with Britain, form an alliance with the advocates of UDI, oppose internment, shift with the tide, and yet shape the world with a fundamentalist vision that maintains the issues of the Reformation as touchstones to conduct. All this, in any case, does not concern author Marrinan who in often baroque language with righteous moral indigna- tion—a quality presently in excess in Ireland—dissects Paisley bigotry, defines his responsibility for the present chaos and in the end produces a polemic not a biography. Perhaps that is all Paisley is worth, and perhaps not.

While there are still a few biographies to be written if every single story is to be told, increasingly it appears as if every aspect of the Troubles has been or is about to be covered, quickly if not adequately. Much of the often fugitive results is seldom available even for review in the United States.[2] For example, George Target is reputed to have finished *Bernadette Devlin* (London: Hodder and Stoughton, forthcoming) and Vincent Browne has long been at work on the Provos but neither work has reached American shores. In some cases such works barely reach the Irish market much less the American one, for Dr. Rona Fields' *Society on the Run* (Harmonds- worth, Middlesex: Penguin Books, 1973) for reasons unsatisfactory to the author was recalled and ten thousand copies shredded. At least a second edition is promised. After its early successes in instant Irish paperbacks, Penguin seems to have run into trouble, for Eamonn McCann, like Fields, complained about the editing of his *War and an Irish Town* (1974) and then discovered that Eason's, one of Ireland's leading book wholesalers, will not stock the book or supply an explanation.

Publishing, too, has become part of the problem. For the American reader, there is a single exception in that the Provisional IRA's *Freedom Struggle,* seized and banned in Ireland (North and South), has been re- published and distributed by Irish Northern Aid.[3] The counterweight to Provisional propaganda, equally unconvincing, would be David Barzilay's

The British Army in Ulster (1972), available from the Century Service in Belfast for the truly curious. That IRA propaganda is readily available is examined in Ian Greig's *Subversion: Propaganda, Agitation and the Spread of the People's War* (London: Tom Stacey, 1973—now defunct, which goes to prove Greig's point if not improve his royalties). And despite the obstacles and rush of time, there is something for nearly everyone except the American reader.[4] John McGuffin in *Internment* (Tralee: Anvil, 1973) has momentarily exhausted the subject in an indignant study. Sir Arthur Hezlet gave us *The "B" Special* (1972), also a victim of the collapse of Tom Stacey but rescued by Pan paperbacks, and Richard Clutterbuck the view from the center in *Protest and Urban Guerrilla* (London: Cassell, 1973). Paul Arthur has turned his master's thesis into *People's Democracy* (Belfast: Blackstaff Press, n.d.).[5] Cathal B. Daly in *Violence in Ireland* (Dublin: Veritas, 1973) opposes all violence in Ireland—except, of course, that of the 1916–22 period, a posture that, however illogical, is still congenial to many. And that few of these are available may be one of the smaller blessings of the Troubles—not that McGuffin is not interesting nor Hezlet useful, only that even the spirit falters at each new entry.

At first glance at least some of the new works offer considerable promise. After all there are still many dark contemporary corners in Ireland. Such difficult corners appear likely to remain dark. David Boulton in the *UVF 1966–1973* (Dublin: Torc, 1973) has managed to elaborate a 1972 interview with Gusty Spence into a book. Despite the author's interest in Ireland and his eight Irish documentary films, he has managed a nonbook. A review of the events surrounding the 1966 Malvern Street shootings, a quick history of Ulster events, the rise of Protestant militancy during 1972, plus the interview, combined and touched up do not make a "history." Until Spence's kidnapping in June 1972, the UVF was little more than an unorganized collection of bloody-minded bigots. Spence's exposure to IRA prisoners, his fascination with more rigorous revolutionary strategy and tactics, and his return to the UVF may have indeed helped form a more stable organization in competition with Vanguard, the UDF, and the other free-lance vigilante groups. The weight of evidence suggests that this supposedly most secret army was never an army and probably is still not despite the sprinkling of military titles and rising pretensions after 1972. The world of the UVF is fluid, composed of ad hoc squads, self-appointed assassins, leadership struggles over drifting followers, in-house violence, area commanders with local support willing to come under the umbrella—an army, even in the IRA sense, it is not. Therein lies Boulton's difficulty in fashioning a coherent volume about an incoherent group of vigilantes, filled with grievances and suspicions but beyond organization or basic ideology.

There have been as well a series of works less closely focused on the specific Troubles but clearly not unmindful of recent events.[6] In some cases the suspicion remains that these books have been written back to front, explaining the past with present perspective. In others the major purpose of publication has been to examine aspects of Irish history previously ignored and recently of crucial interest. A prime example of the latter would be Tony Gray's *The Orange Order* (London: Bodley Head, 1972), which seeks to fill an obvious historical gap for there is no definitive history of the entire organization. Gray makes no pretensions to original scholarship, but as a journalist has the wit to interview members of the various orders. Thus, his book is more than potted history but far from the last word. There is, indeed, much to be done not only on the modern Orange Order but also on the Protestant community, and it is cheering that, as rumor has it, several younger scholars have been so attracted. A second work *Secret Societies in Ireland* (Dublin: Gill & Macmillan, 1973), edited by T. Desmond Williams, should have been more promising on straight academic grounds—and intriguing on title alone; however, as has often been the case with the Thomas Davis lectures, broadcast on Radio Eireann, the result is more entertaining than enlightening. In this case the definition of secret society has been stretched, the individual approaches are often less than rigorous, and several contributors have been preempted by others elsewhere or drawn a congenial but apparently novel subject. Still Williams' introduction is a good beginning and Kevin B. Nowlan's conclusion a decent ending. Perhaps someone will be sufficiently motivated by the exercise to use a deeper plow. A third work is P. Berresford Ellis' *A History of the Irish Working Class* (London: Victor Gollancz, 1972), a socialist history by a committed author. The work is based almost entirely on secondary sources, spiced with the odd newspaper, and covers, academically speaking, no new ground. Alternating between straight narrative and occasional radical explanation, the result, beginning with Celtic communism and ending with the Northern Troubles, still is novel in that not since Connolly has the "Working Class" been so examined. Yet the study is conventional in narrative and predictable in explanation:

> The basis of Northern Ireland's creation was the uneven development of capitalism in Ireland, the fear of the northern capitalists of losing their imperial markets. Since the establishment of the Six Counties statelet had its basis on a real conflict of class interests it will only be moved on that basis.

All three books are flawed to a considerable degree, but it is probably better that the subject be treated limitedly than not at all. The Thomas Davis lectures have helped bring contemporary Irish history to academic respectability; the journalists have been damned for publishing but have challenged the scholar to do better. So if one disagrees with Ellis' Irish "Working Class" there is an opportunity to produce better.

Fortunately here and there "better" has been produced. A more serious general work in the American Foreign Policy Library is Donal Harman Akenson's *The United States and Ireland* (Cambridge, Mass.: Harvard University Press, 1973), which belies the title in that its major purpose is to explain Ireland to Americans. And the effort is directed toward the general reader: no footnotes, a few charts and graphs in the appendix and an annotated Suggested Readings. Akenson, who has written three books on Irish social and religious issues, pivots the narrative on the events of 1920–23 and produces for most of the text no surprises but the welcome addition of the serious treatment of matters often ignored in conventional political narrative: religion and values, social flux and social management, and a very welcome chapter on Irish diplomacy. Then, just before the end, we inevitably come upon "Once Again an Ulster Question," and Akenson, no more than any other scholar, cannot deny himself. Where in the other, more conventional chapters the complaints are minor academic quibbles (Saor Uladh was not the IRA's military arm in Ulster in 1956–62) and detract not at all from an admirable presentation, Akenson on the North arouses grumbles. The Provos are most assuredly not avowedly sectarian but in leadership and ideology Wolfe Tone Republicans. It is quite true that there are Provo bigots who would not disagree with the Provo scenario Akenson presents, but this is another matter. Then, too, it would appear, despite Akenson's contention, that many Irish Americans have well-articulated plans, simple-minded and innocent perhaps but real enough. The same is true with at least some members of the Dublin government who have slipped beyond the old hypocrisy to support the present British initiative. This is not to suggest that Akenson's analysis is wrong or warped, only that it is no better than that projected by the involved. Scenario writers tend to project aspirations (i.e., civil war or my plan, zero-sum games). Still in forty pages he, perhaps better than anyone, makes the Ulster turmoil explicable. So it is a good, sound book; it breaks no new ground but fulfills splendidly the mission assigned by Harvard to explain Ireland to the American reader. This success is, in part, beyond Akenson's demonstrable virtues, because the book was a legitimate academic exercise. There was no rush by the author to stand on his *Education and Enmity: The Control of Schooling in Northern Ireland* and write a swift script explaining all—an expanded "Once Again an Ulster Question." Consequently, he produced a sound and useful work rather than a provocative and inevitably contentious one. Given the elegance of *The United States and Ireland,* the latter avenue might now be worth the author's exploring.

It has been an avenue heavily trod by the whole spectrum of contemporary academicians. There is now a considerable collection of articles scattered from the *Journal of Contemporary History* to the *South Atlantic Quarterly* and points in between that might be termed instant academic analysis.[7] Each with a slightly varied perspective deals with the historical background, then addresses an aspect of the present problem, and ends with an exhortation for accommodation and/or a series of scenarios. Except where the article includes novel material few will be of lasting value, for largely they do no more than inform interested academic colleagues. There are, of course, several more ambitious efforts to analyze the Irish situation; for example, two interesting new treatments of partition have just appeared: Ned Lebow in *Divided Nations in a Divided World* (New York: McKay, 1974), edited by Lebow, Gregory Henderson, and John Stoessinger, which will still be read in ten years for theoretical if not Irish reasons; and Thomas E. Hachey in *The Problems of Partition: Peril to World Peace* (Chicago: Rand McNally, 1972) who is somewhat less dispassionate than Lebow.[8]

A variety of scholars, who bring in their luggage—assuming they feel the necessity to come to Ulster at all—a clutch of contemporary tools have discovered a useful or challenging case study. The results of the social scientists' interests have been various indeed ranging from Anders Boserup and Claus Iversen, "Rank Analysis of a Polarized Community, A Case Study from Nothern Ireland," Peace Research Society (International) *Papers,* vol. VIII, 1969; H. D. Rankin, "On the Psychostasis of Ulster," *Psychotherapy and Psychosomatics,* XIX (1971), 160–74; through full-dress studies like Morris Fraser's *Children in Conflict* (London: Secker & Warburg, 1973); and Rona Fields' *A Society on the Run*—both unavailable in America. A few like Fields, committed to a certain Irish perspective, become in effect part of the problem; others drift on to other congenial case studies, uncertain of the value of the Irish experience, but apparently still convinced of the value of their discipline.

A not atypical social science exercise evolved from a group of Americans who decided to bring together in neutral Scotland a group of fifty-six Protestants and Catholics from Belfast for a workshop "structured to give the participants greater knowledge of how groups and organizations function and greater competence of their own behavior within groups and organizations." Given the events of the Belfast summer of 1972, when the workshop took place, the level of suspicion and intimidation, the continuing violence, and the relative ignorance of the investigators on Irish matters, the project went more smoothly than might have been anticipated. The end results, however, proved moot, beyond quantification in any case, although the authors are convinced that "intervention even in the most bitter quarrels is worth risking."[9] The risks, however, are unevenly shared. While there might be academic advantage to such investigation, if at grave risks, the prospect even of repeated workshops offers little hope to a polarized province addicted to the myths and fears of the past, fearful of the present, and uncertain of any future.

Although somewhat outside the contemporary analysis of the Troubles, a new scholarly current can be detected: Irish history is being revised from 1969 backward. The anguish and shame arising from the Northern violence have engendered serious scholarly effort not so much to explain away the Troubles or depict a contemporary culprit but rather to insist that such events are not the natural and inevitable end result of Irish history. The *real* history of Ireland is seen as largely accommodating in political matters, not even focused on separatism, and not a matter of endless centuries of confrontation with Britain. This revisionist movement extends deep into Celtic history—interpreted not as a time of violence we are informed, despite vague recollections of sagas on cattle raids, personal combat and such, but an era of cooperation and communal bliss. There are, too, suggestions that Catholicism and Nationalism merged in the nineteenth century (i.e., efforts to bomb one Ireland—Protestant—into another—Catholic—are futile and ahistorical). As a result, Robert Kee's huge 877-page *The Green Flag, The Turbulent History of the Irish National Movement* (New York: Delacorte Press, 1973) has received an enthusiastic revisionist welcome, especially because its advent had been unexpected—Kee is a television journalist—and partly because the work had a scholarly foundation including rarely used provincial newspapers. No one can, of course, define Irish nationalism to the satisfaction of all, but Kee's work indicates that the Republican current, a new one in Irish history, has always been thin and the advocates of physical force few. Even separatism and the rejection of the Crown were unpopular with most. Thus, the rebel generations that followed Tone were outside the Irish mainstream, occasionally attracting sympathy but seldom support until the 1916 executions. This for the conservative and conventional translates into The-IRA-is-an-Irish-Aberration. Kee, however, holds no brief for the concept of two Irelands except insofar as by the right of survival the North has acquired a natural status.

In the ranks of One Ireland, he is joined by a curious company that includes Jack Lynch of Fianna Fáil (two communities, one nation),[10] the Provisional IRA (one people, one nation), the official IRA (one working class, one island), and a variety of serious scholars outraged with the two Irelands: Conor Cruise O'Brien, the New Ulster Movement, the Northern Ireland Labour Party, the British and Irish Communist Organization (Stalinists), and the new revisionists. An interesting and germane study, again unavailable in America, engendered by this controversy is Padraigh O.

Snodaigh's *Hidden Ulster, The Other Hidden Ireland* (Dublin: Clodhanna Teo, 1973), which seeks in large part successfully to show that the Gaelic language is an integral part of Ulster's heritage and, in this case particularly, Protestant Ulster. Most Orange ancestors were when planted perhaps more Celtic generically than the natives, and many spoke Gaelic. The case is complex and the arguments far from simple, but the academic origin of much of the present dispute—apparently cited unread in some cases—is probably the justly famous *The Irish Border, A Cultural Divided* (Assen, Netherlands, 1962) by the Dutch geographer M. W. Heslinga. Snodaigh points out that Heslinga agrees there was no clear-cut language division between the immigrants and the natives in the seventeenth century. The clear-cut distinction today, however, between the two Irelanders and the advocates of one nation has little to do with painstaking and dedicated research, value-free analysis, Dutch geographers or the Snodaighs of academe, but simply reflects political predilection most easily served by one or the other of these "historical" concepts.

Not unexpectedly the most useful and revealing work for the serious-minded makes no effort to chronicle the violence, lay the blame, test a scholarly tool, or manipulate the past to present purpose—and curiouser yet the work is neither political nor historical but a straightforward academic study in social anthropology. Begun over twenty years ago in 1952 and eventually published by Manchester University Press in 1972, Rosemary Harris' *Prejudice and Toleration in Ulster, A Study of Neighbors and "Strangers" in a Border Community* (Totowa, N.J.: Rowman and Littlefield, 1972) presents conclusions, both subtle and rigorous, that are worthy of more note than simple, if lavish, "academic" praise. With elegance and feeling, dissecting the nature of prejudice in its manifold forms in a single small village in the west of Northern Ireland, she has well and truly revealed the nature of Ulster's Troubles. The conclusions give scant comfort to anyone, least of all the optimistic, for in "Ballybeg," despite internal differences, there are two Irelands, intractably suspicious, incapable of perception beyond stereotype, and at best maintaining no more than an uneasy toleration ever on the edge of violence. There are, of course, and always have been two Irelands depending on the focus: rich and poor, urban and rural, Briton and Gael, Catholic and Protestant, North and South; thus, neither the advocates of unity nor the backers of partition should—they will of course—snatch up *Prejudice and Tolerance* in Ulster as new evidence for their side. Very diverse peoples, Croats and Serbs, Swiss who speak French and those who speak German, Ukrainians and White Russians, live in unitary states under varying formulas if not always in total fulfillment. Equally special people from the Basques in Spain to the Ibos in Nigeria have opted to fight. Hence, Harris' evidence offers no conviction that at the grass roots there should be two Irelands or could be one, but only how complex the problem, how fragile at best the peace, how deep the prejudice, and how distant an Ulster society that will placate everyone.

An equally successful work is the far more ambitious *Belfast: Approach to Crisis, A Study of Belfast Politics, 1613–1970* (New York: St. Martin's Press, 1973) by Ian Budge and Cornelius O'Leary. The authors have combined a detailed historical analysis of Belfast politics with five opinion surveys, two in the city and three in Glasgow, for crosscutting. The authors thus address various facets of Belfast politics, political recruitment, political communication, popular reaction to parties, for example, that would lie outside a simple historical survey. Although at the time of the first survey in Belfast in 1966, survey research was a novel tool, at least in Ireland, the conclusions presented are surprisingly conventional. In fact they represent the common wisdom, hardly alien to any qualitative or intuitive eye: in Belfast violence and intransigence have been endemic (as the common newspaper reader has surmised), class feeling is low (as the IRA discovered waiting for the conversion of the working class), and denominational loyalties are more intense (as the walls along Shankhill or the Lower Falls can attest). This is not to suggest that the conclusions are facile for they arise out of an intimate knowledge of Belfast political history as well as out of the survey results—results that add concretely to the knowledge of Belfast politics. It is, nevertheless, somehow fitting that almost the last sentence eschews the intricacies of crosscutting or the sum of voter attitudes to quote:

> The good lack all conviction, while the bad/ Are full of passionate intensity.

Yeats aside, the two books here that appear most useful in approaching the Ulster Troubles, no matter for what purpose or from what angle, have been Budge and O'Leary's *Belfast* and Harris' *Prejudice and Toleration*. The reason for this is not particularly complex. Both are first-rate studies arising from conventional academic disciplines dedicated to the truth. Neither was at conception concerned with the Troubles: the Belfast project arose from the possibilities of survey research and Harris in 1952 was attracted to "Ballybeg" in order to focus on a divided society then at relative peace. Both used conventional academic tools. Both have on publication indicated in only the most limited ways the relation of their conclusions to the origins of the Troubles, since the major purpose of both studies lay outside such an explanation. As a result, more than the plain tale of events, more than the instant histories, fast studies, innocent applications of popular academic formulas, and surely more than the rationalizations and orthodox versions, Harris, Budge, and O'Leary have at a minimum defined the problem, and this is a beginning. It is notable that the best of the first wave of analysis, Richard Rose's *Governing Without Consensus: An Irish Perspective* (Boston: Beacon, 1971) also fits this pattern—even to the extent that Rose ended not with Yeats but, as an American, with the Lincoln "malice toward none" quotation.

Despite the hopes of the scholars, the North remains a repository for excess malice and passionate intensity. Somehow matters have stumbled along without living up or down to anyone's expectations. All the scenarios from the judicious to the self-serving have proven faulty. There have been regular surprises, mostly unpleasant. Stormont has gone and the Assembly arrived, Faulkner and Fitt share power, and the Provos bomb the centers of Belfast and Armagh and Derry. The Officials still trust in the working class and the UVF gunmen in the guilt of all Catholics. The Protestants vote for a hard line and London and Dublin seek to encourage moderates.[11] The death toll passes one thousand. No one believes the center will hold and yet life goes on. After all, last year 225 lives were lost in the Troubles while over 300 died in automobile accidents on Ulster roads. Perhaps an accommodation can yet be founded on mutual exhaustion; perhaps the malign scenarios misread the prospect of civil war; perhaps the British will leave; perhaps the Protestants will make a deal or the Provos collapse. No one, of course, knows, least of all those involved who so seldom understand their society or themselves, who have wanted to be entertained by old myths rather than enlightened about present realities. Almost all remain vulnerable bit players in a tragedy with apparently endless acts. And little written and less published on Irish matters in recent years has greatly revised the script, depicted the real forms behind the sound and fury, or outlined a viable final act.

There has at least been a beginning. Serious work has been done and serious questions asked. The chaff has not smothered all the wheat, and if the seeds are few some have sprouted. Irish historiography will never be the same again and perhaps with a little luck neither will Irish politics. In the meantime the car bombs still go off, the assassins will lurk at the end of the lane, the vices of man will be everywhere present, and in the din there will be no dialogue. Reasonable men may be better off writing books than in the streets, for the gunmen have no time to read. A moment will surely come when truth will have a taker in Ireland, when academic analysis need no longer end in anguish or poetic despair, and violence sponsor the printed page. Until then, there seems no end in sight for the chroniclers of the Irish tragedy or present role for analysis beyond the enlightenment of the distant and distraught. Circulation figures and shelf space may comfort the pragmatic, the orthodox version the committed, but amid the rubble it is a cold comfort indeed for most men of good will.

A Tragedy in Endless Acts

Remorselessly, and apparently inevitably, as 1976 ticks away, the death toll in the tangled Irish Troubles creeps higher, faster this year than any time since 1972—the vintage year for blood and turmoil. Except for the threatened, no one any longer seems greatly to care. Murder must be peculiarly grisly or quite spectacular to warrant more than cursory coverage in any but Irish journals. The dramatic detonation of a mine under the British ambassador's Jaguar outside Dublin in July briefly engendered media interest. Ambassadors are not assassinated every day, but in Ulster ordinary people are—or nearly every day. There have been too many no-warning bombs in pubs to remember, too many sprawled bodies discovered by pedestrians to concern any but the devastated relatives. The Provisional IRA's self-imposed truce has eroded and again there are bombs in Belfast, land mines in South Armagh, snipers in Derry. The British army and especially the Ulster police have become prime targets. Yet the Republicans feud among themselves. The Loyalist paramilitaries still pursue a strategy of random assassination and thus have unleashed a vicious, seemingly irreversible, cycle of tit-for-tat murders. Politicians, warders, and judges are targets of assassins of various faiths. And the violence has been exported. There are bombs in Manchester and Birmingham, assassins in Kensington and gunmen firing into restaurants in London's West End, explosions in the underground, firebombs in the shops. The Loyalist paramilitaries have carried their war into the Irish Republic with explosions in crowded streets. The elegant Gresham and Shelbourne hotels have been bombed in Dublin and lesser resort establishments hit elsewhere. The greatest single slaughter, twenty-six people killed, came in a Dublin street, not in Belfast or Derry. No one sees an end. Even the hope that mutual exhaustion might bring an end to violence has flickered out.

The British and then the Irish governments have passed emergency legislation, filled the prisons with the suspected or convicted, and undertaken elaborate and costly security initiatives. The gunmen still contest the streets, deny the authority of the state, murder for the cause, and recruit a new and more deadly generation. The Irish government has pleaded for the Irish diaspora to end their aid to the IRA, and the Armalite rifles still appear along the lanes of Armagh and the housing estates of Belfast. No one pays attention to Dublin desires, least of all Irish Republicans. The British government has apparently run out of political initiatives, opted in despair for a policy of drift, hinted at disengagement and soldiered on. The experiment in power-sharing was brought down in May 1974 by a Protestant general strike that gradually shut off electrical power until ruin faced the province. Britain was forced to impose direct rule. Then there was a

Northern Ireland Convention to create a new provincial government. There was no compromise and soon no convention. There was no reasonable middle ground. The dearest aspirations of the Loyalist denied those of the Republicans. Ulster was a perfect zero-sum game—or so perceived by the more violent players—in that there could be *no* mutual benefits in any political matter. Every British strategy has seemingly been employed, endless carrots and sticks, promises and more promises, elections and plebiscites, parliamentary reports, carefully constructed reforms, novel institutional structures, conventions, conferences and overtures, even a formal cabinet meeting with the Provisional IRA. More troops were deployed and then fewer. There were secret deals and trial balloons. The Special Air Service was sent over and in Belfast troops sent back. All aborted. Much of the British government and an increasing proportion of the British public are sickened by the Irish tangle, yearn to withdraw from the revolting Irish bog, perhaps with honor, perhaps without. To the south the government in Dublin is equally sickened and perhaps more frightened, for such a withdrawal might entail still more dangers than does the present slaughter, even when the killing regularly sloshes over into the Republic. The prospect of a united Ireland with one million angry and violent Protestants and half that number of violent and radicalized Catholics holds little charm for the comfortable in Dublin. No one wants a united Ireland but the IRA. And no dedicated Protestant will consider such a possibility—many feel that to "impose" such a solution would guarantee the long-feared doomsday of a civil war, and many feel that to delay guarantees worse. So the British stay without hope and without direction. Dublin waits, but for what except bad news no one knows. And there is always bad news.

Out of the horrors, there have been a few secondary benefits, a few lessons for others at a distance, a few novel, if sterile, political innovations and the odd technical discovery in counterinsurgency. We know a bit more about how children act under stress and men under torture. There have been some good poems, several thrillers, a couple of plays, but they might have been written in any case and without recourse to such a costly muse. At least, it would seem, unwittingly the Irish have once more fashioned turmoil in such a way as to permit distant and disinterested investigation, learned probes into their contemporary chaos. After nearly a decade of repeated exposure, of endless explanations, of special pleading, official investigation, and preliminary analysis, the academics should at least be able to discern the form behind the fury, offer if not effective answers then useful questions. Certainly in 1968, when, more or less, the present Troubles began, contemporary Ireland had been ignored by academics, especially Irish academics, except in matters of literature. Tim Pat Coogan's fascinating but flawed *Ireland Since the Rising* (New York: Praeger Press,

1966) was a journalist's attempt to fill a vast lacuna, for many felt that writing seriously about the Irish present only exacerbated old quarrels. A decade later all is changed utterly, for contemporary Irish events have engendered intense interest and investigation, assured participants of an audience, even a market for their special story, and provided a staging ground, albeit an unsteady one, for various scholarly exercises. The end results may not be, surely are not, worth the cost in human terms, but at the least, the very least, in some few cases the Troubles have assured academic benefits, if very secondary benefits indeed.

A decade ago even the raw materials of modern Irish history were elusive. There was a scattering of published government documents (London, Belfast, Dublin), the parliamentary speeches and papers, the newspapers (the pamphlets and press of the splinter dissenters difficult to acquire), and there were a few good monographs and a few interested people, but not many of either. Now the books on modern Ireland cover a good-sized wall, for the Troubles have focused attention not only on the six bloody counties but on the long, complex background to the present. There have been new biographies, new interpretations, newly trained people with novel means and novel results. Irish history and Irish historiography will never again be the same. Although much of what has been written has been done from back to front, evoking the past to explain the present, much of the finished work is, nevertheless, powerful and provocative. Whether it is the church in the last century, the rise of republicanism, or the nature of nationalism, there are new views that, had Ulster been as tranquil as Kent, might not have surfaced. And besides the quickening of interest in the history of Ireland, the spate of studies focused on events since 1968 continues unabated. For historians and sociologists and political scientists, for specialists in conflict bargaining or ethic perception, Ulster has practically become an essential case study.

By 1976 even the raw material has been transformed, ordered, catalogued, displayed in readily available forms. Of course, a great deal is not available. Some of it, like cabinet papers, won't be available for years. Police records won't ever be. Still, for the industrious scholar there have been new aids: Arthur Maltby's *The Government of Northern Ireland 1922-1972, A Catalogue and Breviate of Parliamentary Papers* (New York: Barnes and Noble, 1974) is a quite splendid example. And there are published papers and reports churned out by Her Majesty's Stationery Office, the crumbled bricks of unbuilt bridges. *The Northern Ireland Constitution* (Comnd. 5675, London, HMSO, July 1974), for example, once a white hope, now a historical shard, concludes in part:

These proposals offer a new opportunity to all the people of Northern Ireland to contribute directly, and in their own way, to the solution of their own problems. The need is for a joint and stable society. It can be achieved by the people of Northern Ireland with their awareness of the realities of the situation. Failure will bring defeat to all. Success will bring the only real victory.

Urging "realities of the situation" on the people of Northern Ireland by one of a series of governments that over a great many years have had little if any grasp of Irish realities brought no victory for the British—or for their colleagues in Dublin, or for those perpetually optimistic Ulster moderates, repeatedly smashed down in the middle of the road by high-speed militants. Anyway, the parliamentary papers are there to be read, savored by the cynical, even if most bear only tangential relation to Irish realities.

More cheerfully, perhaps one of the most important and impressive of all Irish scholarly endeavors undertaken in recent years—if you can't change reality at least record it—has been the micropublishing programs of Irish Microforms Ltd.,[12] taken over from Irish University Press in 1974. These microform publications mean in effect that at a reasonable cost archival material previously concentrated in one or two places or massive in quantity can now be acquired and stored conveniently. For present purposes the most important program is *Political Literature of Northern Ireland, Phase I: 1968-1972* and *Phase II: 1973-1974* drawn from the unique collection of the Linenhall Library in Belfast. Neatly collected is the entire spectrum of political opinion expressed in the haphazard press, the party papers, pamphlets, and broadsheets.[13] This ephemeral material has too often been just that, ephemeral. In the midst of chaos and mayhem, it is the rare reflective man who husbands the smudged proclamations and hastily issued assaults on authority. And here, courtesy of Irish Microforms, for a bit over $200, a library can have a whole collection—including the nine issues of the *Ardoyne Freedom Fighter* or the twenty-four pages of Clifford Smyth's *The IRA, Eire and the Church of Rome—The Axis Against Ulster.* There in film are the publications of the Provos and the Officials, the Communists and the People's Democracy, the fulminations from the wilder shores of the Woodvale Defense Association or the feral prose of the Rev. Dr. Ian R. K. Paisley. The conventional and conservative may regret the passing of the printed word and the arrival of the microfiche, but these programs mean that the distant now have access to crucial material, the artifacts of crisis, without the necessity of a trek to the Linenhall, no small gift given the obstacles to research in Belfast.

Another set of works makes readily available material that will be of considerable importance to those concerned with more mundane matters: elections. And it should be remembered that along with violence Ireland has been inflicted with an astonishing number of elections and plebiscites in recent years—for Westminster, for Stormont, for the Dublin Dáil, for or against the border, for this body or that. Nicolas Baxter-Moore and James Knight have been underwritten by the Arthur McDougall Fund of London to report much of the results, largely statistical, crosscut often with highly useful commentary. Thus, we have Knight and Baxter-Moore, *The Republic of Ireland, The General Elections of 1969 and 1973* (London: McDougall, 1973); Knight and Baxter-Moore, *Northern Ireland: Elections of the Twenties* (London: McDougall, 1972); the Irish Republic up to and including the election of 1948 published the results; Knight, *Northern Ireland, The Elections of 1973* (London: McDougall, 1974); Knight, *Northern Ireland, The Elections of the Constitutional Convention, May 1975* (London: McDougall, 1975). There is a special advantage to the Irish electoral system: the single transferable vote in several-seat constituencies. The weakest candidate's votes, if so designated, are divided up, revealing to some extent the sources of his attraction, his backers' links, and the subtlety of the Irish electorate. And for others there is the inevitable trivia as well. In the Irish Republic's general election in 1973, two independents each received one vote apiece—no report on their marital state. More seriously for Irish matters, the volume provides not just statistics but also some indication of the schisms and predilections of those mythical people for whom the gunmen kill and die. Revolutionaries, of course, rarely resort to the polls as a valid revolutionary exercise. When the official Sinn Féin ran candidates pledged to take their seats in 1973 in the Dublin Dáil, all but one lost their deposit—one reason why most revolutionaries chose to look into their own hearts rather than the election urn to discover the desires of the people.

A perhaps even more welcome endeavor for those more concerned with Irish matters and less with the charms of the Single Transferable Vote has been the Northern Ireland chronology of events by Richard Deutsch and Viven Magowan published by Blackstaff Press in Belfast.[14] Presently *Northern Ireland: A Chronology of Events* has reached three volumes: 1, 1968–71; 2, 1972–73; and 3, 1974; with the distressing news that there may be no more, partially because of the inevitable fiscal reasons but also, apparently, because of exhaustion on the part of the compilers. The chronology, which comes as close as possible in uncertain times to being a definitive record, can be buttressed by the Diary of the Year in *Hibernia* (Dublin),[15] a crucial journal of opinion, and the chronology in the superb *Fortnight,* published since September 1970 in Belfast.[16] Both are required reading for the concerned. The Blackstaff chronologies by Deutsch and Magowan, however, have the virtue of portability and hence will surely become tools for the advocates of aggregate data, those who count and seek constants and variables. For those uncommitted to counting but concerned with a structure to the plain tale of Northern events, the volumes are vital, and if a labor of love, most assuredly not love unrequited.

For those who do not want to start at the beginning, who find parliamentary papers and election statistics daunting and time-consuming and yet want the feel of raw material, there have always been readers and collections and selections. Ulick O'Connor has brought together in *Irish Liberation* (New York: Grove Press, 1974) what might be called an all-star cast from Yeats and O'Casey to Jimmy Breslin and Pete Hamill. There are a few selections difficult to acquire in the original, such as Egan Bowes and Vincent McCormack on the Burntollet bridge incident, where it might be said the trouble started. But the major virtue of the collection is as a deep background for someone familiar with the actors and plot. Short, inexpensive, illustrated, and dramatically produced, it is ideal collateral reading. A new and most interesting but more academic compilation is John Magee's *Northern Ireland: Crisis and Conflict* (London and Boston: Routledge & Kegan Paul, 1974), intended mainly for students "in sixth forms, Colleges of Education and Universities." There are fifty selections beginning with extracts from T. W. Moody's *Irish Historical Studies* article on "the treatment of native population under the scheme for the plantation in Ulster" and concluding with Prime Minister Edward Heath's statement to the people of Northern Ireland on a visit to Belfast 29 August 1973, as published in the *Irish Times,* 30 August 1973, and including the product of the HMSO, memoirs and diaries, various historians and a letter to the BBC. With a judicious introduction and tied together with commentary it should form, as intended, an excellent teaching aid—and would not be a bad general introduction—but is not a dramatic exercise, nor intended to be.

For those students less enthusiastic or with other academic priorities, there are two shorter background studies. Most interesting, M. A. Busteed's *Northern Ireland* (London: Oxford University Press, 1974), one of a series, "Problem Regions of Europe," edited by D. I. Scargill, places "the problem" in a geographic context. Thus, in a fifty-page case study only ten pages are devoted to the political problem, a welcome and interesting approach although—alack—politics does still creep in elsewhere. The geographic focus guarantees that Busteed's work has more than the originally intended pedagogical value. The finest short survey to date is David Schmitt's *Violence in Northern Ireland: Ethnic Conflict and Radicalization in an International Setting* (Morristown, N.J.: General Learning Press, 1974), which in thirty-five pages covers the crisis with rigor, touches all the bases, provides an insight into more general implications, and concludes with a bibliography. For those who seek brevity, who demand coherence without commitment to a long reading program, and to those instructors who want a foundation for generalization or discussion, Schmitt's "Modular Study" is first-rate, the best inclusive case study readily available.

Somewhat more exciting—and intended to be—and thus a finer if less academic introduction to the Irish problem is W. H. Van Voris' *Violence in Ulster, An Oral Documentary* (Amherst: University of Massachusetts Press, 1975). Taped between 1972 and 1974 by a professor of English at Smith College—with no easily visible track record in Irish political matters[17]— the result is a fascinating medley, a mix of recrimination, instant anguish, special pleading, resignation, and analysis, all beautifully woven together to insure chronology, ready comprehension, and the raw taste of Ulster. The old familiar names are there: Lord Brookeborough, Bernadette Devlin, William Craig, representatives of the Officials and Provos, the British army and People's Democracy, important people and obscure, the articulate and the vindictive. The commentary may not be profound (whatever that is), but there is no better introduction to Irish matters than the Irish—for better or worse—and here Van Voris lets them speak for themselves and they provide a much more intimate and richer mine than the fifty documents or the selected statements that buttress most lectures on "The Northern Irish Problem." *Violence in Ulster* might not be the very first book to read on Northern Ireland, but for those avid to know what it all means, there is no better explanation of the difficulties in supplying meaningful answers.

One long-promised volume that many anticipated would supply insight if not answers into one aspect of the problem, Seán MacStiofáin's *Revolutionary in Ireland* (London: Gordon Cremonesi) finally appeared in 1975. There had been rumors of delays and publishing difficulties (not for the first time) for Rona Field's *A Society on the Run* was apparently withdrawn from circulation by Penguin (a revised edition is in press at Temple University Press, Philadelphia), and its advent in America was less than spectacular. The memoirs of a man who had been chief of staff of the Provisional IRA from its creation in December 1969 until his arrest in November 1972—particularly 372 pages of memoirs—should reveal much of the inner workings of the IRA. Should, but they do not, although they revealed somewhat more about MacStiofáin who had always been a difficult man to know. Throughout the book there is a tone, not always pleasant, that appears legitimate, not simply the result of a rather stilted prose style (after all it *is* his first book). This is the carefully edited tale of a dedicated, closed man with the conviction of the converted who in many ways as leader of the Provos found briefly his one true calling. Most fascinating is the problem of marrying and bringing up a family as a revolutionary—the time spent in prison, the legal harassment when out, the demands of the movement, and the constant fear of retaliation. Even more than the unfolding of the campaign, the wrangles, feuds and successes—the history and the news—the family dimension, matter-of-factly discussed without special elegance or warmth on the page, remains with the reader. Also intriguing is his remarkable display of revolutionary discipline, a commitment to a movement that had discarded him, had no use for his talent, and in private mocked his sacrifices, for there is almost nowhere overt criticism of the Provisionals. The grumbles are few, the hard word absent. There are, of course, historically useful bits of information: the activities of the lean years, the split, especially in his relations with his Official counterpart Cathal Goulding, and something of the flavor of the inside. But this is very much a book written for a political purpose: to establish the Provisionals as a legitimate revolutionary movement and to display the ideals and aspirations of the Irish Republicans within the body of a memoir that was thought to have reader appeal. It will hardly convince some, perhaps most, that the Provos are not terrorists, nor convert many to MacStiofáin's own luminous and narrow vision of the future. Through it all, the nature of the man comes through only flickeringly, although the problems of such a "career" more readily. It is less an intimate memoir, less really even an autobiography, but rather more a Republic biography for Republican purposes—not always well served, and yet it *is* fascinating no matter how read or with what preconceptions.

There have been a half dozen or so other books produced as memoir-history in the last two years, each, as always, dispatched from a very special viewpoint, almost always if the author played a prominent part, an apologia, and yet in their separate ways interesting. Eamonn McCann's *War and an Irish Town* (Harmondsworth: Penguin, 1974), like the works of many of his colleagues on the left of the civil rights movement, is better than it ought to be. "To make the revolution we need a revolutionary party. This book is intended as a contribution to discussion of how best to build it." No matter, he can't help but make Derry, before and during the Troubles, interesting; he can't help but skewer the pompous and recall with intensity the days of confrontation. It is not meant to be a "fair" book, but cannot help but be an interesting one. Paddy Devlin, the bullfrog—green with red spots—of Ulster Nationalist politics, who started out in the IRA and ended up sharing power at Stormont, has like McCann produced his own authorized version. While Penguin, apparently with many second thoughts, published *War and an Irish Town*, Devlin published himself, and *The Fall of the Northern Irish Executive* (Belfast: Paddy Devlin, 1975) is just that, not really a book but scraps and patches and explanations, especially on the wonders of power-sharing. There is no real order—certainly not chronological—but a useful inside account of the fall of the Northern Ireland executive from where Devlin sat, some odds and ends and an attack on his

villains: Ian Paisley, Harry West, William Craig, Sir Henry Tuzo, and Brigadier F. E. Kitson, but without the cunning word and cruel phrase that
come so easily to so many Irishmen. Another very personal exercise with
anticipated results is *The Genesis of Revolution* (Dublin: Kelly Kane, 1976)
by Captain James Kelly, who was led up the garden path during the Great
Arms Smuggling caper in 1969–70. Here the best bits are found in his
dissection of the "Republican" government and policy of Fianna Fáil, who
to be fair in this area at least deserve most of what they get. Other than that,
it is a routine jog through the present Troubles to the inevitable prescription—a united Ireland (which Kelly explains would not evolve into a Cuba
or a Vietnam), for after all every other solution (short, one assumes, of
genocide or forced emigration) has failed.

One the other side of the barricades or peace-line as the case might be are
two Loyalist works, and to a degree "serious" Loyalist works are always
welcome if for no other reason than to balance the dead weight of the other
side. John Biggs-Davison, a Catholic Conservative and Unionist, grandson
of a Presbyterian Liberal Home Ruler from Down, has written of Ulster
from the *Tain Bo Cualgne* to the fall of Stormont (*The Hand is Red*
[London: Johnson, 1973]). Surely a man of good will, Biggs-Davison presents the case against a united Ireland, against the identification of Catholicism with republicanism—and calls in 1972 for "what Unionism needs
today is unity. A system lies in ruins. It is time to rebuild." He preaches to
the converted, delighted to hear Catholic sense. T. E. Utley in *Lessons of
Ulster* (London: Dent, 1975) addresses, apparently, the British establishment in London, once more seat of Ulster's ills, in a long, historical survey
of British incompetence in recent Irish matters. A journalist who contested
the Westminster February 1974 election in North Antrim as an Official
Unionist against the Rev. Ian Paisley, his book is a detailed, contenious
argument for direct rule as the only remaining acceptable solution—
London having frittered away the more desirable options and the separation of Ulster from the United Kingdom being, for Utley, quite unthinkable. Both exercises, if not especially convincing or particularly felicitous in
style, have the virtue of revealing the intractability of many of the actors,
even those of good will.

Two other nonofficial exposures to Ireland are Simon Winchester's *In
Holy Terror* (London: Faber and Faber, 1974) and Richard Howard
Brown's *I Am of Ireland* (New York: Harper & Row, 1974). Winchester is a
perceptive and knowledgeable reporter for the *Guardian* who first arrived
in Ireland in 1970. Brown is the most innocent abroad, a partially Irish
American searching the Troubles for his roots. Brown's wandering through
the Irish diaspora and the Troubles, never dreadfully interesting, reveals
only the holding power of Celtic myths. At the end there is no feeling that

the author knows any more about Ireland and the Irish despite his wanderings than he does about himself. It is a strange and futile book brightened, if that is appropriate, only by the cameo of a group of Irish Americans playing IRA in a New York suburb with guns purchased for The Cause—there were even Polaroid photographs, nothing being real for many Americans unless captured on film. Winchester's *In Holy Terror*, despite a tendency for trendy journalistic character sketches, is a fascinating eye-level view of Irish violence. He spent long enough in Ulster to know the actors all too well and to annoy many, especially the British army who considered his skepticism a positive asset for the IRA. Military press officers prefer those journalists—and the chaps at Lisburn barracks get them in wagonloads—who are delighted with the authorized word and dispatch the handout all but intact. Neither, it might be added, did Winchester delight many Republicans; in fact, by the end he had annoyed a great many people, a rather dangerous procedure in a place like Belfast. There, if enough people in differing quarters are irritated, it is surely an indication of editorial fairness; it may also be time to ask for a transfer. On 9 September 1972, Winchester took the boat down the Lagan on his way to a new assignment in Washington. And his Irish experience in *Holy Terror* is not potted history, a long prescription, a deep insight into the Ulster psyche, but rather a tale of thirty bloody months—good, often spectacular journalism, perhaps even fair.

Somewhat less disinterested are two new entries in the biography stakes. Both, curiously, appear at the very moment their subjects, Bernadette Devlin and Brian Faulkner, appear to have faded from the Ulster scene, the turmoil moving on leaving them still household names, but irrelevant ones. G. W. Target's *Bernadette—The Story of Bernadette Devlin* (London: Hodder and Stoughton, 1975) is a rather lengthy and painful stage-Irish exercise in hagiology. While the book may have virtues in detailing at length the Devlin story, the innocent tone and bright green Celtic prose will turn away all but true believers. In passing, Bernadette Devlin has inadvertently become the litmus paper for most observers of the Irish scene—a few words on Bernadette and it is possible to point to the appropriate niche in the Ulster spectrum (and the cruelest cuts of all have often been by old friends, none so bitter as a Trotskyite scorned). The other script, David Bleakley's *Faulkner, Conflict and Consent in Irish Politics* (London: Mowbrays, 1974) tells us very little new—or believable—about Faulkner but a bit more about Bleakley, who as a member of the Northern Ireland Labour Party was a minister of community relations in 1971 and subsequently a member of the 1973 Assembly—a man of moderation who in this work has attempted to drag the cunning and proven bigot through the needle's eye and upon a pedestal of moderation. Certainly Faulkner's trans-

mutation into an advocate of power-sharing and a man of sweet reasonableness was—is?—curious. Perhaps the change can be explained solely as
opportunism or misguided ambition, better to serve in Stormont as prime
minister, albeit with Fenians, than wander in popular exile. Just how unpopular Faulkner became with his old friends and just how little room for
maneuver remained in the middle of the road are all too clearly revealed in
the response in Stormont to his speech on 14 December 1973 defending the
Sunningdale Conference—included by Bleakley in the appendix and the
saving grace note of an effort in political alchemy.

Along with the memoirs, oft disguised as history, and the biographies,
usually steeped in gall or honey, a continuing genre has been works on the
Irish, and often so titled. This time there have been entries from a variety of
authors, mostly journalists like Tim Pat Coogan (*The Irish* [London: Phai-
don, 1975]), Cecil King, and one Thomas J. O'Hanlon, a member of the
Irish diaspora in America. His *The Irish, Sinners, Gamblers, Gentry,
Priests, Maoists, Rebels, Tories, Orangemen, Dippers, Heroes, Villains and
Other Proud Natives of the Fabled Isle* (New York: Harper & Row, 1975) is
one long, highly readable grumble. The final sentence is as follows: "And
you will be given honorary citizenship in the ancient land of the ever young
if you leave the gathering after hours of entertaining blather with the balmy
blessing 'Things could be worse.'"—not, however, according to the gospel
of O'Hanlon. Mind you, he used a lovely sharp hatchet and did all his own
cutting. Cecil King notes that "for historical facts I have picked the brains
of others. The opinions are my own" (*On Ireland* [London: Jonathan
Cape, 1973]). And everyone, sooner or later, seems to want his own Irish
opinions in print, often with a bundle of fine photographs tipped-in. The
very finest photographs—with commentary tipped in—issued from an unlikely source, Leon and Jill Uris, *Ireland, A Terrible Beauty* (Garden City,
N.Y.: Doubleday, 1975) contains some of the most stunningly beautiful
photographs ever taken of the Irish scene. Even the Northern photographs—now a set piece for photographers (graffiti, Free Derry, Belfast
children, Ulster politicians, riots, each a compulsory exercise with a ritual
form)—are splendid.[18] Leon Uris' commentary is standard prose-backing,
sympathetic to the Irish and Irish aspirations, but no match· for the photographs. At this point, it might be well to acknowledge that on the Irish
Troubles Leon Uris will reach more people than the combined readership
of every book under review in all three of these articles. Literally millions
of people will read *Trinity* (Garden City, N.Y.: Doubleday, 1976) and take
away the orthodox version according to Uris. Sociologists and political
scientists, pop journalists and even popular politicians publish and largely
perish, read by the few or the faithful. Uris writes for the millions and
although *Trinity* ends before the Easter Rising, the millions will parse from

Uris the roots and meanings of what remains for many the inexplicable slaughter under banners bearing strange devices.

Perhaps the most effective attempt recently to make the slaughter explicable has been Patrick O'Farrell's *England and Ireland Since 1800* (New York: Oxford University Press, 1975). In less than two hundred pages O'Farrell, a professor of history at the University of New South Wales, Australia, blocks in the major areas of conflict. What is so useful is the stress on images and perceptions that created an asymmetrical relatic ıship between Irish social problems and English political solutions. Everyone has long stressed the weight of Celtic myths, the Irish burden, but O'Farrell notes the crucial importance of English perceptions and the subsequent policy decisions based on these perceptions, on English priorities, on factors and fallacies long ignored by most Irish investigators limited by their own perceptions and priorities. A narrower but more intensive pioneer study is Richard Ned Lebow's *White Britain and Black Ireland: The Influence of Stereotypes on Colonial Policy* (Philadelphia: Institute for the Study of Human Issues, 1976), which in little more than one hundred pages reveals the English talent for balancing morality with pragmatism. These books should be required reading for all those in Dublin and Belfast and London who have and will again transfer prejudice into law, perceptions into policy.

There have been three new attempts to outline the Northern Ireland problem—from 1171 to Bloody Sunday and beyond—each from quite different perspectives. Gary MacEoin, Irishman and journalist, resident of the American diaspora, in *Northern Ireland: Captive of History* (New York: Holt, Rinehart & Winston, 1974) has prepared well, returned to talk to the involved, covered the same old ground, maintained a reasonable balance, and ended with some uncertain prescriptions. MacEoin, like everyone else, by this time recognizes most "solutions" as nonstarters. He hopes for some sort of united Ireland, perhaps a federal one not unlike Switzerland, perhaps with United Nations or American involvement—all quite vague and uncertain and in a spirit of good will so clearly lacking on the part of those with a veto. It is not that MacEoin is innocent or his book without considerable virtue but, by now, so much has been said about "money, religion, and politics from the Boyne to Bloody Sunday" that one more survey, one more decent man's hegira in print that offers neither novel insight into the unending crisis nor hint of an effective future strategy palls. Thus in a way, Roger H. Hull's *The Irish Triangle, Conflict in Northern Ireland* (Princeton: Princeton University Press, 1976) is a far less rigorous study, divorced in any case from the most jagged edges of Ulster reality, but has the blessing of an unusual construction. Hull, a lawyer, attempts to present three different perspectives (Dublin, Belfast, and London), focused on the conflict points and simultaneously seeking a role for the law. The end result is interesting but unconvincing, certainly worth the effort, but the ultimate wisdom is little different from that to be found in MacEoin—maybe the United Nations, continue the status quo, end sectarian education,[19] maybe sometime, somehow Irish unification. The third attempt is novel and not especially prescriptive. Michael Farrell in *Northern Ireland, The Orange State* (London: Pluto Press, 1976) has written an anti-imperialist, socialist survey of the Northern Ireland state, complete with dark printed quotes to stress his point if not his program. It is not meant to be an academic book or impartial but "a guide to action." A member of the People's Democracy—what a seedbed of the printed word that group proved—who ultimately moved with the PD into an alliance with the Provisionals, Farrell's work has been criticized by those on the left who scorn his politics and by those more academic who see his history as a warping of reality for Socialist purposes. The latter at least have something going for them since *Northern Ireland* is constructed with a special determinism and is a Socialist history, a very good socialist history. Farrell's vision may be too special, his alternatives too bleak, his aspirations forcing the pace of history, his shaping of the past for present purpose too apparent, but the exercise was well worthwhile. And there are those who see his bleak alternatives as far more likely than the initiatives of the men of good will—a United Nations presence or an end to secular schooling or "unification" sometime. For Farrell there are no such vagaries.

> The choice in Ireland has become devastatingly simple: between, on the one hand, a semi-fascist Orange statelet in the North matched by a pro-imperialist police state in the South, and, on the other hand, an anti-imperialist and socialist revolution.

It is not especially surprising that the three newest entries in the history stakes are by an Irish-American journalist, an American academic attorney, and an Ulster Socialist out of the People's Democracy. Each would by nature be attracted or involved. The magnetism of the Troubles, however, is no longer limited to the scholarly specialist or the articulated participant. The Troubles are now universal property, an event for all, and nothing so reveals the new universality than a slim book entitled *God Save Ireland! The Irish Conflict in the Twentieth Century* (New York: Macmillan, 1974) by Patricia Bunning Stevens. A quite conventional title, two hundred pages, and an adequate bibliography, seemingly it is one more trot through the violent bog, one more individual's authorized version, one more script with no special merits that does no particular harm. *God Save Ireland!* however, is the special American genre called the juvenile—not a case study for the serious student, not background, not elegantly written history open to the literate of whatever age, but a special exercise for the immature, too old to be children, too young to want adult treatment, or perhaps not competent to assault the arcane prose of academia or the long pages of mature type. So the American juvenile now has access to the Troubles—for uncertain purpose—and, to be quite fair, *God Save Ireland!* is quite fair, a decent job, smoothly done. What these mysterious juveniles will make of it all is open to question, but what is not is that Macmillan, no mean publisher, felt such a market existed. *O tempora. O mores.*

Juveniles aside, several of the committed or involved have produced works of narrower scope. Another, like Farrell, who years ago innocently started out on that road to a socialist revolution under the banner of the People's Democracy, Paul Arthur has paused to write an admittedly academic study, *The People's Democracy 1968-73* (Belfast: Blackstaff Press, 1974). He has combined a participation in his subject and a commitment that varied over the period investigated with a capacity to write analytically. The result, even if the perspective is narrow, is an extremely valuable study of a radical organization evolving in the midst of political turmoil, a study most useful even for those with no interest in Irish matters. Like a book on crocodiles, it may tell one a bit more than one wants about the subject, but for the concerned *The People's Democracy* is a welcome addition to the literature of the crisis, the more so because a conscious effort was made to avoid the same kind of commitment that makes Farrell interesting. At the opposite pole, Geoffrey Bell in *The Protestants of Ulster* (London: Pluto Press, 1976) in one hundred and fifty pages takes the majority and their evolution as his subject:

> The Protestants of Northern Ireland are the most misunderstood and criticised community in Western Europe. They do not deserve to be misunderstood; this book explores whether they deserve to be criticised.

And Bell, not surprisingly, finds they do deserve criticism, even (if not especially) the beloved working class—for whose conversion generations of Irish radicals have waited. Stressing the manipulation of the Protestants largely for class advantage, Bell, however, as most before him, gives the orthodox version of bigotry. We have yet to be shown the Northern Protestant as he sees himself, for most Northern Protestants are not UVF assassins, frothing bigots, not evil incarnate but decent enough Christians, neighborly, advocates of liberty, often bewildered and embittered by what appears ill-informed, self-serving attacks. Bell's detailed, factual indictment of Ulster Protestants, convincing, coherent, focused on the politics of bigotry, ignores the Protestants' own perceptions. And, oddly enough for those swamped with the images of Paisley's preaching, the Orange parade and the institutionalized pogroms of the past; there is no greater advocate of free thinking than a thoughtful Ulster Protestant.

There is in Ulster little opportunity these days for the thoughtful Protestant. One of the reasons is that in 1974 the activists in one of the most remarkable displays of political organization once more washed away the middle ground, maintained the polarized society, revealed the benefits bestowed by defiance. In *The Point of No Return: The Strike Which Broke the British in Ulster* (London: Andre Deutsch, 1975), Robert Fisk details at length the Protestant general strike that forced the collapse of Faulkner's power-sharing Assembly and a return to direct rule. The almost unknown Ulster Workers' Council gradually shut down the province, easing off the amount of electric power until absolute disaster loomed. The security forces, for various ill-defined reasons, proved impotent, the Provincial Assembly irrelevant, and the Westminster government incapable of affecting events. Fisk foresees the prospect of similar strike actions by militant minorities holding democratic governments to ransom. Certainly in Northern Ireland the Loyalists—loyal to what was no longer quite so clear—in a most remarkable display of imposed discipline, inspired propaganda and by largely nonviolent means closed down the power-sharing Assembly, ended the Sunningdale agreements with the hateful Irish dimension and in the process revealed the suspicious reluctance of the British Army to impose order by confronting Protestant power. Fisk may describe the strike in greater detail than seems warranted, but the implications that arise from the actions of a few hundred power station employees that defied all constitutional authority and the capacities of the security forces, Fisk feels are very serious indeed. However serious they may be elsewhere, the strike—if there need be further evidence—indicated, as would the subsequent futile Convention, what "not-an-inch" meant in institutional terms, just how little the "Loyalists" were willing to surrender, just how foolish—again— had been those who wagered on moderation, reason, and compromise.

A more formal academic exercise is *Law and State, The Case of Northern Ireland* (London: Martin Robertson, 1975) by Kevin Boyle, Tom Hadden, and Paddy Hillyard. Essentially, they make a strong case that the supposedly blind justice dispensed in the province has been an instrument to maintain the existing order. Seeking a more universal relevance in legal practice, they, nevertheless, have produced a work that has caused most parochial concern in Northern Ireland both because of the implications and because of the challenge to other studies with more comforting results for the establishment. The authors do not imply that the law has been consciously used to maintain the regime, harass dissent, and thwart actual rebellion—a strategy proposed by Brigadier Frank Kitson—but rather that the law is in subtle alliance with a sectarian, unstable state, a state that has depended on coercion rather than conciliation.

> If there is any lesson to be learned from the five years of conflict from 1969 to 1974 it is that the choice of a security response to a crisis of intercommunal relations is likely to impede the restoration of stability.

While Boyle, Hadden, and Hillyard, and their conclusions, may be included in that intercommunal crisis whatever their effort at disinterest, there are those with no apparent commitment except to a special methodology, the alien eyes of academics replete with models and theories. Many have already appeared in print, but for the average, common reader much of their work remains buried in discipline-oriented journals, obscure—to the public at least—monographs, and even for the interested not all the rumors of work in progress reach interested ears. Just as Boyle, Hadden, and Hillyard have their doubts about the smooth course of Northern Irish justice so, too, does an article by Edmund A. Aunger of the University of California ("Religion and Occupational Class in Northern Ireland," *Economic and Social Review*, vol. 7, no. 1 [October 1975], 1–18), based on the results of the 1971 census. On the distribution of occupation, he finds a marked tendency for the Protestants to dominate upper-occupation classes. While there has long been a tendency to accept that "everyone" knows the details of discrimination in Northern Ireland, there have been too many Irish "facts" that everyone knows but of which no one can cite convincing printed proof. Now there is far firmer evidence of not only occupational status but also unemployment rates. That the Catholic male appears more susceptible to unemployment than even Catholic women—5 percent for Catholic women, 7 percent for Protestant men, and 17 percent for Catholic men—creates very serious social problems in a society where the stereotype is a dominant, assertive male. According to the psychiatrist Morris Fraser, this stereotype arose as a result of the colonial-settler traditions that are similar in other frontier communities. In fact, R. Douglas Scott (Scott and Barry M. Schultz, *Natives and Settlers: A Comparative Analysis of the Politics of Opposition and Mobilization in Northern Ireland and Rhodesia* [Denver: University of Denver, Social Science Foundation and Graduate School of International Studies, 1975]) has applied Professor Louis Hartz's model of a "fragmented" society to Northern Ireland. Hartz suggests that migrants, after conquering and settling, freeze their society, maintaining the loyalties and values under siege as the home country moves on. Clearly the Ulster Loyalist, like his counterpart in Rhodesia, has given ample evidence that his loyalties are not to the individuals and programs of those now in power in London or to the British society of the

1970s. In any case, Scott presents a conceptual framework to examine the Northern Ireland crisis as a whole—and at times models like cookie cutters give neat end results but leave something behind on the breadboard—while Aunger focuses on one very special and very important aspect in detail. They represent the two ends of the scholarly spectrum. A good many academic works, of course, fall into the soft center of explanation tied to a narrow crosscut on one side or general assertion on the other.

In any case, there have been a variety of academics recently at work, arriving with model or methodology under arm. Northern Ireland has been particularly attractive to those involved in peace studies, in conflict resolution, in encounter workshops and community relations. The results, as the newspaper headlines indicate, have not always been effective on the Ulster ground, but according to Leonard W. Doob and William J. Foltz of Yale "intervention even in the most bitter of quarrels is worth risking," at least for the academics. Another general area of attention has been that of race or ethnic separatism in relation to political matters. Again there are two ends of the spectrum. For example, Sarah Nelson in "Protestant 'Ideology' Considered: The Case of 'Discrimination,'" in *The Politics of Race*, ed. I. Crewe, the British Political Sociology Yearbook, vol. 2 (London: Croom Helm, 1975) has a narrow focus and more original results, while Paul F. Power in "Conflict and Innovation in Ulster," in *Ethnicity and National-Building: Comparative, International and Historical Perspectives*, ed. W. Bell and W. E. Freeman (Beverly Hills, Calif.: Sage Publications, 1974) is hampered by the need to fashion a special case study focused on political innovation. There are, as well, still those at work using survey research, interviewing politicians and the paramilitary Protestants, collecting the folklore of conflict, tracing the lines of interest into the diaspora, assaying the British response to provocation, the nature of Anglo-Irish relations since 1969, and the implications of Irish insurgency to British stability. In time their work will appear in print for, one assumes, the common academic good.

One of the more concise attempts to explain what it all means, or rather what those academics who write on the Irish Troubles *think* it all means and consequently what might effectively be done (the universal assumption remains that the present must be prologue since matters cannot go on as they have, which, of course, they have for some while) is Arend Lijphart's (University of Leiden, Netherlands Institute for Advanced Studies) "Review Article: The Northern Ireland Problem: Cases, Theories, and Solutions," *British Journal of Political Science*, 5:83–106. Focusing on the most substantial of the academics—Denis Barritt and Charles Carter, Ian Budge and Cornelius O'Leary, Conor Cruise O'Brien, Liam de Paor, Rosemary Harris, and Richard Rose—he delineates "The Ten Northern Irelands":

ten different conceptual cases: (1) Binational or Multinational State, (2) Religiously Divided Society, (3) Plural Society, (4) Biracial Society, (5) Colony, (6) Fragment Society, (7) Arena of Guerrilla Warfare, (8) Arena of Class Struggle, (9) Pseudo-Democracy, and (10) Besieged Democracy. And these largely remain the major typologies. Lijphart then goes on to list the contributions to theory: Political Stability, Congruence, Cross-Cutting, Consociational, and Linkage Politics. The most detailed exposition is on the implications of consociational democracy. The conclusion, somewhat less relevant because of the passage of events, is, inevitably, Recommendations for Policy-Makers. It is the finest, most concise survey of the first impact of the Irish Troubles on the academic community. The innocent, the ignorant, the trendy, and the transient are excluded as are participants, with the exception of Conor Cruise O'Brien, who has academic credentials to offer. Although the last book reviewed was published in 1973 on material ending in 1970, the article remains valid and appears likely to have a still longer shelf life than most review articles warrant.

Finally, as the reviewer's choice, the best comes last: Richard Rose's *Northern Ireland, Time of Choice* (Washington, D.C.: American Enterprise Institute for Policy Research, 1976). The analysis of the existing options is wrapped around a detailed account of the Northern Ireland constitutional convention membership elected on 1 May 1975,[20] convened on May 8, deadlocked by November and, despite a six-month British extension, now irrelevant as direct rule continues.

> The people of Northern Ireland must play a crucial part in determining their own future. No political structure can endure without their support. [British Government White Paper, July 1974]

And time and time again, the polarized people have been unable or unwilling to compromise their differences, to build bridges or discover common ground. More often than not the divided people have tolerated or encouraged private armies rather than political parties, have if not taken the wrong turn certainly been "on the wrong course for years, for decades, or for centuries." So Rose has in extensive detail focused on that moment of choice on 1 May 1975, marshaled the numbers, charts and graphs, the results of survey research, the previous polls, and the present wisdom, traced the curious twists and turns and transformations during the brief course of the convention and arrived at "The Limits of Choice." And there in three sentences is the wisest summary yet of the "problem."

> Many talk about a solution to Ulster's political problem but few are prepared to say what the problem is. The reason is simple. *The problem is that there is*

no solution—at least no solution recognizable in those more fortunate parts of the Anglo-American world that are governed with consensus.

In his final chapter Rose sums up the alternative ways of coping, and details the permutations of each.

(1) Self-government within the United Kingdom
       Rule by a Loyalist Majority
       Rule by a Broad Unionist Coalition
       Power-Sharing within a Parliamentary Framework
       Power-Sharing by a Nonparliamentary Representative Government
(2) Direct Rule from London
       Continuing Direct Rule
       Integration with Great Britain
(3) An Independent Northern Ireland
       A Unilateral Declaration of Independence by a Group of Loyalists
       Negotiated Independence
(4) Unification with Southern Ireland
       A Federal Ireland
       British-Irish Condominium Rule
       Transfer of Northern Ireland to the Republic of Ireland
(5) The Destruction of Northern Ireland
       Repartition by Local Option Ballot
       Doomsday

And so there in *Northern Ireland, Time of Choice* are all the prescriptions and all the prospects, improbable or bleak or both and the overwhelming and depressing thought is that there is no solution.

For Northern Ireland all comfort is cold and all benefits have been secondary. Yet even Rose can foresee someday, somehow, a restoration of civil government although "it may be difficult to say who has won. We will only know that the Troubles have once again ended because of the palpable, even brutal, evidence that someone has lost." There does, indeed, seem no resolution to the conflict, only lesser losers whose sacrifices have paid petty returns. Despite all, despite the sudden reasonableness of a Brian Faulkner or William Craig after long years of no surrender, despite the unexpected conversion of the SDLP to responsibility, despite the men of good will, the ingenuity of the Crown, the persistence of the security forces, and the overtures and contacts between the private armies, despite the demonstrative communities of interest, there is no peace, and doomsday waits at the bottom of the lane. Some of the green fields and quiet suburbs are and have been untroubled, but a new violent generation has come of age, appetites have been whetted, the wages of violence counted out. The Troubles have become institutionalized, the killing like that on the roads, deplored but tolerated. And this time there have been too many killed and too many who have had to kill, according to the IRA spokesmen. This time after eight hundred years an end must come and out of the carnage must rise the United Ireland phoenix. And to this deathless dream the men at the other end of the lane who seek to perpetuate their way of life, so little different from that of their Catholic neighbors to the alien eye but so precious in its symbols of conquest and superiority, respond with "No Surrender." Perhaps there will be toleration by exhaustion. Perhaps the British in disgust will withdraw—at the very least putting fewer British lives at risk. Perhaps there is someplace the saving formula. Perhaps there some-day will be a recess sufficiently long to convert the gunmen to the easy life—but probably not. There is still no scholarly consensus on an appro-priate conceptual framework of analysis, no consensus of any sort on the most likely eventuality. Rather there is an inclination to predict disaster, boundaries ill-defined, unless a cherished prescription is followed. For now and for tomorrow, the problem is that there is no solution.

Another Decade On, 1986

In the last decade of analysis nothing has changed utterly, nothing has even changed very much. The Troubles remain, more Ulster than Irish, turbulent, dangerous, still often novel and spectacular, but always deadly. And so the contestants continue to deploy their old assets and seek new ones, gunmen want more guns and the benefit of the ballot; the politicians want their initiatives to clear the stage of the violent; the dedicated want vindication, and many want vengeance. So despite the twists and turns, massacres, assassinations, elections, and surprises of a decade, Ulster as subject remains attractive. And the results are not unlike the first waves, much that is awful but some that is very good, a few unexpected delights and much paper shelved. The readily available books now stretch on groan-ing shelves down a whole section instead of being piled on a bedside table. There would be no point, now, in reviewing the steady stream of very good history on modern Ireland; Ireland is now quite well served by scholars working out of released documents or, if need be, more scattered sources coupled with interviews. And the rewriting of earlier Irish history is worth a volumn. On contemporary Ulster most of the prominent have written of their experiences or been written about, most parties and programs and special crises have a chonicler. Even the elusive and often inarticulate and occasionally unpleasant Loyalists have been brought to the pages of *Ulster's Uncertain Defenders, Loyalists and the Northern Ireland Conflict* (Belfast:

Appletree, 1984) by Sarah Nelson. It might be wise to give some indication of the variety and scope of published concern by those who write on the area.

There are various disciplines easily focused on the Ulster Troubles—often of a kind rarely found in Irish universities where funds and chairs are limited and recent academic fashions often suspect. Thus, those involved in conflict resolution, a world that involves the grand (global order studies) as well as the very specific (crowd security at sports events) have come to Ulster to watch, to write, and at times to become involved. For the most part, like many academics, they tend to write for each other, and unlike most academics, they plow hilly fields far from the bottom lands of orthodoxy. The result is that David Bowman or Irv Goldaber or Denis Barritt are best known to their own. For example, Alfred McClung Lee has produced *Terrorism in Northern Ireland* (Bayside, N.Y.: General Hall, 1983) to no roll of drums, but based on a decade of work known only to specialists, published largely in specialist journals. No matter how suspect the traditionalists may find "field experiences in Northern Ireland" or the concerns of social scientists in alien fields, Lee's work on Ireland is typical of many who approach the Ulster Troubles from special academic ring-forts; his results surface in journals like *Social Problems, Group Tensions, International Journal of Group Tensions, International Review of Modern Sociology, Church & State, Journal of Sociology and Social Welfare, Social Research, Critica Sociologica,* and *Research in Social Movement, Conflicts, and Change,* with titles such as "Mass Media Mythmaking in the United Kingdom's Interethnic Struggles," "Insurgent and 'Peacekeeping' Violence in Northern Ireland," and "Northern Irish Socialization in Conflict Patterns." Mostly done in prose, all with hope for better days, each in a way typical of the vast social science industry churning away in universities far removed from Unity Flats or the Creggan.

While Irish writers are not immune to academic fashions and a specialist approach, they tend to be more committed to the politics arising from the turmoil; after all they are Irish and hence even though far from Ulster involved (and few of the Irish, whatever the mileage, are very far from Ulster). Most works await easy pigeonholes: lift Padraig O'Malley's *The Uncivil Wars, Ireland Today* (Boston: Houghton Mifflin, 1983) and put it in decent-Dublin learning toward the orthodox in contrast to Kevin Kelley's *The Longest War, Northern Ireland and the IRA* (London: Zed, 1982) from the same Irish-American ethnic stable but needing quite a different site as new-Left-sympathy-for-the-Provos. The Irish-Irish, as well, tend to use categories, but a glance through *The Crane Bag, The Northern Issue* reveals the scope and variety of that interest—even though at times disinterested concern:

Michael McKeown, *Chronicles: A Register of Northern Ireland's Casualties 1969-1980*
Percy Allum, *The Irish Question*
Barre Fitzpatrick, *Interview with Andy Tyrie*
Ed Moloney, *Paisley*
David McKittrick, *The Class Structure of Unionism*
Michael McDowell, *Removing the British Guarantee—A Policy Based on Rigour or Rhetoric?*
Seamus Deane and Barre Fitzpatrick, *Interview with John Hume*
Peter Taylor, *Britain's Irish Problem*
John Bowman, *Sinn Féin's Perception of the Ulster Question: Autumn 1921*
Roger Faligot, *Special War in Ireland*
Richard Kearney, *The IRA's Strategy of Failure*
Eamonn Deane, *Community Work in Northern Ireland in the Seventies*
Barre Fitzpatrick, *Interview with Brian Smeaton and Des Wilson*
Timothy Kearney, *The Panter and the Gael: An Interview with John Hewitt and John Montague*

All this relates more to high journalism than social science methodologies, but it is no less useful and surely more readable. In any case, good journalists have often done valid work (e.g., Tim Pat Coogan's less than disinterested *On the Blanket, The H-Block Story* [Dublin: Ward River, 1980]), while the academics have followed their own strange banners into irrelevance and fancy.

Some of the academic work is not quite so academic nor irrelevant, although often fancy. In fact, there are two large schools of analysis that have become part of the problem: the Radical Marxists, largely domiciled in British universities and polytechs eager to apply revolutionary caliphers to Irish violence; and the Union Jack strategists (Brian Crozier, Richard Clutterbuck, Paul Wilenson, et al.) who find the Irish revolting, harbingers of decay within Great Britain. A typical sample of less committed analysis can be found perusing the table of contents of *Terrorism in Ireland* (London: Croom Helm, 1984), as shown below, produced by Yonah Alexander, who has engendered a cottage industry in editing books on terror (a Hardy Boys series on violence) and his colleague Alan O'Day, a sensible scholar hidden in the history department of the Polytechnic of Northern London, site of various British ideological struggles. These range from proforma feminist fashions to Crenshaw's report for the U.S. State Department, the two ends of relevance as well as competence:

Michael McKinley, *The International Dimensions of Terrorism in Ireland*
Raymond J. Raymond, *The United States and Terrorism in Ireland, 1969-1981*

Tom Gallagher, *Scotland, Britain, and Conflict in Ireland*
Suzann Buckley and Pamela Lonergan, *Women and the Troubles, 1969-1980*
Ken Heskin, *The Psychology of Terrorism in Northern Ireland*
Tom Corfe, *Political Assassination in the Irish Tradition*
Sheridan Gilley, *The Catholic Church and Revolution in Nineteenth Century Ireland*
D. G. Boyce, *Water for the Fish: Terrorism and Public Opinion*
John Kirkaldy, *Northern Ireland and Fleet Street: Misreporting a Continuing Tragedy*
Ken Ward, *Ulster Terrorism: The U.S. Network News Coverage of Northern Ireland, 1969-1979*
Philip Schlesinger, *Terrorism, The Media and the Liberal Democratic State: A Critique of the Orthodoxy*
Paul Bew, *The Problem of Ulster Terrorism: The Historical Roots*
Martha Crenshaw, *The Persistence of I.R.A. Terrorism*

Such published work tends to represent rather general presentations by the concerned and competent.

And so it has gone for ten years more, and so it still goes—largely without doing any active harm, largely without humor and lasting worth. Still, recent Irish history now exists on paper, recent Irish politics is no longer a virgin field, even if presently often plowed to cross-purpose, and, indeed, some very good works, have appeared. There is no final chronicle, no ultimate analysis, no conclusion, no last chapter to a tragedy in too many acts, but there is hope. Gerry Adams (one-time Provo C/O of Belfast, delegate at the IRA-British conference in London in 1972, reputed chief of staff, target of a painful but failed assassination attempt, president of Sinn Féin) produced *Falls Memories* (Dingle, Ireland: Brandon, 1982), a work hastily bought with great interest by security officials, by the police and the army in Ireland and the United Kingdom, by eager social scientists of all persuasions and by journalists of every bias. If not a general best seller it often, like Adams, was a most-wanted item. Then the readers discovered that the memories were only of his childhood: if a radical gunman can write on halcyon days along the Falls Road perhaps there is some hope yet.

Appendix: List of Papers

The following list of selected papers presented at meetings of the European Consortorium for Political Research indicates the concerns of academics focused mostly on political matters rather than public policy, sociology or anthropology, or even economics and history. Some reveal work in progress, a few a single Irish venture; collectively the titles indicate that from 1973 to 1985 Ireland remained of considerable concern to those analysts close to the scene.

Allison, L. (Warwick), The Irish in Britain [Aarhus 1982—The Politics of Immigration]

Arthur, P. and Jeffrey, K. (Ulster Polytechnic), Conflict studies in Northern Ireland [Lancaster 1981—European Approaches to War and Peace Studies]

————. (Ulster Polytechnic), Elite interviewing in a "paranocracy": the Northern Ireland case [Aarhus 1982—Elite Interviewing]

————. (Ulster Polytechnic), Policing and crisis politics: Northern Ireland as a case study [Salzburg 1984—The Politics of Policing Democratic Societies]

Aughey, A. (Ulster Polytechnic), Militant Protestantism: the limits of exit, voice and loyalty [Florence 1980—Terrorism in West European Liberal Democracies]

————. (Ulster Polytechnic), European Community: regional policy, justice and the Northern Ireland case [Aarhus 1982—European Policies on Regional Development]

————. (Ulster Polytechnic) and McIlheney, C. (QUB), Law before violence? The Protestant paramilitaries in Ulster politics [Freiburg 1983—Violence and Conflict Management in Divided Societies]

Baker, S. (EUI, Florence), From economic nationalism to European integration: a study of political succession from Eamon De Valera to Sean Lemass in the Fianna Fáil party [Salzburg 1984—Political Succession]

————. (EUI, Florence), The Industrial Development Authority and the politics of industrial subsidization in Ireland: the case of Raybestos Manhattan [Barcelona 1985—The Politics of Industrial Subsidies]

Carroll, T.G. (St. Catherine's, Ontario), Ends and means in Northern Ireland [Louvain-la-Neuve 1976—The Politics of Multi-Cultural Societies]

————. (LSE), Language, religion, national identity and secession: an outline of some parallels in the European experience [Louvain-la-Neuve 1976—The Politics of Multi-Cultural Societies]

————. (LSE), The strategy of cultural interest groups: an Irish-Norwegian comparison [Berlin 1977—Interest Group Strategy]

————. (NIHEL), The referendum and popular participation in the Irish political system [Lancaster 1981—Referendums as New Forms of Political Participation]

————. (NIHEL), The state, the educational system and problems of national identity: the case of Ireland [Aarhus 1982—National Identification Processes]

————. (NIHEL), Prime-ministerial succession: the Irish experience [Freiburg 1983—Political Succcession]

————. (NIHEL), Political succession on the peripheries of Europe, 1918–1939: national-building and political change in Ireland, Finland, Czechoslovakia and the Baltic States [Salzburg 1984—Political Succession]

————. (NIHEL), The ethnic revival in modern, industrialised societies: implications of the Northern Ireland evidence [Barcelona 1985—Centre-Periphery Structures and the Revival of the Peripheral Nationalism in Western Democracies]

Cohan, A.S. (Lancaster), Toward a multi-cultural society: perspectives of the Irish political elite [Louvain-la-Neuve 1976—The Politics of Multi-Cultural Societies]

————. (Lancaster), The confluence of political and cultural movements in the Irish revolution [Berlin 1977—Social and Political Movements in Western Europe]

Collins, N.A. (Birmingham), Some considerations on Irish politicians and brokerage politics [Florence 1980—Clientelist Political Systems]

———. (Birmingham), The European direct election campaign in the Republic of Ireland [Florence 1980—Direct Elections to the European Parliament]

———. (Liverpool), The relevance of federal ideas in contemporary Ireland [Salzburg 1984—comparative Federalism and Federation in Western Europe]

———. (Liverpool), Metropolitan government in Ireland [Barcelona 1985—Metropolitan Government]

Dinneen, D. A. (NIHEL), Anti-unemployment policy in Ireland during the 1970s [Aarhus 1982—Policy Responses to Unemployment in Mixed Economies]

Gallagher, M. (TCD), The composition of governments in the Republic of Ireland 1959-1980 [Florence 1980—The Composition of Governments in Parliamentary Regimes]

———. (TCD), Societal change and party adaptation in the Republic of Ireland 1960-1981 [Lancaster 1981—Party Adaptation to Societal Change]

———. (TCD), Electoral behaviour at different level elections in the Republic of Ireland [Aarhus 1982—Voting Patterns in Multi-level Electoral Systems]

———. (TCD), The political consequences of the electoral system in the Republic of Ireland [Salzburg 1984—Comparing Electoral Systems]

———. (TCD), The selection of parliamentary candidates in the Republic of Ireland [Barcelona 1985—Candidate Selection in Comparative Perspective]

Garvin, T. (UCD), Dublin: periphery-dominated centre [Strasbourg 1974—Varieties of Regional Differentiation]

———. (UCD), The destiny of the soldiers: tradition and modernity in the politics of De Valera's Ireland [Berlin 1977—Social and Political Movements in Western Europe]

———. (UCD), Factionalism in Fianna Fáil: the Haughey succession [Florence 1980—Factionalism in the Political Parties of Western Europe]

Girvin, B. (NIHEL), Industrial policy and economic development in Ireland: the experience of an open economy [Aarhus 1982—Industrial Policies in OECD Countries]

———. (UCC), Government intervention and the nature of interdependence in Ireland [Freiburg 1983—Politico-Economic Interdependence in the Highly Industrialised Democracies]

———. (UCC), Consensus and change in a recessionary environment: the determinants of economic strategy in the Republic of Ireland [Salzburg 1984—Proposals to Cope with the Economic Crisis in Western Europe: the Politics of Economic Strategies]

———. (UCC), Change and stability in Irish democracy: the impact of nationalism [Barcelona 1985—The Stability and Instability of Democracies]

Guelke, A. (QUB), The "ballot bomb": the Northern Ireland Assembly elections and the Provisional IRA [Freiburg 1983—Violence and Conflict Management in Divided Societies]

Hainsworth, P. (Ulster Polytechnic), A Europe for the regions? A Northern Ireland case study [Aarhus 1982—European Policies on Regional Development]

Higgins, M.D. (UCG), Irish patrons and brokers: the clientelist perspective in Irish political science research assessed [Florence 1980—Clientelist Political Systems]

_____. (UCG), Coalitions in theory and Ireland. The Fine Gael/Labour coalition of 1982 [Salzburg 1984—Political Parties and Coalitional Behaviour in Western Europe]

Hillyard, P. (Bristol), State responses to terrorism [Florence 1980—Terrorism in West European Liberal Democracies]

Huber, C. (EUI, Florence), Political parties of Ireland and European integration [Berlin 1977—Parties and European Integration]

Katz, R.S. (Johns Hopkins), Preferential voting and factionalism: a theory and three test cases [Florence 1980—Factionalism in the Political Parties of Western Europe]

Keatinge, P. (TCD), Transnationalism and autonomy: the case of Ireland and Anglo-Irish relationships [Grenoble 1978—Transnational and Trans-governmental Relations and International Outcomes]

Laffan, B. (NIHEL), The women's movement in Ireland and its impact on women's participation in politics [Lancaster 1981—Political Socialisation of Women and Men]

_____. (NIHEL), Job creation schemes in the Republic of Ireland: a study of adaptive implementation [Freiburg 1983—Policy Evaluation: Assessing and Explaining Policy Effects]

Laver, M.J. (Liverpool), Rational choice *in extremis*: an interpretation/analysis of party and voter behaviour in the 1973 Northern Ireland Assembly election [Strasbourg 1974—Participation, Voting and Party Competition]

_____. (Liverpool), Cultural aspects of loyalty: social loyalty and the Ulster loyalist [London 1975—Language and Religion in Politics]

Lee, J.J. (UCC), Taxation and its discontents: the Irish case [Salzburg 1984—The Politics of Taxation]

Lyne, T. (Warwick), The Irish Labour Party: the "tricky game" of neutrality [Salzburg 1984—Social Democracy and Defence]

_____. (NIHEL), Voluntary associations, politics and social change in Ireland: the Gaelic Athletic Association and the Community Games [Barcelona 1985—Voluntary Associations in the Democratic System]

McAllister, I. (Strathclyde), Political opposition in a divided society: a note on the Northern Ireland SDLP [Berlin 1977—Trends and Tensions in European Social Democracy]

_____. (Strathclyde), Nationalist ideology and party organisation: Scottish, Welsh and Northern Irish evidence [Grenoble 1978—Mass Political Organisations]

_____. (Strathclyde), Centre-periphery within Northern Ireland: a model for the development of a party system [Brussels 1979—The Politicisation of Peripheral Identities]

McAllister, I. and Mair, P. (Strathclyde), Territory, class and intra-party tensions: the Labour Parties of the British Isles [Florence 1980—Factionalism in the Political Parties of Western Europe]

Mair, P. (Strathclyde), The Irish Labour Party: a weak alternative in the Irish party system [Berlin 1977—Trends and Tensions in European Social Democracy]

Marsh, M.A. (TCD), Localism and candidate selection in the Irish general election of 1977 [Grenoble 1978—Mass Political Organisations]

_____. (TCD), Electoral volatility in Ireland 1948–81 [Lancaster 1981—Electoral Volatility in Western Democracies: Problems of Measurement, Explanation and Comparison]

_____. (TCD), The voters decide? Preferential voting in European list system [Salzburg 1984—Comparing Electoral Systems]

_____. (TCD), Nominating unattractive candidates: small businessmen in Irish political recruitment [Barcelona 1985—Candidate Selection in Comparative Perspective]

Mickley, A. (QUB), The Northern Irish peace movement and its external effects [Berlin 1977—Power and Influence in International Politics]

Moxon-Browne, E. (QUB), Irish political parties and European integration [Berlin 1977—Parties and European Integration]

_____. (QUB), The relationship between the Irish parliament and the European parliament from 1973 to 1977 [Grenoble 1978—Changing Patterns of Relationships between the European Parliament and the National Parliaments]

_____. (QUB), Terrorism in Northern Ireland: the case of the Provisional IRA [Florence 1980—Terrorism in West European Liberal Democracies]

_____. (QUB), Human rights and the law: a case study from Northern Ireland [Aarhus 1982—Civil Liberties in Advanced Industrial Societies]

_____. (QUB), Human rights and the law: the case of gay rights in Northern Ireland under direct rule [Freiburg 1983]

_____. (QUB), Peripherality in the United Kingdom: the case of Provisional Sinn Féin [Barcelona 1985—Centre-Periphery Structures and the Revival of Peripheral Nationalism in Western Democracies]

Nelson,S. (Strathclyde), Ulster Protestant ideology reconsidered [London 1975—Language and Religion in Politics]

O'Carroll, J.P. (UCC), The politics of the 1983 "abortion referendum debate" in the Republic of Ireland [Salzburg 1984—The Politics of Abortion]

_____. (UCC), Business and government in the Republic of Ireland [Barcelona 1985—Politics and Business in Western Democracies]

O'Neill, H. (UCD), Organisational structure of Irish development cooperation [Freiburg 1983—Organisations for Development Policy in European Countries: Strategies, Social Environment, Administrative Constraints, Political Control]

O'Malley, L. (UCG), Personal data information and the right to information in Ireland [Barcelona 1985—Confidentiality, Privacy and Data Protection]

Orridge, A. (Birmingham), Peripheral nationalisms [Berlin 1977—Social and Political Movements in Western Europe]

Pyne, P. The political role of the Irish bureaucracy and the environmental factors shaping this role: an outline [Mannheim 1973—Comparative Administration]

Roulston, C. (UUJ), "Socialising the national question": the dilemmas of Irish communism [Barcelona 1985—Inside Communist Parties in Western Europe]

Sacks, P. (Colby College, Maine), The role of parties in regional differentiation: the case of Ireland [Strasbourg 1974—Varieties of Regional Differentiation]

Seiler, D. (UCD), Culture, region and party system in western Europe [Strasbourg 1974—Varieties of Regional Differentiation]

Sinnott, R. (EUI, Florence), The quid pro quo of industrial subsidies: the politics of a proposed "hands on" approach to indigenous Irish industry [Barcelona 1985—The Politics of Industrial Subsidies]

Smyth, J. (QUB), Terrorism in Ireland: the limits and bases of support [Florence 1980—Terrorism in West European Liberal Democracies]

_____. (QUB), The welfare state in Northern Ireland: dysfunctional reform? [Aarhus 1982—Society and the Political Economy of the Welfare State: What Kind of Linkages, What Kind of Features?]

———. (QUB), Civil liberties and riot control in Northern Ireland [Freiburg 1983—Civil Liberties/Civil Rights in Industrial Society]

———. (QUB), Politics of policing in democratic societies [Salzburg 1984—The Politics of Policing Democratic Societies

Stadler, K. (Munich), Religion and the conflict in Northern Ireland [London 1975—Language and Religion in Politics]

Taylor, M. (UCC), Police service and satisfaction [Salzburg 1984—The Politics of Policing Democratic Societies]

Whyte, J. (QUB), The Catholic factor in the politics of democratic states [London 1975—Language and Religion in Politics]

———. (QUB), Interpretations of the Northern Ireland conflict [Louvain-la-Neuve 1976—The Politics of Multi-Cultural Societies]

———. (QUB), Patterns of Catholic politics [Brussels 1979—Religion and Politics]

———. (QUB), The permeability of the United Kingdom—Irish border: a preliminary reconnaissance [Freiburg 1983—The Politics of Frontiers and Boundaries]

Wright, S. (Lancaster), The campaign of the British army in Northern Ireland: a case of self-legitimation [Grenoble 1978—Politics and the Military]

Notes

1. Besides the Ulster conference, the Institute for the Study of Conflict has produced three issues of *Conflict Studies* on Ireland: no. 6 by Iain Hamilton, no. 17 by Hamilton and Robert Moss (whose more extensive report on Ulster may be found in *The War for the Cities* [New York: Coward, McCann & Georghegan, 1972]) and no. 36, June 1973, *Ulster: Politics and Terrorism.* The analysis is essentially the view from conservative London based in large part on authorized sources, suspicious of "revolution" and without a grasp of the Irish perspective. Despite the flaws, the publications of the Institute are handy, concise—but not in the Irish case purely disinterested analysis.

2. There is a vast collection of party papers (*The United Irishman* of the Official IRA or *Combat* of the UVF), neighborhood newssheets, broadsides, theoretical journals published erratically, pamphlets, weeklies produced in Belfast or London or New York (*The Irish People*)—all largely only the concern of the professional scholar, various security forces, and the faithful.

3. Another far more elegant effort at propaganda—sympathetic reporting—is P. Michael O'Sullivan's *Patriot Game* (Chicago: Follett, 1972), largely a book of photographs buttressed with an unfortunate text (as told to Don Johnson, whatever that may mean).

4. Another massive category of works on Irish matters is here ignored in that there has been a rush in foreign parts to publish on Ulster. The Troubles can be fitted into various existing niches—Left politics or Catholic loyalty. Repeatedly journalists have returned to Italy or Germany to write of their Ireland. A typical example would be *Tortura in Irlanda* (Rome: Napoleone Editore, 1972), edited by Angelo Puggioni—mostly a collection of translated declarations and documents. There is probably no harm done, although all those old familar names do look odd in the midst of paragraphs in grandiose Italian journalese or dense German analysis.

5. So far the greatest contribution of the thesis-dissertation group has been to

previously ignored areas of Irish history rather than examination of events since 1968. In 1972–73 in the United States there was only one Irish dissertation (Kathleen Kenny, "The Political System of the Irish Republic: Two-and-a-half Parties in a Developing Nation," Syracuse) in political science and only a single proposal dealing with the Troubles (Robert F. Mulvihill, "Attitudes Toward Political Violence: A Survey of Catholics and Protestants in Londonderry, Northern Ireland," Pennsylvania). Given the course record, this restraint is unlikely to continue and rumor of various projects, particularly in British universities, is rife.

6. The old faithfuls, mostly potted sociology on "The Irish" are still about, ranging from the serious and good (Robert E. Kennedy, Jr., *The Irish: Emigration, Marraige and Fertility* [Berkeley: University of California Press, 1973]) to the usual trot through the Irish character and countryside. A saving grace to date has been a general reluctance to trot through the Troubles.

7. There is an obvious need for a thorough bibliography of the Troubles, but as yet there has been no hint of such a project. At least efforts are being made in Belfast to collect the most fugitive material, but an authoritative listing of academic analysis is yet to be made.

8. Richard Ned Lebow, "Civil War in Ireland: A Tragedy in Endless Acts?" *Journal of International Affairs*, vol. 27, no. 2 (1973), 247–60, and Thomas E. Hachey, "One People or Two? The Origins of Partition and the Prospects for Unification in Ireland," ibid., 232–46.

9. L.W. Doob and W.J. Foltz, "The Belfast Workshop: An Application of Group Techniques to a Destructive Conflict," *Journal of Conflict Resolution*, vol. 17, no. 3, pp. 489–512, and "The Impact of a Workshop upon Grass-Roots Leaders in Belfast," ibid. (forthcoming, June 1974).

10. Lynch's single contribution has been "The Anglo-Irish Problem," *Foreign Affairs*, vol. 50, no. 4, (July 1972).

11. British strategy is to invest in a center that will reward moderation and stability while threatening the Protestants with the evacuation of the province and the Provos with perpetual occupation. So far the rewards have been insufficient, the Protestants truculent and the Provos determined. Dublin's strategy is to support London and deplore violence.

12. Irish Microforms Ltd., 35 Kildare Street, Dublin 2.

13. One of the more arcane reference works to appear is *The Last Post, The Details and Stories of the Republican Dead, 1913/1975* by the National Graves Association (Dublin, 1976), an updating of the first 1932 edition. For the specialist the inclusions and exclusions are intriguing, but for others the exercise does, indeed, have a significant import for Irish Republicans. They serve without uniform, pension prospects, or great hope of temporal recognition; thus next to the ballads those who lose in the patriot game can be assured their sacrifice, if in vain, will yet not be forgotten.

14. Blackstaff Press, Ltd., 16 Donegall Square, Belfast.

15. *Hibernia*, 206 Pearse Street, Dublin 2.

16. *Fortnight*, 7 Lower Crescent, Belfast.

17. There is a clue in that a Jacqueline Van Voris published *Constance de Markievicz: In the Cause of Ireland* with the University of Massachusetts at Amherst in 1967.

18. Cf. John Cooney and Lenore Cooney (prose), Leif Skoogfors (photographs), *The Most Natural Thing in the World* (New York: Harper Colophon, 1974); and Colman Doyle, *People at War* (Dublin: F.D.R., 1975).

19. It must be noted that the suggestion to introduce sectarian schools has been a cherished formula for some time but considered by the pragmatic as a non-starter for the immediate future. Dr. William Philbin, Roman Catholic bishop of Down and Connor, has announced that he would refuse to confirm children who went to state or Protestant-dominated schools. Msgr. Patrick Joseph Mullally, chairman of the Down and Connor Maintained Schools Committee, which covers the Belfast area, insisted the proposal is "as phony an issue as you will ever encounter. The issues here are housing and employment, not schools, and there's no evidence at all that education is part of the trouble here" (*New York Times*, 5 August 1976). Although the response, confirming Protestant prejudice and revealing the charming parochialism of the Irish Church, was less than felicitous, Mullally is largely correct in assessing the paucity of evidence that indicates separate schooling produces bigots (some of Richard Rose's data, albeit limited, suggest that familiarity does not breed toleration). The concept of secular, unified schools is a touchstone for many liberal, democratic Americans, but in Ireland it is a contentious concept, guaranteed to engender further passion. As always in Northern Ireland, well-meaning and perhaps even valid prescriptions fall on fallow and bitter ground.

20. Cf. Ian McAllister, *The 1975 Northern Ireland Convention Election* (Glasgow: University of Strothclyde, Survey Research Center, Occasional Paper Number 14, 1976).

22

The Troubles as Trash:
Shadows of the Irish Gunman on America

A most popular form of modern reading continues to be the thiller, composed to entertain rather than enlighten, although there is ordinarily a dash of exotica and the odd arcane detail. Like the western or the closed-room mystery, the script follows a formula. Most are in fact extended chases through foreign places by characters few readers or authors are likely to meet: MI-6 or KGB agents, Mafia godfathers, assassins or Palestinian fedayeen. The classic practitioners, old and new—Eric Ambler, Graham Greene, Frederick Forsythe—all made do without Irish gunmen.

In many of the distant corners of the world Ireland is noted, if at all, not as the home of saints and scholars but rather the fount of the Irish Rebel. With the rise of the present troubles in Ulster, a new interest has been shown in the contemporary IRA gunmen. It was not necessary to understand very much about Ireland or Ulster in order to insert the gunmen into the plot, but like all crafts, time, loving care, and a focus on detail ultimately produce a finer product. And those who construct thrillers have their aspirations as well. Thus, with varying degrees of success, authors have attempted to flesh out their gunmen. In so doing they reveal something about the laic perceptions of the Irish troubles just as—to a degree—Agatha Christie reveals the customs of her tribe or Zane Grey the nature of the frontier.

The resulting image of the IRA volunteer fashioned at a distance from reality often resembles cardboard rather than Celt. Robert Charles is engaged in a series of "Counter-Terror" tales (*The Flight of the Raven, The Prey of the Falcon, The Hour of the Wind,* New York: Pinnacle Books, 1974-1976). He follows a set formula, apparently writes more than he reads, and has a less than felicitous prose style: "she was a woman, a mere slip of a girl, only nineteen years old, but one who could turn his wild blood to fire and his young heart to anguish." Still, he has created what might be considered—for thriller purpose—the three types. First is the hard-man, the gunman of limited ideas and often malice, basic IRA, a killer doomed to die who often barely has a speaking part. Second is the soft-man, the idealist whose political background is drawn in a paragraph or two, who gradually realizes the futility of violence, and thus may be ultimately saved. And third, the good-girl who like the soft man joined the movement for decent purposes in the civil-rights days and sickened by terror seeks to convert the soft-man.

For more effective narrative there must be more depth—the soft-man needs hard spots. Max Franklin in *The Fifth of November* (New York: Ballantine, 1975) has crafted an anti-hero in Hennessy, who, after his wife and daughter are murdered in Belfast, sets out against IRA instructions to blow up the Houses of Parliament on opening day. Hunted by everyone, Hennessy—and the action—have little to do with Ireland. His end is assured, a hard-man, turned by tragedy, a victim of "a dirty business."

John Cleary in *Peter's Pence* (New York: Pyramid, 1975) has gone Franklin one better in operational ambition, for during a raid inside the Vatican to raise money for the IRA, the pope is kidnapped. Once again there is the soft-man—McBride, whose father was crippled in the Tan War and then killed in a failed ambush in Ulster in 1956; he is more American than Irish, more uncertain and has the good-girl Luciana to prod him down justice's path. His colleagues, more complex and dedicated than the usual hard-men, come to the anticipated end and McBride saves Pope Martin the Sixth, himself, and a future after a tangle of adventures. But from the first he, the soft-man, was placed on the angels' side: "Violence has its own backlash. Freedom isn't worth the lives of innocent people."

John de St. Jorre and Brian Shakespare, formerly in the British diplomatic service and presently London journalists, include a great deal more Irish material, names, places, and the odd accent. In *The Patriot Game* (Boston: Houghton Mifflin, 1973), they combine the lone wolf hard-man Hennessy and the saved soft-man McBride. Their IRA gunman, Grogan, disgusted with Irish inefficiency, goes off to fight his own war in London, sought by all, including the IRA. He has a soft-girl, proves terribly competent, draws back at the last moment, and ends up in Stockolm with a blonde. Unlike the other exercises, *The Patriot Game* is about the Irish—but they serve only as background for the ritual chase.

Gerald Seymour, in *Harry's Game* (New York: Random House, 1975), has drawn on his experience as a correspondent in Belfast to write on the duel between Harry, coming to the end of the line as a career British anti-insurgency specialist, and "The Man," an IRA hard-man exhausted by the troubles. There are lots of specific Irish details—place, accent, habits, descriptions—and the odd clanger. Harry gets "The Man" and is killed by his own. Unlike *The Patriot Game*, Harry and The Man have nothing much to do with politics or patriots, but rather with illicit violence, and they both are tired of playing deadly games. While Eric Ambler calls the book "a superb thriller"—which it is—Knopf subtitles it a novel—which it is. But The Man is simply the hard-man gone soft, not from a distate for violence but an excess.

In Seymour's latest novel, *The Glory Boys* (New York: Random House, 1976) the focus is on a group of international terrorists opposed to the British Security Service and some Israelis—something for everyone, including the hard IRA gunman McCoy. Although McCoy has a major part, mostly he does things, says little of importance, and except for the odd, sketched-in background, has little to do with Ireland. This time Eric Ambler calls it a considerable novel and a superb thriller. The latter is certain, but *The Glory Boys* has substituted action for characters and the locale is London. McCoy does not last the route, shot and given up to the police by the soft-girl.

A thriller phenomenon has been Jack Higgins, who has taken off after some twenty-five novels. Higgins, a Belfast Protestant with Catholic relatives out of Yorkshire and the Horse Guards, has produced two books with Irish themes, *A Prayer for the Dying* and *The Savage Day* (New York: Holt, Rhinehart & Winston, 1973, 1972). *A Prayer for the Dying* is the formula of the gunman guilty of an unintended atrocity wandering about—this time in England—seeking salvation. Fallon, as usual with hard-men turned soft, finds his in death.

The Savage Day is much more Irish—a British officer, Vaughan, the undoomed hero is dispatched through various adventures to confound the enemies of the Crown. Along the way he encounters three people who, more than is usually the case, have a foundation in reality. The Small Man, Michael Cork, is the old idealist—rather a hard-man with a soft center—and Binnie Gallagher is the young idealist with a somewhat smaller soft center who dreams of dying for the Republic. Both of course do die as required but in an appropriately heroic manner. Our hero notes, "The IRA didn't just consist of bomb-happy Provos. . . . There were also genuine idealists there in the Pearse and Connolly tradition. Always would be." Which is about as close to praise as the IRA gets anyplace. The third character is the required woman, Norah, who at the very end turns out to be a hard-woman dedicated absolutely to violence, even the death of innocents, and is thus killed on the last page. And in Ireland there are far more hard women than our other authors have indicated. Women who have chosen not to wait and knit under the guillotine but take up the gun have often proved the most deadly of the Irish rebel species.

A composite picture of the Irish Troubles can be gleaned by these thrillers, written by both the innocent and the informed. It is hardly profound but may represent the wisdom of the commom reader. The present violence apparently arose from legitimate grievances, not too specifically detailed, of the Catholic community; the Protestant complication is largely avoided. The IRA, however, focuses almost entirely on the struggle for a united Ireland. Mostly the IRA is the Provisional IRA. The Officials appear only once or twice, and Higgins, in *The Savage Day,* invents his own organization.

As a revolutionary organization no one has much time for the Provos: Bloody but inefficient, lacking in vision, heartlessly cruel, redeemed if at all by a few idealists (the soft-men). Membership for any length of time as an idealist sufficiently corrupts so that salvation usually may only come through death—The Man, the Small Man, Michael Cork, Binnie Gallagher, even the one hard-woman Norah is dispatched with a boat-bomb by the hero. The moral nearly every time is that violence corrupts both the cause and the man. The more complex the man corrupted, the better the thriller but never, never is there an indication that violence in fact may pay decent wages in the coins of political power. The common reader is not yet ready for a politically successful "terrorist" organization as once he was not for the American Indian.

As far as can be discerned from the usual indicators of American public opinion, the real public agrees with the authors. The Catholics had legitimate grievances and used effective means (civil disobedience), but gradually the IRA extremists took over and their use of violence has contaminated a just cause. The IRA, the odd misguided idealist aside, is a collection of mindless bombers and gunmen whose operations are counter productive. The Irish rebel has become a terrorist. The British army and security forces are simply trying to maintain order. And this is more or less what the editorial writers of the *New York Times,* overt political opinion beyond the reach of Irish votes, and the concerned at Washington cocktail parties believe. Here and there outside the Irish diaspora there is sympathy for the IRA and distaste for the British, but not to any extent in the English-speaking world.

In the thrillers and out of them, the IRA has blotted its copy book with no-warning bombs, assassinations, cycles of civilian deaths—all the techniques of terror. This image of the IRA is not to their advantage. They have no patrons as do the fedayeen or quixotic cause as do the Japanese Red Army, but a chance, if slight, at power that requires the organization to seek a certain aura of legitimacy.

In part what has happened to the IRA is a visibility made posible by the technological elegance of the communication industry—including thriller production—which displays in living color, often personal and close up, the tactics of terror. In the old days rebels hacked out thier campaigns in the bush or away from the media's eye. Now a global audience is flooded with live violence. For the fedayeen this is splendid; with no real hope of power, they seek prominence. For the IRA it has been a disaster, forcing the Army Council to chose between restraint that guarantees dwindling impact and tactics that erode legitimacy.

Thus, in some strange, small way the thrillers on Irish matters may have played a part in the British campaign to restore order, if not justice, to Ulster. In both strokes of black and white, they have painted the jolly ploughboy, the Irish rebel, the romantic gunmam, as a terrorist, futile, brutal, at best misguided, at worse a callous killer. Surely, the British could ask for no more.

So it would appear that everyone who approaches the Troubles with intent, determined on new surveys, new probes, even new thrillers, is likely to become part of the experience rather than handmaiden to history. Many not only see but also demand relevance, application, action, an effect on policy ranging from the resolution of conflict in one lane to the validation of decades of policy, from a brief background on the IRA for the State Department to a paper weapon in the hands of ideologically appropriate rebels or defenders. Many want no part of advocacy, and assume that they can speak without teaching, write without prejudice, and need not be a scholar *engagé*. They have enlisted in no army, preach no gospel, and probe only for the truth. They are seldom welcomed by the frantic, the fanatical, the victims, or even, as Hugh Munro pointed out, the other observers.

> Through their safe one-way mirrors they savor all the passion, all the vio-
> lence, all the love, all the hate, but they are not involved. As long as the
> intelligentsia persist with the notion that to comment usefully on the North
> you must adopt a lofty attitude and show that you are above mere tribal
> passion, for so long will the intelligensia do more harm than good.

So even those of other tribes with dispassionate qualifications, equipped with good will and taking no delight in special models, special pleading, politics, or power, may do no harm, but certainly no good. Voyeurs of violence thus may not be limited to terror junkies, television crews, combat cameramen, or nomadic rebels; anyone who approaches Ulster has a part, a role that awaits them and if improperly played, could damage the drama and harm the cast.

For the most part, those who have trooped into Ulster in pursuit of the truth, in search of example or experience, eager to write rather than make history, hopeful that there might be lessons to be learned or applied, have done no great visible damage. Perhaps, almost certainly, they have done some real good; they have written good history, often good politics, solved few real world problems, but then people and governments have never taken easily to academic analysis or learned much from history or acted on general principles based on scholarly writ. Perhaps, given the spectrum of potential advice out of Ulster, the menu of urgent choice suggested, the visions and fanatasies fashioned as real, the simple rules made turgid by the arcane language of social science sorcery, it is just as well. Many do not want any reality that violates accepted canons. Rationalization, not truth, has takers. History as dreamed and the past as presently fashioned by patriot gunmen and cunning politicians wants no rivals. Those involved under whatever analytical banner and to whatever purpose, emboldened or limited by conversion to whatever ideology or political purpose, are engaged in what may be good works; they may produce good or harm, they write well and analyze brilliantly, but they have not totally monopolized analysis. There is room for those *not driven* by tribal passions or lofty attitudes, have not signed up with a secret army or the passionate. There are still different perspectives open that may do no harm and may even do good, if inadvertently.

Epilogue: A Political Memoir

Politicians and bureaucrats are not alone in wanting clear, precise explanations as to why matters are presently amiss and what may occur in the future so that appropriate actions can be undertaken. The interested want to know the nature and tides of history, the direction and pace of the currents, and the proper site for practical, inexpensive dams and weirs in order to channel the turmoil into pleasant pools. They do not want to know about complex eddies and unmapped turbulence. The purpose of scientific analysis is to reveal the uniformities underlying surface turbulence: Why are there Ulster Troubles? What is really happening in Ireland? What can be done, swiftly and effectively, to introduce stability and general contentment? Given a generation of contentious violence, how is general justice, peace with honor, to be achieved? Those who seek merely to explain the plain tale of events are thought irrelevant, and those who would advocate particular policies are suspect, part of the problem. In a real sense the prospects for disinterested analysis close to the arena are dim; the reception is usually related not to the message but to a heavily marked wish list. The past is magically transformed from brief reading to prologue for present postures; existing events are to be seen through special spectacles, and the future is threatened as dire retribution and agreed truth are denied.

A trained historian and once practicing politician like Conor Cruise O'Brien can hence declare that 1916, and all of that, was unnecessary to establish a free Ireland, that there is no need for the present violence since Protestant Ulster is not of the main and never will be, and that great harm lurks in certain, bloody civil war if there is too great a movement toward Irish unity. The past will be rewritten, the present interpreted, and the future awesome unless right action is taken. O'Brien is merely more articulate, more authoritative, than most who insist on the need for analysis but listen only for their voice's echo. Seldom, in fact, has so much been written over so short a time about agreed upon events without visible consensus on any aspect of the drama: why the play began, the nature of the players, their motives, the meaning of the plot, the reason for the length of the drama (scenes into endless acts), or the probable outcome. No one denies the dates

336

of atrocities, the roles of the victims, the names of the actors, the figures on the bottom line or strung across the charts of violence. All, even and especially the distant and uninvolved, want only the simple truth and decent advice, perhaps only fair warning. History so far has taught nothing nor, apparently, have the involved learned anything or forgotten anything. Consensus, like conciliation and accommodation, has found no Ulster home nor past a proper meaning nor future an outline. Analysis, however well-meaning, however disinterested, like Ulster remains victim to turmoil, frantic passion, and special interest—an audience with most lessons learned, the special past absorbed, the present simple and deadly, and the future possessed. And much analysis is neither well-meaning nor disinterested, so that the mystical common reader seeking not retribution or vindication but truth is often denied. Still, the obstacles have seemingly deterred few; the seminars are filled; the dissertations are undertaken; the shelves groan, and the conferences meet. Just as there are now bibliographies of bibliographies on Troubles' texts, so too are there those who focus solely on interpretations of interpretations, the trouble with those troubled by investigation of the turmoil.

Just as there is difficulty in writing the final chapter to any book on the Ulster Troubles, much less the Gun in Politics, there is no agreement on first causes—the moment of prologue. The innocent begin far in the past and rush through potted history to the advent of the civil-rights campaign. The more professional have increasingly investigated aspects of modern Irish history relevant to the present disturbances: economic structures, peasant aspirations, tribal rites, electorial results, political development or social attitudes. In part the search is for the causes of chaos; when the roots disappear in the past is, perhaps, less important than the nature of the plant studied. Everyone now accepts the long roots, but the scramble for first causes continues. Why has Ulster been so troubled? Why Ireland? Why now? Some answers are simple, even simple-minded, but perhaps compelling even to the complex. Others are alien models imported by converts and true believers. Some have served time for scholars elsewhere or regularly appeared as explanation for civil crisis—thus relative deprivation or outside agitators. In any case, a crucial question is why a dramatic prologue suddenly led to an unforeseen violent first act.

Even a partial listing of the answers to the casual questions without exposition is an extensive task, for nearly every commentator in print including the most hastily dispatched journalist as well as the amply prepared Irish historian has answered in some form why. Some answers have been compelling, many relevant, and others primitive.

1. For many, especially in the early years and at all times for some of the

simple and innocent, the Troubles are an inexplicable religious war near the end of a secular century: primitive Protestants versus Papish Catholics. All the complexities of Republican ideology, the civil-rights struggle, economic and social grievances, historical pressures are thus simple facets of a sectarian struggle. There are those who identify with Catholic defenders or Protestant liberties and others who see simply different bigots running amok under irrelevant banners.

2. A quite different approach is taken by those who see the Province of Northern Ireland as Britain's last colony, held more firmly and with less reason, therefore. Ulster history is thus to a large degree simply following the course laid down in Palestine and Cyprus and Kenya and the rest. There were then often ethnic problems, religious divisions, that Britain exploited to stay (for awhile, not too long) in India or Nigeria. Westminster uses the same rationales, the same tactics, even some of the same experts in anti-insurgency, and so Ulster is imperialism's last stand, religious division a facet of colonial control and Irish history less important than British experience.

3. Some academics have deployed specific theories that have proven useful models elsewhere. Thus, some suggest that the Northern Ireland problem is one of a fragmented society, frozen in place at some special period in the past so preventing any political flexibility (rather like a Celtic Rhodesia). Others note that as social and economic conditions began to improve in the 1960s, the denied Nationalists suddenly realized how deprived they had been; ambition whetted they took to the streets, led, for example, by the first generation of Catholic university students—a typical example of relative deprivation. These are certainly reasons why other men have rebeled and incorporate the existing religious strife and imperial legacy, but as less than compelling single causes.

4. Other academics, some Irish, many British of varying neo-Marxist schools, embedded in the polytech-university scene, have wheeled in the tools of class analysis, often militant, often for specific Ulster use, often swiftly disseminated by Irish activists. Essentially the Troubles are a class struggle, detailed with great scholarly cunning by the competent and broad daubs and splotches by those with more urgent priorities. Still, the optimism of some of the proclaimed Republican Marxists that in Ulster class would overcome creed often resembles nothing so much as the Christian belief in the conversion of the Jews. Some class analysis may have much to offer; some is even divorced from special pleading, but often, on the ground, the simple radical socialism of the activist seems more relevant and the academic analysis no more real than the fragmented society—even if truly difficult to place in the turbulence of warning bugle calls down in the lanes.

5. Simpler, and sufficient to set to bugle calls, is the contention that the IRA struggle is but one more battle for national liberation; Ireland may or may not be a colony, but it should be a nation once again despite the

manipulated opposition of the Protestant Loyalists and without regard for academic theorists or Marxist logic. This explanation has many takers among the Irish-American diaspora, unconcerned with the refinements of theory, the complexities on the ground, or the details of recent history. And wars, especially of national liberation, are more often won by sacrifice for slogans than love of theory.

6. Some, a differing some at differing times, feel that the years of murder come not as a result of the tides of history or great social movement but at the hands of psychopathic criminals. This descent into chaos is even a manifestation of individual original sin. Mad-dog killers have been on the loose, fanatics of all faiths moved not by nature's laws or class interest but inherent evil.

7. For others it is not simple sin or a lust for blood that has caused the Troubles but a continuation of Celtic violence, a historical, racial, societal violence rooted in the Irish—violent Paddies all. This proposition has takers not only along the Shankhill but also in London clubs and Tory conversations; Ireland may seem a Western Cornwall, but it is really a European Congo; look see what they did to Mountbatten in the Republic. And a good number of pages have been written to refute this theory indicating instead that the ancient Celts were a decent enough people despite the cattle raids and battles, that all Irish history is not a blood-stained prologue to Ulster murder but rather a plain tale of agreement, compromise, accomplishment, and movement toward democracy and social justice. The Protestant Loyalists, too, have had to defend their nature—biological bigots, a historical society of vigilantes and state terrorists, incapable of conciliation or compromise, only driven to dominance and violence. By nature Ulster's Loyalist would insist, like the Celts' heirs, that they have been misunderstood and stand for liberty and justice (especially against the bigotry of Rome).

8. And there are those who press conspiracies as prime cause: the Pope's hand or those of the Jesuits, the Masons, the CIA, the KGB, Imperialist capitalism, and the various contemporary forms of the devil. Everyone accepts, after all, that Ulster is surely plagued by the Orange Order and secret armies, is surely filled with agents and operators, and must be the crux of conspiracy. And if the plots are not true, the conspirators' only fancy, such plots *ought* to exist and at least thus *explain* the present, a simple explanation, perhaps primitive, but more compelling than relative deprivation or ancient Celtic grievance. And the Pope does plot and the KGB and the CIA, and the Great Satan is not entirely a figment of Shi'ite demonology.

In fact, all the analytical explanations seem valid but partial explanations, real enough but not enough. All the labels—race as destiny or conspiracy as cause—are possible but hardly provable. Yet if no cause can be wholly excluded and no cause alone will do, the curious, not to mention the concerned, are left with either a vacuum or a prologue too complex to consider. Why has there been no satisfactory answer, not just for all, but for anyone?

Certainly between 1967 and 1968, there were, looking backward, long dominant historical considerations, trends that shifted and swung but could be identified as relevant: Republican aspirations, Loyalists fears and arrogance, British institutions in Ulster and innocence in London, demographic changes, shifts in education and ambitions, world trends and fashions in politics, lots of factors that made up Ireland in 1969. These were the proximate conditions that when extended in time—into 1970—did not give Ireland or Ulster a surprise-free future. The institutionalized injustice of Northern Ireland was all but certain to come under challenge; that Stormont had not come under challenge was simply or largely due to Irish isolation, a time-lag in trends, and parochial immobility. There was going to be change, perhaps simply action and reaction and a return to the touchline. Yet television and emigration patterns, economic investment, generational priorities, world fashions, all would mean movement. There was in fact much discussion of change even and especially when Dublin's Seán Lemass met Stormont's Terrence O'Neill. Some potential change could be resisted: Christian piety in the countryside would hedge rapid social shifts that would run unchecked, and unnoted, in Dublin. Some seemingly could not be stemmed, even if there had been a desire—the rush to live in Dublin, the drop in emigrants, the boom in construction that devastated both the countryside and inner-Dublin.

In 1967 all these proximate conditions, a challenge to the Northern Ireland establishment by a new generation of young, educated activists who were humiliated and outraged and convinced that change was possible—not just possible but probable. That the tactic would be civil disobedience was likely and that it would have a profound effect on the entire Loyalist spectrum almost sure. What the events of 1967–70 forced or permitted was a logical extension of certain institutions' existing intentions; this potential for action, the implication of avowed aims, had been ignored by many of the activists and discounted by most observers. The IRA was thought moribund, irrelevant, incapable of recovery. The more primitive Orange machinery was considered outdated, raw, unorganized, a symbolic leftover from other days, the obverse of the IRA coin. The Stormont establishment was given credit for vision, skill, even cunning, actual power that proved to be lacking. No one imagined that the British government would prove inept, ignorant, determined only on policies that would placate no one, enrage the involved, and serve no purpose but the fueling of violence. Everyone assumed Dublin would be a force for order, a monitor, a power to conjure with in plotting the future of the North. Thus, the proximate conditions for change were relatively clear, but the powers and potential of those concerned misread; the concerned tended to read their own hearts for other's motives, accept wisdom, control, and conciliation in all as a given, and deny the avowed and violent programs of many of those involved. No one wanted to know the real nature of the actors because they might refuse the roles penciled in by the various playwrights. Nearly everyone in 1970 knew what they wanted to discover in the next act and could not easily admit the problems of production. No one since has been able to limn to general satisfaction the four main players: the IRA-Republicans, the Orange-Loyalists, the British establishment at Westminster, or the Irish in Dublin. No one agrees on the players' motives or even what play is being acted. No one understands why the play persists or what the next act, much less the last act, will be. And none can be sure what part the violent tragedy plays in the long sweep of Anglo-Irish history: aberration or culmination. Is the gun a conventional and necessary part of Irish politics or an exception, a sudden mutant, an irrelevance in the long stream of parochial peace and justice done? Why the Troubles? What really has happened? What will happen? What does it all mean? These are still open questions.

The Players

The IRA

In a volatile and violent arena in the midst of armed revolt, whatever the level, the key player is the rebel; without the IRA the only relevant guns would be locked in police barracks with the army withdrawn and the Loyalists content, Dublin distant and London elsewhere occupied. With the gun very much present in Irish politics, the IRA stars in the dismal drama, and it would be easy to assume that there would be an agreed portrait of the IRA volunteer or at maximum two sides to a profile. Not so, not so simple. Those who abhor the IRA see the members as simple (or not so simple) criminals (not patriots with a scattering of psychotic gunmen), death lovers, maniacal, homocidal freaks; the IRA is a mix of ghetto-terrorists who have institutionalized evil into an apolitical underground. Those dedicated to the Ireland out of patriot history, often residing far from the battle and complexities of motives, see the volunteers as national liberators mostly without fault or flaw or reproach, crusaders to liberate the island from history and British imperialism—laical Knight Templars. Both tips of the spectrum might concede a few, very few, shades of grey in the stark portrayal, but the burden is on black and white, good and evil, the cardboard characters from Irish history in a classic comic book.

1. The IRA as wicked, evil men is a position held at various times by a

variety of those opposed to either the means or aims of the organization. It remains a category; even those not demonstrably wicked encourage their evil colleagues who commit regular horrors. Such an analysis, particularly in a country comfortable with the language of religion, has maintained a certain hold and popularity. And given some of the authorized operations or attendant atrocities of the IRA, a few of the volunteers might very well be wicked and some surely incompetent.

2. Others see the Troubles as the result of mad, mindless men, killers, criminals, psychopathic gunmen who slaughter for sport under a patriotic banner. That revolutionary organizations want effective idealists, not the psychotic, not those who have been bought, and not criminals, does not mean that a few will not slip through the sieve. But after a generation, the evidence would suggest that madmen do not direct the IRA nor are the killings mindless, brutal without purpose, ruthless for private pleasure.

3. At various times a large constituency, favoring at some time, in some form, at little cost, a united Ireland, have deplored the means of the IRA, patriotism stained by squalid murder or innocent death, without indicating that the volunteer need be either mad nor wicked, only misguided.

4. The IRA's security opponents are more likely to accept the volunteer as criminal surely, incompetent at times, skilled at others, dedicated, persistent, ruthless, limited in vision—at times a poor Paddy at others an urban guerrilla—but oddly, almost as a natural artifact of Ireland, inexplicable in any but island purpose, a difficult, narrow, nasty opponent for uncertain cause, *sui generis.*

5. Far harsher are the old friends and/or contemporary radical rivals who see the Provos as the bitter end of the pure Republican tradition, corrupting ideals as pawns of imperial, Capitalist-class masters safe in Dublin and London: green bigots, neo-Fascists. Conventional party Republicans in the island drop, mostly, the militant language of the Left to talk of changing times, democratic responsibility, and the brutal arrogance of the IRA gunmen who would improperly speak for and from the common past. And whatever their radical opponents may contend and their distant advocates claim, some conservatives contend the Provos are not only flawed Republicans using the unsavory means but also militant socialists, red-commie-killers wrapped in a green cloak, unwitting pawns of the KGB busy at Moscow's work.

6. Within the province of Northern Ireland, the Loyalists, particularly the more primitive, would agree to all of these attacks under the patina of analysis, but stress that the crucial element is the Catholic nature of the IRA— no matter what the Army Council says, or the radicals of the Workers Party on one side and the conventional politician of the orthodox parties (North and South) on the other, or the categories of the academics, or the opinions of the British army and government, the IRA is the Pope's pawn. Perhaps it is several times removed, but the

whole lot seeks a Catholic, Celtic Ireland—look only at the fate of the Protestants in the South, the imposition of pious morals as public policy by the Dublin government, the power of the bishops and parish priests, the wording of the 1937 Constitution. United Ireland is a code for Catholic Ireland.

7. The militant Republicans see their army as a community of idealists, dedicated to the historic Republican principles, heirs to Irish history, determined that the united nation shall protect those of no property and restrict only exploitation, certainly not civil liberties, particularly those of the Protestants who have given Irish Republicans so many heroes. The means—"Physical force"—is a result of Bristish intransigence and always is focused on legitimate targets.

8. Others, friends, advocates, neighbors, have seen the IRA as a necessary Catholic defender against pogroms, Protestant police, and all manner of intrusions. Others less concerned with the legitimacy of the defense have stressed the radical social ambitions of the Provos—civil activists, traditional agitators unlike the strange artificial mix of splinters jerry-built into the Workers Party. The IRA for these is intent on liberating more than just a nation, running up a flag and running home while the gombeen men gather once more for the spoils. The IRA volunteer is thus a radical Socialist Republican (except while touring the conservative Irish-American diaspora in search of petit-bourgeois funds).

Eliminating the slanders, slings, and outrage of their opponents and the daubed labels of the patriot game, the IRA leadership at times is not all that sure of their banner or the nature of their crusaders. Certainly the flawed do not last long; there is no place for the criminal, the mad, the romantic gunman, or the greedy in a secret army; certainly idealism must adjust to the erosion of cordite; certainly persistence may pay some reward; yet the real profile of an activist within the IRA amid the Ulster Troubles, once beyond census statistics, is not an easy one to draw. There are surely many political reasons to volunteer, many economic ones, often too many, and by this time there is no prospect for great glory, only sacrifice and risk and dismay in non-Republican homes. So the ideal must play a part, as well as the vision and the lack of options for sacrifice and adventure. The dream remains compelling as does the need for retribution. Once enlisted the major thrust of the IRA has always been clear—the dominance of the national issue; bleeding principles down into tactics and techniques provides the driving force. Social justice, civil liberties, the language, and socialism have always been there but swept along with the grail of the Republic, Ireland a nation once again, a united Ireland.

The Loyalists

The Orangeman—the dedicated Protestant, the Loyalist, far more mysterious than the IRA volunteer, no broth of a rebel boy, no hero of a

Hollywood film, no warmth, and little grace—for nearly as long as the Republican dream has been manifest has denied the legitimacy of that grail, denied the nation, decried and island that could be united only over the heaped bodies and the smashed culture. For the Republicans, often for the IRA, until recently for all proper Dublin, the Loyalist has been invisible, an unsavory hobgobblin fashioned for British establishment purposes at crucial moments and then boxed away; he is not Irish, not a part of national calculation, and not real, he is invisible and obsolete and dangerous—and best avoided. Given the power and prominence of the Loyalists, their wont to run rampant when provoked, their friends in London, their obdurant Irish presence for three centuries, this has been a remarkable feat. Once after 1922, when the Free State became somewhat free and almost a state, few ventured North and then not for long, few wanted to sacrifice for the abandoned Northern Nationalists; no one wanted to learn more of the invisible men, appalling pawns, cutting orange cards for another's game. You could read books about Republican heroes or the secret army; volumns on the nature of the Irish were annual events. Everyone knew of the real Irish, the romantic IRA, the Irish rebels, none cared to learn about the Orangemen. No knowledge was to prove a dangerous thing.

To the disinterested the Ulster Loyalist was an anachronism, unappealing, schismatic, seized on old quarrels and irrelevant issues, colored grey by primitive belief, colored orange once a year in arrogance and bombast. There were all sorts of Loyalists of course: the rich and elegant, almost English, off to Oxford and Bond Street, responsible for governance, rural in inclination; allied to the merchants, richer but less elegant, perhaps Presbyterian not Anglican, urban if not urbane. They might be the peak of the working class pyramid of Derry and Belfast from bowler and watch chain or at the bottom the sweeper with sweet tea and chapel, and far from the rural world of small farmers, some comfortable and conservative on inherited acres, some marginal. To each other they were different tribes, different classes, different people in various pews united in what they were not and what they risked, rarely visible on an alien island. They, in different manners, sought liberty in schismatic churches, often built out of the timber of a single voice; they were suspicious of government, even their own. They produced a society that to the untrained eye appeared rigid, stratified, all spontaneity circumscribed, children at prayers and not play, hours kept and homes tight, class close and class conscious, suspicious of the feckless and light, opposed to play and sloth, the swings locked on Sunday and the heart all week; they seemed a grave and sober people, inflamed rarely by God's message but at times by alcohol.

For them liberty seemed all defensive. All speculation returned to the fundamentals; ideas were primitive but popular, available to the pious. The

poor had the righteousness of the self-saved, often born-again and possessed of truth. Theirs was a fragile triumph over the world, over wealth,
over elegance and education, over opposing dreams and historical tides.
Theirs thus was a unique heritage of those seeking salvation. This version,
grasped in simple plain chapels and narrow hearts, was identified with the
tribe, was in turn self-perpetuating; it need not be exported or transferred
beyond the redeemed land, need not be transferred to the alien. Possession
was, of course, vulnerable to general sin, to alternatives of pomp, wealth,
elegance, display, artifice disguised as beauty, and hearsay cloaked as education. Salvation was always at risk and no more so than on a wild island
filled with fools and fanatics. These native people of no property, no prospects, long lost to Rome, beyond salvation, corrupted by far institutions,
were determined to breed or batter their way to power, and thus to disaster,
for their own and for those loyal to the truth, to the one God, not of Rome
but of the one Book, found not through formula but by singular effort. So
believing in liberty, dedicated to freedom, the community of the saved
organized to defend their own, who were so vulnerable, so easily lost and
hard won.

The defense in depth imposed rigidity on every level, from the single
soul, through the family, and on to each social institution—change was
risk. Truth was pure and seamless. One misstep could lead to an avalanche,
so not-an-inch was given. There was no need and little opportunity to
move to the offensive, no call for a mission of conversion on a stunted
island that would be Rome thwarted. No, defense was the key against a
vast, undifferentiated opposition, all-powerful, expansive, compelling, possessed of lures and magnets, eager to exploit any chink with the rewards of
decadence. In the past then, the Loyalists had grasped the truth. This
historical splendor of salvation had to be protected. In the campaign of
legitimate defense, all the political, economic, and social weapons were
increasingly deployed, at times silently and secretly, with barely a nod to
conventions held across the waters in Great Britain. Thus, when observers
came among the Loyalists, isolated in their semi-island fortress, hearts
frozen on ancient fancies, minds shut to novelty, dour, closed, narrow
people in a Northern province, they found no pleasant rounds to be made,
no charm, nothing to reward curiosity. So few ventured beyond the golf
courses and government offices. Few understood Northern fears and faiths,
not in London, not in Dublin, and often not in Catholic homes in the six
counties. When the Troubles began, the Loyalists were suddenly visible,
demonstrably awful, pious spokesmen of violence, erupting Biblical arguments for self-interest, and wanton, brutal vigilantes in police uniforms;
they were Orange caricatures come to life.

The Loyalists felt misunderstood, victims of a satanic plot, their talents and toil taken advantage of, prey to forces distant and deadly. And in part they were right, few understood their special, long heritage of fear and faith; few admired their undeniable virtues; few even wanted to hear their anguish, too often made manifest in cruel sermons or shrill lectures. And the Loyalists were also wrong. Many could recognize that in defending their own truth advantage had been taken, excused at first by the proper voices of rural squires and then by the bombast of gunmen on the make. The others—the Fenians—had been, whenever possible, denied, degraded, excluded from all but minor roles and regular persecution—not to keep the Orange faith, or protect the Protestant truth, but rather to reward ones own. The Loyalists claimed to be misunderstood, their opponents' pawns in far political schemes, equally greedy and vicious. The Orangemen denied all guilt, found justification wherever possible just as had the Boers in South Africa, the Democratic Party in Alabama, or the European of Rhodesia. They had remained loyal to the old gods—truth, justice, hard work, culture—and how were they rewarded? Their mighty fortress was built on a single acre; they feared to give an inch for losing the whole. So they explained, accused, and sought to fashion for public consumption illusions of equality, a justice system for all or institutions based on democracy. The results were strange to those gathering observers (the massed media with recorders and cameras, investigatory committees, transient academics, and politicians), a police state with insufficient police, a judicial system that insured injustice, a democratic government that guaranteed many of the people would be surpressed and denied.

The Loyalists could foresee only stark alternatives: withdrawal from the province that they had made their own, exile for the chosen, defeat on the ground and absorption into the Celtic mass, or victory. Seemingly London would not permit victory but would not close off the horrid alternatives as forever unthinkable. So the Loyalists soldiered on, defensive, desperate, alternately arrogant and fearful, capable of any brutality to defend salvation won. The saved were determined on ultimate justification with the triumph of the right, but secretly they were sure that while there might be no surrender there would be no victory at the end of Ulster's long night.

The Orangeman who would actually use an unauthorized gun to defend the past, protect the system, deny surrender, assure present importance, is relatively rare. Many march, others serve their own special gods within the system as police or militia or simply employers; others are eager to protect, to agitate, to vote for the extreme, to tolerate if not abet their violent few. Such toleration, a great warm ocean fed by many streams (some quite respectable), permits horrors by the more immediate and primitive, the passionately intense who strike at representatives of whole categories at times of stress or anguish. The few and violent are without restraint, without remorse, moved by slogans and often by unsavory pleasures in their proclaimed duty. Murder along the Belfast peace line or in the mixed countryside comes at the hands of these few who seek to make their limitations into virtues, their declared opponents tremble, and their own lives real and important. There are no rural squires, bank managers, or decent working people to be found in the murderous gangs, simply the ideas and ideals of the Loyalist community whittled down for murder. The murderous gang is the Loyalist ethos of these troubled times carried to a logical bloody conclusion—atrocity as witness to communal fear, a fear no longer fully hidden by public arrogance, no longer eroded by power and accomplishment. Ambivalence is rampant. Loyalty is no longer properly rewarded; the island fortress rests on quaking ground, defended by fearful men, guilty men who are misunderstood, misquoted, violent pilgrims gone astray.

The British

The Orange pilgrims move backward under the trappings of a loyalty increasingly denied by those across the waters who, like most of the distant, find the Loyalists (except for the few of their own) dreadful, properly relegated to that awful Ulster place. The security forces may regard the IRA as an obstacle of Celtic nature, beyond Albion understanding. But what of the Loyalist (theoretically his own) draped in the Union Jack, singing the proper songs, giving tea and toasts, Royalists each and every one? In turn the British from trooper to minister were expected to defend jobbery, corruption of justice, communal murder, religious nepotism, gerrymandering and intimidation—the Orange system no longer hidden by the proper, even articulate, defense of the squires and the comfortable. The Loyalists are often difficult to swallow in Britain, especially for those with no special affection for squires or Ulster comforts. They are often thought devoid of common sense and compromise and, worse for the Orangemen, are often lumped with the Irish whole, one more island tribe. The most violent tribe, the avowed enemy, the gunman of the lanes, the guerrilla-killer, remains the IRA volunteer, a strange and deadly native in a world never understood, certainly not by the British government and rarely by the British army. All these gunmen of Ulster are drawn on the political map as dreadful "Monsters" and, except from time to time, have no politics, green or orange, recognizable in London.

Essentially, with rare exception, the British are agreed on one single, overwhelming truth: they do not understand the Irish. Orange, Green, rich, poor, Celtic, or cunning, none make much sense in London and most of London and the rest of Great Britain does not care to make more of an effort to understand them. The result, down through the long centuries of

Irish peace and prosperity, pocked by risings, famines, and turmoil, has been that the government at Westminster has not handled the island effectively. All the political philosophers, skilled statesmen, justices, negotiators, overlords, generals, agents, commissions and boards, and lawmakers of the Empire have not managed to cope with the Irish; empires have been built, lost, regained, British democracy established, justice institutionalized, and British genius in government displayed everywhere except across the Irish Sea, where every decade of triumph leads only to sullen disobedience or open revolt by the irreconcilable. And so even, or especially, the English accept, grudgingly, their special and peculiar incompetence.

> The moment the very name of Ireland is mentioned the English seem to bid adieu to common feeling, common prudence, and common sense, and to act with the barbarity of tyrants, and the fatuity of idiots.
> —Sidney Smith, 1810

There are today many involved in the Ulster Troubles who agree. Worse than barbarity, British efforts at conciliation or accommodation, seemingly well-meant, decent doing by a decent people, have proved disastrous. London has caused killing by kindness. Cromwell at least slaughtered by conviction to affect policy. London has for a generation had no policy but a desire for the easy life achieved by technical maneuver and vague delays, and thus inspires those with frantic conviction to kill.

When civil order began to decay in Northern Ireland in 1969, the degree of ignorance within the London establishment concerning the island was so great as to be beyond subsequent belief. There was no residue knowledge of Irish history, no contemporary experience, no accepted cast of characters, and worse, no realization that Ireland was very different, not simply an outland that provided jokes, construction workers, good fishing, golf, Guinness, and poets. The Irish spoke English, the Loyalists were loyal, and Northern Ireland tranquil for fifty years but for a few mad bombers, and the Republic (*Eire*) a further Wales under a tricolor, beachtowel flag. Even after 1969, except for the evening news and the detailed killer lists of the British army, the responsible still had little grasp of Irish reality. It took forever for London to realize that an ally existed in Dublin; *any* Irish government had much to gain by cooperating with London as long as the alignment was discreet. And never did British spokesmen learn that the accent and assumptions of their establishment read in Ireland like late-Colonel Blimp—arrogant, ignorant. After all that had gone before, it still boggles the imagination that Prime Minister Thatcher, in a single sentence, could make the hapless Dublin effort seem relevant if not powerful. Two years wasted in an afternoon, co-operation postponed, enemies never to be lost now all accomplished with the three hard words "Out! Out! Out!" Everyone in Ireland, except a few easily convinced politicians, knew that the Irish Forum was a necessary public relations exercise, not an agenda for action. In a war, politicians are easily driven from the "political" stage by gunmen and are understandably eager to play a role, even a paltry one. This blunder was simply one in a very long line: concessions posed as innocently poisoned packets, accommodation coupled with arrogance, lies repeated before the knowledgeable, and the truth offered to those who wanted lies. Seemingly every British initiative was a shoddy package wrapped in thorns, not worth the opening.

The combination of the burden of history's errors and contemporary ignorance created a cultural clash when the British were forced to deal with serious Irish matters for the first time in forty years. The first immediate response was delay, a refusal to act, thus permitting the escalating extension of violent intentions: agitation, insurgency, and vigilante murder. Thus made awful, the Irish problem seemed still amenable to the usual imperial mix disguised as domestic initiative: firm security measures (a fix many, including the Loyalists, felt insufficient unless more Draconian) and a mix of political concessions previously decried as unneeded or beyond London's competence. By the end of 1971, London accepted that the Ulster crisis was a very serious matter, but not so serious as to require true sacrifice either fiscal or psychic nor amenable to authorized murder; rather, a tolerable level of violence, ultimately achieved, would do. Over this small regional disaster, a swift and elegant curtain of democratic reasonableness was drawn: justice was *not* debased but adjusted; torture was not used nor brutality made policy; the violence came at gunmen's hands and accommodation came only by British sponsorship. Those who loved and admired Britain, the legacy of Churchill and Kent's green fields, The Poet's Corner, civility the invisible constitution, could only agree that in a nasty situation the calm and articulate British, democrats all, heirs of Locke and Coke, would do right, tell no lies, and seek justice. And thus Britain had for friends uncritical, innocent admirers resident in newspaper offices, government ministries, and great universities. Having drifted into crisis and remained for dubious purposes, the government in London (any government) thus had few external critics beyond the Irish diaspora. As long as the IRA did not raise the stakes or the Loyalists ignite civil war, London could maintain the United Kingdom inviolate, ignore or insult Dublin, pursue the Republican gunmen, threaten the Loyalist fanatics, pay the bills, and turn to more congenial matters. The Ulster Troubles simply did not greatly trouble Whitehall or Westminister; it is a distant dire province without potential reward, with no gifts for the Crown, no careers to be made, not even military, no plums, best forgotten. So mostly the British managed to forget, to evade contemplation of the enormous emotional cost of withdrawing from the last colony—the last terrible psychic defeat reducing the empire to one small island, the establishment to parochial irrelevance, the mission and destiny of a great people gone, the last banner snatched by the Paddies. Instead, Ireland could be put aside—a matter of technicalities, public relations, low-intensity security, a tactical factor in domestic politics not worth the trouble to study. No matter the past errors, no matter the present blunders, the bloody riots and ritual murders, no matter the risks, Ireland ignored was an Ireland irrelevant. And an irrelevant Ireland—an acceptable level of violence, some local truce, money spent—remained year after year British policy and British purpose; an Ireland important was beyond grasp, a threat that must be ignored, denied, a final fate not real for Britain, a nightmare undreamed.

The Dublin Irish

In the Irish Republic, the dangers of Irish dreams became swiftly apparent once Ulster—and for a time seemingly the entire island—slipped toward civil war without certain sides. In 1969 the more orthodox and ambitious saw the movement in the North as the end to partition, the last act of the first Troubles, an opportunity. This enthusiasm to manipulate those daring to act, a determination to encourage or abet the secret army of the Republic eroded as the risks became more apparent; conservative support would not mean conservative results; chaos in the North would bleed the South and did in fact turn historic Ulster into a free-fire zone. The Northern nationalists began to look as dangerous as Northern Loyalists—dark, radical Ulstermen who cared little for the nature of the bit of tin worn on a policeman's badge if he served gombeen law. How could a united Ireland absorb the embittered, radicalized Nationalists? How could a united Ireland be united with a seething, violent Orange million who would not surrender? How could the comfortable, pious conventions of the Republic withstand an Ulster onslaught? How could those who flourished in Celtic Ireland, whether in dubious business, petty Dáil politics, flaccid semistate corporations or protected firms, cope in a united island floating off cut-throat Europe? What would real freedom mean? The dreams of the militant Republicans could produce an awful reality—revolution, civil strife, Protestant car bombs, economic depression—sacrifices beyond potential repayment. For years it had been possible to forget the six counties of Ulster, never visited, little known, never discussed, seldom taught.

Between the first protest march in 1969 and Bloody Sunday in Derry in January 1972, the Irish establishment in Dublin, with little dissent, decided to go back to the starting line, forget the patriot game, draw an invisible line to the nation's march. The IRA was, as the conservatives suspected, a real danger to Irish tranquility, and so again Dublin rushed to limit the Republican radicals. The Loyalists were indigestable as well as horrid and now not easily ignored, and certainly unwanted. The British were seen as foolish, unable to read the nod-and-the-wink, slow to grasp there was no nettle in Dublin to grasp, only urgency to put the genie back in the bottle. Britain could manage with a carefully crafted, articulately explained policy of inaction, fearful of the implications if Ireland were a truly lethal problem instead of simply an awful place best forgotten between atrocities. Dublin, however, could not avoid the nightmare that had transformed the nation's dream as easily as could London. It would take years before the patriot game had no players. Oratory at the church gate only slowly became muted and the old myths lost their urgency. Soon, finally, no one was troubled jailing the IRA seeping south out of Ulster to rob and kill, now everyone feared the Loyalist gunmen to come. Thus, Dublin's difficulty was the persistence of the old myths and the Irish inability to effect Ulster reality. Dublin, despite the expectations of all, including the innocent in the government, had no power and no leverage. The only option left open would be counterproductive—intervene in the north—and would require sacrifices neither people nor politicians wanted to make. Thus unlike London, Dublin was forced to ponder the national dream turned nightmare and ever so slowly awaken to the cold contemporary Ireland, a twenty-six county nation without power or prospect of altering the real Ulster world. Thus for different reasons, Dublin, like London, wanted the Ulster Troubles to go away, disappear behind the smoke of tribal war, isolated, diminished, the final flare of obsolete aspirations. London wanted minor provincial troubles that could be ignored. Dublin wanted no trouble until the province could be relabeled in Irish hearts as Well Lost!

The Play: The Troubles

In sum, then, the motives of the players were often hidden in the public script. Each actor scribbled in a role and played a slightly different part. Ireland did not want to play at all, especially the patriot game, had not time, will, nor talent, but must appear on stage. Britain insisted the stage was theirs; Ireland was a tolerated intruder in a family skit. The Loyalists agreed. Ireland was an unwanted, illicit intruder in a family drama, who insisted the play was of enormous importance, where giants struggle for the future; it was not just a skit. Not so for the IRA, the stage is all-Ireland, an island warped by British presence, disgraced by Irish acting, troubled by Loyalists paid and cued by alien London interests, and the play is assured an endless run unless freedom for all thirty-two counties comes in a final act. In the medley of crosspurposes, real ambitions, denied motives, during a deadly quarrel with the past howling off-stage and few watching out front, there is no wonder that alien critics despair. Not to fret, the IRA wants freedom and retribution, the Loyalists ancient dominance, the British vindication and the easy life, Dublin peace and piety. And each player carries special weapons, certain limitations, a private script and a public speech, determined with varying degrees of sincerity and dedication to continue what has become a tragedy in endless acts. It is too complicated to be a zero-sum game, too long running, too embittered for easy denouement. The closer to the center of the stage, the more determined the players to persist, sacrificing the present for a future founded on a dream, bedded in an edited past, unreal but to the faithful.

And so the gun seems assured of a future in Irish politics, in the Ulster Troubles, for of all the cast, the IRA volunteers accept that the last scene can be writ by those willing to suffer the most. They cannot, as yet, be intimidated or purchased, deterred, driven from the Ulster arena as presently constructed. Perhaps someone will tear down the Ulster theater, discover a *deux ex machina* to blend the contradictions to general satisfaction, dialectic triumph or perhaps not. Surely there will be more surprises, atrocities, spectaculars, sacrifices and cunning political initiatives; perhaps, too, another generation of obdurate militants and old myths made real. There is always something new in the Ulster Troubles, each act novel but rooted in the play, but no one seems likely to write out the gun or write in a curtain call for all.

There are many who still see that gun as alien, the Troubles as aberrant, Irish politics as conciliatory and largely tranquil, conservative and accommodating. Except for the most active players, few see the Ulster violence as the culmination of Irish history, a low-intensity Armageddon, the national drama made manifest. But rather they see this present conflict as a narrow, parochial anachronism. If there had been more time, more vision, there would have been little violence. Lemass and O'Neill had begun a process of conciliation that with a will could have continued, justice done without recourse to gunmen.

From afar what happened was a general misreading of the power of the past, nourished by decades of little change in an Ireland isolated from movement, rural, conservative, parochial, regularly fed on old myths by old men. The 1960s revealed the potential of change, new money, new buildings, new opportunities, but not new myths (yet), not new politics (yet), not new reassurances for old fears. Potential, however, was actual, and the indicators were there: the movement toward Dublin, the impact of secular customs, the lure of easy money, the shifting society no longer easily bound by the parish and the past. Politics, and more important the national dreams, the totems of the tribe, remained static, unmoved, monuments in the quickening tides. And the responsible found this convenient, a comfort in times past. Few saw that a mix of new pretentions, new ambitions and the old ways and the old dreams would not easily be adjusted as time rushed by in a world alien to the parish pump, the Landbeg drum, and the doldrums of the Dáil. Thus, those who see the long sweep of largely peaceful change, the triumph of Irish democracy, the common decency, lack of crime, organized or violent, the odd sport of Northern intolerance aside, miss the fact that the institutions on the island only claimed legitimacy—they did not possess it. Northern Ireland had been imposed on the entire island; the Free State arose on civil war and the denial of the Republic. Compelling force had been the ultimate architect. The IRA accepted this; the fault of all evil was Britain, the means to ameliorate this physical force, and the desired result the Republic. Simple. Even the Loyalist position—what was done is done and cannot now ever be undone—could not convince even their own. The British having forced a solution insisted the result was voluntary, fair and irreversible—history's just judgment. The Free State and all its descendents having accepted the result, willingly or until a better day, denied the reality of island conditions. And all the players, then, had forty years of relative tranquility to consolidate their positions. Dublin hypocrisy kept the IRA alive, but barely, and British power, delegated, kept the Loyalists loyal, but foolishly.

Because the whole people of Ireland by 1969 had not been transformed by the rewards of prosperity, distracted by getting and spending the various and variegated consumer wonders of the wired-world of the postindustrial globe, they had not become Europeanized or Americanized. Tempted, only they did not all swing to the top of the pops or whistle the same tune yet, and their priorities did not all change or change at all. Worse, many traditionalists clinging to the old ways and old dreams saw the tides running the wrong way, the language threatened, the faith under attack from the telly, the old respect going, and the old ties frayed. In the rush for the new, civil justice was but one more banner, the spine of those Loyalists seemingly threatened by the new stiffened: not an inch. For old Republicans the politics of protest seemed an opening to insert the old question. Events occurred too quickly to absorb easily, to adjust attitudes, to make needed concessions, to contemplate; suddenly, barriers were down, and the potential inherent in the faithful became obvious. In a world moving toward consumption and indulgence, an era of the spectator and the transient, real vocations under old totems had compelling power. A rich, sated Ireland, comfortable, the result of decades of growing prosperity and new myths, might not have been transformed into an island theater of violence. In the

1960s a convulsion of trends, directions, rewards, opportunities, and novelties also saw a rush to the sure rocks of the past. Time passed very quickly and the responsible responded with conventional lethargy, assumed that time had rewarded them with legitimacy, that the patriot game had no losers, and that the Orange drums could drown the rattle of protest placards. The new Irish establishment believed in the new rewards, the new boundaries and saw no dangers in the public proclamation of the old myths and pieties. The Loyalists soon saw nothing but threats, a nation bought by color television, the faith endangered by trendy slogans parroted by dangerous children. The British saw nothing across the Irish Sea but an island reserved for vacation and sport, irrelevant to swinging London and the real world of NATO and Europe and partisan politics. And the IRA sudddenly saw their chance and moved on stage with an old script.

Everyone was suprised at the Troubles. The Loyalists were outraged that anyone would dare what they had long feared. The IRA believed that persistence would pay soon and swiftly. The men in Dublin found that the myths had reality and in London the government dithered over novel Irish parochial matters. And while the Troubles were thus a surpirse—and in their intensity and persistence remained surprising—they were not an aberration or for that matter a culmination but an aspect of the much longer Irish drama. The Ulster Troubles had occurred because Irish development had been sudden, sporadic, unexpected, and monitored by those with limited talents—bad luck in Dublin, bad luck in London, bad luck in Belfast.

The rules of the history game do not permit readjustment; the tape cannot be stopped, rewound, and started over. "If this" and "if that" are wondrous beginnings to laic sentences, no real concern of the professional. The fact is that the chaos after 1969 had many fathers, each with a long lineage. Some warned might have played a different part, but a generation of patriot speakers, enthusiastic and contented listeners, bugle calls without responsibility, drum rolls at no cost indicte a most general satisfaction with old myths. And these "myths" had a reality in their potential; this was after 1969 made manifest. There were too many volunteers in front of the bugler and bodies were soon scattered by the drummers. Time had not given Ireland an opportunity to become addicted to new realities, to leave in far fields the bugler, to neglect the drum rolls for more pleasant fancies. Forty years of habit is not so easily shed, the traditions of violence were real; those in power in Dublin and Belfast had wanted both legitimacy and the rewards paid by the tribal totems. They spent their capital, wasted time, and scattered hypocrisy: Eire was not the culmination of Easter week; Stormont was not eternal, a just rock in a Papish sea. The men in Dublin in the 1960s had at last crept toward recognizing that far to the north of the Liffey lay a reality that need be named. The men in Belfast had at last recognized that institutionalized bigotry had to be eroded; it was bad business, was understandable but improper. And there was more money and more opportunities, new glass buildings and a general quickening of purpose. It was also little more than a year or so of recess, a thaw between the frozen past and the boiling future. Everyone who had waited too long to grow up and to grow wise could thus act only in small incremental steps easily overlooked. And so the way was opened to all the furies, and would have been open even without the thaw unless luck had postponed a proximate cause—the contingent and unforeseen incident that would lead inevitably to civil violence beyond swift oppression or immediate remedial action.

Elsewhere similar furies were loose, marginal men who feared that in a homogeneous world their special people would be absorbed—no future or Basques in Spain or Palestinians in their homeland, no place for South Moluccans or Moros or the Naga. So unless the wave of change, the rip tide into the postindustrial world was enormous, sweeping all the Irish into a world they never made but could enjoy, then perhaps the old myths would have persisted, wisdom or no, long thaw or no. And so there was no time for the new realities. And there were the same old players who felt not just a right but also the responsibility to use that gun, to make real their myths, to deny the new realities hawked by the smug and purchased. There was no hope for the new men to write out the part, to take back the gun, to explain that times and priorities had changed, to urge piety, moderation, the easy life and patience. They had spent their years easily, fed four decades of hypocrisy with martial Republican music or bigotry tolerated beneath the drum beat.

The present tragedy, then, has been bought on the installment plan over a long time. Foolish pennies yearly tossed on the scales for narrow purpose, for an easy life, for return payment on some other day. And always a British thumb heavy with distant and forgotten purposes or no purpose at all, a careless addition to a delicate balance. Those who do not know their history are supposedly doomed to repeat it. The Irish have made their history back to front and their present Troubles a little at a time over long years—a mysterious and special process, an island alchemy transforming an authorized version of past dreams into a present conflict underwritten by power unused and misused.

There was always hope that somehow, someway something could be done, a path to accommodation found. The politicians, too often made irrelevant by the bombs, persisted, fashioned forms and formulas that devoured time and interest but produced no change easily visible in the continuing conflict. Each time with the advent of a new initiative, there was enthusiasm within various establishments and on the part of those distant from the island who wanted only to see peace and quiet and prosperity for all the Irish. The Council of Ireland, the Irish Forum, and the Anglo-Irish agreement signed at Hillsborough were each greeted with general enthusiasm except within Northern Ireland where the committed remained blind to other options, other visions. And a great many in American at least did not want to read more bad news, learn of another political disaster followed by escalating atrocities. Most, understandably wanted good news, so writing for those even marginally concerned with Irish matters was no simple matter leading to disgruntled readers or negative editors ever hopeful that some momentary bright patch in the Irish clouds would spread—that there would be good news, just as their editorials and commentaries had for years promised.

The good news often seems to be trivial or transient, sports events, Patrick's parade, the euphoria of the peace people or a drop in the numbers at the bottom of this year's butcher bill. Ireland, when notice is taken, remains for most distant observers a most distressful country, if green, soft with rain and literary memory still presently a tragedy in endless acts. The year 1986 began on January 1 with a bomb in Armagh town and the death of a member of the security forces; one more death, hardly worth notice in foreign newspapers, one more funeral to cover for local television, novel only because of the date. The year was supposed to have begun more hopefully, for once more there had seemingly been some good news out of the island in 1985. The British and Irish governments had signed an agreement that in effect would permit a Dublin involvement in Northern Ireland events in return for renouncing claims to rule the entire island. Vague in detail, as often is the case with effective agreement, Dublin's role was as uncertain as the claim to speak for all thirty-two counties. Still, there was real enthusiasm in Westminster, in the Dublin Dail, except by Charles Haughey, the leader of the main opposition party Fianna Fail, and especially delight in Nationalist circles in the North eager to find room to manuever between the uncompromising Unionists and the Sinn Féin's (Gerry Adams, Martin McGuinness, and Danny Morrison) supporters of the IRA military campaign, who by November would be willing to take their party into any parliament—new rivals. In protest all the Unionist members of Westminster resigned and in a regional by-election in January all but one were, as expected, re-elected to underline Protestant distaste. The party of the Catholic Nationalists reduced Sinn Féin's vote and elected one of their own—a seeming triumph for moderation or at least an indication that many would vote for something rather than everything. In the South polls indicated that even within Fianna Fail only thirty-four percent supported Haughey's opposition. Despite the continuing IRA campaign, largely against security posts in smaller towns, and the anger of the Protestants, the year seemingly, indeed, augered well. No one had anticipated that the IRA would go away. No one assumed that Unionists would—at first— embrace *any* change, support any initiative that would not give them, the majority, real control of the province. The problem of what next, what a long view would reveal, was not one to unduly trouble politicians in London or Dublin. Movement had been seen to take place; agreement was historic; the moderates in the North would be rewarded—had in the by-elections been rewarded. The new Anglo-Irish Inter-governmental Conference met three times by the end of February; IRA violence was no worse; the Protestants had neither taken to the street nor resorted to murder, seventy-two percent of Northern Catholics approved of the agreement—matters moved along. There was guarded optimism.

Mostly those in the Irish Republic concerned about politics, any politics, were delighted to let the North drift along on that guarded optimism. Something had been done, had been seen to be done. Mostly those in Dublin wished, ever so devoutly, that there were no North at all. In this they were one with the British who had taken an inordinately long time to grasp the Republic's distaste with the Troubles. Dublin wanted nothing so much as to stand idly by without responsibility or undue guilt. Mostly those in the Irish Republic faced enormous and seemingly intractable economic and social problems that could not be ignored nor ameliorated. Ireland is in the best of times the least of the advanced, on the fringe of the industrial world, marginal, vulnerable to any ill-wind. It has the credit of the Dutch and the debts of Zambia. For some years economic difficulties have increased, spending to create jobs has failed, stringent budget cuts have devastated entitlements, world conditions have assured a spiraling unemployment, agricultural difficulties, and an erosion of hope. By January 1986 there were 240,000 people out of work, an all-time high, nearly eighteen percent of the labor force, a gross disaster.

An entire generation appeared redundant. In the boom years the countryside had emptied out leaving the profitable big farms and a rural slum where the deserted scenery could be sold to tourists. The future was Dublin and hi-tech industry and offices. And so Dublin was razed. Vast ticky-tack suburbs were run up outside the city, beyond amenities and transport. The Georgian city was vandalized, pocked with ugly, jerry-built glass boxes, derelict sites, and car parks. New "industries" were brought into the country at great cost to the state but with unalloyed enthusiasm. And then the end came. A ruined Dublin was a monument to greed with a million square feet of empty office space surrounded by a ring of alienated workers without work. The trendy branch factories kept closing and the tourists discouraged by high prices and the Troubles did not make up the difference. Tens of thousands flee to America to jobs taken without work visas. Matters might well improve. The fine Gael-Labour coalition government of Dr. Garrett Fitzgerald, a decent if limited lot, insists this is the case. Fianna Fail of Haughey, too, having presided over the slide into these troubles, has a solution, if unstated, to reverse the drift down. He wants an early election, scents power and office. And yet the polls indicate some enthusiasm for Desmond O'Malley's new party the Social Democrats with the major visible assets of being new if filled by old failures and frustrated Haughey-rivals. No one with power or prospects really offers much of a solution and no one at all wants to examine the long-term effect of gross unemployment unrelieved by emigration—alienation, violent crime, the patriot game, unpleasant options all.

The economic troubles and the ensuing social chaos may not be amenable to Irish political initiatives—but could be to an improvement in Europe or the world. Low oil prices help the dollar balance. The hi-tech option is not closed. Ireland has many virtues as a site for post-industrial development: safe, scenic, a well-educated work force, a sound infra-structure, in times the phones may even work properly. Even just *some* reduction in the length of the dole line would help—hope is nearly as important as a new branch office letting in an empty glass box in Ballsbridge. So no matter what combination of conservatives sit at the center in the Dublin Dáil, there could be good news and the really bad news, the impact of another decade of alienation from a system that fails to provide as promised, can be considered tomorrow.

As for the Northern Troubles it is easy enough for London, if less so for Dublin, to think on other more pressing matters much of the time. A spectacular atrocity or a mass protest may bring out the foreign journalists, the mini-cams and public statements, but this is now ritual. The Troubles have been institutionalized at an acceptable level of violence. Terror is limited to a few intractable areas and dire scenarios of some future wars. The hard core is likely to remain hard and any real security benefits from the new Anglo-Irish Agreement will be long in coming. Nearly everyone but the militants now recognize that there is no visible solution. And as long as the violent zero-sum game is played out only locally, often very locally, the losses can be tolerated and ignored.

A decade ago it appeared that the assets of the IRA or the Orangemen were wasting, the old totems eroding, the old loyalties of the patriot game or bigotry sooner or later to be replaced. The new Ireland, North and South, had jobs, careers, the retail trinkets to be consumed and new directions to be explored. If color television with six channels and a new ticky-tack house would not do in violence, then new values, a new toleration, a new vision would replace the old legends and lies. And at the end of the decade, the hire purchase has taken the telly, the ticky-tack house is decrepit, the mortgage overdue. New values have led not to toleration but fortunes in speculation presided over by the same drear politicians—and there is no new vision. The partiot game offers, if at great cost, an old dream and a new career, a way out of alienation and boredom. The combination of idealism, still undimmed by the reality of no-warning bombs and innocents shot down by error, and the new dole line both offer much to the IRA. And for the bigot of whatever color, time so far after centuries has not eroded the sharp edge of island hate. So at the heel of the hunt, these are surely not the best of times for Ireland but then they are not the worst— the worst could be yet to come or maybe not. If the moderates, the optimists, the comfortable and cynical are right then, perhaps, the Anglo-Irish Agreement means the worst is over. There will be a last act ahead to the patriot game. The problem will find a solution. It would be rash, however, to count on sun over an island, often soft and comfortable, always conservative, also often an arena for slaughter, that has suffered a drizzle of blood, a reign of terror, for centuries.

And this Ireland of the sorrows pleases no one. Americans are not alone in wanting good news, an end to trouble. And so more often than not while the messenger is not killed, the bad news is not believed, not published, not read. The Troubles have lasted too long, a generation of gunmen without sufficient power to make a revolution. The militants of all varieties have left a bloody trail but no pointers for the future. Ireland has become a most distressful country but why, to what purpose?

So at the end there is no simple insight, no clear slogan or even easy access to the role of the gun in Irish politics, certainly no solution to the present Ulster Troubles, no real lessons to deploy for the practical nor cunning models for the analysts. It is not simply that the reel of history runs on—no last act, no coda—but rather that as at the beginning for the innocent, the matter is complex, tangled, replayed, and rewritten. And more so than most historical tragedies. Ireland is a narrow, tight, stone-strewn, a past-haunted island, small, often bitter, regularly swept by new tides and new peoples but enduring, indomitable, implacable. Nothing is remembered properly and nothing much forgotten. Every century many leave taking away a special swift frozen Ireland that only years, not distance, melts into a bright green blur under a blue bowl, sparkling clear with a thin west wind, a land of dreams darkened only by mists of vengeance never easily dispersed. Those who stay live in a crafted world not unlike the exile's image. Out of the mix of real blood and real events, bad lessons, history written with thick crayon, old violence and change and long soft periods of accommodation, a tower-Ireland has been raised by the involved, more real than real, more compelling than simple pleasures, a dismal responsibility. And those who merely want to get on with matters, collect the taxes, feed the children, sail ships, play games, make daily rounds, seem to the militant a different island race, tranquil, smug, safe, advocates of law over justice, order over liberty, untouched by lethal quarrels and responsibilities bred in the bone.

Those who do not read the books of revelations as received and skip across the druid ditches of the true believers are irrelevant—scholars *manaque*, alien ideologists, apologists for conformity. So that the lessons that might be learned have few Irish takers, who have learned too much already.

Abroad there are Irish lessons, for the island players have done more for others than the aliens have done for them. The eager and ambitious do note and long remember Irish experience: nations are more than new flags and ministerial limousines; liberation goes forward on many fronts, only one peopled by guerrillas; the weak must exploit the strong; the poor make do with nasty means; and the rewards of persistence may be a heart grown cold. The Irish have taught the fanatics to look into their own narrow hearts for justification of atrocity, have taught the benefits of suffering and the joys of defeat, have taught that a surface calm may erupt when dappled with the drops of a blood sacrifice. Thus the Irish gunmen have encouraged a motley crowd (good, indifferent, evil) in far places that a beginning must be made, that persistence is crucial, that victory elusive, and that the struggle an epic; at worst they are an example for poets and at best a means to power, able to act on history, to live free and to die proud. These are not always lessons the comfortable want learned. The gun in politics pays dividends of various sorts beyond power; the costs may be high, especially for the gunman, but the returns *are* real if various. And, too, the Orange killers, pathological murder done by the ignorant, reveal, alack, that even the most unsavory acts do pay political coinage as well. And it is likely that none in power want to consider the costs of hypocrisy that have come due in Dublin or the damage done by years of London indifference, ignorance, and delay. These scattered coins and wasted years have often been the very stuff of good, democratic politics—bows and bobs to the old gods in order to placate obsolete believers, a love of patience when other options came with a price tag, a confidence in tomorrow because yesterday has passed safely.

Muddle did not in the end pay, nor tenure assure wisdom or legitimacy for the men of office. The times changed but not fast enough. Too few were co-opted to the new ways, too few understood the lasting power of the old habits—the compelling attraction of the Republican dream, the centuries of Orange fear styled into arrogance, the awesome power of spite and malice grown rank. So after 1969, once more the gun, a few no-go ghettos, small wars in the countryside. The players were young, the roles old, often comfortable; there were no surprises; the causes were manifold, the results appalling, hard to accept, no better for quick labeling or swift analysis from scholarly texts or smudged tracts. And no end to the masque. No appropriate admonitions. Few lessons and no solution. And yet there has always been a recess when the frantic withdraw, a pause (often a long pause) not only of peace but productivity. Perhaps the tangled, violent threads can be woven whole by the wise, by time, or by the unexpected. Sometime soon, perhaps, Sundays won't be bloody or roads cratered, or armor sitting in the town corners. Perhaps, even this time the secret army will reach the end of the long drama, find a means to absorb the anger, conciliate the alien and fearful, establish one island at last indivisible, and then disband and let others rule as permitted. Perhaps others will find a new plot to disarm the gunmen, close the play, and empty the arena at last. Long wars do end. Elsewhere guns have grown rusty on cupboard shelves and secret armies rise only for reunions. Perhaps there will be pleasant surprises, even mutual exhaustion, the toleration of the frantic heart grown still, and perhaps not. Island history is still not whole. Secret armies still manuever out of sight. The gunmen has a role. The play goes on and on, and speculative finales find no takers and excite only bought claques. The future still is beyond prediction.

Index

Printed in the United States
by Baker & Taylor Publisher Services